PRENTICE HALL

HISTORY OF MUSIC SERIES

H. WILEY HITCHCOCK, editor

fourth edition

MUSIC
IN THE UNITED STATES
A Historical Introduction

H. WILEY HITCHCOCK

Distinguished Professor of Music emeritus,
City University of New York

with a final chapter by Kyle Gann

PRENTICE HALL, Upper Saddle River, New Jersey 07458

Library of Congress Cataloging-in-Publication Data

HITCHCOCK, H. WILEY (Hugh Wiley).
 Music in the United States : a historical introduction / H. Wiley
Hitchcock : with a final chapter by Kyle Gann. — 4th ed.
  p. cm. — (Prentice Hall history of music series)
 Includes bibliographical references and index.
 ISBN 0-13-907643-3 (pbk.)
 1. Music—United States—History and criticism. I. Gann, Kyle.
II. Title. III. Series.
ML200.H58 2000
780'.973—dc21
                  99-42121
                  CIP

Editorial director: *Charlyce Jones Owen*
Publisher: *Norwell F. Therien*
Senior acquisitions editor: *Chris Johnson*
Project manager: *Carole R. Crouse*
Prepress and manufacturing buyer: *Ben Smith*
Copy editor: *Carole R. Crouse*
Marketing manager: *Sheryl Adams*
Cover design director: *Jayne Conte*

This book was set in 10.5/12 Caledonia by Prepare Inc./Emilcomp S.R.L.
and was printed and bound by Courier Companies, Inc.
The cover was printed by Phoenix Color Corp.

Cover art: William Sidney Mount, American, 1807–1868. "The Power of Music," 1847.
    Oil on canvas, 43 × 4 × 53.5 cm. Copyright The Cleveland Museum of Art,
    Leonard C. Hanna, Jr. Fund, 1991.100.

ISBN 0-13-907643-3

PRENTICE-HALL INTERNATIONAL (UK) LIMITED, *London*
PRENTICE-HALL OF AUSTRALIA PTY. LIMITED, *Sydney*
PRENTICE-HALL CANADA, *Toronto*
PRENTICE-HALL HISPANOAMERICANA, S.A., *Mexico*
PRENTICE-HALL OF INDIA PRIVATE LIMITED, *New Delhi*
PRENTICE-HALL OF JAPAN, INC., *Tokyo*
PEARSON EDUCATION, ASIA PTE. LIMITED, *Singapore*
EDITORA PRENTICE-HALL DO BRASIL, LTDA., *Rio de Janeiro*

CONTENTS

FOREWORD

Students and others interested in the history of music always need books of moderate length that are nevertheless comprehensive, authoritative, and engagingly written. The Prentice Hall History of Music Series was planned to fill these needs. It seems to have succeeded: revised and enlarged editions of books in the series have been necessary, and now a new cycle of further revisions is under way.

Five books in the series present a panoramic view of the history of music in Western civilization, divided among the major historical periods—Medieval, Renaissance, Baroque, Classic, and Twentieth-Century. The musical culture of the United States, viewed historically as an independent development within the larger Western tradition, is treated in another book, and in yet another pair of books, the rich folk and traditional musics of both hemispheres are considered. Taken together, these eight volumes are a distinctive and, we hope, distinguished contribution to the history of the music of the world's peoples. Each volume, moreover, may of course be read singly as a substantial account of the music of its period or area.

The authors of the books in the Prentice Hall History of Music Series are scholars of international repute—musicologists, composer-critics, and teachers of exceptional stature in their respective fields of specialization. Their goal in contributing to the series has been to present works of solid, up-to-date scholarship that are eminently readable, with significant insights into music as a part of general intellectual and cultural life.

H. WILEY HITCHCOCK, *Editor*

PREFACE

Since the publication of the first edition of this book, about thirty years ago, general knowledge of, and interest in, the music and musical life of the United States have increased exponentially. The past decade has also seen major developments in American music; and there has been an extraordinary upsurge of American-music scholarship—and by that word I mean not only writings about the American musical past (up to yesterday) but also editions and recordings of American music, through a very wide spectrum of periods, genres, and styles.

My own conception of our musical history has been altered, inevitably, not only by the passage of time but also by this scholarship, which is reflected on virtually every page of this new edition of *Music in the United States* (known and used by enough readers of earlier editions to have gained the faintly amusing acronym *MinUS*). For a new final chapter, on American music between the late 1980s and the late 1990s, I thought it would be appropriate to turn to Kyle Gann, who has been immersed in contemporary American music during the last dozen years or so; a composer himself and the longstanding new-music critic for the New York City weekly *The Village Voice*, he is also author of the unique historical account *American Music in the Twentieth Century* (Schirmer Books, 1997).

This is a book based on primary sources: almost without exception I have studied the scores or listened to performances of the music cited herein (or done both). My debts to other scholars are, however, many; these are partially acknowledged in bibliographical notes at the end of each chapter, which will help readers reach out beyond this book to other sources. In footnotes, too, I have attempted to cite primarily works that can serve as further references. Whenever possible and appropriate, I have quoted composers on their own (or sometimes others') music.

A powerful resource, to which I urge readers to turn, is *The New Grove Dictionary of American Music* (London and New York, 1986)—herein abbreviated colloquially as *"AmeriGrove"*—of which I was fortunate enough to be coeditor with Stanley Sadie. I occasionally refer specifically to entries therein, but let me remind the reader that for almost every composer or topic touched on in this book an entry exists in *AmeriGrove*, usually with a helpful bibliography. (Although the dictionary includes many cross-references, it is not, regrettably, indexed; thus one must be resourceful and imaginative in searching for possible topic titles.)

Four other basic reference works that every reader should be aware of are the unique, massive *Resources of American Music History: A Directory of Source Materials from Colonial Times to World War II*, ed. D. W. Krummel et al. (Urbana: University of Illinois Press, 1981); Krummel's *Bibliographical Handbook of American Music* (same publisher, 1987); the exceptionally valuable annotated bibliography by David Horn (revised version with Richard Jackson), *The Literature of American Music in Books and Folk Music Collections* (Metuchen, NJ: Scarecrow Press, 1988); and Thomas E. Warner's classified and annotated bibliography, *Periodical Literature on American Music*, 1620–1920 (Warren, MI: Harmonie Park Press, 1988).

I cite here with pleasure other significant recent additions to the historiography of American music. First among these are the considerably revised third edition of Gilbert Chase's *America's Music* (Urbana: University of Illinois Press, 1987) and *The Cambridge History of American Music* (Cambridge: Cambridge University Press, 1998), a 650-page book of essays (by a total of nineteen scholars, astutely chosen by editor David Nicholls). Richard Crawford turned his 1985 Bloch Lectures into an idiosyncratic and illuminating view of *The American Musical Landscape* (Berkeley and Los Angeles: University of California Press, 1993). Two standbys should also be mentioned here: Charles Hamm's *Music in the New World* (New York: W. W. Norton, 1983) and Daniel Kingman's *American Music: A Panorama*, 2nd ed. (New York: Schirmer Books, 1990). Scheduled to appear in late 1999 is a major contribution by Richard Crawford, *America's Musical Life: A History* (New York: W. W. Norton)—also to be abbreviated as a textbook. An essential complement to these histories, and to this one, is Eileen Southern's seminal work *The Music of Black Americans*, now in a third edition (New York: W. W. Norton, 1997). And, at the risk of seeming immodest, I must point to an unusually interesting gathering of essays by thirty authors and brief music compositions by eleven composers: *A Celebration of American Music: Words and Music in Honor of H. Wiley Hitchcock*, ed. Richard Crawford, R. Allen Lott, and Carol J. Oja (Ann Arbor: University of Michigan Press, 1990).

Three valuable books address twentieth-century American music. The most recent, and the most specifically focused, is the work by Kyle Gann cited above. The others deal with Western music in general: Robert P. Morgan's *Twentieth-Century Music: A History of Musical Style in Modern Europe and America* (New York: W. W. Norton, 1991), with an accompanying anthology furnished with analytic commentary (*Anthology of Twentieth-Century Music*), and Eric Salzman's companion volume in the Prentice Hall History of Music Series, *Twentieth-Century Music: An Introduction*, 3rd ed. (Upper Saddle River, NJ: Prentice Hall, 1988).

Valuable series of earlier American music scores, in both facsimile and fresh editions, have proliferated. I refer from time to time to compositions in specific volumes of these; let me here just enumerate them by series title: Dover Publications in American Music; Earlier American Music (*EAM*; Da Capo Press); Recent Researches in American Music (*RRAM*; A-R Editions), the later volumes of which are coclassified with the American Musicological Society's Music of the United States of America (*MUSA*; A-R Editions); the twelve-volume Three Centuries of American Music (*3Centuries*; G. K. Hall); and the fifteen-volume Music of the New American Nation ("Sacred Music from 1780 to 1820") and sixteen-volume Nineteenth-Century American Musical Theater (both Garland Publishing).

This edition of *MinUS*, like the last, cites phonorecordings, but almost exclusively those available in early 1999 and likely to remain so for some time to come—specifically, releases from New World Records, Composers Recordings, Inc., and the Smithsonian Institution. New World is gradually reissuing on compact discs (CDs) recordings from its unique U.S. Bicentennial series of one hundred long-playing discs (LPs)—the "Recorded Anthology of American Music"—and consistently adding new CDs to its catalogue; I cite herein both original "NW LP" discs (assuming that many students and teachers will have access to these through their institutions' music libraries) and remastered or brand-new "NW CD" recordings. Composers Recordings, Inc., similarly, steadily reissues on CDs music from its huge repertory of "American Masters" (originally issued on LPs), as well as producing substantial numbers of new CDs; I cite the availability on "*CRI* CD" recordings of works discussed or mentioned in the text. The Smithsonian's recordings program has curtailed its catalogue (except for releases from the Folkways legacy), but at this writing it maintains stock of its boxed sets, the "Smithsonian Collection of Classic Jazz," revised version (*SCCJ*), and the "Smithsonian Collection of Classic Country Music" (*SCCCM*), which I also cite (whenever relevant to works discussed herein).

Helpful discographies include *American Music Recordings: A Discography of 20th-Century U.S. Composers*, ed. Carol J. Oja (Brooklyn: Institute for Studies in American Music, 1982), for concert-music works from about

1900 through 1980; and *American Music before 1865 in Print and on Records: A Biblio-Discography*, rev. ed., comp. James Heintze [*ISAMm* 30] (Brooklyn: Institute for Studies in American Music, 1990).

My approach to nineteenth-century American music has focused on what I have termed "cultivated" and "vernacular" traditions. In dealing with the latter, as with secular music in the earlier Colonial and Federal eras, I discuss much music now considered "folk music"—but as the *popular music* of earlier times (see Chapter 3); American folk music, as such, is considered more broadly by Bruno Nettl and Gerard Béhague in their companion volume in the Prentice Hall History of Music Series, *Folk and Traditional Music of the Western Continents* (3rd ed., 1990). In discussing twentieth-century American music, I have emphasized the principal stylistic trends and the predominant musical attitudes. Many fine composers and performers have thereby gone unmentioned; they have had to make way, with my regrets, for those who seem to me to be the ones to have addressed the major issues of the century's American music most clearly, boldly, and influentially. I make no apologies for devoting an entire chapter of a comparatively brief book to Charles Ives: his thought and his music continue to stand as provocative, stimulating, and fertile challenges to American musical evolution.

In the first three editions of this book I acknowledged the support and help of many students, colleagues, and friends, to whom I remain most appreciative. For this edition I was helped in many different ways—by some of the same, again, and by others, especially Edward A. Berlin, George Boziwick, Tom Brodhead, J. Peter Burkholder, J. Bunker Clark, Austin Clarkson, the late Sidney Cowell, Richard Crawford, Kendall Crilly, Carole Crouse, Jody Dalton, Elizabeth A. Davis, Diane De Grazia, Suzanne Eggleston, Susan Feder, Chuck Garrett, Marion Gottlieb, William Holab, Kathleen Mason Krotman, Judith Kuppersmith, David Nicholls, Carol Oja, Vivian Perlis, Katherine Preston, K. Robert Schwarz, James B. Sinclair, Susan Sommer, Joanne Swenson-Eldridge, Jeff Taylor, Richard Teitelbaum, Mark Tucker, Todd Vunderink—and, of course, Kyle Gann.

Once again, I am indebted to many libraries, especially the New York Public Library and the Music Research Division of its Performing Arts Library; the Music Division of the Library of Congress; the library of the City University of New York's Graduate School and University Center, and the music libraries of Columbia University, New York University, and Yale University.

My final acknowledgment remains essentially as before. To my wife, Janet, I am grateful for many things, among them the model of her own impeccable scholarship; her contributions to whatever accuracy and grace of expression may be found herein; and her good-humored and cheerful sufferance, for many years, of my humming, whistling, singing, playing through, and listening to three and a half centuries of American music.

To my students, who over five decades have never failed to challenge, inspirit, inspire, and indeed teach me, I wish to dedicate my part of this new edition of *Music in the United States*.

H. W. H.

COVER ART: The reproduction serving as cover art for this edition is *The Power of Music*, by William Sidney Mount (1807–1868), now in The Cleveland Museum of Art. Mount, not only an artist but also a musician (fiddler and collector of fiddle tunes), spent his whole life in Stony Brook, New York. The subjects of his art—mainly portraits and genre paintings of Long Island scenes—were often neighbors, friends, and relatives. In *The Power of Music*, the fiddler is Mount's fifteen-year-old nephew; the two older white men, friends; the black man, freeman Robin Mills, a neighbor, standing in a pose long employed by portraitists to suggest grace, dignity, even nobility. Said *The Literary World* sensitively in 1847 (after *The Power of Music* was first publicly displayed):

> The triumph of the picture is the negro standing outside. [He] listens critically, at the same time delightedly. We never saw the faculty of listening so exquisitely portrayed as it is here.

ABBREVIATIONS

AM	*American Music* (1983–)
AmeriGrove	*The New Grove Dictionary of American Music*, ed. H. Wiley Hitchcock and Stanley Sadie (London: Macmillan Press Limited and New York: Grove's Dictionaries of Music, Inc., 1986)
CRI	Composers Recordings, Inc. (New York, 1954–)
EAM	*Earlier American Music*, ed. H. Wiley Hitchcock (New York: Da Capo Press, 1972–)
ISAMm	Institute for Studies in American Music monograph (Brooklyn: Institute for Studies in American Music, 1973–)
JAMS	*Journal of the American Musicological Society* (1948–)
MQ	*The Musical Quarterly* (1915–)
NW	New World Records [Recorded Anthology of American Music, Inc.] (New York, 1975–)
PNM	*Perspectives of New Music* (1962–)
RRAM	*Recent Researches in American Music*, ed. H. Wiley Hitchcock, 1976–94; John Graziano, 1995– (Madison, WI: A-R Editions, Inc., 1976–)

MUSA	*Music of the United States of America*, ed. Richard Crawford (Madison, WI: A-R Editions, Inc., for the American Musicological Society, 1993–)
SCCCM	*The Smithsonian Collection of Classic Country Music* (Washington, DC: Smithsonian Institution, 1981)
SCCJ	*The Smithsonian Collection of Classic Jazz*, rev. ed. (Washington, DC: Smithsonian Institution, 1987)
3Centuries	*Three Centuries of American Music, A Collection of American Sacred and Secular Music*, ed. Martha Furman Schleifer and Sam Dennison (Boston: G. K. Hall, 1992–)

part one

The Colonial and Federal Eras (to 1820)

ONE

SACRED MUSIC IN NEW ENGLAND
AND OTHER COLONIES

In his poem *The Gift Outright*, Robert Frost remarked that "the land was ours before we were the land's. / She was our land more than a hundred years / Before we were her people." Acknowledging that there must have been an "American music" of long standing among the native American Indians; that French Huguenots doubtlessly sang psalms and made other music on their arrival in Spanish Florida in 1564; that Englishmen under Sir Francis Drake would have enjoyed music in Spanish California in 1579; and that there is evidence of the use of trumpets and drums, and the performance of popular and religious song, by the English settlers of tidewater Virginia very early in the 1600s, we still must recognize that the heart of "our land ... before we were her people" was New England. It is with the music of early New England that our historical introduction begins.

The musical world left behind by such New England colonists as those of Plymouth, Massachusetts Bay, and New Haven was a rich one. At court and in the mansions and manors of the British peerage was heard elegant, sophisticated music of many kinds—madrigals, balletts, ayres, canzonets, and other songs by such Renaissance masters as William Byrd, Thomas Morley, Thomas Weelkes, and John Dowland; variations, dance pieces, preludes, and other fanciful works for harpsichord by Elizabethan virginalists such as

Orlando Gibbons, John Bull, and Giles Farnaby; fantasies and suites for ensembles of viols and other instruments. The music at the Chapel Royal and in the great cathedrals was elaborate and magnificent: both Catholic and Anglican services were permitted under Elizabeth I's long reign (1558–1603); choirs of good size performed intricate and resonant motets and Mass settings in the former, anthems and great services in the latter.

The American colonists, however, could hardly maintain such kinds of music in the New World. Almost none of them were of the wealthy aristocracy that had supported such music in England. The leisure necessary to enjoy such purely artistic music was hardly their lot; in fact, almost none of them could even *read* that kind of music. Cargo space was at a premium on the tiny colonial ships, and large instruments such as organs or harpsichords could not be accommodated. Thus, the colonists could enjoy only music that was quite simple and functional: social music and worship music. Of the former we have few specific details; of the latter we know more. The history of "American music," in the first century of British colonization, may best begin with New England worship music, specifically the *psalmody*, sung in religious meetings and at home, that had originated in mid-sixteenth-century Protestant sects of western Europe.

PROTESTANT BACKGROUNDS

John Calvin, austere leader of the Swiss-French Protestant movement, believed that the only proper music for the church had to be based on the Psalms, the lyric poetry of the Bible. Like Martin Luther, Calvin encouraged congregational singing in the language of the people, not a choral music in the ecclesiastical Latin of the Roman Catholic Church. But, unlike Luther, Calvin thought that polyphonic music, instruments, hymns, and other non-biblical texts were too much associated with Catholicism; he replaced them with unaccompanied congregational singing of psalms, translated into metrical French verse. By 1562 the Calvinists had published in their center at Geneva the complete psalter—all 150 psalms—in translations by Clément Marot and Théodore de Bèze (Beza, in Latin), with melodies composed or adapted by Louis Bourgeois. Similar psalters for congregational use were prepared by Dutch Protestants; and in London, in 1562 (the same year as the Geneva psalter), the printer John Day published a complete English psalter, with translations of the psalms by Thomas Sternhold and John Hopkins and with melodies partly of English origin, partly of continental—the latter brought back, after Queen Elizabeth I's ascendancy, by English Protestants who had sought asylum in Geneva during the brief reign (1553–58) of Queen Mary I, a Catholic.

The music of these Protestant psalters was adapted from a variety of sources. Some melodies were derived from popular songs of the day; some were older hymn tunes; some were altered versions of Catholic chants. They must have been sung with fervor and gusto: apparently because of their sprightliness, the French Huguenot psalms were dubbed "Geneva jigs" and "Beza ballads"; Shakespeare, in *The Winter's Tale* (Act IV, scene 3), has the clown say, "Three-man song men all [i.e., singers of polyphonic "part-songs"], and very good ones... [only] one Puritan amongst them, and he sings psalms to hornpipes!"

In view of the character of this music and considering the popularity of part-songs in the sixteenth century, it should not surprise us that polyphonic arrangements of psalm tunes, for enjoyment and edification at home, were soon forthcoming. In England, Daman's psalter of 1579 ("to the use of the godly Christians for recreatying them selves, in stede of... unseemly ballades") contained four-part settings, and in 1592 Thomas East enlisted the aid of prominent composers of the day (John Dowland, Giles Farnaby, Michael Cavendish, and others) to provide polyphonic settings for his psalter. Two later and very popular collections of harmonized psalm tunes were Richard Alison's of 1599 and Thomas Ravenscroft's of 1621.

EARLY NEW ENGLAND PSALMODY

That the fiercely devout New England colonists regarded the singing of psalms as an integral part of life is suggested by a comment of one of the little group of Pilgrims that sailed for the New World from Delftshaven, Holland, in 1620:

> They that stayed at Leyden feasted us that were to go at our pastor's house, [it] being large; where we refreshed ourselves, after tears, with singing of Psalms, making joyful melody in our hearts as well as with the voice, there being many of our congregation very expert in music; and indeed it was the sweetest melody that ever mine ears heard.[1]

The "joyful melody" sung by "many... very expert in music" was doubtless a group of the psalms collected, translated, and published in 1612 for his congregation by Henry Ainsworth, the pastor of the English Separatists at Amsterdam. Ainsworth's psalter included both prose and poetic translations, copiously annotated, of the entire Book of Psalms; it also included thirty-nine melodies borrowed by Ainsworth from "our former Englished Psalms [and from] the French and Dutch Psalms." In variety of length, meter, and rhythm Ainsworth's choices were remarkable: compare, for example, the lilting asymmetry of Psalm 21, which is of English origin and which Ainsworth probably got from Daman's psalter, with the powerful, stomping regularity of Psalm 44, a Huguenot tune first printed in Genevan psalters, then taken over in the Sternhold-Hopkins English psalter (Example 1–1).

---

[1] Edward Winslow, *Hypocrisie Unmasked* (1646), quoted in Waldo Selden Pratt, *The Music of the Pilgrims* (Boston: Oliver Ditson, 1921), 6.

EXAMPLE 1–1.   *Psalm 21* and *Psalm 44* (first verses of text only) from Ainsworth's psalter (1612), after the Amsterdam edition of 1618: *The Psalmes in Metre* (no author, place, or publisher given). The music is the same as that of the first edition: H[enry] A[insworth], *The Book of Psalmes: Englished both in Prose and Metre. With Annotations* ... (Amsterdam: Giles Thorp, 1612).

Used by the Pilgrims of the Plymouth colony and also by settlers at Ipswich and Salem, Ainsworth's psalter was finally replaced in the 1690s by one that came to be universally known as the Bay Psalm Book (its real title: *The Whole Booke of Psalmes Faithfully Translated into English Metre*). This was the first book-length work to be printed in the British colonies (at Boston, in 1640). The committee of Puritan colonists that compiled it sought to make "a plain and familiar translation" of the psalter more accurate than the Sternhold-Hopkins version they had brought with them from England. The Bay Psalm Book originally included no music but directed that most of its verses could be sung either to Ravenscroft's tunes or to those of "our english psalm books"—that is, Sternhold-Hopkins. Enormously popular, the Bay psalter was published in almost thirty New England editions by 1760. To the ninth edition of 1698 (or possibly to an earlier one, now lost) were appended thirteen melodies, with basses as well, which the unknown compiler had borrowed from various editions of John Playford's *Introduction to the Skill of Music* (London, 1667 and later).

That only thirteen melodies could suffice for all 150 psalms suggests that the psalms of the Bay psalter were less diverse metrically than those of earlier psalters, and perhaps that the New England congregations of the late seventeenth century were less "expert in music" than their forebears. Indeed, "almost all this whole book of psalmes," declared the Preface of the first edition of 1640, was composed in three meters: Common Meter (8, 6, 8, and 6 syllables for the four-line stanzas), Long Meter (8, 8, 8, 8), and an irregular meter of 6, 6, 8, 6. The decline in the number of psalm tunes regularly sung was a reflection of a general decline in the quality of psalmody in the colonies.

By the early eighteenth century, Puritan ministers were raising horrified outcries at the poor singing in their churches; one complained in 1721 that "the tunes are now miserably tortured, and twisted, and quavered... into an horrid Medly of confused and disorderly Noises." Precentors were appointed to "line out" the psalms for the congregation—that is, to set the pitch and remind their fellows of a psalm tune by chanting it, line by line, echoed by the group. But the precentors were altering the melodies at will: "every Leading-Singer would take the Liberty of raising any Note of the Tune, or lowering of it, as best pleas'd his Ear, and add such Turns and Flourishes as were grateful to him," wrote Rev. Thomas Symmes of Bradford, Massachusetts, in 1720. He was repelled by what came to be called the "Old Way" of singing—a folkish oral tradition that paid little heed to the notated music on which it was based.

The New England ministers set out to reform the music in their churches by encouraging their congregations to replace the Old Way with a "New Way" based on singing the notes as written. In doing so, they created the first music instruction books in America, established a unique kind of musical education, and paved the way for the first school of American composers.

First came sermons, pleading for "regular" singing, by note instead of by rote; one such plea was Symmes's sermon on "The Reasonableness of Regular Singing" (1720). The earliest practical attempt to improve matters, and the first American music textbook, was a small volume by Rev. John Tufts of Newbury, Massachusetts, *An Introduction to the Singing of Psalm-Tunes*, first published in 1721. Tufts wrote a brief preface explaining the rudiments of music and a new method of musical notation that he had devised (by letters rather than by musical notes), and he followed these with a collection of English psalm tunes (without texts). The fifth edition of 1726, the earliest extant, includes thirty-seven such tunes, with two other harmonizing parts. Among them is one, *100 Psalm Tune New*, that has not been found in earlier publications and may perhaps be claimed as the first American composition; whether Tufts wrote it himself we do not know. The little piece (Example 1–2) is worth a brief look: not ungraceful, it has nevertheless an angularity of melody (the Cantus part has the principal air) and a predilection for unisons, octaves, and bare fifths—not to mention the

EXAMPLE 1–2.   J. Tufts, *100 Psalm Tune New, An Introduction to the Singing of Psalm-Tunes* ... The Fifth Edition (Boston: Printed for Samuel Gerrish, 1726), 10. The Medius part is to be sung an octave lower than notated.

parallel fifths at the end of the third "measure"—which distinguish it from British psalm tunes of the period. As we shall see, these were precisely the features that were to characterize native American music of the later eighteenth century.

At almost the same time that Tufts first published his *Introduction*, another manual appeared, also including a number of psalm tunes with accompanying parts. This was *The Grounds and Rules of Music Explained* (Boston, 1721) by Rev. Thomas Walter of Roxbury, Massachusetts, a nephew of the well-known Cotton Mather and, like Tufts, a graduate of Harvard College. These two "tunebooks" (as such works came to be known, even after they were furnished with texts as well as "tunes" and subsidiary melodic lines) were eminently successful: Tufts's went through eleven editions between 1721 and 1744, and Walter's was still in print (as part of another book) almost a half-century after it was first published. They marked the beginning of a significant movement in American music, that of the singing school (to which I shall turn in a moment), and were the first of more than five hundred American tunebooks that were to be printed by 1810.

The same period saw an expansion in the nature and sources of texts for Protestant American worship music. As mentioned, John Calvin had limited the texts of church song to biblical psalms in metrical vernacular translations. The other great leader of the Protestant Reformation, Martin Luther, had not been so restrictive; from the beginning he had permitted, and even composed himself, original sacred poems that came to be termed *hymns*. Hymnody flourished under Lutheranism, and even before the eighteenth century it found its way into the English Puritan services. The first significant writer of English hymns was the Reverend Dr. Isaac Watts (1674–1748). In 1707 he published his first major collection, *Hymns and Spiritual Songs*; in 1715, his *Divine Songs* (the first children's hymnbook); and in 1719, *The Psalms of David Imitated* (including "O God, our help in ages past" [see p. 19]). For more than a century, Watts's works were the most popular sources of texts for English and American congregational worship music. A further impetus to hymnody was provided, from the 1730s on, by the evangelical movement of Wesleyanism and by the series of evangelical "awakenings" and "revivals," beginning with the "Great Awakening" of 1735, that studded the evolution of American Protestantism.

THE SINGING-SCHOOL MOVEMENT

As we have seen, agitation among Puritan ministers for better singing in their churches resulted in the first American music instruction books. At their call, too, was instituted the first kind of American music school. Thomas Symmes asked in 1720,

> Would it not greatly tend to promote singing of psalms if singing schools were promoted?...Where would be the difficulty, or what the disadvantages, if people who want [i.e., lack] skill in singing, would procure a skillful person to instruct them, and meet two or three evenings in the week, from five or six o'clock to eight, and spend their time in learning to sing?

That is precisely what happened. As early as March 1722, Boston had a Society for Promoting Regular Singing, with a core of about ninety who had learned to read music. From that time on, *singing schools*—convened to learn, practice, and demonstrate the skill of reading music at sight—became an important institution in the colonies, social as well as musical. Although originally their aim was to improve church music, and although their music was for the most part religious, the singing schools were as much secular institutions as sacred, as much social outlets as pious assemblies. One student at Yale College in New Haven, for example, wrote to a friend:

> At present I have no inclination for anything, for I am almost sick of the World & were it not for the Hopes of going to the singing-meeting tonight & indulging myself a little in some of the carnal Delights of the Flesh, such as kissing, squeezing &c. &c. I should willingly leave it now.[2]

---

[2] Quoted in Irving Lowens, *Music and Musicians in Early America* (New York: W. W. Norton, 1964), 282.

In a society that recognized no split between religion and everyday life, the singing school was a popular meeting ground for both. Not only in New England but also in the more southern colonies, singing-school instruction became popular in the eighteenth century: we hear of it in South Carolina in 1730, Philadelphia in 1753, New York in 1754, and Maryland in 1765.

A broadside or a newspaper advertisement would alert a community that a singing school was to be organized. Arriving on the scene, the singing master would enroll students for classes once or twice a week for a month or more. Their texts were sometimes manuscript copybooks, into which they laboriously wrote the music they were learning to sing, or sometimes printed tunebooks, partly composed by the singing master, partly borrowed from other sources. (Copyright was nonexistent until late in the eighteenth century, and piracy was as common among literary landlubbers as on the high seas.)

Characteristically oblong (thus sometimes called an "end-opener") and headed by some such sociable title as *The Chorister's Companion*, *The American Singing Book*, *The Rural Harmony*, or *The Easy Instructor*, the typical tunebook was a how-to-do-it manual, containing an introduction to the rudiments of music theory and notation, and also a what-to-do anthology, with a collection of psalm tunes (and later in the century, of hymns, anthems, and sometimes even secular songs), harmonized in three or four parts for men's and women's voices. No instrumental accompaniment was provided; the old Calvinist suspicion of instruments as belonging not to the Lord but to the Devil (or the Catholics) died hard, and the prejudice died only gradually during the eighteenth century.

The classes of a singing school would typically culminate in a "singing lecture"—essentially a choral concert embellished by a sermon from the local minister—or a "singing assembly," without the sermon. Having taught his pupils to sing accurately by note, having enlarged his reputation and the use of his tunebooks, and probably having got in a few licks for some other business interest (most of the singing masters were veritable prototypes of the Yankee peddler or worked at some trade), the singing master would move on to another community to begin a new singing school.

In this way the first group of American composers developed. They forged a distinctive style of music—rugged, powerful, and homogeneous (if also, as we shall see, awkward-seeming and archaic-sounding to later, more genteel ears).

THE FIRST NEW ENGLAND SCHOOL
OF COMPOSERS

Singing schools of the middle decades of the eighteenth century relied on reprints of earlier tunebooks (such as Tufts's and Walter's) and the Bay Psalm Book; the next important new book was published only in 1761—*Urania*, a "choice Collection of Psalm-tunes, Anthems, and Hymns" compiled by the New Jersey–born James Lyon (1735–94) and published in Philadelphia. Lyon apparently culled most of the ninety-six compositions in the work from various English tunebooks in circulation at the time. Among the seventy psalm settings are some of special interest to us: they are "fuging psalm tunes" (the adjective is pronounced "fyooghing") with a form and a texture that were to be taken up lustily by New England tunesmiths. The V *Psalm Tune* (Example 1–3), borrowed perhaps from Abraham Adams's *Psalmist's New Companion*, 6th ed. (London, ca. 1760), is characteristic: beginning with a four-part setting of the tune (in the tenor voice), it reaches a cadence (here on the dominant) in measure 12; then it starts afresh with imitative entries for the individual voices—the so-called "fuge" (pronounced "fyoog") or "fuging section"—and soon leads to a final cadence. Aside from some peculiarities of harmony—for instance, the characteristically British use of cross-relations (F♮ vs. F♯, successive in measure 1 and simultaneous in measure 2, and the clash of soprano and alto in measure 16), there is a smoothness about the little piece that betrays its transatlantic origin; American fuging tunes would tend to be simpler in rhythm, more angular in melody, less chromatic in harmony, and in some ways stronger in general effect.

EXAMPLE 1–3.   The V *Psalm Tune*, in J. Lyon, *Urania* (Philadelphia: William Bradford, 1761), 42–43.

In the 1760s, following the publication of Lyon's *Urania*, the pace of American tunebook publications quickened considerably, and by the 1770s a whole group of composers were busily at work in the Northeast. The First New England School of American composers, as the group may be called (see p. 150 ff. regarding a second one), was centered in Connecticut and Massachusetts. Its members consisted of journeyman composers (some have termed them "Yankee tunesmiths"), most of whom, as remarked earlier, practiced other trades or professions. The first to make his mark, and the most prominent of the group, was William Billings (1746–1800), a Boston tanner turned singing-school master and composer—as such, the first American to attempt to make music his sole profession—and one of the most picturesque personalities in American music. Billings's first tunebook, *The New-England Psalm-Singer; or, American Chorister*, was issued in 1770. It was a landmark. Hardly more than a dozen tunes by native Americans had previously been published, and with this collection of 127 pieces, all of his own composition, Billings increased the number tenfold. (Ultimately, his compositions were to number 338.) The title page of *The New-England Psalm-Singer* was engraved by Paul Revere, which reminds us of Lexington and Concord, of the colonies versus Britain, of growing national consciousness and the spirit of independence during the Revolutionary decade of the 1770s. In his prefatory comments "to all musical practitioners," the twenty-four-year-old composer made no bones about *his* independence:

> Nature is the best Dictator, for all the hard dry studied Rules that ever was prescribed, will not enable any Person to form an Air any more than the bare Knowledge of the four and twenty letters, and strict Grammatical Rules will qualify a Scholar for composing a Piece of Poetry, or properly adjusting a Tragedy, without a Genius. ... I don't think myself confin'd to any Rules for Composition laid down by any that went before me.

Warming to the analogy between music and poetry, Billings went on: "[As I] have often heard of a Poetical Licence, I don't see why with the same Priority there may not be a Musical Licence." Here spoke the rebellious, self-confident young American of 1770. Nevertheless, despite his stated conviction that "I think it is best for every Composer to be his own Carver," Billings proceeded to instruct his readers in the rudiments of music, and even to make some qualifications in his eulogy of native genius:

> Perhaps some may think I mean and intend to throw Art intirely out of the Question, I answer by no Means, for the more Art is display'd, the more Nature is decorated. And in some sorts of Composition, there is dry Study requir'd, and Art very requisite. For instance, in a *Fuge*, where the Parts come in after each other, with the same Notes; but even there, Art is subservient to Genius, for Fancy goes first, and strikes out the Work roughly, and Art comes after, and polishes it over.

Many years later—in the preface to his last tunebook, *The Continental Harmony* of 1794—Billings was still the self-confident autodidact, putting his faith not in dry-as-dust rules declared by others but in himself, and insisting on the preeminence of self-expression and of "fancy":

> Musical composition is a sort of something, which is much better felt than described (at least by me). .... But in answer to your question, although I am not confined to rules prescribed by others, yet I come as near as I possibly can to a set of rules which I have carved out for myself; but when fancy gets upon the wing, she seems to despise all form, and scorns to be confined or limited by any formal prescriptions whatsoever.

The New-England Psalm-Singer contains 108 psalm and hymn settings and 15 anthems and canons for chorus. The *Canon 4 in 1* "When Jesus Wept" (*NW* LP 80552) is one of Billings's loveliest melodic inspirations (Example 1–4); similar to it in style is another four-part canon, "Thus saith the high, the lofty one." These canons suggest Billings's flair for graceful melody. But perhaps it was his patriotic pieces that accounted for Billings's early popularity. Among the pieces in *The New-England Psalm-Singer* was one, *Chester*, that so caught the fancy of young America that it became a rallying song of the Revolution. When he published his second tunebook, *The Singing Master's Assistant* (Boston, 1778), at the height of the Revolutionary War, Billings reprinted in it the stirring, stomping, marchlike tune of *Chester*, and to its patriotic text (his own) he added new verses that spoke for—shouted for—his whole generation (in *3Centuries* 7, 21).

> Let tyrants shake their iron rod,
>   And Slav'ry clank her galling chains,
> We fear them not, we trust in God,
>   New-england's God for ever reigns.

Later verses went on with even more fire and sarcasm:

> Howe and Burgoyne and Clinton too,
>   With Prescot and Cornwallis join'd
> Together plot our Overthrow,
>   In one infernal league combin'd.

> The Foe comes on with haughty stride;
>   Our troops advance with martial noise,
> Their Vet'rans flee before our Youth,
>   And Gen'rals yield to beardless Boys.

The Singing Master's Assistant also includes an address, "To the Goddess of Discord," with a short choral piece, *Jargon* (in *3Centuries* 7, 21), accompanying it. Apparently Billings had been criticized for the bland harmony of

EXAMPLE 1–4. W. Billings, *Canon 4 in 1* ("When Jesus Wept"), *The New England Psalm-Singer* (Boston: Edes and Gill, 1770).

his first tunebook: he begins his manifesto to Lady Discord by saying, "I have been sagacious enough of late, to discover that some evil-minded persons have insinuated to your highness, that I am utterly unmindful of your Ladyship's importance." But he affirmed his fealty to *concord*: "I shall be so condescending as to acquaint your uglyship, that I take great pleasure in subscribing myself your most inveterate, most implacable, most irreconcilable enemy." Then follows the notoriously dissonant *Jargon*, a musical joke full of harsh intervals and awkward harmonic progressions. The text is a brief quatrain:

> Let horrid Jargon split the Air,
> And rive the Nerves asunder,
> Let hateful Discord greet the Ear,
> As terrible as Thunder.

Billings gives mock instructions for its performance with a rough humor that prefigures some of the salty marginal comments of another, much later American composer, Charles Ives (see Chapter 7):

> In order to do this piece ample justice, the concert must be made of vocal and instrumental music. Let it be performed in the following manner, viz. Let an Ass bray the bass, let the fileing of a saw carry the Tenor, let a hog who is extream hungry squeel the counter, and let a cart-wheel, which is heavy loaded,

and that has been long without grease, squeek the treble; and if the concert should appear to be too feeble you may add the cracking of a crow, the howling of a dog, the squalling of a cat; and what would grace the concert yet more, would be the rubbing of a wet finger upon a window glass. This last mentioned instrument no sooner salutes the drum of the ear but it instantly conveys the sensation to the teeth; and if all these in conjunction should not reach the cause [i.e., suffice], you may add this most inharmonical of all sounds, *"Pay me that thou owest."*

By 1781 Billings had published two more tunebooks. The first, *Music in Miniature* (1779; the title referred to its unusually tiny size), included mainly reprints of successful earlier pieces. The second, *The Psalm Singer's Amusement* (1781; *EAM* 20), had plenty of new pieces, among them two that must have been great favorites in the singing schools. One, *Consonance*, is a setting of a poem by Mather Byles entitled "On Musick" (in *EAM* 20, 81). It begins, "Down steers the Bass with grave majestick air / And up the Treble mounts with shrill career." Billings is at his most melodious as he graphically "explains" each of the lines in a technique of musical word painting that goes all the way back to the madrigal composers of Elizabethan England. The other, *Modern Music* (in *EAM* 20, 72), explains several musical matters even more explicitly, commencing with the lines "We are met for a Concert of modern invention. / To tickle the Ear is our present intention." The singers chant liltingly that "we all agree / To set the tune on E, / The Author's darling Key / He prefers to the rest," and they go on to present, in various meters, modes, and textures, a naive but engaging demonstration of "modern" American music.

Billings was to offer to the public two more tunebooks, *The Suffolk Harmony* in 1786 and *The Continental Harmony* in 1794. In the preface to the latter, he exclaimed ecstatically over "fuging music," which he had been composing since *The Singing Master's Assistant* of 1778:

> There is more variety in one piece of fuging music than in twenty pieces of plain song. ... The audience are most luxuriously entertained, and exceedingly delighted; in the mean time, their minds are surprizingly agitated, and extremely fluctuated. ... Now the solemn bass demands their attention, now the manly tenor, now the lofty counter [i.e., alto], now the volatile treble, now here, now there, now here again—O inchanting! O ecstatic! Push on, push on ye sons of harmony.

Why was Billings so excited about "fuging music"? The most likely answer: Billings (and after him many other Yankee tunesmiths of the First New England School) was rediscovering the pleasures of counterpoint. Their predecessors, the earlier compilers of the pre-Revolutionary period, had been content to offer singers nothing but simply harmonized versions of traditional psalm tunes, but the idea of contrapuntal imitation between the voice parts seemed to offer a much better world of musical pleasure than had the old "plain song." No wonder Billings called the idea of imitative counterpoint—not a new idea, by any means, but one with which most Americans had lost contact—a "most ingenious and ... most grateful" one. It may be true, but it is certainly irrelevant, that neither Billings nor, perhaps, any of the other Yankee tunesmiths had the background or the technical skill needed to write *real* fugues—which is why it is useful to preserve the archaic spelling and thus to distinguish from the "fugues" of contemporaneous European music the New Englanders' "fuging tunes." What the latter were after, and what they achieved, was music grateful to perform—music that would give every voice a good tune to sing. It was enough for them that the regular, foursquare chordal texture of the music would occasionally give way to a "fuge," and, as Billings put it, each part would seem to be "mutually striving for mastery, and sweetly contending for victory."

Billings has captured the imagination of American music historians by virtue of his colorful personality, his apostleship of artistic freedom and individuality, his sense of humor, and his flair for tuneful melody. He symbolizes perfectly the cheerful, unselfconscious pride, the honest journeyman excellence of our nation's first composers. Nevertheless, he died "poor and neglected"; other composers, from outside the Boston area, had even more successfully caught the popular fancy in the post–Revolutionary War period. Like Billings, they were singing masters and singing-school tunebook compilers.

Daniel Read (1757–1836) was one of the most active and gifted composer-compilers. Born in Massachusetts, he moved to New Haven, Connecticut, in 1782, establishing a general store there and becoming a manufacturer of horn and ivory combs. His immense popularity as a composer can be suggested by the fact that his pieces were pirated time and again by other tunebook compilers; one of his Christmas hymns, for instance, *Sherburne* (NW CD 80205), was reprinted (with or without permission) seventy-eight times between 1785, when it first appeared in Read's *American Singing Book*, and 1810 (see Figure 1–1); others by him—such as *Calvary, Greenwich* (NW CD 80205), *Judgment, Lisbon, Russia, Stafford, Windham,* and *Winter*—also became staples in the "core repertory" of early American psalmody.[3] Timothy Swan (1758–1842) of Worcester, Massachusetts, worked mainly in the Connecticut River valley as a singing-school master (also hatter and merchant); his pieces *Bristol, Montague* (NW CD 80255), and *Rainbow* were successful enough to figure in the core repertory, though in later

---

[3] That repertory—the 101 sacred compositions most often printed (and/or reprinted) in America between 1698 and 1810—was established by Richard Crawford and edited by him, together with complete "tune biographies," in *The Core Repertory of Early American Psalmody* (RRAM 11–12).

FIGURE 1–1.   Daniel Read's fuging tune *Sherburne* (1785), as printed in shape-notes in an 1802 edition of *The Easy Instructor*. Courtesy of the Music Research Division, New York Public Library; Astor, Lenox and Tilden Foundations.

life he was termed "poor, proud, and indolent" by an acquaintance. Supply Belcher (1751–1836) was a tavernkeeper in Stoughton, before he moved to the northern frontier, published his *Harmony of Maine* (1794; *EAM 6*)—which includes his *Anthem of Praise* and *Heroism* (both on *NW* CD 80255)—and came to be known as the "Handel of Maine." Justin Morgan (1747–98) is perhaps best known as breeder of the Morgan horse; he was also known in West Springfield, Massachusetts, and later in Vermont as a schoolmaster, tavernkeeper—and singing master. Andrew Law (1749–1821) was a minister, with several college degrees, but eventually all his energies went to organizing singing schools and to engaging in endless angry correspondence with musical pirates who were, he claimed, "pillaging my books"—his tunebooks, of which he was the most prolific compiler among the American singing masters.

Other flourishing composers and compilers of music for the singing schools (and a few of their representative tunebooks, most of them anthologies including compositions by others as well as by themselves) were Jacob French (1754–1817; *New American Melody*), Jacob Kimball (1761–1826; *The Rural Harmony*), Samuel Holyoke (1762–1820; *Harmonia Americana* and *The Columbia Repository*), Jeremiah Ingalls (1764–1838; *The Christian Harmony, or Songster's Companion* [*EAM* 22]), Oliver Holden (1765–1844; the last three editions of *The Worcester Collection*, 1797–93),

Stephen Jenks (1772–1856; his collected works are in *RRAM* 18, including the contents of all his tunebooks, from *The New-England Harmonist* [1799] to *The Harmony of Zion* [1818]), and many others.

The kind of piece the New Englanders liked best was the fuging tune; about one-quarter of their total production is made up of this characteristic type—which, as we have seen, was modeled on English fuging psalm tunes of the sort Lyon had introduced to the New World in *Urania*. The typical American fuging tune usually proceeds like this: beginning like a choral hymn, in three-part or four-part harmony with the principal air in the tenor voice, it gives way about halfway through to a series of staggered entrances by each of the voice parts (the fuging section), which are then led to a full close; then the "fuge" is repeated. A good example, and one very popular during the Federal era (it was "borrowed" for reprinting 102 times before 1810, after its initial publication in 1782) is *Greenfield* by Lewis Edson (1748–1820) of Bridgewater, Massachusetts. Example 1–5 gives the piece one whole tone lower than its original pitch, to facilitate comparison between the Yankee musical style in fuging tunes and the style of their British prototypes, as represented in Example 1–3.

Some fuging tunes are strophic settings of metrical psalms or hymns; the same music serves for each of the poetic stanzas. Similarly strophic are *plain tunes*, which are syllabic settings of one poetic stanza, with three- or four-part harmony throughout, no fuging section, and the principal air in the tenor voice; see, for example, Billings's *Conquest*, Read's *Windham*, or Swan's *China* (the last-named in Example 1–6). The New Englanders essayed larger types of works also: the *set piece*, a through-composed setting of poetry longer than a single stanza, and the *anthem*, a through-composed setting of a prose text, often from Scripture. Whereas the set piece is typically chordal throughout, like an extra-long plain tune, the anthem is characterized by varied textures—now a chordal passage, now a fuging section, now individual voice parts in alternation. These longer pieces are not always successful: the Yankee tunesmiths had a very limited vocabulary of harmony and virtually no concept of modulation, and their attempts to build larger formal structures often become tedious for lack of harmonic variety.

The melodies of all these pieces are apt to be of a folkish quality, now simple and flowing, now angular and rhythmically powerful, if somewhat rigid. They derived partly from the Anglo-Celtic folk-song tradition, and indeed in many of the tunes can be heard echoes of such folk songs as *Greensleeves* and *Lord Randal*. One of the most striking is that of Swan's *China*, a piece that so caught the fancy of New Englanders that it was sung at funerals "down East" for about a century after its composition in 1790. Example 1–6 gives the entire piece; the air is in the tenor voice.

The harmony of the Yankee fuging tunes and other works is perhaps the most characteristic feature of their style. Abounding in open fifths, parallel fifths and octaves, modal inflections, and surprising dissonances, it seems almost a throwback to a much earlier style of European music, long before

EXAMPLE 1–5.   L. Edson, *Greenfield*, as first printed in Simeon Jocelin's tunebook *The Chorister's Companion* (New Haven: T. and S. Green, 1782), 18.

EXAMPLE 1–6. T. Swan, *China* (1790), after the version printed in William Little and William Smith, *The Easy Instructor* (Albany, NY: Websters & Skinner and Daniel Steele, 1809), 99.

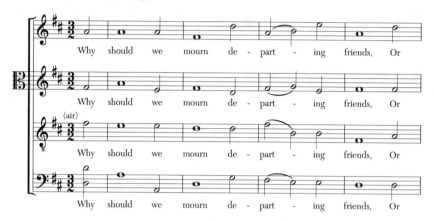

the development of the highly organized tonal syntax of the century of Handel and Haydn. Yet the Americans were consistent in their taste, and their music is perfectly homogeneous stylistically; in its own terms, it is as "stylish" as the more complex and sophisticated European music of its time.

In performing these choral pieces, some women usually doubled the leading tenor part in a higher octave; conversely, some men might double the trebles an octave lower. Thus the New England style often resulted in an organlike sonority of six parts. Sometimes, if the composer wrote "choosing notes" (more than one note to a part), the texture was even richer; Billings's *Chesterfield* (termed by Richard Crawford in his liner notes for *NW* CD 80255 a "boulderlike drone of a piece") is an especially powerful example. Billings emphasized the desirability of a really solid bass: he complained in *The New-England Psalm-Singer* that "in most Singing Companies I ever heard, the greatest Failure was in the Bass," and he cautioned that "in order to have good Music, there must be Three Bass to one of the Upper Parts. So that for instance, suppose a Company of Forty People, Twenty of them should sing the Bass."

Most of the texts found in the Yankee tunebooks are, of course, religious. Isaac Watts was by far the most popular source for the hymns and fuging tunes. His doughty translations and paraphrases of the psalms fit the rough-hewn, forthright New England music perfectly, and on occasion he could rise to greatness; witness a stanza of his that was set as a hymn by Justin Morgan under the title *Amanda* (in *3Centuries* 7, 30):

> Death, like an overflowing stream,
> Sweeps us away; our life's a dream;
> An empty tale, a morning flow'r,
> Cut down and wither'd in an hour.

Watts employed the meters of balladry in his "imitations" (for which read "paraphrases") of the psalms; thus, in his hands Psalm 90, which in the King James version of the Bible begins "Lord, thou hast been our dwelling place in all generations," turns into the rock-firm, memorable Common Meter quatrain:

> Our God, our help in ages past,
> Our hope for years to come,
> Our shelter from the stormy blast,
> And our eternal home.

Nahum Tate and the Wesleys were also favorite poets, and so was John Newton, whose *Olney Hymns* (1779) were full of powerful (some said extravagant) imagery and emotionalism.

Patriotism and religion were often intermingled. One can imagine the political overtones that singing schoolers must have read into Supply Belcher's lusty *Jubilant*, set to a text by Charles Wesley and published not long after the United States was proclaimed a new constitutional republic:

> Blow ye the trumpet, blow
> The gladly solemn sound;
> Let all the nations know,
> To earth's remotest bound:
> The year of jubilee is come,
> Return, ye ransom'd sinners, home!

Stephen Jenks voiced the same sentiments even more directly in his fuging tune *Liberty* (in *RRAM* 18, 119):

> No more beneath th'oppressive hand
> Of tyranny we groan;
> Behold a smiling happy land,
> That freedom calls her own.

In 1775, Andrew Law found appropriate verses for *Bunker Hill*—the music of which may be by him but is more likely by one Sylvanus Ripley—in a poem, "The American Hero," written just after the outbreak of the Revolution by the American-born Nathaniel Miles:

> Why should vain mortals tremble at the sight of
> Death and destruction in the field of battle,
> Where blood and carnage clothe the ground in crimson,
> Sounding with death groans.
>
> Life, for my country and the cause of freedom,
> Is but a trifle for a worm to part with;
> And if preserved in so great a contest,
> Life is redoubled.

We may find Billings's paraphrase of Psalm 137 amusingly presumptuous, but certainly it was no smiling matter to him when, remembering the siege of Boston, he wrote,

> By the Rivers of Watertown we sat down and wept,
> when we remember'd thee, O Boston. . . .
> God forbid! Forbid it Lord, God forbid that
> those who have sucked Bostonian Breasts
> should thirst for American blood!

Such a piece as the last-mentioned—Billings's *Anthem: Lamentation over Boston* (1778; *NW* CD 80276)—points to one of the most appealing aspects of the singing-school music of the Yankee tunesmiths: this was a music completely in tune with the society for which it was written. These journeyman composers had a secure and respected function in Colonial and Federal-era life in general; viewed historically from a point two hundred years later, theirs was a sort of golden age of musical participation in which teachers, composers, singers, and populace in general worked together fruitfully. If ever there was truly a popular music, the music of the New Englanders was popular: it arose from deep traditions of early America; it was accessible to all and enjoyed by all; it was a plainspoken music for plain people; and assessed on its own terms, it was a stylistically homogeneous music of great integrity—and the first indigenous music of the newborn United States.

Diffusion of the Yankee idiom outside New England was aided by the peripatetic singing masters—Andrew Law, for instance, conducted singing schools not only in his native New England but also in New York, New Jersey, Pennsylvania, Maryland, and even the Carolinas—and also by the evangelistic revival movements, such as the "Great Revival" of 1800. It may also have been encouraged by the development of new systems of music notation, especially the *shape-note* notation of William Smith and William Little, in whose tunebook *The Easy Instructor* (Albany, 1801) the musical notes were shaped differently according to their position in the scale (see Figure 1–1 on p. 15). At that time, instead of *do, re, mi, fa, sol, la, ti, do,* the syllables *fa, sol, la, fa, sol, la, mi, fa* were used; hence, four shapes sufficed to distinguish the syllables: ◣ (*fa*), ○ (*sol*), □ (*la*), ◇ (*mi*). Little and Smith's invention, reminiscent of other, less successful American attempts to make easier the task of learning to read music—both earlier (e.g., Tufts's) and later—had the simplicity of genius. Their four-shape notation was widely adopted in other tunebooks: it would seem that Andrew Law, who claimed shape-notes as his own idea, borrowed them from *The Easy Instructor* for his *Art of Singing* (4th ed., 1803; two tunes from it—*Delaware* and *Old 100*—in 3*Centuries* 7, 57); and other tunebook compilers followed suit, especially those who favored the New England style of music.

But not every post-Colonial American did favor it. With the new wave of immigration that followed the successful establishment and consolidation of the United States of America came a new wave of foreign influence in American music. In the cities along the eastern seaboard, wealth began to accumulate about 1800, and so did a taste for European standards of culture—and cultural models as well. The tendency of more-or-less aristocratic Americans to look to Europe for "lessons in living well" had been latent for some time; it was reinforced as some, especially in the eastern cities, sought increasingly to act "urbane" or cosmopolitan. Ironically, in the very place that had seen its beginning, and for the same reason—cultural improvement—the Yankee music began to be attacked. One articulate spokesman for reform was John Hubbard, a sometime composer himself but also professor of mathematics and natural philosophy at Dartmouth College in New Hampshire. Hubbard's *Essay on Music* of 1808 was a harsh criticism of the New England style and its artisan composers. It attacked the "common fuge" as a music that "can never be of more consequence than an oration well pronounced in a foreign language," and as for the tunesmiths,

Almost every pedant, after learning his eight notes, has commenced author. With a genius, sterile as the deserts of Arabia, he has attempted to rival the great masters of music. On the leaden wings of dullness, he has attempted to soar into these regions of science, never penetrated but by real genius.[4]

Elias Mann, whose tunebook *The Massachusetts Collection of Sacred Harmony* appeared in 1807 in Boston, made a point of saying in its preface that he had included "none of those wild fugues, and rapid and confused movements, which have so long been the disgrace of congregational psalmody, and [have earned] the contempt of the judicious and tasteful amateur." Andrew Law, after a lengthy career as partisan of the native style, turned his back on it completely. Increasingly, as his knowledge of the "sublime and beautiful compositions of the great Masters of Music" grew, he sought to substitute "serious, animated, and devout" music for "that lifeless and insipid, or that frivolous and frolicksome succession and combination of sounds" that the New Englanders had created. Even Daniel Read, perhaps the most gifted of the Yankee composers, felt the impact of the new wave. Read never became, as did Law, a self-styled reformer; nevertheless, in some touching words written in his old age, he confessed to changed musical values:

> Since studying the writings of such men as D'Alembert [and others], since carefully examining the system of harmony practically exhibited in Handel's *Messiah*, Haydn's *Creation*, and other similar works … my ideas on the subject of music have been considerably altered; I will not say improved.[5]

In later chapters, we shall see how the music of the First New England School was submerged beneath the new wave of musical taste in the eastern United States—but not drowned out completely.

SOUTH OF NEW ENGLAND

If the British colonists of the New World must, because of their predominance among the early settlers, be considered the mainstream of early American culture, there were nevertheless important minority groups very early. In general, these groups—notably German Pietists in Pennsylvania and Moravian brethren in Pennsylvania and the Carolinas—were culturally insular;

---

[4]John Hubbard, *An Essay on Music* (Boston: Manning & Loring, 1808), 17–18. Not surprisingly, Hubbard was one of the founders, in 1807, of the Handel Society at Dartmouth.

[5]Quoted in Lowens's seminal essay "Daniel Read's World: The Letters of an Early American Composer" (1952), reprinted as chap. 8 of his *Music and Musicians in Early America*. The fullest biographical study of Read is Vincent C. Bushnell, *Daniel Read of New Haven (1757–1836): The Man and His Musical Activities* (Ph.D. diss., Harvard University, 1978). See also the introductory essay by Karl Kroeger and Richard Crawford in Daniel Read, *Collected Works* (*MUSA* 4 [= *RRAM* 24]).

their communities tended to remain "foreign" enclaves even in a land of immigrants. Nevertheless, their musical cultures deserve brief mention.

A number of Protestant German sects settled in Pennsylvania for religious motives. Each differed in its worship-music practice, but all were alike
in their emphasis on congregational song, especially hymns (stanzaic poems
to original, not scriptural, texts). To Germantown in 1694 came a group of
Pietists under the leadership of Johannes Kelpius (1673–1708). Known as
the Hermits of the Ridge (or Wissahickon Mystics, or True Rosicrucians),
they sang hymns, psalms, and anthems and apparently used instrumental accompaniment. Kelpius compiled for his flock a hymnbook with the Pietist title
*The Lamenting Voice of the Hidden Love at the Time when She Lay in Mis-
ery and forsaken* (the manuscript is now at the Historical Society of Pennsylvania), containing ten hymn tunes, seven with basses, of a harmonic
richness unknown to the New England Puritans.

Conrad Beissel (1691–1768), who emigrated to Pennsylvania in 1720,
founded in 1732 a semimonastic community at Ephrata, in what is now Lancaster County, sixty-five miles from Philadelphia. Urging on his band an active musical seventh-day observance, Beissel turned from Pietist and
traditional hymn sources to original compositions, some of great length and
in as many as eight voices. In 1747 he published in Ephrata a massive collection of sacred texts for choral singing, with a German title that may be
translated as *The Song of the Lonely and Forsaken Turtle Dove, namely the
Christian Church*. This lacked any actual music, but in its foreword Beissel
outlined his theory of composition and singing, which was realized in many
choral compositions passed on through oral tradition.[6]

The richest and most sophisticated musical culture in colonial America was that of the Moravians in Pennsylvania and the Carolinas. They came
from German-speaking Bohemia for the most part, members of the Uni-
tas Fratrum—the first independent Protestant sect, founded in Bohemia
and Moravia in the mid–fifteenth century. The first Moravians to reach
America came to the West Indies in 1732; a sizable community settled in
Bethlehem, Pennsylvania, in 1741. Other Moravian centers were created
at Lititz and Nazareth in Pennsylvania and at Salem (now Winston-Salem)
in North Carolina.

The musical life of the Moravian brethren was extraordinarily intense.
Theirs was the first concerted sacred music in America: instruments joined
soloists and choirs in anthems, sacred arias, motets, and hymns. At the major
Moravian musical centers, Bethlehem and Salem, brass ensembles serenad-
ed the communities of brethren and played for weddings, christenings, funerals, and other solemn occasions. Collegia Musica—groups meeting
regularly to practice music, especially instrumental music—were organized,

---

[6]The largest and most stunning of the Ephrata Cloister manuscripts of hymn texts, once pos-
sessed by Benjamin Franklin, is in the Library of Congress.

and substantial libraries of European music of the seventeenth and eighteenth centuries accumulated. Some of this country's earliest and best instrument makers helped to supply the Collegia; especially notable is the organ builder David Tannenberg (1728–1804), who designed and constructed more than forty organs for Lutheran and Roman Catholic as well as Moravian churches.

Like most of the Yankee composers to the north, many of the Moravian composers were occupied in other tasks for a living. Indeed, some might never have composed at all had not a demand for new music existed. Jeremiah Dencke (1725–95) arrived from Germany in 1761 as pastor and business manager in Bethlehem. He was the first in America to compose sacred music with instruments, notably three sets of sacred songs for soprano, strings, and organ, among them the sturdy chorale *Meine Seele erhebet dem Herrn* and the lovely aria *Gehet in dem Geruch Seines Bräutigams-Namens* (both on *NW* CD 80467), both written for a festival of young girls (*Mägden-Fest*) in 1767. Johannes Herbst (1735–1812) came to Pennsylvania in 1786, was pastor at Lancaster and later Lititz, and was pastor and bishop at Salem in the last year of his life. The most prolific of the Moravian composers, Herbst wrote about 180 anthems and some 145 sacred songs, including, among the latter, *Abide in Me* and *Thanks Be to Thee* (both on *NW* CD 80467). John Antes (1740–1811), born near Bethlehem, was a string-instrument maker who was later ordained a pastor and sent to Egypt as a missionary; he eventually settled in England, where he published three attractive trios for violins and cello about 1790 (*NW* CD 80507), the earliest chamber music written by a native American.

Johann Friedrich (John Frederick) Peter (1746–1813), who came to America from Germany in 1770, was probably the most gifted of the Moravian composers. He wrote more than one hundred works, mostly anthems and sacred arias but also six string quintets (Salem, 1789; *NW* CD 80507); the quintets reveal him as a sensitive and highly expressive minor master of the early Classic style.[7] David Moritz Michael (1751–1827), a German who was in Pennsylvania from 1795 to 1815 in various administrative posts, put his firsthand knowledge of woodwind instruments to good use in fourteen *Parthien* and two sets of *Water Music*—suitelike works, mostly for wind sextet (*NW* CDs 80490 and 80531; *Parthia* 8 in *3Centuries* 12, 48–58).

The Moravian culture was essentially insular: although it was known and spoken of admiringly by other Americans in the eighteenth century (Benjamin Franklin, for one), it had little influence outside the Moravian communities themselves. On the other hand, the music of the American Moravians has a special stamp, the result of the New World environment. One specialist in their music cogently describes the source of this "American" quality:

---

[7]The sacred aria *Leite mich in deiner Wahrheit*, perhaps Peter's earliest work (first performed in 1770 a few months after his arrival in the New World), is on *NW* CD 80467.

The Moravians were devout people. Colonial life for them had a religious purpose and religious ideas dominated their activities. This gives their music a special character. In Europe, the average late 18th century composer wrote an occasional piece of church music between the symphonies, sonatas, operas, and other secular works which were his chief concern. To the Moravian musicians in America, however, church music was the most important expression of their inner lives. Their music therefore is better suited to the purpose and more touching than most religious music written in Europe during the same period.[8]

The story of sacred music in the Middle Atlantic and southern British colonies is less well documented than in New England or the German-speaking communities to the south. Little is known of sacred music in the Quaker centers of Philadelphia until the 1760s; Virginia, almost wholly an agricultural colony, has left us almost no colonial music; in South Carolina, especially its largest city, Charleston (Charles Town at the time), an active secular music life has somewhat obscured any special activity in sacred music.

Two native-born composers figured in the sacred music of Philadelphia in the early 1760s. These were James Lyon and Francis Hopkinson (1737–91; see p. 41). Lyon began the history of Philadelphian music publishing in 1761 with *Urania* (see p. 8). He indicated in the Index that six of the pieces in it were "completely new" (and thus perhaps the earliest publications in standard music notation of works by an American composer); five of these may have been composed by Lyon himself, but the music for *The 23rd Psalm* (Example 1–7) is by Hopkinson, better known as a cultivated dilettante specializing in secular music. One of the hymns in *Urania* (*Whitefield's*) is a setting of a text from the 1757 *Hymn Collection* of the famous British Methodist revivalist George Whitefield; its music is the first American publication of the tune *God Save the King*, later (1831) to be used as the melody for Samuel Francis Smith's "My Country 'tis of Thee" in the unofficial national hymn *America*.[9]

Charleston, by 1775 the largest city south of Philadelphia, was a brilliant center of church music, as it was of secular. Free from the restrictions on instruments observed in Puritan New England, Charleston's Anglican churches of St. Philip's and St. Michael's allowed organs to be heard, and peals of bells. Organist at St. Philip's from 1737 until his death was Charles Theodore Pachelbel (1690–1750), son of the famous Nuremberg composer and organist Johann Pachelbel. Of Charles Theodore's music we have only a fine *Magnificat* for two choirs and organ—written, however, before the composer left Germany for America.

[8] Hans T. David, ed., *Ten Sacred Songs. Music of the Moravians in America ... No. 1* (New York: New York Public Library, 1947), v.

[9] The tune has been put to many various uses, over many years, by Americans; one version from the Federal period begins with the words "God save great Washington," another with "God save America."

EXAMPLE 1–7.   F. Hopkinson, *The 23d Psalm Tune*, in J. Lyon, *Urania* (Philadelphia: William Bradford, 1761), 50, measures 1–12. The cut-time signature reversed indicates a quick $\frac{2}{2}$ tempo.

BIBLIOGRAPHICAL NOTES

Richard Crawford has published invaluable writings on much of the material in this chapter; see in particular his lengthy introduction to the monumental *American Sacred Music Imprints 1698–1810* (Worcester, MA: American Antiquarian Society, 1990), begun by Allen Britton and Irving Lowens, completed by Crawford; the chapter "William Billings and American Psalmody: A Study of Musical Dissemination" in his *The American Musical Landscape* (Berkeley and Los Angeles: University of California Press, 1993), 111–50; and "A Historian's Introduction to Early American Music," *Proceedings of the American Antiquarian Society* 89/2 (October 1979): 261–98 (with an accompanying LP sound sheet). Irving Lowens's important articles, especially a group of seminal bibliographical studies, are reprinted, in revised versions, in *Music and Musicians in Early America* (cited in note 2).

Nicholas Temperley's *The Music of the English Parish Church* (New York: Cambridge University Press, 1979) is a detailed study of the British antecedents of early American psalmody; complementing it, in dealing with the American repertory, is his article "Psalms, metrical" in *AmeriGrove*. Richard Crawford's "Psalmody," also in *AmeriGrove*, is a masterly summary.

The music of Ainsworth's psalter is reproduced in facsimiles and transcriptions in Lorraine Inserra and H. Wiley Hitchcock, *The Music of Henry Ainsworth's Psalter* (*ISAMm* 15 [1981]). Chapter 2 of Lowens's *Music and Musicians in Early America* considers "The Bay Psalm Book in 17th-Century New England." Zoltán Harazti's *The Enigma of the Bay Psalm Book* (Chicago: University of Chicago Press, 1956), with a facsimile of the first edition of the psalter, discusses it from the textual standpoint, and Richard G. Appel's *The Music of the Bay Psalm Book* (*9th Edition* [1698]) (*ISAMm* 5 [1975]) contains facsimiles and transcriptions of the tunes as first printed in New England. D. W. Krummel briefly reviews the history of this historically important edition in "The Bay Psalm Book Tercentenary, 1698–1998," *[MLA] Notes* 55/2 (December 1998): 281–87.

Nicholas Temperley has culled American publications preceding Billings's *New-England Psalm-Singer* for pieces not traced in any earlier printed source; see his "First Forty: The Earliest American Compositions," *AM* 15/1 (Spring 1997): 1–25.

David McKay and Richard Crawford wrote the definitive monograph *William Billings of Boston: Eighteenth-Century Composer* (Princeton: Princeton University Press, 1975); Crawford alone, *Andrew Law, American Psalmodist* (Evanston, IL: Northwestern University Press, 1968; repr. New York: Da Capo Press, 1981).

The Complete Works of William Billings, ed. Hans Nathan (vol. 1) and Karl Kroeger (vols. 2–4) (n.p.: American Musicological Society and Colonial Society of Massachusetts, 1977–90), is notable as the first scholarly edition of an American composer's complete works. Kroeger went on to edit Daniel Read's *Collected Works* as *MUSA* 4 (= *RRAM* 24). Nym Cooke has published (as *MUSA* 6 [= *RRAM* 26]) the complete *Psalmody and Secular Songs of Timothy Swan*, with a generous prefatory essay. Facsimile editions have been issued of Billings's *The Psalm Singer's Amusement* (*EAM* 20) and *The Continental Harmony* (Cambridge: Belknap Press of Harvard University, 1961); also of Supply Belcher's *The Harmony of Maine* (*EAM* 6) and Ingalls's *The Christian Harmony* (*EAM* 22). A 15-volume series titled Music of the New American Nation (Sacred Music from 1780 to 1820), overseen by Karl Kroeger (New York, Garland Publishing, almost complete in 1999), contains singing-school music of the First New England School.

White Spirituals from the Sacred Harp (NW CD 80205) includes pieces by Billings, Read, and Ingalls in twentieth-century folkish performances that may come closer to the "Old Way" of psalmody than the more polished choral performances on NW CD 80255.

TWO

SECULAR MUSIC IN NEW ENGLAND
AND OTHER COLONIES

We have very little hard evidence of secular music making in the Colonial period, at least until the late eighteenth century. As Oscar Sonneck (1873–1928)—the first great scholar of American music—commented in his monumental bibliography of early American secular music, "Before 1790 practically nothing but psalm and hymn books were published, with here and there an issue of secular character as in the various 'Almanacks' and literary periodicals—also a very few songsters with music" (as opposed to the great majority of songsters—pocket-sized booklets that included song texts only).[1] But it is impossible to believe that the colonists, for all the strictures of Calvinist and Puritan leaders, did not enjoy secular songs and dances along with psalmody (and, as we have seen, psalmody was often put to secular, social use in the singing schools). And, in fact, there is plenty of circumstantial evidence that they did.

---

[1] Oscar George Theodore Sonneck, *A Bibliography of Early Secular American Music* (*18th Century*), rev. and enl. William Treat Upton (Washington, DC: The Library of Congress, Music Division, 1945; repr. New York: Da Capo Press, 1964), 575.

BRITISH-AMERICAN FOLK AND POPULAR SONG

To begin with, there is the large repertory of Anglo-Scottish-Irish "folk songs" that have come down to us. These were, of course, the "pop songs" of the day—a living music of everyday use by all. During the Colonial period, virtually none were written down: not only were they part of an ages-old tradition whereby popular music was transmitted orally from performer to performer and from one generation to the next, but also the press, in early America, was almost entirely in the control of the clergy, and the clergy had no interest in propagating or memorializing secular music. Nevertheless, the "underground" popular culture of the American colonies was a very lively one indeed. This is suggested, for instance, by the fact that about one hundred of the three-hundred-odd traditional British story-telling "Child ballads" have been traced (because they are still sung) in this country—more than in living British tradition. ("Child ballads" are named after Francis James Child [1825–96], their great collector and commentator.) The colonists were selective: older songs on themes irrelevant to the Colonial experience, such as courtly or chivalric themes, tended to be dropped; and many that were preserved have to do with sexual rivalry as seen through feminine eyes (*Barbara Ellen*, *The Gypsy Laddie*, *Little Musgrove*, *Jimmy Randall*) or relate directly to the New World experience (*Captain Kidd*, *The Golden Vanity*). The colonists changed the details of many British songs in terms of the American context and developing character. One example is a song from southern England (known also in Ireland), "My Jolly Herring" or *The Red Herring Song*, which was transformed into a tale of Yankee resourcefulness and thrift (with a comic note) as "The Sow Took the Measles."[2] Another is *The Foggy Dew*, of which the original explicit sexuality ("I rolled my love all over the foggy dew") was tempered by Puritan sensibility ("The only thing I did that was wrong / Was to keep her from the foggy dew").

Against the background of this British ballad tradition, Americans of course created their own popular ballads. The earliest that can be dated with certainty is *Springfield Mountain*, a re-creation in song of the death by snakebite on August 7, 1761, of Timothy Myrick of Springfield Mountain (now Wilbraham), Massachusetts (Example 2–1).[3]

In addition to British ballads and other songs brought to the New World and preserved through oral tradition, the colonists had copies of various British publications containing popular and traditional songs and tunes. One was Thomas Ravenscroft's three-part collection of 1609–11: *Pammelia* (the earliest British printed collection of catches and rounds), *Deuteromelia* (which includes the first published version of "Three Blind Mice"), and *Melismata: Musicall Phansies*. Others were John Playford's *The English Dancing Master* (1651; many more editions, as *The Dancing Master*, through 1728),

---

[2] Some of these points (and the specific example of this song) I owe to Alan Lomax, *The Folk Songs of North America in the English Language* (New York: Doubleday, 1960), xv–xxii.

[3] Lomax, *The Folk Songs of North America*, 6; the other verses of this version of the song are on 13.

EXAMPLE 2–1. *Springfield Mountain*, as collected by Alan Lomax in Townshend, Vermont (1939); stanza 1 of text only. After Alan Lomax, *Folk Songs of North America* (Garden City, NY: Doubleday, 1960), 13.

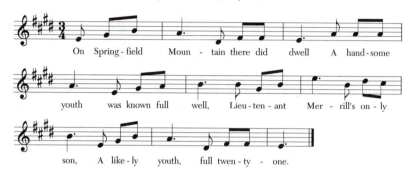

our largest single source of ballad tunes; Thomas d'Urfey's six-volume collection, *Wit and Mirth*; *or Pills to Purge Melancholy* (1719–20); John Watts's *The Musical Miscellany*, also in six volumes (London, 1729–31); and John Walsh's *The Compleat Country Dancing Master* (1731).

Examples from one or two of these printed collections of British popular tunes can suggest the sturdy musical stock from which sprang early American secular songs and dances. *Newcastle*, from Playford's *English Dancing Master* (Example 2–2 [a]), is a bold stomping tune with a short-long iambic syncope ("x" in the example) that we shall meet again in several later kinds of American popular music. The traditional *Packington's Pound* tune (Example 2–2 [b]) is the basis for anonymous verses about the "gallants of Newgate"—denizens of London's most notorious prison—which were printed in Watts's *Musical Miscellany*; the tune alternates between minor and modal flavor (now using E♮, now E♭) and at one point broadens out marvelously from $\frac{3}{4}$ to $\frac{3}{2}$ meter (bracketed in the example).

EXAMPLE 2–2. (*a*) *Newcastle*, my transcription from John Playford, *The English Dancing Master* (London, 1651 [recte 1650]), No. 77; the original is a minor third higher. (*b*) *Newgate's Garland*, anonymous verse to be sung to the tune *Packington's Pound*, John Watts, *The Musical Miscellany* (London, 1729–31), V, 42.

With *Newgate's Garland*, which relates to London's underworld—as does the first popular English "ballad opera," *The Beggar's Opera* (1728) of John Gay and Christopher Pepusch (and the song's tune, *Packington's Pound*, is used for Air 43, in Act III)—we approach a more formal kind of secular music than the ballads of oral tradition: music that was heard in concerts and on stages in American cities along the eastern seaboard from about 1730 on. These cities had developed remarkably in size and wealth during the first three-quarters of the eighteenth century. If by 1590 substantial towns had been established at Boston, New York, Philadelphia, Charleston, and elsewhere, by 1774—on the eve of the Revolution—they had mushroomed into real cities, which grew even more rapidly in the next quarter-century. The following table[4] shows the growth during this period.

[4] Adapted from Charles A. and Mary R. Beard, *A Basic History of the United States* (Philadelphia: The Blakiston Company, 1944), 44, and Russell B. Nye, *The Cultural Life of the New Nation*, 1776–1830 (New York: Harper & Row, 1960), 124

	1690	*1774*	*1800*
New York (founded 1625)	3,900	25–30,000	60,000
Boston (founded 1630)	700	20,000	25,000
Charleston (founded 1672)	1,100	10,000	18,000
Philadelphia (founded 1681)	4,000	40,000	70,000

Other growing cities were Salem, Providence, New Haven, Perth Amboy, Baltimore, Richmond, and Savannah. Although the population of these cities was only a small fraction of the total population of the colonies, their concentration of wealth and of social, political, and intellectual activity made them the cultural centers of the new land. Though primarily commercial cities, they tended to reflect the artistic life of similar European cities, with which they had close contacts. Thus, among other kinds of art, art-music gained its first Anglo-American expression in the cities, where from about 1730 we have records of concerts, operas, and other secular music.

THE RISE OF CONCERTS AND OPERA

The New World was hardly behind the Old in the establishment of a secular music culture based on public concerts. This would be a matter for nationalistic pride were it not for the fact that public concerts in Europe were a reflection of the rise of the middle class as patron of music, in contrast to the traditional aristocratic and churchly patronage; lacking a true aristocratic class, American culture was basically middle-class from the beginning, and it was natural that some of its musical energy was directed very early into public concerts. Thus—disregarding such isolated events as a public performance of music in Philadelphia at the consecration of the Gloria Dei church in 1700, or a "consort at Mr. Broughton's" in New York noted by the Reverend John Sharpe in his journal in 1710—genuine public concerts are reported as beginning as early as the late 1720s. The first of these we know about was announced in the Boston *Gazette* of February 3, 1729, as a "Consort of Musick [to be] performed on sundry Instruments, at the Dancing School in King-Street."[5]

Opera, too, was heard in America from the 1730s—not, of course, the lavish, costly, and aristocratic courtly Baroque operas, but English ballad op-

---

[5] See Cynthia Adams Hoover, "Epilogue to Secular Music in Early Massachusetts," *Music in Colonial Massachusetts 1630–1820*, II, ed. Barbara Lambert (Boston: Colonial Society of Massachusetts, 1985), 715–868; the *Gazette*'s notice is reproduced on 410. This concert was presented more than two and a half years before the one commonly cited as the earliest (at Boston, in "Mr. Pelham's great room," in December 1731), first by O. G. T. Sonneck, *Early Concert-Life in America* (Leipzig: Breitkopf & Härtel, 1907), 251.

eras, plays with songs (prophetic of the much later American musical comedies), which had captivated London's public with the immensely successful
run in 1728 of *The Beggar's Opera*. To John Gay's text, which satirized the
social, political, and musical establishment, Johann Christoph Pepusch adapted well-known popular songs and ballad airs—also, with tongue in cheek,
some music from Italian operas by Handel and other composers. (The satiric thrust of *The Beggar's Opera* and its many imitations, and their use of preexistent music, were gone from English operas later in the eighteenth century;
those were largely sentimental or comic dramas with newly composed songs
interpolated in them.) New York audiences heard *The Beggar's Opera* in
1750 and 1751, as produced by a company of "comedians from Philadelphia." But the record of ballad opera in America had begun even before that
with *Flora, or Hob in the Well* (abbreviated from a British work of 1729, with
text by Colley Cibber and musical interpolations arranged by John Hippis-
ley); it was produced at Charleston in 1735 during the first theatrical season
in that city. Also produced at Charleston, in 1736, was *The Devil to Pay* (1731)
by the Irish composer Charles Coffey. Other English ballad operas that were
to become popular in America included Cibber's *Damon and Phillida* (1749),
Henry Carey's *The Honest Yorkshireman* (1736), and Henry Fielding's *The
Mock Doctor* (1732). Probably the most popular opera of the entire Colonial
and Federal eras was *The Poor Soldier* (London, 1783), a comic opera with
a text by the Irishman John O'Keeffe and original music by the English composer William Shield, plus many airs to be sung to well-known popular tunes.
The Poor Soldier was first produced in America in December 1785, by the
Old American Company in New York, and had an unprecedented run of
eighteen more performances in the spring and early summer of 1786.

The operatic centers of America in the eighteenth century were the
cities from New York south: at Boston, an antitheater "blue law" of 1750 had
put an effective check on the establishment of ballad opera there. By the
end of the eighteenth century, two major opera companies were well established. One was William Hallam's London troupe, which started its American career in 1752 at Williamsburg, moved to New York, named itself the
American Company (and later the Old American), went back to England
during the Revolution, then returned after the war to New York. The Old
American Company's rival was the New Company founded in 1792 at
Philadelphia by Thomas Wignell, English actor and singer, and Alexander
Reinagle (see p. 36). The Wignell-Reinagle company played in the celebrated
New Theatre on Chestnut Street, a handsome hall with a stage 36 feet wide
and 71 feet deep and with some two thousand seats, nine hundred of them
in two tiers of boxes, above which was a large balcony area.

Early American concerts and ballad operas were understandably dominated by immigrant professional musicians, unlike the singing schools, which,
arising from a native tradition, were led by American-born journeyman composers. The cities could support these emigrant "professors" of music, particularly in the post-Revolutionary Federal period of economic and

commercial consolidation between 1783 and 1812, and in fact their standards and taste were to have a shaping influence on American musical culture in general. They were aided by (and indeed they led) the remarkable development in the late eighteenth century of music publishing in America. In little more than a half-century before 1820, American publishers issued an estimated 15,000 separate works in sheet-music editions, plus more than 500 printed "songsters," with their collections of song texts. Instrument manufacture was also on the rise; the simpler instruments had probably been made in America almost from the beginning, but we learn of a harpsichord builder as early as the 1740s, Gustav Hesselius of the Old Swedes' Church in Philadelphia, and of piano builders from 1775, when John Behrent of Philadelphia announced the manufacture of "an extraordinary instrument, by the name of the pianoforte, in mahogany in the manner of a harpsichord."[6]

Concerts and opera performances in the cities were paralleled by a dramatic rise of secular music in the urban home. "Almost every young lady and gentleman, from the children of the judge, the banker, and the general, down to those of the constable, the huckster and the drummer, can make a noise upon some instrument or other, and charm their neighbors with something which courtesy calls music," wrote a correspondent in the Philadelphia *Mirror of Taste and Dramatic Censor* in 1810.[7] Even if professional musicians could not make a living solely by performing, they could eke out an existence by hanging out a shingle as teachers or as proprietors of music stores—"magazines" or "repositories," as they were more often called. In short, secular music was becoming a real business in America as the eighteenth century closed and the nineteenth opened.

We should not, however, expect to find in the secular music of eighteenth-century America anything to match the scope or seriousness of purpose of, say, the music of Vienna, Rome, or Paris. The American ballad opera was an unpretentious entertainment with simple songs, enjoyable to all. The American concert was a mixture of short instrumental pieces, delivered by a few performers, and songs or duets of no great dimensions. American music publishers addressed themselves mainly to amateurs: like the singing-school tunebooks, the thousands of sheet-music publications and songsters were aimed at the modest abilities of music makers at home, to offer them practical or topical sources of mild diversion. It remained for a later generation to distinguish between such "popular" music and a more self-consciously high-flown "classical" music with serious artistic pretensions.

Representative of the socially useful and surprisingly diversified output of our early publishers is one collection of the 1790s with the informative title page *Evening Amusement, Containing fifty airs, song's, duett's, dances, hornpipe's, reels', marches, minuett's, &c., &c., for 1 and 2 German flutes or violins. Price 75 cents. Printed & sold at B[enjamin] Carr's Musical*

---

[6] Arthur Loesser, *Men, Women and Pianos* (New York: Simon & Schuster, 1954), 442–43.
[7] Quoted ibid., 456–57.

repositories, Philadelphia and New York, & J[oseph] Carr's, Baltimore. Published in 1796, this grab bag of pieces designed for "evening amusement" typifies the kinds of secular music enjoyed by American townspeople of the early Federal period. In it, traditional popular songs (we would call them folk songs today) of the English, Scottish, and Irish past are well represented, among them *Soldier's Joy*, *The Irish Washerwoman*, and *O Dear, What Can the Matter Be?* Newer songs, many of them from operas, are present, such as *What a Beau your Granny Was*, *Thou Softly Flowing Avon*, and *How Happily My Life I Led* (the last taken from the brief comic opera *No Song, No Supper* of the English composer Stephen Storace). Patriotic songs furnished tunes for several of the items: *God Save Great Washington* (see p. 25, note 9); *Yankee Doodle*; Reinagle's *America, Commerce, and Freedom*; and *The Marseilles Hymn*. A variety of dance tunes appears—several hornpipes, a highland reel, a "minuet de la cour," *Mrs. Fraser's Strathspey*—and so do marches, including *General Washington's March*, *The Duke of York's March*, and a march from *The Battle of Prague* by the Czech-English composer František Koczwara (d. 1791). Joseph Haydn is represented by a minuet and "airs" from two symphonies.

Here, then, is what our early urban secular music comprised: martial and patriotic music, traditional songs and opera airs, dance tunes, and a smattering of programmatic or absolute instrumental music.

MARCHES AND PATRIOTIC SONGS

As we might expect, both the Revolutionary and the Federal periods produced their share of military music, including marches and patriotic songs. Sometimes the two were combined, as in *Hail! Columbia* (in *3Centuries* 1, 174–75), popular in early America but virtually forgotten today. Its text by Joseph Hopkinson (son of Francis Hopkinson; see p. 41) was written in 1798 to be sung to the tune of *The President's March*; the latter, a sturdy foursquare tune, was the work of Philip Phile, who may have composed it after George Washington's inauguration as president of the new United States in 1789 but published it only in 1793 or 1794. *The President's March* (*3Centuries* 12, 26) was very popular: arrangements for two flutes and for piano duet appeared, as well as many other versions adapted from Phile's original piano setting; Ezekiel Goodale (1780–1828?) honored it in *The Instrumental Director* (1819) by placing it first of the sixty instrumental pieces in the volume (*3Centuries* 12, 59–60).

Yankee Doodle has all the earmarks of a march, too, and in fact, the earliest known separate edition of the song, published in England in the 1780s, carries the mocking title *Yankee Doodle, or (as now Christened by the Saints of New England) The Lexington March*. A subtitle instructs: "NB. The Words to be Sung thro' the Nose, & in the West Country drawl & dialect"—a jibe at the rural, plebeian backgrounds of most English emigrants to America. Popular here even before the Revolution,[8] *Yankee Doodle* as a *song* was first published in this country in 1797 or 1798, with bold new words, by the press of James Hewitt, the leading New York composer in the post-Revolutionary period (see p. 48).

The song destined to become our national anthem was anything but patriotic to begin with. Addressed "To Anacreon in Heav'n," the tune later sung as *The Star-Spangled Banner* originated as a British drinking song, celebrating the twin delights of Venus and Bacchus. Taken up by Americans, it was given new patriotic words in 1798 by one Thomas Paine (not *the* Thomas Paine), who sang of "Ye sons of Columbia, who bravely have fought / For those rights, which unstained from your Sires had descended." The *Star-Spangled Banner* text, written in 1814 by Francis Scott Key after the bombardment of Fort McHenry by the British, was applied to the old tune, and the resulting song was eventually made the national anthem (though not until 1931).

OTHER SONGS AND OPERA AIRS

The song *America, Commerce, and Freedom* found in *Evening Amusement* has a patriotic text, but it originated as a theater air. The composer was Alexander Reinagle (1756–1809), who came to New York in 1786 from his native England but soon moved to Philadelphia, where he dominated the musical scene for over two decades. An indefatigable composer, pianist, arranger, conductor, and impresario, Reinagle typified the immigrant professional musicians of the Federal period. A competent if not extraordinary composer, he wrote many of the airs for the operas produced at the New Theatre on Chestnut Street, where he was musical director. (Its opening concert of February 2, 1793, offered an elaborate program of overtures, concertos, symphonies, songs, a quartet, and glees.) *America, Commerce, and Freedom* was composed for the "ballet pantomine" *The Sailor's Landlady*; lusty and virile, it is one of Reinagle's best songs. Example 2–3 gives the beginning of the verse and the sturdy refrain.

More characteristic of the American opera air than *America, Commerce, and Freedom* was a tender, lyrical effusion in the tradition of English or Irish love songs, modeled on the pleasant if somewhat effete airs by middle- and late-eighteenth-century English composers of light operas and songs for the "pleasure gardens" of London, such as Thomas Arne (1710–78), Charles Dibdin (1745–1814), James Hook (1746–1827), William Shield (1748–1829), and Stephen Storace (1762–96). Reinagle surely contributed

---

[8] It is mentioned in the libretto of *The Disappointment: or, The Force of Credulity* (New York, 1767), as the tune for Air IV of that ballad opera (which seems to have been the first ballad opera actually written in America). The work, with music realized by Samuel Adler, is published in *RRAM* 3–4; its preface should be read in the light of Carolyn Rabson's later research, published as "*Disappointment* Revisited: Unweaving the Tangled Web," *AM* 1/1 (Spring 1983): 12–35, and 2/1 (Spring 1984): 1–28.

EXAMPLE 2–3. A. Reinagle, *America, Commerce, and Freedom* (Philadelphia: B. Carr, 1794), measures 9–16, 29–42.

many of this kind to Philadelphia productions, although few of his airs are extant today: virtually all his music was lost in a fire that consumed the New Theatre on April 2, 1820.

The general nature of the "tender" airs, and of their usually vapid poetry, is well seen in *Why, Huntress, Why?* composed by Benjamin Carr (1768–1831) for an opera on the tale of William Tell (*The Archers; or, the Mountaineers of Switzerland*), produced by the Old American Company in New York in 1796. Carr, who came to New York from London in 1793, established with his brother and his father a chain of music stores in Philadelphia, New York, and Baltimore and was a prolific publisher as well. He also had a nice, if modest, talent as a composer of songs, as suggested by his *Hymn to the Virgin* ("Ave Maria"), No. 3 of *Six Ballads from the Poem of "The Lady of the Lake"* (Philadelphia, 1810; three, including "Ave Maria," recorded on NW CD 80467), to texts from Sir Walter Scott's popular work; some nine minutes long, with an accompaniment stylishly written for harp, the "Ave Maria," though not perhaps bearing comparison with Schubert's well-known setting, is one of the most impressive American songs before Stephen Foster's. On a much smaller scale is Carr's sensitive little setting of the "Willow Song" from Shakespeare's *Othello*. It is so inconclusive, however, as to suggest that it was not intended as an independent work but as an interpolation in the play (Example 2–4).

Lacking a lyric theater tradition, New England did not produce a large body of secular song in the eighteenth century, at least not of the sort I have been discussing. The Yankee singing-school tunebooks served, as noted previously, for secular diversion even though their contents were mainly sacred; and into them, as the eighteenth century neared its close, secular texts crept more frequently. Supply Belcher's *The Harmony of Maine* (Boston, 1794) included no fewer than eight secular, nonpatriotic songs to texts in the English lyric tradition; and the songbook was explicitly intended for use in both "singing schools and musical societies." Belcher meant by the latter term those rivals of the singing schools that were beginning to be organized in the cities—choral or instrumental groups established (usually under immigrant professional musicians) to perform the "new, scientific" music of Europe. The most famous of these was Boston's Handel and Haydn Society, organized in 1815 by Gottlieb Graupner (1767–1836), who, born in Germany, emigrated first to London; then moved to Prince Edward Island, Canada; next to Charleston, South Carolina; and finally to Boston early in 1797. There he became an influential entrepreneur of concerts and musical organizations, and Boston's leading music publisher and dealer. The invitation that Graupner sent out to the organizational meeting of the Handel and Haydn Society was explicit about its aim: "... cultivating and improving a correct taste in the performance of sacred music, and also to introduce into more general practice the works of Handel, Haydn, and other eminent composers."

EXAMPLE 2–4.   B. Carr, "Shakespeare's 'Willow,'" *Musical Journal* (Philadelphia: Carr and Schetky, 1800; repr. Wilmington: Scholarly Resources, 1972), I (Vocal Section), 22.

Organist of the Handel and Haydn Society was the well-trained, mature, and magisterial British immigrant George K. Jackson (1757–1822), deemed the most learned musician of Boston. Composer of an affecting *Dirge for General Washington* with a complementary *Dead March* for instruments, Jackson also wrote "songs, serenades, cantatas, canzonetts, canons, glees, &c., &c.," as we read in the subtitle of his undated collection

New Miscellaneous Musical Work. One of its songs, *Cancherizante* (Example 2–5), suggests he was indeed musically learned: planned as a demonstration of *cancrizans* (crablike) or retrograde melodic technique, it is, as Dr. Jackson pedantically explains at the head of the music, "a song to be sung forwards & then backwards beginning at the last note & ending with the first." Pedantic or not, the little song comes off rather well, its music matching nicely the gentle pastoral text. His setting, for vocal trio, violin, and piano, of Alexander Pope's "celebrated ode" *The Dying Christian to His Soul* (ending "Oh, grave, where is thy victory? / Oh, death, where is thy sting?")—also set by Billings as an anthem—shows Jackson in a more dramatic vein (*NW CD 80467*).

EXAMPLE 2–5.   G. K. Jackson, *Cancherizante, New Miscellaneous Musical Work* (n.p., n.d. [after 1800]), 9.

Gilbert Chase neatly pinpointed the two kinds of musicians who fostered eighteenth-century urban secular music: "immigrant professionals" and "gentleman amateurs."[9] Among the latter, best known (though for activities other than music) are Thomas Jefferson, who if not a practicing musician or composer was still an aristocratic patron of art-music, and Benjamin Franklin, who was a practicing musician on the guitar, the harp, and the musical glasses—and, in fact, invented an improved version of the glasses, which he called an "armonica." Franklin may also have composed music (although probably not the string quartet sometimes claimed to be his). Another prominent "gentleman amateur" was Francis Hopkinson (1737–91). According to John Adams, Hopkinson was a "pretty, little, curious, ingenious" man, "genteel and well-bred." He was something of a poet (his *Battle of the Kegs* is well known) and a political figure (his signature is on the Declaration of Independence, and he was our first Secretary of the Navy). Hopkinson's interest in music extended beyond performance and composition to mechanical improvements for the harpsichord (somewhat belatedly, since the instrument was already being superseded by the pianoforte).[10] In 1788 Hopkinson dedicated a set of *Seven Songs for the Harpsichord or Forte Piano* to George Washington (an eighth was added after the title page was set in type), remarking in the dedication that "I cannot, I believe, be refused the credit of being the first native of the United States who has produced a musical composition." Hopkinson probably knew the music of the New England Yankee tunesmiths, some of whom doubtless antedated him as native-born composers, but he must have adjudged his genteel songs for the "republican court circle" of Philadelphia as *real* music, compared with the folkish singing-school tunes of his northern contemporaries. Nevertheless, the first composition we can unequivocally attribute to a native American is a manuscript song by Hopkinson dated 1759, *My Days Have Been So Wondrous Free.* The music does not quite live up to the charm of its first verse line; it is a bit stiff, if innocuously pleasant. The *Seven Songs*, written (or at least published) almost thirty years later, show hardly any advance in style or technique, although one of them, *My Gen'rous Heart Disdains* (in *3Centuries* 1, 391–92), is a lilting rondo of considerable verve and wit; Example 2–6 is its refrain.

Songs and instrumental music were combined in a special way in a few turn-of-the-century theater works that mingled the English ballad-opera tradition with the descriptive incidental music of French and German "melodrama," a term at that time denoting a play with background music. Such a

---

[9] *America's Music*, 3rd ed. (Urbana: University of Illinois Press, 1987); the quoted terms are the titles of chap. 5 and 6.

[10] In March 1771, Thomas Jefferson wrote to his agent in Philadelphia, sending a list of purchases to be made in Europe. Nine weeks later he wrote again to the agent, who was by then in England, correcting the list to include a piano: "I have since seen a Fortepiano and am charmed with it. Send me this instrument instead." Quoted in Oscar G. Sonneck, *Suum cuique* (New York: G. Schirmer, 1916), 51.

EXAMPLE 2–6.   F. Hopkinson, *My Gen'rous Heart Disdains, Seven Songs . . .* (Philadelphia: Thomas Dobson, 1788), No. 7, measures 21–48.

mélange was the historically intriguing "operatic melodrame" *The Indian Princess*, by the American playwright James Nelson Barker and the British-born actor-composer John Bray (1782–1822), produced at the Chestnut Street Theatre in Philadelphia in 1808. The first surviving play on the story of Captain John Smith and Pocahontas, *The Indian Princess; or, La Belle Sauvage* (NW CD 80232) contains an overture, solo airs, choruses, and vocal ensemble numbers in the manner of ballad opera; it also has snippets of instrumental music sounding in the background of the spoken dialogue to underscore the drama and heighten its emotional impact. Open-ended, to be repeated as many times as needed during a given scene, these mood-music miniatures are the precursors of later American background music for drama and films, and they point to the dawning Romantic era's impulse to exaggerated emotionalism—that is, to "melodrama" in the later sense—and to a programmatic, narrative musical aesthetic.

DANCE MUSIC

One of the least-studied areas of early American music is that of the dance. Yet the colonists, even the earliest ones, were great dancers. Hawthorne's tale of *The Maypole of Merry Mount* is partly legendary, but its essence is confirmed by William Bradford's contemporary account (1647) of the revels at the Merry Mount settlement in colonial Massachusetts, where "they also set up a May-pole, drinking and dancing about it many days together." Throughout the Colonial and Federal periods, journals and letters are full of references to dancing. The eminent justice Samuel Sewall of Boston refers in his diary in 1685 to "a Dancing Master who seeks to set up here and hath mixt dances"; by 1716 the *Boston News-Letter* was advertising instruments, instrumental instruction books, and ruled paper (presumably music paper, with printed staves) "to be sold at the Dancing School of Mr. Enstone." Eighteenth-century concerts often concluded with a march, which served then to introduce a postconcert ball.

The main reason, of course, that the actual music of early American dances is not better known is that little of it was published or even written down: like most of the world's dance music, it was not transcribed but improvised by musicians according to the needs of the moment, elaborating upon, extending or shortening, repeating or varying the current repertory of dance tunes. Popular dancing, moreover, is traditionally done to the accompaniment of whatever instruments or voices are at hand. Thus, when dance music is written down, it usually appears as a bare-boned skeleton, to be given flesh and blood in actual performance; the written music is often merely a cue sheet for the musicians. Ultimately, composers may base a fully realized work on a well-known tune, a dance rhythm, or a typical dance form (J. S. Bach,

Chopin, and Scott Joplin come to mind); but their music presents a somewhat flossy and stylized, if artistically valid, image of a particular dance.

By the late eighteenth century, however, American dance music had found its way into manuscript and even printed music sheets. Some of the pieces are stylized versions for pianoforte of well-known dance types. Such is the "Tempo di Menuetto" movement of a *Sonata for the Pianoforte with an Accompaniment for the Violin* (1797?; on *NW* CD 80299, together with its other movement, an "Andante"); this is by Rayner Taylor (1747–1825), a teacher of Alexander Reinagle and active in Philadelphia's musical life from 1793, a year after emigrating from his native England. Many, however, are practical dances written out, usually in abstract format, on treble and bass staves (although often just the treble tune is given), to be fleshed out by actual instrumentation and improvisation on the spot.

The dances in the *Evening Amusement* collection of 1796 (mentioned earlier) suggest the types favored by the late eighteenth century: hornpipes, reels, minuets, strathspeys, and marches. To these might be added the gavotte, the allemande, the country dance, the cotillion, the quadrille, and the waltz (which was a great novelty in the period). The music of a "line dance," such as the country dance (or "contra dance"), was often the same as for a "square dance," such as the cotillion or the quadrille; hornpipes, reels, cotillions, strathspeys served equally well for these dances of British origin. On the other hand, the minuet, the gavotte, and the allemande, introduced from France, each had its own tempo, steps, and rhythmic character.

Cotillions and country dances were the most popular in the late-eighteenth-century American cities. The music comes as a surprise to present-day listeners, since it is obviously the forerunner of square-dance and other "country" music that we think of as rural, not urban. It is not hard to hear *Harriet's Birthday* or *Jefferson's Hornpipe* (Example 2–7) as lusty, ongoing fiddle tunes, pattering along in running eighth notes until, at the phrase endings, they land stompingly on repeated cadence chords.

EXAMPLE 2–7. Two country dances, from James Hewitt, comp., *A Collection of the Most Favorite Country Dances* (Philadelphia: J. Hewitt, 1802), 5, 17.

(a) Harriet's Birthday

(b) Jefferson's Hornpipe

Fitz James (Example 2–8) is a lively dance tune from a collection of "the most favorite cotillions" published in Philadelphia about 1804. The collection is interesting, not only for the verve and unpretentious excellence of its tunes, but also for its arrangement in "sets" showing the actual order that the dances followed, and for the "figures" (directions for the dances) that follow each tune. *Fitz James* turns out to be a miniature group of variations on its first strain, which then returns at the end to round out the form neatly. The "figure" for this dance is

> The leading couples chassez to the right—back again—chassez across each couple with your partners and back again—right and left.

Simple as such dance music is, it has a vitality, an infectious appeal, and a kind of rawboned integrity that transcend much other music of the period.

OTHER INSTRUMENTAL MUSIC

Aside from marches, dances, and some opera overtures, very little instrumental music was published in colonial America. With the Revolution and the stimulus that the little bands attached to units of the military gave to band music elsewhere, more instrumental music began to appear in print. The following Federal era saw rather extensive publication of it, mostly by European composers: by 1825, American presses had issued about 170 works by Mozart, almost 80 by Haydn, over 50 by Handel, and about 30 each by Beethoven and Weber. More highly favored than sonatas or even the flowery sets of variations coming into favor in the late eighteenth century were programmatic pieces of all kinds, especially "battle" pieces. The prototype among these, at least in terms of the number of American editions published, was *The Battle of Prague* by Koczžwara (see p. 35), described as late as 1880 by Mark Twain in a hilarious account of its performance by a young Arkansan bride:

> The bride fetched a swoop with her fingers from one end of the keyboard to the other, just to get her bearings, as it were. ... Then, without any more preliminaries, she turned on all the horrors of the "Battle of Prague," that venerable shivaree, and waded chin deep in the blood of the slain. ... The audience stood it with pretty fair grit for a while, but when the cannonade waxed hotter and fiercer, and the discord average rose to four [notes] in five, [and] when the girl began to wring the true inwardness out of the "cries of the wounded," they struck their colors and retired in a kind of panic.[11]
> There never was a completer victory. ... This girl's music was perfection in its way; it was the worst music that had ever been achieved on our planet by a mere human being.

[11] *A Tramp Abroad*, chap. 32, 341–42, of the first American edition, repr. in facsimile in *The Oxford Mark Twain* (New York: Oxford University Press, 1996).

EXAMPLE 2–8. *Fitz James* ("First Set, No. 1"), from *A Collection of the most favorite Cotillions* ... (Philadelphia G. E. Blake, 1804?), 2.

The *Battle of Prague* (ca. 1788) was rearranged constantly by American musicians to fit their instrumental resources; one Boston program in 1810 proudly announced that its version would include "double-basses, cymbals, French horns, kettle drums, trumpets, cannon, etc." (The tiny "Turkish Quickstep" section is performed by winds and a field drum on *NW* CD 80299.) Other battle pieces were also popular: the French composer Bernard Viguerie's *Battle of Marengo* came out in an American edition (1802) as "a military and historical piece for the piano forte," with cannon shots (expressed by the symbol ⊗ to be produced "by stretching the two hands flat on the three lower octaves in order to sound indistinctly every note." Like other battle pieces, *The Battle of Marengo* is an episodic work, its various sections entitled "March," "Word of command," "Trumpet call," "Cries of the wounded," and such. The whole work ends with a gigantic ⊗.

One American composer of battle pieces was James Hewitt (1770–1827), who came to New York in 1792 as "leader of the band" for the Old American Company. The first concert he organized in New York (September 21, 1792) included not only an overture by Haydn, a quartet by Pleyel, and a flute quartet by Stamitz but also his own *Overture in 9 movements, expressive of a battle* and an *Overture in 12 movements, expressive of a voyage from England to America* by Joseph Gehot (born in Brussels in 1756), who had indeed just made such a voyage, having immigrated to America with Hewitt and some other "professors of music from the . . . Professional concerts under the direction of Haydn, Pleyel, etc. London." Hewitt also composed a *Battle of Trenton*, dedicated to George Washington (1797; in *RRAM* 7), which he enlivened with quotations from *Washington's March* and *Yankee Doodle*. This was not the first American publication of *Yankee Doodle* in instrumental guise, for in 1794 Benjamin Carr had included it along with the *Marseillaise*, *Ça ira*, *O Dear, What Can the Matter Be?* and other popular tunes in a patriotic potpourri called *The Federal Overture*. Carr, too, reflected the fashion for battle pieces in *The Siege of Tripoli* (1804/5; in *RRAM* 1), its finale a "Yankee Doodle arranged as a Rondo," and he could write a graceful Haydnesque miniature for keyboard, if the six sonatas in *A New Assistant for the Piano-Forte or Harpsichord* attributed to him are indeed his (Example 2–9).

Carr's tiny sonata movements were aimed to instruct (the fingerings of Example 2–7 are those of the original edition). Much more lengthy and probably written for his own performance are four sonatas left in manuscript by Alexander Reinagle (*RRAM* 5). (Its editor, titling them *The Philadelphia Sonatas*, claims them as "the first real piano music . . . written in the United States".) One of these may have been played by Reinagle at a concert in June 1787, heard and noted in his diary for June 12 by George Washington, who was then in Philadelphia as a delegate to the Constitutional Convention. Example 2–10 shows the beginnings of the movements of Sonata III, a charming if somewhat overextended essay in the style of C. P. E. Bach.

Musical education up to this time had been almost completely limited to the classes of the singing schools; instrumental training, if done at all, was on an informal tutorial basis. But the rise of instrumental music was reflected in the publication also of the first American methods for learning to

EXAMPLE 2–9. B. Carr (?), Sonata 1, *A New Assistant for the Piano-Forte or Harpsichord* (Baltimore & Philadelphia: B. Carr, 1796), second movement.

play instruments. One of the most significant was Samuel Holyoke's *The Instrumental Assistant* of 1800 (followed in 1807 by a second volume); it contained "instructions for the violin, German flute, clarionett, bass viol and hautboy" and also "a selection of favourite airs, marches. &c."—sixty-five of them, culminating in a sonata—set as duets and trios in open score. A similiar tutor is Joseph Herrick's *The Instrumental Preceptor* (1807; printed, like Holyoke's volumes, at Exeter, New Hampshire). Two other collections

EXAMPLE 2–10.   A. Reinagle, Sonata III, *The Philadelphia Sonatas* (1780s?), beginnings of the three movements.

of 1807 are *Martial Music*, by the former Revolutionary War bandsman Timothy Olmstead (1759–1848), and *For the Gentlemen*—"written chiefly in four parts, viz. two clarionetts, flute and bassoon, or two violins, flute and violincello"—by the leading musician of Providence, Rhode Island, the blind Oliver Shaw (1779–1848).

BIBLIOGRAPHICAL NOTES

Charles Haywood's *Bibliography of North American Folklore and Folksong*, 2nd ed. (New York: Dover, 1961), and Ray M. Lawless's *Folksingers and Folkways in America*, rev. ed. (New York: Duell, Sloan and Pearce, 1965), are basic guides to music once popular, now folk. Alan Lomax's book on North American English-language folk songs (cited in note 2) includes the music of 317 songs.

Besides Francis Child's own fundamental work of 1883—*The English and Scottish Popular Ballads* (repr. New York: Folk Lore Press, 1957)—two other studies of British ballads are important: B. H. Bronson, *The Traditional Tunes of the Child Ballads*, in 4 volumes (Princeton: Princeton University Press, 1959–72), and Claude M. Simpson, *The British Broadside Ballad and Its Music* (New Brunswick, NJ: Rutgers University Press, 1966). A classic is Cecil J. Sharp and Maud Karpeles, *English Folk Songs from the Southern Appalachians* (1932), 2nd ed. (London: Oxford University Press, 1952).

Several of the seventeenth- and eighteenth-century British publications of popular music are available in modern editions. Ravenscroft's *Pammelia, Deuteromelia*, and *Melismata* have been separately reprinted by Broude Brothers (New York: Publishers Facsimiles, 1998). Playford's *Dancing Master* is similarly reprinted, with an introduction and notes by Margaret Dean-Smith (London: Schott, 1957); a transcription of the music has been made by Leslie Bridgewater and Hugh Mellor (London: H. Mellor, 1933). D'Urfey's *Wit and Mirth* was published in a new edition in 1876; a facsimile of that edition, with an introduction by Cyrus L. Day, is published in 3 volumes (New York: Folklore Library, 1959). The most extensive discussion of popular songs of this period—and for that matter, up to the 1970s—is Charles Hamm's *Yesterdays: Popular Song in America* (New York: W. W. Norton, 1979).

Good studies of musical life in American regions and cities are all too few. Three that are rich in material relevant to the present chapter are Wiley L. Housewright's generous *History of Music and Dance in Florida, 1565–1865* (Tuscaloosa: University of Alabama Press, 1991); Charles Kaufman's *Music in New Jersey, 1655–1860* (Rutherford, NJ: Fairleigh Dickinson University Press, 1981); and H. Earle Johnson's *Musical Interludes in Boston, 1795–1830* (New York: Columbia University Press, 1943). Another long-neglected area of research, that of music publishing, was boldly invaded by Richard J. Wolfe with *Early American Music Engraving and Printing: A History of Music Publishing in America from 1787 to 1825 with Commentary on Earlier and Later Practices* (Urbana: University of Illinois Press, 1980).

The national songs of America (among many others) are presented engagingly, with well-researched accounts of their origins and publication histories, in James J. Fuld's *The Book of World-Famous Music: Classical, Popular, and Folk*, 4th ed., rev. & enl. (New York: Dover, 1995). Vera Brodsky Lawrence's *Music for Patriots, Politicians, and Presidents* (New York: Macmillan, 1975) is full of superb illustrations. The origins of the tune of *The Star-Spangled Banner*, which eluded researchers for a long time, were tracked down by William Lichtenwanger in "The Music of the Star-Spangled Banner," *College Music Symposium* 18 (1978): 34–81.

NW CD 80293 offers dance music of the period: Thornton Hagert's liner notes for the album are exceptionally informative.

The two basic sources on the early development of American concert music and opera, still unsurpassed, are by Oscar Sonneck: *Early Concert-Life in America* (Leipzig: Breitkopf & Härtel, 1907; repr. New York: Musurgia, 1949) and *Early Opera in America* (New York: G. Schirmer, Inc., 1915; repr. New York: R. Blom, 1963). The basic resource on the British composers of most early American operas is Roger Fiske's mammoth *English Theatre Music in the Eighteenth Century* (London: Oxford University Press, 1973). Cynthia Adams Hoover offers an illuminating account of "Music in Eighteenth-Century American Theater," *AM* 2/4 (Winter 1984): 6–18; following historically, for the Federal-era music theater, is Susan L. Porter's *With an Air Debonair: Musical Theater in America 1785–1815* (Washington, DC: Smithsonian Institution Press, 1991). (See the informed review of the Porter book by Victor Fell Yellin in *[MLA] Notes* 49/3 [March 1993]: 1061–64.) Yellin has written on "Rayner Taylor" in *AM* 1/3 (Fall 1983): 48–71, and on "Rayner Taylor's music for *The Aethiop*" in *AM* 4/3 (Fall 1986): 249–67, and 5/1 (Spring 1987): 20–47. Stephen Siek discusses thoroughly "Benjamin Carr's Theatrical Career" in *AM* 11/2 (Summer 1992): 158–84. On *The Indian Princess*, see H. Wiley Hitchcock, "An Early American Melodrama: *The Indian Princess* of J. N. Barker and John Bray," *[MLA] Notes* 12 (1955): 375–88.

Anne McClenny Krauss covers "Alexander Reinagle, His Family Background and Early Career" in *AM* 4/4 (Winter 1986): 425–56. Reinagle as composer of popular sheet-music songs and concert-music piano sonatas is discussed provocatively in Richard Crawford's "Teaching and Composing," chap. 2 of his *The American Musical Landscape* (Berkeley and Los Angeles: University of California Press, 1993); see especially 58 ff.

The grass roots of American instrumental ensemble music, in the field music of the Revolution, are the subject of Raoul Camus's *Military Music of the American Revolution* (Chapel Hill: University of North Carolina Press, 1976); *3Centuries* 12 includes many examples of this music (as well as later works for winds), edited by Camus. Taking up where Sonneck-Upton's *Bibliography of Early Secular American Music* (see note 1) leaves off is Richard J. Wolfe's 3-volume bibliography, *Secular Music in America 1801–1825* (New York: New York Public Library, 1964).

For opposing views as to the composer of a famous string quartet, see W. Thomas Marrocco, "The String Quartet Attributed to Benjamin Franklin," *Proceedings of the American Philosophical Society*, 116/6 (December 1972): 477–85, and M. E. Grenander, "Reflections on the String Quartet(s) Attributed to Franklin," *American Quarterly* 27/3 (March 1973): 73–87.

"Battle music" is dealt with in an article (so titled) by J. Bunker Clark, in *Ameri-Grove*; he treats early American keyboard music in general in *The Dawning of American Keyboard Music* (New York: Greenwood Press, 1988).

Several volumes of *EAM* are relevant to this chapter, especially Belcher's *Harmony of Maine* (*EAM* 6); *The American Musical Miscellany*, a 1798 collection of more than one hundred songs (*EAM* 9); *Riley's Flute Melodies* (I, 1814–16, and II, 1817–20), containing more than seven hundred tunes (*EAM* 18); and Benjamin

Carr's *Musical Miscellany in Occasional Numbers* (1812–25; *EAM* 21), which includes more than eighty vocal and instrumental pieces by European as well as American composers.

The *RRAM* series includes several volumes of early American secular music. On Andrew Barton's comedy *The Disappointment* (*RRAM* 3–4), see note 8. O'Keeffe and Shields's opera *The Poor Soldier*, ed. William Brasmer and William Osborne, comprises *RRAM* 6. Thirty-one compositions by James Hewitt (mostly songs and keyboard pieces), ed. John W. Wagner, make up *RRAM* 7. Eve R. Meyer has selected and edited a fine selection of more than twenty songs by Carr in *RRAM* 15; see Karl Kroeger's perceptive review in *Notes* 45/1 (September 1988): 149–50. J. Bunker Clark edited thirty-six keyboard works for *RRAM* 1–2 (*Anthology of Early American Keyboard Music 1787–1830*). The *Philadelphia Sonatas* by Alexander Reinagle (with a chronology of his known works) are in *RRAM* 5, ed. Robert Hopkins. And Karl Kroeger has gathered together the music for the New York and Philadelphia theaters published in twelve monthly *Columbian Melodies* (Philadelphia, 1812) by Victor Pelissier (*RRAM* 13–14).

3Centuries 12 includes marches from Samuel Holyoke's *Instrumental Assistant* (pp. 7, 8, 23, 24), Joseph Herrick's *Instrumental Preceptor* (9, 10), Timothy Olmstead's *Martial Music* (11, 12), and Oliver Shaw's *For the Gentlemen* (13, 14–15).

part two

The Romantic Century
(1820–1920)

THREE

CULTIVATED AND VERNACULAR TRADITIONS, AND THE IMPACT OF ROMANTICISM

Americans distinguish colloquially between two broad categories of music: they speak of "classical" and "popular" music. The terms may be poor ones, especially the former (because of its several meanings), but they bespeak a common realization of the existence of two major traditions in American music. These I call the "cultivated" and the "vernacular" traditions, and I shall explain what I mean by these terms in a moment.

There is, of course, yet another great category of American music: folk music. This body of music, whether as a legacy of older musical tradition still to be found in cultural backwaters (and at times taken up somewhat self-consciously by the more sophisticated) or as traditional communal music made by various immigrant or ethnic minority groups, is not treated, as such, at any length in this book—not by any means because this music is unimportant in American cultural history, but because it is dealt with by Bruno Nettl in a companion volume in the Prentice Hall History of Music Series: *Folk and Traditional Music of the Western Continents*, 3rd ed. (1990).

However, as we have observed (see p. 29), whether one speaks of a certain music as "folk" or "popular" often depends on the time being considered. The British ballads of the Colonial era and the songs and dances of the Federal era were in every sense *popular*, not "folk" music; many of them still survive, but *now* as folk music (in the first sense described). Conversely, some folk music occasionally becomes popular: think of "folk singers" or country-music performers in recent decades and the music they have diffused so widely—nationalized, in effect—that it has become truly a "popular" music, a music of the populace. For that matter, some "classical" music may also become a popular music: in Germany and Austria, this has happened to some of Schubert's songs; in the United States, to some of Stephen Foster's. The rapidity with which such shifts in social function and "status" of various musics have occurred in the United States is one of the most striking things about our dynamic musical culture (reflecting, of course, our culture at large)—in fact, as far as I know, it is unique.

To return to cultivated and vernacular American-music traditions: I mean by the term *cultivated tradition* a body of music that America had to cultivate consciously, music faintly exotic, to be approached with some effort, and to be appreciated for its edification—its moral, spiritual, or aesthetic values. By *vernacular tradition* I mean a body of music more plebeian, native, not approached self-consciously but simply grown into as one grows into one's vernacular tongue, music understood and appreciated simply for its utilitarian or entertainment value.[1]

As America entered the nineteenth century, a distinction between cultivated and vernacular traditions was hardly visible. The music of the ballad operas at New York and Philadelphia was also the music of broadsides and songsters, as it was of the popular products of sheet-music publishers. The fuging tunes of the New England Yankees aimed to improve church singing and thus to be spiritually edifying, but they served also as a popular social music for secular entertainment. The Alexander Reinagles of the late eighteenth century brought a cultivated professionalism to the New World, but they wrote and played and sang to the populace at large as well as to the gentlemen and gentlewomen.

However, as the nineteenth century unfolded we can distinguish with increasing clarity two bodies of American music, two attitudes toward music: cultivated and vernacular traditions become visible; an eventually profound schism in American musical culture begins to open up. On the one hand there continued a vernacular tradition of utilitarian and entertainment music, essentially unconcerned with artistic or philosophical ideals; a music based on established or newly diffused American raw materials; a "popular" music in the largest sense—broadly based, widespread, naive, and unselfconscious—and a music whose "success" was measured not by abstract aesthetic standards

---

[1] My terms "cultivated" and "vernacular" are derived from similar terminology (relating to other aspects of American culture) in John Kouwenhoven's *Made in America. The Arts in Modern Civilization* (New York: Doubleday, 1949). A much later, stimulating consideration of a similar bifurcation in more general American culture is Lawrence W. Levine's *Highbrow/Lowbrow: The Emergence of Cultural Hierarchy in America* (Cambridge: Harvard University Press, 1988); see especially part 2 ("The Sacralization of Culture"), 85–168. See also Paul Charosh's "'Popular' and 'Classical' in the Mid–Nineteenth Century," *AM* 10/2 (Summer 1992): 117–35.

but by those of the marketplace. On the other hand there developed a cultivated tradition of fine-art music significantly concerned with moral, artistic, or cultural ideals; a music almost exclusively based on continental European models, looked to rather self-consciously; an essentially transatlantic music of the pretenders to gentility; a music by no means widespread throughout all segments of the populace but one that its advocates hoped was sophisticated; and a music that in general could not and did not pay for itself but required, for its very existence, some degree of patronage—for its composers if not its performers.

Many factors worked to create this dualistic musical culture in nineteenth-century America, among them the rapid geographical expansion of the nation and distinctive new immigration patterns. Perhaps most significant were the impact of Romantic attitudes and ideals and the continued growth of public concerts as a primary source of musical experience.

The extraordinary territorial growth of the United States in the nineteenth century accelerated a split between cultivated and vernacular traditions in American music because it diversified the cultural possibilities of American society. Dominating the entire social and cultural situation was the moving frontier, constantly pushing westward and leaving behind it an ever widening area of newly settled towns, with the older urban centers of the eastern seaboard behind *them*. Necessarily, musical life was different in the pioneer settlements along Horse Creek in Wyoming, between the Mormon and Oregon trails; in a relatively new but well-established and growing town such as Pittsburgh, just beyond the Allegheny Mountains (its population increasing between 1810 and 1850 from less than 5,000 to more than 70,000); and in an "old" urban center such as New York or Boston. Music of cultivated taste was taken up first in the older eastern cities, which were closest in spirit and space to Europe's centers of an art-music tradition. The music formerly enjoyed in such cities by all levels of society then tended to become both a slightly déclassé "popular" music and part of a vernacular tradition accompanying the westerly push of Americans across the land. By 1853, for instance, a Boston writer remarked of the Yankee singing-school tunebooks, once enjoyed by Bostonians great and small, that "if used at all, [they] have been crowded to the far west, mostly out of sight and hearing."[2]

The frontier settlements had virtually no contact with the developing cultivated tradition of the eastern urban centers. However, the newly established towns in between, rapidly growing in numbers, in population, in stability and ease of life, did have some contact and sought still more. But, lacking the urbanity, wealth, leisure, and comforting traditions of the eastern-seaboard cities, they were at once envious, fearful, and resentful of the culture "back East." The men, only one step removed from pioneering, viewed time spent on nonproductive, inutile art as wasteful or effete: land and money

---

[2] Nathaniel Gould, *Church Music in America* (Boston: A. N. Johnson, 1853), 55.

needed cultivation, not their sensibilities. Music, the most intangible and "useless" among the arts, had their special disdain and hostility. Leave music to the women, or to the immigrant "professors" (most often organists in the local churches, who also gave music lessons privately), or to the occasional touring virtuoso performers and ensembles whose number increased steadily from the 1840s on. Thus crystallized an American view of fine-art music as something that was essentially the province of foreigners or females (or effeminates)—a view still common early in the twentieth century, although it weakened rapidly after World War I.

New immigration patterns during the nineteenth and early twentieth centuries were also of great importance in shaping America's music, particularly that of the cultivated tradition, but ultimately also that of the vernacular. The flow of immigrants was immense—more than 35 million between the declaration of national independence in 1776 and the imposition of immigration quotas in 1924—spurred on by the land-rich, broadening nation and its manpower-hungry industrialization. The overwhelmingly white, Anglo-Saxon, Protestant population of the early United States (always excepting Native Americans and the Hispanics of the Southwest) was augmented by the main immigrations of the 1820–60 period: some 5 million Europeans, 90 percent of them from England, Ireland, or Germany. By contrast, in the 1860–1920 period, during which about 30 million entered the country, the immigrants were mostly non-English, non-Protestant, and from central and eastern Europe (Italy, the Balkans, Poland, and Russia).

The arrival of large numbers of Germans, in the first of these periods, and of other continental Europeans in the second, was critical in the molding of cultivated American taste because it diluted the traditional mainstream of Anglo-American culture and, especially, because it occurred at the peak of the Romantic movement in Europe. Early nineteenth-century America was ripe for Romanticism: indeed, someone has said that the American Revolution itself was perhaps the first and greatest example of Romanticism and, as Lewis Mumford wrote, "pioneering may in part be described as the Romantic movement in action."[3] Ordinary Americans may not have been consciously aware of the philosophic concepts of Romanticism—idealism, imagination, boundlessness, personal freedom, individualism—but their whole way of life and thought reflected them. And their musical attitudes were ready to be shaped along Romantic lines.

Romanticism had its beginnings in both France and England, as well as an early flowering in Germany. Although springing initially from the egalitarian and libertarian ideals of the French Revolution and back-to-nature goals as expressed by Jean-Jacques Rousseau, Romanticism found perhaps its highest expression and made its greatest impact through German music and

[3] *The Golden Day*, 2nd ed. (Boston: Beacon Press, 1957), 20.

musicians. Outside the field of opera, in which Italy maintained a national identity, hardly any kind of nineteenth-century music escaped being touched by German influence; hardly any musician could avoid the impact of Beethoven, Schubert, Schumann, Mendelssohn, Liszt, Wagner. Essentially, the centers of nineteenth-century musical thought were in Berlin, Leipzig, Munich, and Vienna; essentially, the ultimate in fine-art music was considered to be German music.

Even before devastating crop failures and the 1848 revolutions brought a huge wave of Germans to the United States, some Americans—reflecting in part, ironically, trends in the English musical world with which they felt themselves allied—were shifting their musical allegiance to Germany. The influential hymnodist Thomas Hastings spoke for his generation, poised on the brink of submission to German models, when he wrote in 1822 in his *Dissertation on Musical Taste*:

> We are the decided admirers of *German* musick. We delight to study and to listen to it. The science, genius, the taste, that every where pervade it, are truly captivating to those who have learned to appreciate it: but such, we presume, are not yet the *majority* of American or English auditors or executants.[4]

Hastings was writing as one of the first spokespersons for the cultivated tradition of American music. Terms such as *science, genius,* and *taste* bespoke special standards, not for all music, but for the *art* of music; not for music as a utilitarian part of everyday life or a pleasant diversion on the surface of life, but for music as an art whose holy mission it was to edify and uplift. "Appreciation" of such music—admiration for and understanding of it—required cultivation. As expressed by the highly respected editor and critic of the later nineteenth century, John Sullivan Dwight, the aim of such music and of the other arts was to remedy the defects of a materialistic society by "familiarizing men with the beautiful and the infinite." This was the credo of the cultivated tradition. As the exponents of this attitude saw it, German music more than any other achieved the desired goals. One significant result of this view was a rejection of the American musical past, dominated as it had been not only by popular, "unscientific" taste but also by British backgrounds. Both the

---

[4] *Dissertation on Musical Taste* (Albany, NY: Websters and Skinner, 1822), 194. Note that Hastings implies he is speaking from a single Anglo-American music culture, as differentiated from that of continental Europe—a fact elaborated upon cogently by Michael Broyles in his "Lowell Mason on European Church Music and Transatlantic Cultural Identification: A Reconsideration," *JAMS* 38/2 (Summer 1985): 316–48, and chap. 3 ("Lowell Mason: Hymnodic Reformer") in his *"Music of the Highest Class": Elitism and Populism in Antebellum Boston* (New Haven: Yale University Press, 1992). Nicholas Temperley speaks similarly in "Introduction: The Great Divide: Ocean or Channel?" *AM* 8/1 (Spring 1990): 1–11.

friendly, folkish music of the First New England School and the great melodic reservoir of Anglo-American song were spurned as bases for the new "scientific" music of the cultivated tradition.

In their self-conscious, unselfconfident striving toward a transatlantic taste for cultivated music, Americans also tended to reject the American present as a source of musical subject matter. The very aspects of American civilization that were unique had no models in Britain or continental Europe; they found scant celebration in American art-music. Europeans of the early nineteenth century were, after all, infinitely disparaging of American culture: "Who, in the four quarters of the globe, reads an American book, or goes to an American play, or looks at an American painting or statue?" asked the British author-minister Sydney Smith in 1820.[5] Europeans might grudgingly admit to American achievements in industry, technology, and science but considered them, if anything, inimical to art and edification. When the Philadelphia journalist-composer William Fry asked the director of the Paris opera if he might present at his own expense an open rehearsal of his opera *Leonora*, he was refused with the remark, "In Europe we look upon America as an industrial country—excellent for electric railroads but not for art." (Fry's angry retort was that "although we had excelled in making electric telegraphs to carry ideas without persons, it was not a necessary consequence that we built railroads to carry persons without ideas."[6]) The American pianist Louis Moreau Gottschalk had a similar experience: "Zimmerman, director of the piano classes at the Paris Conservatoire ... without hearing me refused to receive me because 'l'Amérique n'était qu'un pays de machines à vapeur.'"[7] Cowed by such attitudes, American musicians of the cultivated tradition were not about to celebrate their electric telegraphs or their steam engines, their reapers or their railroads. (Vernacular-tradition composers—of popular songs, for instance—did, however, celebrate them, as they eventually did American steamboats and streetcars, balloons, baseball, and the Brooklyn Bridge.)

With the European music of Romanticism their main model, and with German music held up as the ideal, nineteenth-century Americans welcomed German musicians. They came in large numbers. Gottschalk heard a volunteer military band in Williamsport in 1863: "Is it necessary," he wrote in his journal, "to say that it is composed of Germans (all the musicians in the United States are Germans)?" A year earlier he had only half facetiously noted, "It is remarkable that almost all the Russians in America are counts, just as

---

[5] Quoted from the *Edinburgh Review* by J. B. McMaster, *History of the People of the United States*, I (New York: D. Appleton, 1883), 82.

[6] *The Musical World and New York Musical Times*, V/13 (March 26, 1853): 196; quoted in *Dwight's Journal of Music*, 2/26 (April 2, 1853): 202. I owe this reference to R. Allen Lott, "Pianos American Style III," *ISAM Newsletter* 15/1 (November 1985): 12.

[7] Jeanne Behrend, ed., *Notes of a Pianist: Louis Moreau Gottschalk* (New York: Knopf, 1964), 52.

almost all the musicians who abound in the United States are nephews of Spohr and Mendelssohn." The figure of the German music teacher came to be a familiar one in American towns; Gottschalk, Paris-trained and something of a Germanophobe (but with a perceptive eye and a sharp pen), wickedly described one:

> I was introduced [in St. Louis in 1862] to an old German musician with uncombed hair, bushy beard, in constitution like a bear, in disposition the amenity of a boar at bay to a pack of hounds. I know this type; it is found everywhere.[8]

It was inevitable that as the cultivated tradition of American music developed momentum in the nineteenth century, under the sway of European music and musicians here at home, young American musicians affluent enough to do so would go to the source for training: to Europe. Not surprisingly, when they went, it was to Germany.

Some aspects of Romanticism, working in combination with a new domination of the economics of music by the middle class, confirmed the dichotomy between cultivated and vernacular traditions in American music. Romantic art-music put a premium on the individuality of the composer and on an apparent subjectivity of artistic expression. One result was a broadening of the vocabulary of art-music, for to the degree that a composer used a vocabulary different from others' he could be viewed as unique, as one who was expressing his innermost thoughts as only he felt and knew them, a sort of extraordinary culture hero. (In that male-dominated age, there was hardly any possibility of *heroines*.) Romanticism encouraged the virtuoso composer. But if individuality and novelty were most highly prized assets of the composer, they also collided with the fundamentally conservative tastes of the mass public, which had become the principal patron of music. The agents of the new patronage were the public concert and the public opera, which had replaced the aristocratic *soirée musicale* and the cathedral or courtly chapel service as the principal forums for musical performance. Public concerts depended for their existence on the approbation of a large, heterogeneous audience. Such an audience, with collective ears less finely tuned, less carefully cultivated than those of the earlier aristocratic patrons of music, tended to resist complexity and innovation in the musical language—just what the Romantic-era composer was striving for. The composer was trapped between the conflicting demands of Romantic individualism and the mass audience. Precisely to the degree that the composer spoke in a uniquely personal language, his or her communication with the public—which liked what it knew and knew what it liked—was attenuated. Inevitably, a fissure appeared between the taste of the composer of art-music and that of the ostensible patron, the public. Inevitably, the fissure widened as the nineteenth century wore on. Ultimately, the fissure now a chasm, the public concert would virtually exclude the contemporary composer; the public concert hall and the

---

[8] This and the previous two quotations ibid., 127, 102, 63 (in order of quotations here).

public opera house would virtually become musical museums. The American composer of cultivated-tradition art-music was forced to find other sources of patronage, or at least other sources of income, to be able to go on composing; as one American-music historian has put it:

> Even as the 19th century approached its end, composing art music had yet to be established as a profession in the U.S. [Such figures as John Knowles Paine, Horatio Parker, and Edward MacDowell], although hired by their universities chiefly for their achievements as composers, earned their livings as pedagogues. The careers of other 19th-century composers of art music confirm the pattern. Anthony Philip Heinrich once described his livelihood as "teaching little misses on the pianoforte, for small quarter money, often unpaid"; William Henry Fry followed a journalist's trade; Louis Moreau Gottschalk toured as a virtuoso pianist; George Frederick Bristow was an orchestral violinist, a church organist, a conductor, and a teacher of private lessons and public school music. Remembered now as composers, all four composed only as a sideline, at that a mostly nonremunerative one.[9]

If the virtuoso composer's lot was a problematic one, the virtuoso performer's was not. Not only were performers a critical success for their unique gifts, which made them appear inspired Romantic individualists par excellence; they were a popular success as well. Technical brilliance is confused with musical profundity in direct ratio to the naiveté of the listener, and the mass-public concert audience of the Romantic era tended to be naive. American concert audiences welcomed the virtuoso, equated virtuosity with artistry, mistook virtuosity for talent. European virtuosos appeared regularly in America. Robert Schumann commented,

> The [European] public has lately begun to weary of virtuosos, and . . . we have too. The virtuosos themselves seem to feel this, if we may judge from a recently awakened fancy among them for emigrating to America; and many of their enemies secretly hope they will remain over there; for, taken all in all, modern virtuosity has benefited art very little.[10]

To America came the Norwegian violinist Ole Bull, who was here for lengthy stays (1843–45, 1852–57), annual winter tours (1867–73), and other visits; the "Swedish nightingale" Jenny Lind, who was brought here in 1850 by the

---

[9] Richard Crawford, "Patronage [in American Music]" (unpublished essay kindly provided by him). He elaborated on this matter (hardly touched by earlier scholars) in two chapters ("Part 2. Economics") of his book *The American Musical Landscape* (Berkeley and Los Angeles: University of California Press, 1993), 41–69 and 70–107.

[10] *Gesammelte Schriften über Musik und Musiker*, 5th ed. (Leipzig, 1914), 2, 134, as translated in Paul Rosenfeld, *Robert Schumann on Music and Musicians* (New York: Pantheon, 1946), 81.

notorious impresario P. T. Barnum and stayed for two years; the German soprano Henriette Sontag, who toured the United States between 1852 and 1854, before going to Mexico; and the virtuoso pianists Leopold de Meyer (U.S. tours 1845–47), Henri Herz (Western hemisphere tours 1846–51), and Liszt's rival Sigismond Thalberg (U.S. tours 1856–58).[11] The British virtuoso pianist Richard Hoffman, a pupil of de Meyer's, immigrated in 1847, toured with Jenny Lind, and remained in this country (see p. 86).

One result of the adulation of virtuosos was an emphasis on the performer of music rather than on the composer or even the music itself—that is, on the means rather than the end. Did it matter what was performed by such virtuosos as Paganini or Liszt or Jenny Lind, so long as they did perform? Symbolic of this view of the musical experience (and still common today) was the listing in announcements of a forthcoming concert not of the music to be heard but only its performer(s). In earlier eras, when the virtuoso was primarily an improviser, virtually composing the music while performing it, such an attitude was hardly peculiar and posed no threat to progressive trends in the musical vocabulary. But in the Romantic era, when the art of improvisation was dying under the effect of the composer-as-culture-hero idea, and when at the same time the conservatism of the mass audience meant resistance to innovation, this attitude tended to freeze the concert repertory and to block any change in the musical vocabulary. In this sense the nineteenth-century virtuoso became the real musical hero, whereas only lip service was paid to the living composer, whose heroism often had to await posthumous recognition after the slowly changing taste of the concert public, finally catching up with the composer's vocabulary, allowed a change in the canonical "standard" repertory.

The virtuoso conductor, a new kind of virtuoso, was born during the Romantic era. He was no longer merely first among equals, a musical chronometer keeping time for his fellow instrumentalists, but a kind of super-performer playing a super-instrument, the romantically expansive symphony orchestra. America welcomed increasingly this kind of virtuoso, as was reflected in a number of visiting orchestras and the development of American orchestras themselves, with a parade of European conductors to lead them, further emphasizing the faint exoticism, the "foreignness" from an American standpoint, of the cultivated tradition.

The premium put on virtuosity tended to create higher performance standards in general, thus to increase professionalism in music of the cultivated tradition. This was mirrored in the establishment of America's first

---

[11] Jenny Lind's American sojourn is thoroughly chronicled in W. Porter Ware and Thaddeus C. Lockard, Jr., *P. T. Barnum Presents Jenny Lind: The American Tour of the Swedish Nightingale* (Baton Rouge: Louisiana State University Press, 1980); similarly, the American years of three European piano virtuosos by R. Allen Lott, "The American Concert Tours of Leopold de Meyer, Henri Herz, and Sigismond Thalberg" (Ph. D. diss., City University of New York, 1986), to which he added later "'A Continuous Trance': Hans von Bülow's Tour of America," *Journal of Musicology* 12/4 (Fall 1994): 529–44. Besides thoroughly documenting the itineraries of these pianists, Lott discusses issues common to all of them, such as audiences, repertory, the role of the impresario, and finances.

musical conservatories (see p. 149). Perhaps more significant in terms of musical attitudes were the increasingly common attempts through private music lessons to train amateurs to professional levels of accomplishment, often with futile and musically disenchanting results, and always with an affirmation of the distinction between cultivated and vernacular music traditions. A later but similar educative aim, one hoping to train people to "professional" levels of musical understanding, lay behind the phenomenon of "music appreciation" lectures, which flourished in the early and mid–twentieth century; the music in question, whose appreciation had to be cultivated, was of course exclusively cultivated-tradition music.

If the rise of the middle class altered the system of musical patronage and accelerated a musical professionalism, it also tended to create a vast new army of amateur performers of art-music, persons with the leisure time to spend on music making and the aspiration to do so, but with only modest talent or artistic judgment. Reflective of this aspect of middle-class musical culture was the rapid growth of the sheet-music-publishing industry, which in America had reached impressive proportions even by the first decades of the nineteenth century (see p. 34) and continued to expand thereafter. The main output of the publishers was naturally music simple enough to be sold in quantity to amateur musicians across the land, music that in one sense of the word would be "popular." At first this published popular music was indistinguishable from the music to be heard on concert programs. This is true, for example, of late-eighteenth-century American sheet music, which more often than not made an advertising pitch by actually citing its use in concert or opera—such as Alexander Reinagle's opera air *Rosa* (1800), "... sung with great applause by Mrs. Merry in the comedy of *The Secret*," or Benjamin Carr's *Federal Overture* (1794) "... as performed at the theatres in Philadelphia and New York." But there, too, a fissure appeared—between the taste and capability of the amateur performer and the music of the professional concert and opera performers. As the latter became ever more professionalized and as virtuosity tended to increase, concert music outstripped amateur ability, and the "popular" music of the music sheets came to be a different thing from the "classical" music of the concerts.

Some of this sheet music was music of the vernacular tradition. But much of it (songs and piano pieces for the most part) had an aura of pretentious gentility about it; it derived from and lay within the cultivated tradition rather than the vernacular, although its accessibility to both performer and listener kept it near the vernacular. As composed by innumerable musical poetasters, it actually represented a subdivision of the cultivated tradition that may be termed "household music"—a term that in fact was used in the period, as in the title of a collection of the 1850s: *Household Melodies, a Selection of Popular Songs, Duets, Trios & Quartettes, Arranged to Household Words,* issued first by W. C. Peters & Sons of Cincinnati and then by other publishers and distributors in St. Louis, Nashville, Cleveland, Pittsburgh, and Louisville. The term "household music" seems appropriate, not only because it indicates the *destination* of such music, but also because it suggests an analogy with the other household artifacts of the period such as silverware, ceramics, glass, furniture, rugs, and draperies—which, although utilitarian, were never acquired solely for their utility but with an eye to their attractiveness and their reflection of fashionable cultivated taste. (Others have termed this repertory "parlor music"; and in the twentieth century it was often called "semiclassical" or "light classical"—terms perfectly characterizing its ambiguous status.)

By that time—let us say from about 1910 on—the two main traditions of American music, cultivated and vernacular, came to be less independent. Some cultivated-tradition music showed the influence of vernacular music (e.g., concert works by such composers as Arthur Farwell influenced by black-American song and dance music); some music based on vernacular traditions showed increased sophistication, artistry, and complexity (e.g., the theater songs of Jerome Kern); and some composers moved back and forth easily between musical genres associated with one or the other tradition (e.g., Victor Herbert between concertos and light opera, John Philip Sousa between band marches and operetta, and George Gershwin between Tin Pan Alley songs and orchestral concert works and opera). By the mid–twentieth century, although distinctions continued to be made among such categories as pop music, rock, country music, jazz, the musical, opera, concert music, sacred music, and still others, interpenetrations among them were so complex and commonplace that to discuss them in terms of a dualistic musical culture of vernacular and cultivated traditions would be simplistic and invalid. Thus, one must declare that cultivated and vernacular traditions, historiographically speaking, hardly existed in our seventeenth- and eighteenth-century American music, materialized beginning in the early nineteenth century, and declined in the early twentieth, when a much more complex variety of subtraditions came into play.

In the following three chapters, we shall consider that period in American music when the vernacular and cultivated traditions diverged and remained more or less separate: from about 1820 until about 1920. It will be most convenient to deal first, in Chapter 4, with the cultivated tradition (including the genteel household music) up to the Civil War; next, in Chapter 5, with vernacular-tradition music during the whole period; and then, in Chapter 6, with cultivated-tradition music from the Civil War through World War I.

FOUR

THE CULTIVATED TRADITION,
1820–1865

American music of the cultivated tradition between about 1820 and the end of the Civil War can perhaps best be approached through a discussion of its main genres: sacred music, song, piano music, orchestral music, and opera.

SACRED MUSIC

As we have seen (pp. 21–22), the First New England School of composers of psalm settings, hymns, anthems, and patriotic pieces, of fuging tunes and other sacred/secular works in a characteristic, indigenous style, came under criticism toward the turn of the nineteenth century. As early as 1791, when Samuel Holyoke published at Boston his collection titled *Harmonia Americana*, he specifically called attention to his omission of "fuging pieces," claiming in the Preface that "the principal reason why few were inserted was the trifling effect produced by that sort of music; for the parts, falling in, one after another, each conveying a different idea, confound the sense, and render the performance a mere jargon of words." But this argument, an old one against vocal counterpoint, was only one of the reasons for the new disfavor in which the Yankee composers found themselves. More significant was the developing taste for "the sublime and beautiful compositions of the great

Masters of Music" (to recall Andrew Law's phrase)—that is, the masters of continental Europe.

Symptomatic of the shift in taste are the collections of church music published by Thomas Hastings (1784–1872), whom we have met (p. 59) as a "decided admirer of German musick" and as a major figure in nineteenth-century cultivated church music. In 1815 Hastings brought out his first compilation, *Musica Sacra: A Collection of Psalm Tunes, Hymns, and Set Pieces.* Along with original tunes and works by other Americans, he included adaptations from the following Europeans: Felice Giardini (to whose melody the hymn "Come Thou, almighty King" is sung even today in Protestant American churches), Henry Purcell, William Croft, Handel (*Messiah*), Charles Burney, and Martin Madan. The English bias is clear; Hastings, like many compilers of collections in England itself, had not yet wholly submitted to "the science, genius, the taste" of Classic-era German music. He (and they) turned to it increasingly, however, for tunes to include in later hymn collections. By 1849 he could even name one hymnbook *The Mendelssohn Collection.* To its main body he added as a sort of appendix a group of older hymns and psalm settings—a concession, apparently, to those who still wanted to sing the old New England favorites. Among them we find Timothy Swan's *China* (see p. 18), but in a completely bowdlerized version. Hastings's condescending footnote reads, "Extensively sung in former times, at funerals. The original harmony was, of course, inadmissible."

Hastings's own output as a hymnodist was considerable: he is said to have written some six hundred hymn texts and composed one thousand hymn tunes. Among the best-known are "Gently, Lord, O gently lead us," "How calm and beautiful the morn," "Return, O wand'rer to thy home," and, most popular of all, "Rock of ages," which appeared as a setting for A. M. Toplady's text in *Spiritual Songs for Social Worship* (1832), a collection compiled jointly by Hastings and the other dominant figure in the cultivated tradition's church music, Lowell Mason.

Mason (1792–1872) arguably had a stronger and more lasting impact on our musical culture than any other nineteenth-century American. His first musical success came with sponsorship by the weighty Handel and Haydn Society of Boston, which aimed not only "to introduce into more general practice the works of Handel, Haydn and other eminent composers" but also to support the publication of approved church music. Upon the recommendation of its esteemed organist, George K. Jackson (see p. 39), the society accepted for publication a hymn collection assembled by Mason, who was working at the time as a bank clerk in Savannah, and in 1822 there appeared the first of many editions of *The Boston Handel and Haydn Society Collection of Church Music;* [and the title continues:] *being a selection of the most approved psalm and hymn tunes; together with many beautiful extracts from the works of Haydn, Mozart, Beethoven, and other eminent composers* (reprinted as *EAM* 15).

Mason's parents were musical, and by the time he had left his native Massachusetts for Georgia, he was proficient on several instruments. In Savannah he was taught by a German-born musician, Frederick Abel, who probably contributed much to his esteem for "scientific" music as opposed to the less suave and polished American sacred style. The 1822 *Boston ... Collection* was based primarily on William Gardiner's English anthology, *Sacred Melodies from Haydn, Mozart, Beethoven and other composers ... appropriated for the use of the British Church* (1812–15). But, besides the Viennese classicists named in its title, Mason tapped other European sources, including German chorales, Gregorian chants, and works of Handel, Gluck, Hans Georg Nägeli, and Ignace Joseph Pleyel; his aim, pursued throughout his career, was to provide church music that was "dignified, chaste, restrained, and in good taste."[1]

The *Boston Handel and Haydn Society Collection* was an immediate and continuing success: twenty-two editions were published between 1822 and 1858. Mason returned to Massachusetts in 1827, to become president of the Handel and Haydn Society until 1832. The next year, together with George James Webb (1803–87) and some other Boston musicians, he founded the Boston Academy of Music; its purpose was to instruct children in music on principles based on the revolutionary methods of the Swiss educator Johann Heinrich Pestalozzi (1746–1827), whose theories in fact laid the foundations of modern elementary education in England and the United States.

Mason continued to compose, compile, and adapt hymns, which he published between 1832 and 1854 in more than thirty collections; a few of the most successful (and lucrative) included *Spiritual Songs for Social Worship* (1831–32; with Thomas Hastings); *The Boston Academy's Collection of Church Music* (1835); *The Modern Psalmist* (1839); and *Carmina Sacra* (1841). Mason also published fourteen books of children's songs and dozens of others for glee clubs and singing schools. With the income from such publications, Mason's fortune was assured; along with it went extraordinary fame and influence.

The musical style of Mason's hymns, based on that of the European Classic era, is one of genteel correctness, neat and tidy in harmony and form, mild in rhythmic vitality and melodic thrust. The airs are now in the tenor voice in the old manner, now in the treble; not infrequently, they are oddly awkward, perhaps because Mason's musical thought as a whole was dominated by considerations of harmony, and as a result even the air is sometimes made to accommodate the harmony rather than fulfilling its own directional impulse. Some of Mason's best-known hymns, such as *Missionary Hymn* ("From Greenland's icy mountains"; in *3Centuries* 7, 34), *Olivet* ("My faith looks up to Thee"; in *3Centuries* 7, 32), and *Bethany* ("Nearer, my

---

[1] See Henry L. Mason, *Hymn-Tunes of Lowell Mason: A Bibliography* (Cambridge: The University Press, 1944). The quotation is from Michael Broyles, *"Music of the Highest Class": Elitism and Populism in Antebellum Boston* (New Haven: Yale University Press, 1992), 73.

God, to Thee"), share this trait. Others, though, such as *Antioch* ("Joy to the world! the Lord is come," after Handel) and *Watchman* ("Watchman, tell us of the night"), are unforgettably lyrical. The texture of all, in general, is unrelievedly homophonic; the "fuging" style of earlier American psalmody is consistently avoided—as are, of course, its folkish harmony and casual counterpoint; in their place are a full triadic vocabulary, functional harmony with occasional seventh chords, and even secondary dominants. The influence on American congregational song of Mason's hymns, along with the similar ones of Hastings, was immense; as one writer puts it (beginning with a quoted fragment from Mason's *Address on Church Music* of 1827),

> The "simple, easy, and solemn" pieces found in the collections of Hastings and Mason ... established a style of Protestant hymnody that has remained virtually unchanged for a century and a half. [Their hymns] are still sung today, in their original harmonization, without arousing the slightest feeling that they are in any way different from other pieces in modern hymnals.[2]

Mason was not only a composer of some twelve hundred original hymn tunes (though we shall perhaps never know the exact number, since he published many without attribution) and an adapter of almost five hundred melodies from other composers; he was also a dedicated teacher. To him must go credit for getting music admitted into the public-school curriculum of Boston, and indirectly into public-school programs over the entire country. The beginning was the Boston Academy, which provided free extracurricular music classes for schoolchildren. In 1838, after years of propagandizing by Mason, the public schools of Boston began to include musical instruction as a part of the regular curriculum, with Mason appointed as superintendent of music for the city system. It was a milestone in the history of American music and musical attitudes; for better or worse, Mason's ideals and tastes, and those of a huge circle of musicians and educators associated with him, could now be directed where they would have the greatest impact: to the children.

Music Education

It may be appropriate here to pause and consider the unique place in American culture that has been held by music education, which since Mason's day has been considered an essential subject in the curriculum of most schools. In fact, from the time of Tufts and Walter early in the eighteenth century to the present, musical indoctrination has been considered a matter of

---

[2] Charles Hamm, *Music in the New World* (New York: W. W. Norton, 1983), 166. Indeed, a number of Mason's hymns are regularly included in "modern hymnals."

importance by Americans. This attitude is uniquely American: as characterized by Allen Britton, a prominent music educator, music education has been "an American specialty."[3]

Significantly, Americans have viewed music education as important not just for itself but also as a means to a higher goal. In the singing-school era, the end was a greater perfection in religious observance; since Mason's time, it has been a kind of aesthetic and moral improvement. Throughout our history, these goals have been sought through education in "better music"— better, that is, than the vernacular music of the period in question. In Tufts's and Walter's day, the "better music" was that on the written page, and their main aim was simply to teach students how to read music. In the early nineteenth century, the "better music" for the reformers among the singing-school masters was almost any music other than "those wild fugues" of the Yankee tunesmiths. For Mason and his circle, and indeed for many music educators up to the present, the "better music" was the music of continental Europe's Classic era (later, also its Romantic era).

At the same time, because of the lag between the musical thought of the composer and the musical understanding of the public (explored in Chapter 3), education in the more complex and "difficult" examples of European art-music was considered unrealistic. Thus, just as folk and vernacular music was rejected by school music teachers, so was the very best of "classical" music. Instead, a bland and bloodless, if correct and irreproachable, music of second- and lower-rate composers was taught. A lasting result was, as Britton remarks, that music education has always operated "at a certain distance from the well-springs of American musical life, both popular and artistic. ... The term 'polite' is perhaps as good as any other to characterize much of the music utilized in schools from the time of Lowell Mason to the present day."

Thus we see a paradox in American educational philosophy: on the one hand, a unique acceptance of music's importance in the education of every American and, on the other, a narrowly restricted kind of music that Americans are to be "educated" in—a music that has little to do with either the American past or the American present or with either the rough-hewn virility of folk music or the craftsmanly elegance of much art-music. The effect on many Americans has been one of disenchantment with music, both as listeners and as participators, in the years after schooling: not only has formal music education tended to dull the impulse to lusty, unselfconscious participation in music making for the fun of it; it has also provided very little understanding, let alone high standards for performance, of any highly artistic music. A great many Americans, since the mid–nineteenth century, have

---

[3] "Music Education: An American Specialty," *One Hundred Years of Music in America*, ed. Paul Henry Lang (New York G. Schirmer, 1961), 211–29. A more comprehensive survey is Britton's "Music Education in the United States of America," *Bulletin of Research in Music Education* 3/2 (July 1982): 91–102; and see also "Education in Music" in *AmeriGrove* ("Schools" by Richard Colwell; "Higher Education" by James W. Pruett).

come to adulthood without much enthusiasm for any kind of music—at least, until the 1960s and later, when the folk-song revival and the supplanting of the piano by the guitar as the principal "household-music" instrument reawakened American youth (at least) to the pleasures of informal music making.

SONG

The Anglo-American tradition of the genteel air was maintained during the entire nineteenth century. Songs were the staples of the mid-nineteenth-century concert repertory; hardly any concert of exclusively instrumental music was to be heard, and most public concerts were essentially song recitals. Up to the Civil War, at least, the songs of the public concerts were also heard in the parlor, the very center of middle-class polite society; there, beside horsehair-stuffed chairs and sofas and polite, instructive family magazines, could be found—ever more commonly as the century wore on—a square or upright piano or a reed organ. There, in the home, their cultural life dominated by the new breed of middle-class woman, nineteenth-century Americans gathered to hear a favorite daughter or bride sing—or play for the family or friends to sing—the latest concert-household songs.

If eighteenth-century American songs only occasionally borrowed the sentimental tone and the high-flown language of James Thomson's *The Seasons* and Oliver Goldsmith's *The Deserted Village*, nineteenth-century songs reflected the tastes of an age that reveled in Sir Walter Scott's poems and Gothic romances, after a turn-of-the-century preparation by way of Samuel Richardson's *Pamela* and Susanna Rowson's *Charlotte Temple: A Tale of Truth*. Almost entirely vanished were the sturdy unforced optimism of Alexander Reinagle's *America, Commerce, and Freedom* or the lightly mocking bow to conventional love of Francis Hopkinson's *My Gen'rous Heart Disdains the Slave of Love to Be*. In their place were set texts of the most extreme sentimentality, often descending to bathos or ascending to manic ecstasy.

Especially important in the background of nineteenth-century American song were the collections of *Irish Melodies* of the poet-musician Thomas Moore (1779–1852)—ten volumes published between 1808 and 1834 in London, each pirated almost immediately by American publishers (unrestrained, in those days, by an effective international copyright law). Moore added new texts of his own invention to traditional Irish melodies, also polishing the latter and providing them with up-to-date harmonizations, to create some of the most enduringly popular songs in the English language. Among the most universally known are *Believe me if all those endearing young charms* (to the tune "My lodging is on the cold ground"), *'Tis the last rose of summer* (to the tune "The Groves of Blarney"), and *The harp that once through Tara's halls* (to the tune "Gramachree"). The dominant theme of Moore's poems is nostalgia for a past better than the dismal present. In one form or another, that theme was to predominate also in American song through the Civil War, and as Charles Hamm has demonstrated persuasively, the wide diffusion of Moore's Irish songs in the period had much to do with this development.[4]

Models for American songs of the period were provided partly by English singers who barnstormed through the eastern half of the country in the 1830s and 1840s. The most successful and influential of these was Henry Russell (1812–1900), who was in America from the mid-1830s to the early 1840s. He left the organ bench of the First Presbyterian Church in Rochester, New York, to make a name for himself as a baritone soloist and songwriter. Mining the vein of nostalgia—especially a subvein that prized old age for its evocation of "the good old days"—Russell concentrated on "old" songs (*The Old Bell*, *The Brave Old Oak*, *The Old Sexton*, *The Old Clock*, *The Old Farm Gate*, and many others), for a total he claimed to be over 800 (but a more likely figure is about 250, some 75 of which were written in the United States). Among the most renowned were *Woodman, Spare That Tree* ("...Touch not a single bough, / In youth it shelter'd me, / And I'll protect it now"; in *3Centuries* 1, 270–75) and *The Old Arm Chair*.

Many details of *The Old Arm Chair*, published in 1840 at the peak of Russell's popularity, illustrate the genre of the antebellum household song. The text is embarrassingly maudlin: the poet gazes on the armchair "with quivering breath and throbbing brow"; religion and filial love are identified ("I almost worshipp'd [Mother] when she smiled, / And turn'd from her bible to bless her child"); the chair itself is an object of sentimental veneration ("I love it, I love it, and cannot tear / My soul from a mother's Old Arm Chair"). The sheet music's cover page, with a lithograph showing Mother and the chair, is characteristic; nineteenth-century song sheets aimed to be visually seductive as well as vocally attractive. The music is quite simple. The form is strophic. The melody is essentially declamatory, in easy $\frac{4}{4}$ rhythms; characteristic are many sighing appoggiaturas, which strive to confirm the text's tone of deep emotion and relate to the Italian opera aria style—that of Rossini (with whom Russell may have studied), Bellini, and Donizetti—that is important in the background of this and others of Russell's songs (even a song of the prairie such as *A Life in the West* [on *NW* CD 80251]: "... the broad prairie, / Where man, like the wind, rolls impulsive and free"). The most frequent harmonic progression in *The Old Arm Chair* is the gentle I–IV–I. One paradox of the song, typical of the genre, is that despite its lachrymose subject it is cast in the major rather than the minor mode.

It would be unfair, however, to let these details of *The Old Arm Chair* stand for all of Russell's songs—especially their subject matter, which ranged far and wide, as one specialist has pointed out:

A single concert might touch upon political history (*Charter Oak*), poverty and social responsibility (*A Christmas Carol*), emigration (*The Emigrant's Farewell*), gambling (*The Gambler's Wife*), the ill-treatment of Indians (*The*

---

[4] See Hamm, *Yesterdays* (New York: W. W. Norton, 1979), chap. 3 ("'Erin, the Tear and the Smile in Thine Eyes'; or, Thomas Moore's Irish Melodies in America").

Indian Hunter), westward migration (*A Life in the West*), marriage (*Not Married Yet?*), insane asylums (*The Maniac*), and temperance (*The 'Total Society*). To leaven the fare he included songs that often featured histrionic display (*Land Ho!, A Life on the Ocean Wave, Ship on Fire, A Leap for Life*) [and] God and motherhood (*My Mother's Bible*).[5]

Russell's songs were extraordinarily influential in virtually establishing "popular song" in America, and they epitomize the concert- and household-song repertory. Far more extreme examples of bathos could be cited than *The Old Arm Chair*, and by composers highly thought of: perhaps the nadir was reached by W. B. Bradbury (1816–68)—primarily a hymn composer, an associate of Thomas Hastings, and a sort of New York City counterpart of Lowell Mason— in *The Lament of the Blind Orphan Girl* (1847). In this song, the doubly afflicted heroine is made to voice her lament in incongruously skipping rhythms and a modest coloratura (derived in part, certainly, from the Italian opera arias that Bradbury would have heard in New York in the 1840s). It is a remarkable lesson in how to turn sentiment into sentimentality (Example 4–1).

EXAMPLE 4–1.   W. Bradbury, *The Lament of the Blind Orphan Girl* (New York: Atwill, 1847), measures 25–30, 73–84.

---

[5] Dale Cockrell, "Nineteenth-century popular music" (chap. 7), in *The Cambridge History of American Music*, ed. David Nicholls (Cambridge: Cambridge University Press, 1998), 158–85 (the passage quoted: 176–77).

round them are twin'd_____ O, when_ shall_ I__

see them?_____ I'm blind, O,___ I'm blind.____

The Lament of the Blind Orphan Girl was published "as sung with distinguished Applause, by Abby Hutchinson." Abby was the female member of the most celebrated American "singing family" for several decades from 1840 on: the Hutchinsons. They were one of a number of American troupes formed in imitation of European family groups, such as the Rainer family from the Tyrolean Alps, which toured the United States during the 1840s and after. The Hutchinsons specialized not only in laments—*Oh! I'm in Sadness, Last Year's Flowers, Give That Wreath to Me, The Guardian of the Grave*—but also in "Alpine" songs. Precisely at the time (1846) that the Donner party battled to get to California across the mountain walls of the Rockies, Americans in the East were hearing about

> The mountain top! the mountain top!
> Oh! that's the place for me;
> I love to mount each craggy steep
> With shout of joyful glee!

And on an Albany program in 1842, the Hutchinsons sang *The Snowstorm*, its concluding verses a classic of American melodrama:

> And colder still the wind did blow,
> And darker hours of night came on,

And deeper grew the drifts of snow,
Her limbs were chilled, her strength was gone.
"Oh God!" she cried in accents wild,
"If I must perish, save my child!"

The Hutchinsons became influential advocates of social reform, espousing such radical causes as antislavery, temperance, women's rights, and universal suffrage. Besides original songs by one or another family member—such as John Hutchinson's suffrage song *The Fatherhood of God and the Brotherhood of Man* (NW CD 80267)—they often used well-known tunes, which only increased their songs' popularity: the abolitionist song *Get Off the Track* (*3Centuries* 1, 131–34) is to be sung to a minstrel-show tune everyone knew, *Old Dan Tucker*; the all-purpose pride-in-America song *Uncle Sam's Farm* (also on NW CD 80267), to another minstrel-show tune, *Walk in de Parlor and Hear de Banjo Play*. The Hutchinsons sang both solo songs and partsongs; for the latter they developed a kind of sweet-sounding, "natural" (i.e., nonoperatic and ostensibly uncultivated) close harmony and informal delivery that were to become standard in American popular music for generations to come.[6]

It is against this background—the nostalgic sentimentality of *The Old Arm Chair*, the crocodile tears of *The Blind Orphan Girl*, the hysterical unreality of *The Mountain Top*—that one must view the household songs of Stephen Collins Foster (1826–64), a few of which so sublime or mitigate the conventions of the genre, and so transcend the songs of his contemporaries, that Foster must be adjudged America's first great songwriter.

Born on the Fourth of July, fifty years to the day after the Declaration of Independence, near the still-small but booming commercial and industrial town of Pittsburgh, Foster had a typical middle-class upbringing in a family of comfortable means to which household music was no stranger: his older sister played the piano, and his father fiddled a bit. Drawn to music from early childhood (his father commented when Foster was sixteen that "his leisure hours are all devoted to musick, for which he possesses a strange talent"), he nevertheless got scant encouragement. Foster's music itself leaves little room for illusions about the extent of his formal training; on the other hand, it reveals an extraordinary ability to absorb various popular-music styles in the United States at the time—Irish, English, German, and Italian, not to mention American—and synthesize them in a totally winning personal style, sparked and dominated by an obvious and undeniable natural gift for melody.

Foster's debut as a songwriter was with *Open Thy Lattice, Love* (1844). Text and music are both remarkably restrained for the period, and we seem

---

[6] See Cockrell, "The Hutchinson Family, 1841–45; or, The Origins of Some Yankee Doodles," *I.S.A.M. Newsletter* 12/1 (November 1982): 12–15. Cockrell also edited and annotated *Excelsior: Journals of the Hutchinson Family Singers, 1842–1846* (New York: Pendragon Press, 1989).

to be back in the very early nineteenth century, with a typically cool if amorous air set to music that reflects Foster's Anglo-Irish descent (Example 4–2).

EXAMPLE 4–2.   S. Foster, *Open Thy Lattice, Love* (Philadelphia: Willig, 1844), measures 5–8.

Within the next twenty years, until his death in New York, Foster was to publish about 150 such household songs. Most are love songs, but the sweetheart is usually unattainable, either dead or distant, and the poet (usually Foster himself) can dwell with her only in a dream of love. Nostalgic yearning for the irretrievably lost is the keynote, but the poet finds the mournful dream delicious. "I dream of Jeanie with the light brown hair," sang Foster in 1854— but Jeanie is gone:

> Many were the wild notes her merry voice would pour,
> Many were the blithe birds that warbled them o'er.

and we see her only through a gentle haze of nostalgia, "floating like a vapor on the soft summer air."

Gentle tenderness, or temperate gentility, characterizes the music as well as the texts of Foster's best household songs. *Gentle Annie* (1856) and *Gentle Lena Clare* (1862) are stereotypes, but both heroines are depicted in memorable melodies (Example 4–3). In one of Foster's most thoroughly composed love songs, *Come Where My Love Lies Dreaming* (1855), it is the sweetheart who is dreaming, hence asleep, hence for the moment unattainable. The song is written, atypically for a household song, for vocal quartet, with the soprano part set in relief against three lower voices and given an arching line that derives from the Italian opera to be heard in New York, where Foster had lived for most of 1854 (Example 4–4). The last love song written by Foster is one of the best, musically: *Beautiful Dreamer*, copyrighted shortly after his death.

EXAMPLE 4–3. (*a*) S. Foster, *Gentle Annie* (New York: Firth, Pond & Co., 1856), measures 5–12 (piano part omitted). (*b*) S. Foster, *Gentle Lena Clare* (New York: S. C. Gordon, 1862), measures 9–16 (piano part omitted).

EXAMPLE 4–4. S. Foster, *Come Where My Love Lies Dreaming. Quartette* (New York: Firth, Pond Co., 1855), measures 13–16.

As in the love songs, nostalgia suffuses an extraordinary proportion of the other household songs of Foster. Perhaps from Moore's *Irish Melodies* and from Henry Russell, whom he had heard sing in Pittsburgh, comes Foster's favorite adjective "old," meaning usually "of the past," not just "aged": *Old Memories* (1853), *When Old Friends Were Here* (1864), *Farewell, Old Cottage* (1851), *My Old Kentucky Home, Good Night* (1853). Beloved ones lost through death are mourned in *Bring My Brother Back to Me* (1863), *Our Willie Dear Is Dying* (1861), and *Little Belle Blair* (1861). In *Ah! May the Red Rose Live Alway* (1850), one of Foster's richest works harmonically, the poet asks "Why should the beautiful die?" (Example 4–5).

EXAMPLE 4–5.   Foster, *Ah! May the Red Rose Live Alway* (Baltimore: F. D. Benteen, 1850), measures 9–16.

There are, to be sure, some happy ones among Foster's household songs. *Fairy Belle* (1859); *If You've Only Got a Moustache* (1864), an Irish reel with coy advice to bachelors; and *There's a Good Time Coming* (1846) are a few. But for the most part a sense of loss and nostalgia for the lost are pervasive. An apostrophe to the family hound, *Old Dog Tray* (1853), leads Foster to mourn a "once happy day":

> The morn of life is past
> And evening comes at last;
>   It brings me a dream of a once happy day,
>   Of merry forms I've seen
>   Upon the village green...

Some historians have seen more than simple sentimentality in the insistent nostalgia of the American mid–nineteenth century, so typified by Foster. The "once happy day," they say, was an unspoiled early America, fresh for clearing and settling, since, as Lewis Mumford put it, "ruin and change lay in the wake of the pioneer, as he went westering." A sense of uneasiness, of dislocation, of transition and change must have permeated post-pioneer life. Mumford reminds us of the fascination the legend of Rip Van Winkle held for the period:

> The old landmarks have gone; the old faces have disappeared; all the outward aspects of life have changed. At the bottom, however, Rip himself has not changed; for he has been drunk and lost in a dream, and ... he remains, mentally, a boy.[7]

Foster, too, perhaps remained a boy—musically, at least, for there is no essential stylistic difference between early works and late ones among his household songs. (There is, however, between his home-and-hearth songs and his minstrel-show songs, as we shall see.) But with his natural talent as melodist, and despite his artlessness, Foster spoke for pre–Civil War America; not for the frontier nor for the seaboard cities, perhaps, but for that broadening span in between—settled but unsettled, no longer a frontier to be pierced and conquered but an America to be made into something else, and perhaps frighteningly so.

Foster's last years coincided with the Civil War, which evoked, even more than most wars, a wave of songs from American composers. Charles Hamm has written insightfully (in both *Yesterdays* and *Music in the New World*) about how, although the war between the states spawned no great painting, sculpture, poetry, or fiction (or large-scale art-music compositions), it did inspire an enormous burst of accomplishment in photography, journalism, and song. Foster contributed a few songs to the Northern cause— *We Are Coming, Father Abraham, 300,000 More*, a poem set by several

---

[7] Both quotations are from Mumford's *The Golden Day*, 2nd ed. (Boston: Beacon Press, 1957), 32–33.

composers, among them Luther O. Emerson (*3Centuries* 1, 209–12; on *NW* CD 80202); *We've a Million in the Field*; and others—but they are of no particular distinction. Two other composers seem to have caught in a few of their songs the militant spirit of the Civil War far better than Foster: Henry Clay Work (1832–84) and George Frederick Root (1820–95).

Work wrote more than thirty war songs, beginning with the antislavery *Kingdom Coming* (1862); in *Marching Through Georgia* (1865), he produced a jaunty valedictory to the war, following on Sherman's unopposed march through Georgia to the sea. Another great success of his was "*Come Home, Father!*" (1864)—captioned "The Song of Little Mary, standing at the bar-room door..." and interpolated regularly in the most famous temperance play of all time, *Ten Nights in a Bar-Room*.

Root, after an early association in Boston with Lowell Mason, moved to New York in 1844 and then in the late 1850s to Chicago, where in the 1860s he was music editor for his brother's important music-publishing firm, Root and Cady. Of his two-hundred-odd songs, almost thirty are Civil War songs, among them *The Battle Cry of Freedom* (1862), *Just Before the Battle, Mother* (1862), and *Tramp! Tramp! Tramp!* ["*The boys are marching...*"] (1864). An amusing and revealing footnote to Root's career: having decided to try for some of the popular household-song market dominated by Foster but taking a patronizing attitude toward it, Root sought a pseudonym; in view of the adulation of German musicians at the time, a German translation of his own name was his choice: G. Friedrich Wurzel.

Another kind of song, the glee, was also popular during the period and, like the solo song, was sung both in concerts and at home. A part-song for three or four unaccompanied male voices, the glee (from the Anglo-Saxon *gliw* or *gléo*: "entertainment, music") had been enormously popular in eighteenth-century England. Settings of friendly doggerel, and not musically complicated, glees were a mainstay of the Hutchinsons' repertory and were written by most of the composers we have mentioned (though not by Foster) for household use and for musical societies, usually made up of amateur musicians, such as the Harvard Glee Club (founded 1828). Many of these were male-only organizations: male chorus singing in America, which preserved the tradition of the glee long after it had waned in England, was stimulated by the influence of the German *Männerchor*; a German singing society of this name was organized at Philadelphia in 1835, and similar groups were formed elsewhere, particularly in the Midwest, where many German immigrants had settled.

Solo songs and part-songs were combined in the secular cantata, which was often cast in dramatic form and sometimes even staged—a sort of homespun genre that to some degree, at least, satisfied the need for musical drama met in European culture by opera. The first such cantatas seem to have been composed by George Root for classes of young women at various educational institutions in New York where he was employed. His earliest was *The Flower Queen, or The Coronation of the Rose* (1851–52), set to a text by his former pupil, the blind poet and author of thousands of hymn texts, Fanny Crosby

(1820–1915); perhaps his best-conceived and best-composed cantata—certainly the most popular—was *The Haymakers* of 1856–57 (part 2 recorded on *NW* CD 80234; the entire work edited in *RRAM* 9–10). Root termed it an "operatic cantata" and provided for it rather elaborate directions for staging; Richard Crawford has described it as being based on "elements of the reformed American hymn tune, the English glee, and the Mendelssohnian oratorio."[8]

PIANOS AND PIANO MUSIC

If any single instrument can be called the preeminent Romantic-era instrument, it is the pianoforte. Indeed, its invention in early eighteenth-century Florence by Bartolomeo Cristofori, its gradual replacement of the harpsichord during that century, its triumphant hegemony among keyboard instruments during the nineteenth, and the decline in its importance during the twentieth reflect a whole cycle in Western musical history.[9] Unlike the harpsichord and the organ, and much more resoundingly than the clavichord, the pianoforte responds directly to the player's touch: it can play not only soft and loud (*piano* and *forte*) but also at all the dynamic levels above, below, and between. Not only is it appropriate for intimate music making at home, but also, as enlarged and extended in range during the nineteenth century, it can rival an orchestra in power. Not only can it simulate the sustained, affective melodic curve of a single voice, but also it can produce dense polyphonic textures. In a period such as the Romantic era, which viewed tonal flux as a musical mirror of life itself, whose centers of music were the small parlor and the large concert hall, and whose favored musical fabric was a blend of cantabile melody and rich harmony, the piano was the ideal instrument. If the organ was still viewed as the imperious king of instruments, the piano was a responsive and versatile queen.

Manufacture and sale of pianos in America boomed in the nineteenth century. It has been estimated that whereas in 1829 about 2,500 instruments were built, or one for every 4,800 persons in the nation, in 1851 more than 9,000 were produced and sold. By 1860 the figures had risen again, to 21,000 pianos manufactured, one for every 1,500 Americans, with sales across the country of 30 pianos every working day.[10] If we take into account

---

[8] *The American Musical Landscape* (Berkeley and Los Angeles: University of California Press, 1993), 171 (in chap. 5, "George Frederick Root ... and American Vocal Music").

[9] And in social history as well, as has been shown with brilliance and wit by Arthur Loesser in *Men, Women and Pianos: A Social History* (New York: Simon & Schuster, 1954).

[10] Ibid., 469, 492, 511. The social necessity of a piano in a proper parlor is graphically shown in the design for an ideal *American Woman's Home* (New York, 1869) suggested by the authors, Catherine Beecher and Harriet Beecher Stowe. On their first-floor ground plan, they indicate only two pieces of furniture, both in the drawing room: one is a sofa, the other a piano. See John A. Kouwenhoven, *Made in America* (New York: Doubleday, 1949), 77.

the longevity of a sturdy pianoforte and its low depreciation and degeneration rates, even the last figures must be low as a reflection of the number of people who had access to a playable piano on the eve of the Civil War.

American piano builders (many of them immigrants, of course) were among the best in the world, making significant improvements in the instrument during the period. In 1825 the Massachusetts builder Alpheus Babcock (1785–1842) obtained a patent for a one-piece cast-iron frame, which, well adapted to the extremes of American temperature (and later to American central heating), became the foundation of all later piano development. From the 1820s to the 1850s the standards of piano manufacture were established by the firm headed by Jonas Chickering (1798–1853) of Boston. Like other American manufacturers, he concentrated on the heavy, horizontal, four-footed "square" (actually rectangular) piano that was most popular in America during the nineteenth century, but he and his sons made wing-shaped "grands" as well, and very grand they were: the virtuoso pianist Louis Moreau Gottschalk commented in his journal in June 1863 on

> two mastodons, which [Thomas] Chickering made expressly for me. ... The tails of these monster pianos measure three feet in width. Their length is ten feet; they have seven and a half octaves.

Piano builders were among the German immigrants of the 1830s and later. Among them were William Knabe, who settled in Baltimore in 1837, and, most celebrated of all, Henry Steinway (1797–1871; baptized as Heinrich Steinweg), who emigrated to New York in 1850 and with his sons established his own firm in 1853. America's own nineteenth-century dynasty of musicians, the Masons, figured in piano manufacturing through Lowell Mason's son Henry, a cofounder of the Mason & Hamlin Company in 1854. Initially the company built melodeons, one American term for small reed organs (also called cottage organs, parlor organs, or cabinet organs; sometimes harmoniums), which, because of their small size and price and their popularity mainly in rural America, Arthur Loesser brightly called "the American piano's little country cousin."

The Romantic fondness for the piano, its versatility and its value both as cultural symbol and as source of entertainment, resulted in an extraordinary output of piano music from American publishers. Most of it was frankly utilitarian, intended for household use as pleasant diversion and without pretensions to high artistic value, though with overt claims to cultivated gentility. Hundreds of dilettante composers appeared in print as writers of airy trifles; almost anyone, it seems, could gain publication in that era of a seller's market for parlor piano music. The nonentities are legion and need not detain us. One among them might be cited, however, partly because his music so completely typifies the kinds of piano music of the period and partly because of his fantastic prolificacy: Charles Grobe (1817?–79).

We know very little about Grobe; having served his purpose as composer of parlor pieces, he was promptly forgotten, all the more quickly because he seems not to have been a performer of any caliber. He is thought to have been born in Weimar and to have come to the United States about 1839. He was appointed music teacher in Wesleyan Female College (Wilmington, Delaware) in 1840, and according to John W. Moore (1807–89), America's first musical lexicographer, "in 1842 his pianoforte publications became known, which are very numerous."[11] Moore was putting it mildly: Grobe's production of piano music, apparently the only genre that he worked in (except for a handful of songs), surpasses that of any other known composer. His first publication (1841) was a march on themes from Bellini's *I Capuleti e i Montecchi*. By 1845 he was only up to Op. 43 with the *United States Grand Waltz* ("dedicated as a Tribute of Respect to the Ladies of the U.S."; recorded on *NW* CD 80257), but then he began to hit his stride. By 1847, with *The Battle of Buena Vista* ("a descriptive Fantasie for the Piano"), he was up to Op. 101; six years later, he had trebled his output: the *Gothamite Quick Step* of 1853 is Op. 352. Another half-dozen years, and Grobe's extensive and thorough *New Method for the Piano-Forte* (Philadelphia, 1859) came out as Op. 1100. Almost in the same breath was issued an *Italian Medley*, Op. 1102, on opera airs by Rossini, Donizetti, Verdi, and others. The mid-century fad for the jog-trot rhythm of the polka was reflected in Grobe's *Tommy Polka* of 1860, Op. 1211, and the Civil War naturally inspired in him an "American Medley," *Music of the Union* (Boston, 1861). Grobe's Op. 1805 borrowed from George Root: "*Come Home, Father!*" *with Brilliant Variations* (1866). Almost two hundred more opus numbers were yet to come, ending finally in 1870 with *Sweet Spirit, Hear My Prayer*, Op. 1998!

Programmatic and patriotic pieces, marches and dances, medleys of popular tunes and opera airs, and above all variation sets were the order of the day, pianistically speaking. When Grobe published in 1854 his *Buds and Blossoms: 60 Sacred Melodies with Brilliant Variations for the Piano*, among the melodies were Mason's *Missionary Hymn*, *Adeste Fideles*, Haydn's "The Heavens Are Telling," an air from Rossini's *Stabat Mater*, another from "Mozart's 12th Mass." On the back cover of *Buds and Blossoms*, the publisher obligingly printed a catalogue of representative compositions by Grobe (Figure 4–1). One could almost write the history of early-nineteenth-century America from the 215 titles listed. The 68 sets of variations outnumber any other type of piece; next come 52 waltzes, 28 duets (mostly dances: waltzes, polkas, and schottisches), 25 marches and quicksteps, 18 "gallops," 11 polkas, and a few each of "piano songs" and "rondos, etc."

The popularity of piano variations reveals several things about the era. One was its love of the imaginative and inventive: to the ordinary

---

[11] Appendix to *Encyclopaedia of Music* (Boston: Oliver Ditson, 1875), article "Grobe." (Moore's *Complete Encyclopaedia of Music* [Boston, 1854] was the first comprehensive American music encyclopedia.)

CATALOGUE

OF THE

COMPOSITIONS OF CHARLES GROBE,

Published by LEE & WALKER, (Successors to George Willig,) 188 Chestnut St., Philadelphia.

WALTZES.

A Home that I Love	12½
Alpine Rose	12½
L'Amarante	12½
Amusement de Salon	18¾
Barcarole	12½
Charity	12½
Chateau en Espagne	12½
Cologne Water	12½
La Confiance	12½
Court Ball	12½
L'Etoile du Matin	12½
Fillmore	25
Home of my Heart	12½
Snow Flake	12½
The Lone Star	12½
The Meteor	12½
Guadalquiver	12½
Hand in Hand	12½
Kate	12½
Ladies' Smile	12½
Mazeppa, (Grand)	25
Mnemosyne, (Valse Brillante)	12½
Monterey	12½
Night and Morning	12½
O Summer Night	12½
Queen of my Soul	12½
Ole Bull's Dream	12½
Orsini, (from Lucretia Borgia)	12½
Pet, (Call me pet names)	12½
Potpourri, (from the Bohemian Girl)	12½
Ray of Hope	12½
Rose Blanche	12½
Sans Souci	12½
Souvenir de Belleville	12½
Souvenir de Cape May	12½
Spring Flower	12½
'Tis Midnight Hour	12½
Ruby	12½
Don Pasquale	12½
Come to the Old Oak Tree	12½
By the Margin, etc	12½
Snails	12½
The Sky Lark	12½
The Magician	12½
Annie Laurie	12½
Couleur de Rose	12½
Thou art gone from my gaze	12½
True Love	12½
El Cabalera	12½
Metamores	12½
United States Grand Waltz	25
Sophie Waltz, (by Strauss)	12½

GALLOPS.

Banisher of Sadness	12½
Fausta	12½
Flying Cloud	12½
Homage aux Belles du Philadelphia	25
Hortensia	12½
Ice Cream	12½
Les plus beau de mes jours, etc	12½
Lucy Neal	12½
Maritana	12½
Pine Apple	12½
Ray of Joy	12½
Sentinel	12½
Strawberry	12½
Unassuming	12½
Ever be Happy	12½
Comet's Flight	12½
Short and Sweet	12½
Orlando	12½

DANCES, etc.

Mirror Dance	38
Les Nymphes	25

MARCHES AND QUICKSTEPS.

Adieu et Retour	12½
Brewer of Preston Grand March	12½
Capuletti i Montecchi	25
Captain Walker's Quickstep	12½
Clay Club Quickstep	12½
General Taylor's Grand March	12½
Les Amazones	12½
Lucrezia Borgia	12½
Old Rough and Ready Quickstep	12½
Philadelphia Gals' Quickstep	12½
Alpine Horn	25
Cuba	12½
March from Lucia	12½
Postal Quickstep	12½
Spider and the Fly	12½
Virginia Rosebud Quickstep	12½
Mr. and Mrs. Jones's Quickstep	12½
March from "Il Crociato"	12½
Cuckoo Quickstep	12½
Swiss March	12½
Sixty Miles an Hour Quickstep	12½
Avant Courier Quickstep	12½
Going Ahead Quickstep	12½
Alpine March	12½
Gothamite Quickstep	25

DUETS FOR TWO PERFORMERS.

Flow gently, sweet Afton	12½
Venetian Gallop	12½
Louisville Gallop	12½
Elfin Waltz	12½
La Belle du Sud	12½
Baden-Baden Polka	12½
Affection Waltz	12½
Grand March from the Bohemian Girl	12½
Flower of America	12½
Hohnstock Polka	25
Mollie's Dream Waltz	25
Morning Star Waltz	25
Evening Star Waltz	25
National Schottisch	25
Redowa Waltz	25
Sounds from Home	25
Henriette Polka	25
Souvenir of Germany, (Schottisch)	25
Emerald Waltz	25
Gipsy March	25
Pet Waltz	25
Jenny Lind Polka	12½
Gertrude's Dream Waltz	12½
'Tis Midnight Hour, (Waltz)	12½
Les Vents, (No. 1, 2, 3, 4,) each	12½
London Polka Quadrilles	50
March Triumphale	25
Le Retour des Heroes	25

POLKAS.

Fidelia	12½
Lucilla	12½
La Mode	12½
My Heart and Lute	12½
Saratoga	12½
Rose Atherton	12½
Bona Fide	12½
Ne Plus Ultra	25
The White Violet	25
Fitzgerald's Gift Polka	25
Leap Year Polka	25

PIANO SONGS.

The heart, the heart, oh, let it be	12½
Kindred Hearts	25
Look how the Stars like jewels glisten	25
The Sabbath Bells	25

VARIATIONS.

L'Amitie, (La Fille du Regiment)	38
Amusement des Amateurs	50
Bachelor Polka	50
Les Bords du Hudson	50
Charity	38
Evening Song to the Virgin	38
Les Charmes de l'Amitie	38
Chasse d'Amour	50
Clochette Polka	62½
Dearest Mae	25
I dream of my Fatherland	38
The False Friend	38
Flow gently, sweet Afton	38
O Susanna	25
Oh! would I were a Boy again	50
Ravel Polka	50
Old Uncle Ned	25
Mary Blane	25
Rosa Lee	25
Virginia Rose Bud	25
Gipsy's Wild Chant	50
Hope and the Rose	50
Leonore	25
Les Ideals	50
Song of the Regiment	38
Salut a Philadelphie	25
Les Amoureux	25
Serenade March	38
Les Troubadours	62½
La Solitude	38
What's a' the Steer Kimmer	25
Come, ye Disconsolate	38
From Greenland's Icy Mountains	38
Jerusalem, my Happy Home	38
Henriette Polka	50
A Life on the Ocean Wave	50
Salut a Baltimore	25
La Liberte	50
Child of the Regiment	38
Song of the Drum	38
Rataplan	38
By the Sad Sea Waves	38
Love Not	25
Les Fleurs du Plaisir	50
Columbia the Gem of the Ocean	62½
Jenny Lind Polka	50
Vesper Hymn	38
I would not live alway	38
Strike the Cymbal	38
Peace, troubled Soul	38
Far, far, o'er Hill and Dell	38
Fading, still Fading	38
Messenger Bird	38
Widow of Nain	38
Adeste Fideles	38
There is nothing true but Heaven	38
Sicilian Hymn	38
Pleyel's German Hymn	38
Pilgrim Fathers	38
Prayer from Moses	38
Prayer from Zampa	38
Prayer from Tancredi	38
Watchman, tell us of the Night	38
Faith ... 38 Hope	38
Washington's March	38
Maretzek's Rondo Finale	50
Yes, I Remember, (answer to Ben Bolt)	38
Wings of a Dove	38

RONDOS, etc.

Bellone, (Polonaise à la Militaire)	38
Diane, (Rondeau de Chasse)	25
El Sinsonte de Camagne	25
La Tendresse, (Rondoletto)	12½
The Talisman, (Rondo Militaire)	50
Love's Influence, (Rondo)	25
Potpourri en forme de Rondeau	25

☞ Just Published, 1st and 2d Nos. of GROBE'S WORLD OF MUSIC, an unsurpassable Collection of Music, consisting of 100 of the most charming Melodies ever offered to the Musical World. ☜

☞ LEE & WALKER'S Publications may be had of the principal Music Dealers in N. York, Boston, Baltimore, N. Orleans, Cincinnati, St. Louis, Louisville, Charleston, Savannah, Pittsburg, Detroit, Chicago, and other Cities of the U. States and Canada.

FIGURE 4–1. A list of piano works (incomplete) by Charles Grobe, on the back cover of the sheet-music publication of his *Wings of a Dove* (1854).

consumer-musician, what could be more delightfully titillating than to hear, through a shower of fanciful passagework, the hidden outlines of a familiar tune? What more suggestive of a composer's invention—tested, as it is in variation sets, against the given material of a theme? Another, closely related, was the era's love of the improvisatory in performance. The concert pianist at that time was still expected as a matter of course to improvise, sometimes on familiar tunes, often on themes called out to him by the audience. Almost by definition, such improvisations took the form of variations; and if not of variations, then of a "fantasy," less formally strict than variations but no less a matter of creating new shapes out of old, or of pouring new wine from old bottles. In a survey of New York piano concerts between 1849 and 1865, one researcher found that one out of every three works presented was a fantasy on popular themes.[12] Variations and fantasies were also the simplest and most foolproof substructure for virtuoso scaffolding, since neither form nor thematic content was problematic and all attention could be paid by both performer and listener to the treatment of the musical material.

It is against this background that some comments made by Gottschalk toward the end of his career about the improved taste of American audiences must be read. He noted in his journal for December 8, 1864, that "at the time of my first return from Europe [1853] I was constantly deploring the want of public interest for pieces purely sentimental; the public listened with indifference; in order to arouse it, it became necessary to astound it; grand movements, tours de force, and noise had alone the privilege in piano music." By the mid-1860s, however, he was finding audiences happy to listen to "pieces purely sentimental"—pieces that, in Gottschalk's terms, had real musical content and "feeling," not just spectacular fantasies and pyrotechnical variations.

If Grobe can represent for us the legion of minor composers of piano music for the household market, a few others of the period before the Civil War emerge as composers with higher aspirations and more distinct musical personalities. Most notable are Anthony Philip Heinrich, Richard Hoffman, William Mason, and Gottschalk.

Heinrich was born in Bohemia (later to be part of West Czechoslovakia) in 1781, emigrated to America about 1810, and died in New York in 1861. He was this country's first—and without a doubt its most wildly enthusiastic—Romantic in music. Intoxicated with the natural grandeur of the New World, fascinated with the history of his adopted country, enchanted with the American Indian as "noble savage," and above all eager to be called an "American Musician," he poured out hundreds of pieces of the most extravagantly bizarre Romantic programmatism. Most of these were on American subjects, although his musical speech remained essentially that of central Europe.

Heinrich came first to Philadelphia, where he was a merchant and served as volunteer director of music at the Southwark Theatre. Beset by financial reverses, in the fall of 1817 he decided to try his lot elsewhere and traveled to Lexington, Kentucky, still virtually a wilderness village. He began composing music—began!—shortly thereafter; to a pathetic plea for funds written late in his life (1856) he added:

---

[12] Andrew C. Minor, "Piano Concerts in New York City 1849–1865" (M.Mus. thesis, University of Michigan, 1947), 475.

P.S. The Composer did not commence writing music until verging upon the fortieth year of his age, when dwelling by chance in the then solitary wilds and primeval forests of Kentucky. It was from a mere accident that music ever became his profession.[13]

Once embarked on composition, however, Heinrich poured out songs, piano works, marches and dances, choral music, and orchestral overtures, fantasies, concertos, and symphonies. His "opera prima," certainly the most extraordinary Opus 1 in the history of music, was published in Philadelphia in 1820. It is titled *The Dawning of Music in Kentucky, or The Pleasures of Harmony in the Solitudes of Nature* and is a huge collection described by the composer as including "Songs and Airs for the Voice and Pianoforte, Waltzes, Cotillions, Minuets, Polonaises, Marches, Variations with some pieces of a national character adapted for the Piano Forte and also calculated for the lovers of the Violin." Heinrich might also have noted that he included a minuet version of *Hail! Columbia* and a waltz version of *Yankee Doodle*; that the "military waltz" *Avance et Retraite* is to be played from beginning to end, then backward to the beginning again (as suggested by the title); that *A Chromatic Ramble, of the Peregrine Harmonist* is a tour de force of harmonic complexity, a piece that literally must be seen to be believed; and that the collection is crowned with a fantastic chamber quintet for piano and strings—a showpiece for its *violino principale* titled *The Yankee Doodleiad*, based on trumpet calls, *Hail! Columbia*, and a set of fifteen variations on *Yankee Doodle* interrupted in midstream by an interlude on *The President's March* labeled "Huzza for Washington!" (Its full title is *The YankeeDoodleiad, A National Divertimento, Dedicated to the very liberal Patrons of the Science in the United States, as a VERY Small Mite of Gratitude from A. P. Heinrich.*)

Heinrich's was an expansive and mercurial muse: he himself characterized his music as being "full of strange ideal somersets and capricios." (The pontifical J. S. Dwight of Boston said it was "bewildering ... wild and complicated.")[14] And this is true of most of his piano music; some of it, however, is gentle, sweet, and direct—for example, "The Laurel Waltz" (*NW* CD 80257), from *The Ellsler Dances* of 1841.

Richard Hoffman (1831–1909) came to America from his native England as a boy of sixteen, having already studied with a constellation of German pianists (but not with Liszt, as is often claimed). He settled in New York, where besides teaching and composing he played concerts. Competent and agreeable ("a perfect musician, a distinguished and modest man ... an artist and a *gentleman*," said Gottschalk with unusual generosity), Hoffman wrote a piano music of flowery grace through almost one hundred opus numbers. *La Gazelle* (1858; in *3Centuries* 3, 328–32) was a favorite, with its Lisztian arabesques (Example 4–6) and its fashionable French title evoking the image of Chopin.

---

[13] Heinrich, manuscript scrapbook, Library of Congress (Music Division), 836.

[14] *The Harbinger*, July 4, 1846. Dwight's lengthy review of a sixty-fifth birthday concert for Heinrich, almost a one-man show, is reprinted in full in W. T. Upton, *Anthony Philip Heinrich* (New York: Columbia University Press, 1939), 199–201.

EXAMPLE 4–6.   R. Hoffman, *La Gazelle* (Mainz and New York: B. Schott's Söhne, ca. 1858), measures 8–15.

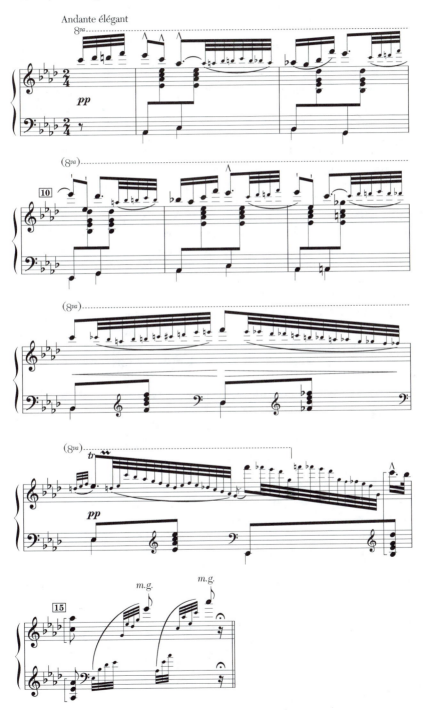

William Mason (1829–1908), the third son of Lowell Mason, was a pupil of Liszt's during the last of his five years' study in Germany (1849–54). His main role, like his father's, was more that of tastemaker and teacher than composer; but he was also a most competent performer. He concertized in the northern states from the East Coast to Chicago, offering solo piano recitals (without the interpolations of song from an "assisting vocalist" that were conventional at the time); and he played music of high caliber, if almost exclusively Germanic, although his recital-closing improvisations might, because of audience demand, have to be based on *Yankee Doodle* counterpointed with *Old Hundred* (the ancient tune sung by Protestants to Psalm 100, "Praise God from whom all blessings flow"). He also formed an influential chamber-music group, the Mason-Thomas Quartet (actually a five-member ensemble—a string quartet plus Mason as pianist). For thirteen seasons (1855–68) they offered New York City its finest chamber music; the very first concert (November 27, 1855) included the premiere performance of Brahms's Trio in B major, Op. 8, as well as works by Schubert, Wagner, Chopin, and Mendelssohn, among others. Mason was also a renowned piano teacher. His own piano music seems most often proper but bloodless, without Hoffman's airy Lisztian flair (an exception being the early *Silver Spring*, Op. 6, recorded on *NW* CD 80257, along with Mason's more typically genteel *Pastoral Novelette* of 1895). Franz Liszt, however, politely called Mason's *Amitié pour amitié* (Example 4–7) "a charming little piece," his *Etude de concert*, Op. 9, and *Valse caprice*, Op. 17, "distinguished in style and of good effect."[15] Chopin's *Berceuse*, Op. 57, was certainly the model for Mason's *Lullaby* of 1857; its reference to "Three Blind Mice" was surely unconscious and unintended.

Without question the most colorful personality, the most articulate intelligence, the most talented performer, and the most provocative composer among the mid-nineteenth-century pianists was Louis Moreau Gottschalk (1829–69). Born in the racial and ethnic melting pot of New Orleans, Gottschalk could claim a cosmopolitan lineage: his father was a cultivated English Jew educated in Germany; his mother was Louisiana-born and of French ancestry (hence "Creole"). Gottschalk grew up in the Vieux Carré quarter, hearing among other kinds of music that of the many blacks and Latin Americans in the southern trade center. In 1842 he was sent to Paris to study, whence he returned to America only in 1853 as a renowned virtuoso and keyboard composer. From then on, his life was virtually one long concert tour, all over the United States, Canada, the West Indies, Panama, Mexico, and South America, where he died at Rio de Janeiro, only forty years of age.

Even as a youth in Paris, Gottschalk was praised by Chopin and Berlioz, and his playing was spoken of in the same breath with that of Liszt and Thalberg. He became the darling of the Paris salons not only for his vir-

[15] William Mason, *Memories of a Musical Life* (New York: The Century Co., 1902), 88, 294.

EXAMPLE 4–7. W. Mason, *Amitié pour Amitié*, 2nd ed. (Boston: N. Richardson, 1854), measures 1–8.

tuosity but also for his early compositions, which were perceived as exotic mélanges of Afro-Caribbean rhythms and Creole melodies, with a Chopinesque overlay of virtuoso passagework. According to a review by Berlioz of a concert in 1851, "everybody in Europe now knows [Gottschalk's] *Bamboula, Le Bananier, Le Mancenillier, La Savane*, and twenty other ingenious fantasies in which the nonchalant grace of tropical melody assuages so agreeably our restless and insatiable passion for novelty."[16]

Back in the Americas and embarked on a career as traveling virtuoso, Gottschalk became a sort of living player piano:

> I have become stupid with it. I have the appearance of an automaton under the influence of a voltaic pile. My fingers move on the keyboard with feverish heat.... The sight of a piano sets my hair on end.

---

[16] Quoted in Jeanne Behrend, ed., *Notes of a Pianist* (New York: Knopf, 1964), xxii.

In December 1862, after finishing his last tour of the year, he wrote:

> I have given eighty-five concerts in four months and a half. I have traveled fif-
> teen thousand miles by train. At St. Louis I gave seven concerts in six days; at
> Chicago, five in four days. A few more weeks in this way and I would have be-
> come an idiot.[17]

In an age of virtuosity, Gottschalk was the virtuoso incarnate. He has also rightfully been called "our first matinee idol": the young American music student Amy Fay lamented in Berlin upon hearing of his death, "The infatuation that I and 999,999 other American girls once felt for him, still lingers in my breast."[18]

Like Chopin and other pianist-composers of the era, Gottschalk published little of his music except solo piano compositions, of which there are just over one hundred. In addition he composed some songs, a few orchestral works, and several operas (their music mostly lost). The pieces mentioned by Berlioz are among the earliest and most interesting of the piano compositions, "New Orleans" pieces published in France and advertised there as the work of "Gottschalk de la Louisiane." Based mostly on black-American and Creole tunes, they tend to begin with marvelously fresh, strong ideas (see Example 4–8), which before long are overwhelmed by showers of scales, arpeggios, passagework of all kinds. Youthful, exuberant, and immensely promising, they nevertheless tend to be overlong and lacking in tonal or formal interest, as the genuinely gifted fledgling composer gives way to the virtuoso prodigy. The slightly later *Le Banjo*, Op. 15 (1854 or 1855; a so-called *Banjo second* was actually composed first), probably has in common with Stephen Foster's *Camptown Races* (see Example 5–8) a source in black-American song (if it was not based on Foster's). Full of ingenious strumming, *Le Banjo* is one of Gottschalk's best works, although even an enthusiast such as the pianist John Kirkpatrick admitted that it has a "characteristic redundance and tonal monotony."[19]

Gottschalk mined other folk and popular song veins as he toured through Spain (*La jota aragonesa*, Op. 14), the West Indies (*Souvenir de Porto Rico*, Op. 31; *Souvenir de la Havane*, Op. 39), and South America (*Grande Fantaisie triomphale sur l'hymne national brésilien*, Op. 69). Only occasionally, as in *Souvenir de Porto Rico* ("*Marche des Gibaros*"), does formal control

---

[17] Both quotations ibid., 102. Gottschalk's journal, written between 1857 and 1868, is a kaleidoscopic account of his travels in the West Indies, the United States, and Latin America.

[18] *Music-Study in Germany* (New York: Macmillan, 1897), 42. The idolatry of Gottschalk as prefiguring that of later stage and screen stars was first suggested by Irving Lowens; see the chapter on the pianist in his *Music and Musicians in Early America* (New York: W. W. Norton, 1964), 223–33.

[19] "Observations on 4 volumes and supplement of the works of Louis Moreau Gottschalk" (typescript; Music Research Division, New York Public Library).

EXAMPLE 4–8.   L. M. Gottschalk, early "New Orleans" pieces. (*a*) *Bamboula*, Op. 2, measures 1–7. (*b*) *Le Bananier*, Op. 5, measures 1–8.

restrain technical exuberance; however, in that piece of 1857–58, based on a native Christmas song (Example 4–9), Gottschalk achieves a minor master-piece with the arching dynamic curve, waxing and waning, of a "patrol" piece and the strong syncopations of Afro-Caribbean dance music (Example 4–10). Perhaps Gottschalk's greatest *pastiche* on folk and popular source materials,

EXAMPLE 4–9.   Puerto Rican *aguinaldo*, beginning, and L. M. Gottschalk, *Souvenir de Porto Rico* (Mainz: B. Schott's Söhne, 1859), measures 17–20.

EXAMPLE 4–10. Gottschalk, *Souvenir de Porto Rico*, climax (measures 189–93).

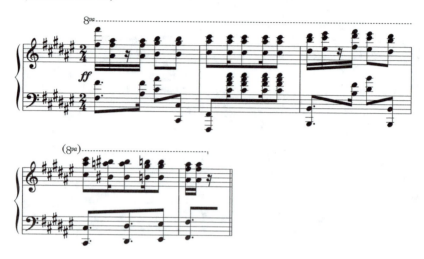

and certainly the noisiest, was *l'Union*, Op. 48 (1852–62), a grand "paraphrase de concert sur les airs nationaux" (*Yankee Doodle, The Star-Spangled Banner, Hail! Columbia*, and some trumpet calls) completed at the height of the Civil War and received in Philadelphia, according to the composer's journal, with "unheard-of enthusiasm ... recalls, encores, hurrahs, etc.!"

Another side of Gottschalk's art was that of the "purely sentimental" piece, as he called it, the genre piece of meditative and "poetic" reflection. Among the most carefully worked of these are *Ricordati* ("*méditation*"), Op. 26, a Chopinesque nocturne; *The Last Hope* ("*méditation religieuse*"), Op. 16 (1854), Gottschalk's monument to pious sentimentality, his most notoriously successful tearjerker, but withal a shrewdly contrived series of daringly chromatic introductions (note the plural) to an indestructible arc of songful melody; *Berceuse*, Op. 47 (ca. 1861), based on a French folk song, *Fais dodo, mon bébé*; and *Suis-moi*, Op. 45 (ca. 1861). *The Dying Poet* (1863?), one of "some contraband pieces that are to be published under the aegis of a borrowed paternity" (as Gottschalk archly described his pseudonym "Seven Octaves"), and *Morte!!* (1868?), which achieved, said Gottschalk, "un succès de larmes" (a triumph of tears), were famous pieces in the vein of *The Last Hope*.

Gottschalk noted in his journal one night in 1865 that his had been a life of "playing the piano, of having composed two or three hundred pieces, of having given seven or eight thousand concerts, of having given to the poor one hundred or one hundred and fifty thousand dollars, [and] of having been knighted twice." The remark may have been one of Romantic hyperbole, but so were Gottschalk's personality and his music.

ORCHESTRAS

The Romantics loved the orchestra. Convinced that instrumental music in general was the purest, most sublime music, they conceived of the orchestra as a kind of super-instrument. And seeking an ever broader coloristic and expressive spectrum, they enlarged it from a smallish ensemble of one or two dozen players into a giant symphonic machine of more than a hundred. If during the era the organ was king of instruments, the piano the queen, the orchestra was emperor.

One of the most characteristic trends in United States music since the mid–nineteenth century has been the proliferation of independent symphony orchestras. Whereas in Europe such orchestras have hardly existed apart from opera houses (although a few, typically state-subsidized, are now virtually independent), in the United States the symphony orchestra has tended to develop as an independent entity, reflecting a public penchant for concerts rather than opera. The American notion of a "permanent" orchestra, and one supported by public subscriptions and box-office receipts as well as private donors, was a by-product of the rise of public concerts and a mass audience that I discussed in Chapter 3. In 1842, two decades before the Civil War, the first "permanent" orchestra still in existence today, the New York Philharmonic, was founded. By 1996–97, the American Symphony Orchestra League could count some 1,200 American "adult" orchestras—excluding, that is, school and college-level orchestras. More than 20 of these were "major" orchestras (with annual operating budgets over $10 million); 10 percent, or about 120, were "medium" ($750,000 to $10 million); and 88 percent—nine out of ten, or about 1,100—were "small" (less than $750,000). To get the whole picture, one must add the thousand or so school/college/university/conservatory orchestras, as well as even smaller, non-"symphonic" regional and community orchestras across the land.[20]

The beginnings of this astonishing development go back to the early nineteenth century, when Gottlieb Graupner (see p. 38), who had been one of the musicians in Salomon's orchestra in London during Haydn's famous visit there in 1791–92, organized a group of Boston instrumentalists into a "Philo-Harmonic Society" to meet informally and play through symphonies of Haydn and others. Notices of rehearsals appeared regularly in the semi-weekly Boston newspapers from October 4, 1809, and the society soon began playing for the public. John Rowe Parker (1777–1844), editor of the first American music periodical, *The Euterpeiad, or Musical Intelligencer* (1820–23), signalized the historic importance of Graupner's instrumental organization (and the other society Graupner helped to found) when he wrote, "Until the formation of the Philo-Harmonic for instrumental, and the insti-

---

[20] These figures, provided by Abby Wilner of the League's Resource Center (to whom I am grateful), derive from its 1996–97 *Orchestral Statistical Report*. The historical development to the mid-1980s is well covered in the *AmeriGrove* entry "Orchestras."

tution of the Handel and Haydn Societies, for vocal performances, regular concerts have never succeeded in this metropolis" (*Euterpeiad*, April 8, 1820). They did not succeed well enough, apparently, for the Philo-Harmonic Society of Boston gave its last concert late in 1824.

Meanwhile, in Philadelphia a Musical Fund Society was organized in 1820 by Benjamin Carr and others; it was active as a choral-orchestral organization to 1857, and more sporadically to the present. In the nearby Moravian center of Bethlehem, a Philharmonic Society was founded, also in 1820, which flourished until about 1839. And in 1842 a group of musicians led by Ureli Corelli Hill (1802–75), Henry Christian Timm (1811–92), and William Scharfenberg (1819–95) founded the New York Philharmonic Society; its first concert included Beethoven's Fifth Symphony, Weber's *Oberon* overture, another overture (by the Bohemian-German composer Johann Kalliwoda), a piano quintet by Johann Hummel, and various vocal solos and duets. Numbering about fifty-five players, give or take the few who found it impossible to give up other jobs to play in the three concerts of the first season (four in each season thereafter through 1858), the New York Philharmonic initially had no single conductor; six of the musicians shared the duties. From the five-hundred-seat hall of the Apollo Rooms on Broadway below Canal Street, the orchestra graduated to Niblo's Theatre (Broadway and Prince Street), then in 1856 further uptown to the elegant Academy of Music at 14th Street and Irving Place.

That our first permanent orchestra should have been established in New York City reflected an important economic and social development: New York's skyrocket rise, stimulated especially by the opening of the Erie Canal in 1825, to supremacy as the nation's first port, largest city, and principal commercial center. As such it became also the nation's center of those performing arts that rested on a foundation of mass-audience support. New York's preeminence as a musical-performance center already by the mid–nineteenth century is confirmed by the fact that not until 1881 would the second permanent American symphony orchestra, the Boston Symphony, be established.

Three other orchestras heard in pre–Civil War America should be cited briefly here for their catalytic influence on American music. One was the Germania Musical Society, a group of twenty-five young musicians who left Berlin in May 1848, heading for the United States "in order to further in the hearts of this politically free people the love of the fine art of music through performance of the greatest German composers."[21] The Germanians' first concerts in New York led to others elsewhere, and the well-trained, well-balanced ensemble was heard, before its dissolution in 1854 (all its members by then American citizens), in more than nine hundred concerts in many American and Canadian cities from Richmond to Minneapolis and

---

[21] H. F. Albrecht, *Skizzen aus dem Leben der Musik-Gesellschaft Germania* (Philadelphia, 1869), trans. in H. Earle Johnson's "The Germania Musical Society, *MQ* 39 (1953): 75.

from Boston to St. Louis (where one young woman, hearing Beethoven's Second Symphony for the first time, remarked, "Well, ain't that funny music!"). American attitudes as to the "standard repertory" of orchestral music were strongly shaped by this group's concentration on Germanic works from Haydn to Wagner.

Another, briefer symphonic visitor was the orchestra brought from London to New York for one year by the French conductor Louis Antoine Jullien (1812–60)—"a splendid, bold, and dazzlingly successful humbug," wrote the New York *Courier and Enquirer*. To his twenty-seven-piece orchestra Jullien added more than sixty local musicians (among them two young violinists named George Bristow and Theodore Thomas, of whom more shortly); on August 29, 1853, after a strenuous advertising campaign, he initiated a series of "Monster Concerts for the Masses" at Castle Garden. The *Courier and Enquirer* had to admit that "the discipline of his orchestra is marvelous." The *New York Clipper* was not so charitable; that lively precursor of *Variety* and *Billboard*, which proclaimed itself "A Weekly Sporting Paper, devoted to the Ring, the Turf, Yachting, Pedestrianism, Cricket, Rowing Matches, Theatricals, Music, and the various sports of the Old World and the New," took up the cudgel against "these 'highfalutin' gimcracks" in its issue of September 3:

> There were not quite 3,000 persons in the building, and perhaps not quite 2,500 who paid for their tickets [at 50¢ each]. ... It is now more difficult to humbug us than it was a few years since. ... With encouragement, America can produce musical wonders as well as reaping machines; an American Forrest [Edwin Forrest (1806–72), American actor] as well as American Clippers ... Several European celebrities have lately returned to their homes, not at all pleased with our reception of them. Stand fast, Americans! encourage those who are with us. ... Monster concerts for the masses, indeed!

The chauvinist tone is of interest: here spoke the vernacular tradition of American culture, weary of the European monopoly over American cultivated taste. In its next issue (September 10) the *New York Clipper* chuckled over the no-more-than-"middling success" of Jullien's nightly concerts, and on September 17, headlining "A Failure in New York" for Jullien, it urged its readers to "encourage our own musicians, and endeavor to do away with the puffing system adopted by foreign professionals." Jullien's concerts had not in fact failed, but he got the message: he began to include on his programs works by American-born composers, among them Bristow and William Fry. It was the first recognition that native-born American composers of symphonic music had had.

A notable graduate of Jullien's orchestra and of nine years' playing experience with the New York Philharmonic (1854–63) was Theodore Thomas (1835–1905). His potential as a director was recognized when he was a violinist in the group organized by William Mason in 1855 for chamber-music evenings: Mason conceded in his *Memories of a Musical Life* that

Thomas's "was the dominating influence, felt and acknowledged by us all." After some tentative beginnings in 1862 and 1863, Thomas initiated a long and brilliant career as conductor of his own orchestra late in 1864. An astute impresario and a canny program builder, Thomas knew how to create and hold an audience with programs that might be called crescent-shaped, with the heaviest fare in the center; thus he might flank orchestral movements by Beethoven, Schubert, Mendelssohn, even the radical Wagner, with simpler music: the waltzes of Strauss, the Bach-Gounod *Ave Maria*, and other crowd-pleasers. It was an original format, which gave up the old reliance on a pot-pourri of instrumental and vocal works to maintain audience interest, and it was destined to become a stereotype. Characteristic is the following program from one of Thomas's Summer Night Concerts in New York's Central Park Garden (August 7, 1868):[22]

Coronation March	Johann Strauss
Overture to *Die Heimkehre aus der Fremde*	Mendelssohn
Waltz from *Masaniello*	Auber

Intermission

Overture to *Tannhäuser*	Wagner
2nd movement, Symphony No. 8	Beethoven
3rd movement (Scherzo), Symphony No. 7 (C major)	Schubert

Intermission

Grand March for the Schiller Centenary	Meyerbeer
Overture to *Mignon*	Thomas
Ave Maria	Bach-Gounod
Waltz, "Die Sphärenklänge"	Johann Strauss
Turkish March [arranged from Piano Sonata, K. 311?]	Mozart

Between 1869 and 1878 the Thomas Orchestra made regular, lengthy tours through the East and the Middle West as far as Chicago, with a roster of about fifty players.[23] Both in New York and throughout the country, its influence on standards of performance and ideas of a standard orchestral repertory was immense. The modern symphonic ideal derives from Thomas's: the

---

[22] Adapted from Rose Fay Thomas, *Memoirs of Theodore Thomas* (New York: Moffett, Yard and Company, 1911), 49. Later programs of Thomas's orchestra had fewer "light" works and included complete symphonies; some were retrospective exhibitions of works by a single composer.

[23] When it played the opening concert of Harvard University's Sanders Theatre, November 21, 1876, the makeup of the orchestra was eight first violins, eight second violins, four violas, four cellos, and four basses, plus woodwinds and brasses in pairs, according to *Dwight's Journal of Music* 36 (March 3, 1877): 398. Presumably there was a percussionist as well.

dozens of players must submit through careful rehearsal to the rigorous, not to say autocratic, direction of the conductor, in the interests of polished perfection. Thomas's ideas on repertory were inevitably governed by an Austro-Germanic bias; nevertheless, he occasionally played music by American composers. They were very few, however; Thomas had high standards and, as he put it, "I do not believe in playing inferior works merely because they are American" (*Memoirs*, 67).

Thomas became conductor of the New York Philharmonic in 1877, resigned for an abortive year as first head of the Cincinnati College of Music, resumed the Philharmonic directorship in 1880, then moved permanently to Chicago in 1891 to become conductor of the newly established Chicago Symphony Orchestra. For the last half of the nineteenth century, he was the acknowledged master of the symphony orchestra, the first American virtuoso conductor.

ORCHESTRAL MUSIC

What about American orchestral music, as opposed to American orchestras, in the period up to the Civil War?

With only a few orchestras in the land and with orchestral music, as distinct from music for solo instruments or small chamber groups, identified mainly with European composers and conductors, it is not surprising that American composers produced comparatively little symphonic music. Nevertheless, a few composers stand out as our first symphonists.

"The Beethoven of America" is what Parker's *Euterpeiad* called Anthony Philip Heinrich in its issue of April 13, 1822. We have met Heinrich previously (see pp. 85–86) as a composer of bizarre and extravagant virtuoso piano music, songs, and chamber works. He also had orchestral aspirations, and in fact his first historically noteworthy act, upon arrival in Kentucky in the autumn of 1817, was to organize a benefit concert—the beneficiary was Heinrich himself—in which he not only played the violin and the piano but also directed the "full band" in a "Simfonia con Minuetto" by Beethoven—perhaps the First Symphony, not one of the bigger, later ones, but certainly an extraordinary kind of work to present in the pioneer town of Lexington, Kentucky, in November 1817.

The major part of Heinrich's orchestral music consists of descriptive symphonies in several elaborately titled movements, or one-movement programmatic fantasies divided into contrasting sections. Their subjects are those of a hyperenthusiastic, Romantic newcomer to America: Indian lore (*Pushmataha, a Venerable Chief of a Western Tribe*, 1831; *Manitou Mysteries; or The Voice of the Great Spirit*, before 1845); American history (*The Treaty of William Penn with the Indians...for a full orchestra, comprising successively 6 different characteristic movements, united in one*, 1834, revised 1847; *Der Felsen von Plymouth; oder, Die Landung der Pilger Väter in Neu-England*,

1858–59); the American landscape (*The War of the Elements and the Thundering of Niagara*, before 1845); hero-worship (*Schiller. Grande sinfonia dramatica*, 1830s, revised with additions 1847; *The Tomb of Genius: To the Memory of Mendelssohn-Bartholdy. Sinfonia sacra*, ca. 1847); and finally, patriotic encomiums (*The Jubilee. A Grand national song of triumph*, for orchestra and chorus, 1840). Heinrich's friendship with the great ornithologist and painter John James Audubon led to two programmatic symphonies, *The Columbiad; or, Migration of American Wild Passenger Pigeons* (1837) and *The Ornithological Combat of Kings; or, The Condor of the Andes and the Eagle of the Cordilleras* (1847, rev. 1856). Heinrich considered the latter (recorded on *NW CD 80208*) his finest work. Subtitled "A grand symphony. Extracted and arranged for a full orchestra, with some deviations, from a descriptive concerto grosso vocale of the same title and subject," the twenty-five-minute piece is in four movements—"The Conflict of the Condor in the Air," "The Repose of the Condor," "The Combat of the Condor on Land," and "Victory of the Condor."

The style of these extraordinary orchestral outbursts is indeed one of "strange ... somersets and capriccios" (to borrow Heinrich's own characterization of his music), mingling simple dance tunes (especially folkish clog-dance Ländler types) and elaborately chromatic melodies; crystal-clear Classic-era harmonies and wildly modulating passages; basically homophonic, diatonic textures and a profusion of decorative chromatic counterpoints (most often solo woodwind voices over a background of strings); predictable, periodic phrase forms and surprising extensions (or, instead of the latter, the opposite: unexpected grand pauses of dead silence).

For a latecomer to composition, Heinrich had a remarkable ear for orchestral color and an expansive imagination that led him to write for unusual instruments as well as the conventional orchestral core. The first movement of *The Ornithological Combat of Kings* (the scoring of which occasionally reaches as many as thirty-seven parts) reveals imaginative use of triangle; the third movement, freshly conceived writing for percussion and for solo woodwinds. Among the instruments called for in the very large orchestra of *The Indian War Council* is a "harmonicon" or "glasschord," the mechanized set of musical glasses that had been improved or perhaps even invented by Benjamin Franklin. *Pushmataha* is a fourteen-minute fantasy for thirty-three orchestral voices including piccolo, basset horn, serpent, contrabassoon, three kinds of drums, triangle, cymbals, and tambourine as well as the normal full orchestra. For reasons unclear (but possibly relating to the first public Independence Day celebration at which S. F. Smith's *America* was sung to *God Save the King* [July 4, 1831]), this paean to a mighty Indian chief culminates with a majestic and exuberantly chromaticized quotation of the tune (Example 4–11).[24]

---

[24] Wilbur R. Maust offers another conjecture in "The American Indian in the Orchestral Music of Anthony Philip Heinrich," in *Music East and West: Essays in Honor of Walter Kaufmann*,

EXAMPLE 4–11.   A. Heinrich, *Pushmataha* (1831), measures 460–65 (reduced from the Library of Congress orchestral-score manuscript).

It might be expected that the intense musical life of the German-speaking communities in Pennsylvania would have inspired some orchestral music, but the Moravians seem for the most part to have been content with European scores, and thus far we know of no orchestral productions of the

ed. Thomas Noblitt (New York: Pendragon Press, 1981), 309–25: "The ... introduction of this tune may be due to the facts that Pushmataha was an ardent supporter of the U. S. and that he was honored at his funeral 'with a great procession and booming guns'." (The quotation is from the entry on Pushmataha by Katherine E. Crane in the *Dictionary of American Biography*.)

other sects. One of the earliest known American orchestral works is a Symphony in D, in two tiny movements, by William C. Peters (1805–86), composed in 1831 for the Harmony Society of Economy, beyond Pittsburgh in western Pennsylvania and hardly more than a frontier settlement in 1831. Charles Hommann (ca. 1800–after 1862) won a prize in 1835 from the Musical Fund Society of Philadelphia for an overture and contributed a four-movement symphony in E♭ and an overture in C to the Philharmonic Society of Bethlehem; these and other works, especially some strong chamber pieces for strings, deserve more attention from conductors and performers than they have had.

George F. Bristow (1825–98) and William H. Fry (1813–64) were the best-known mid-century composers of orchestral music in New York. Bristow was the better trained, a professional violinist and conductor who composed several symphonies in a polished Mendelssohnian style, among them the fine Third Symphony in F♯ minor, Op. 26 (performed by the New York Philharmonic under Carl Bergmann in 1859), and a more lengthy Fourth Symphony ("Arcadian"), Op. 49 (1874), which includes perhaps the first use of an American Indian melody in a work of art-music. The opera *Rip Van Winkle* (1855) and the cantatas *The Great Republic* (1879) and *Niagara* (1898) all have strong overtures. Fry, famous as a noisy champion of American composers amid the deluge of Europeans just before the Civil War, composed four symphonies, *Santa Claus*, *The Breaking Heart*, *Childe Harold*, and *A Day in the Country*, all performed by Jullien's orchestra in 1853–54 and all provided with interminable programs that explain, but do not make coherent, the naive tone-painting and narrative forms of the works; an *Overture to "Macbeth"* (1862) reminiscent of Auber is well scored and never dull.

The Romantic tendency to gigantism, exemplified by Jullien's "monster concerts," is suggested also by two in which Gottschalk was involved in Cuba and Rio de Janeiro. For a concert at Havana early in 1860, Gottschalk composed several works, among them a *Sinfonia Triunfal* (with a vocal/choral finale from a lost opera, *Charles IX*); the orchestra, he reported in his journal, numbered 650, plus 87 choristers, 15 solo singers, 50 drums, and 80 trumpets—"that is to say, nearly nine hundred persons bellowing and blowing to see who could scream the loudest." And at Rio in November 1869, for a concert that included the Andante of his *La Nuit des tropiques* (1858–59), Gottschalk dreamed of "eight hundred performers and eighty drums to lead."[25] He got about 650, made up from bands of the Brazilian National Guard, the Imperial Navy, the Army, and the War Arsenal, and from three orchestras assembled for the occasion. *La Nuit des tropiques*, though subtitled *Symphonie romantique*, survives in only two movements, Andante (*La Nuit*) and Finale (*Une Fête sous les tropiques*); Gottschalk's biographer has characterized it as "at once a sophisticated symphonic poem in the tradition

[25] Octavia Hensel, *Life and Letters of Louis Moreau Gottschalk* (Boston: Oliver Ditson, 1870), 174.

of Berlioz and a raucous dance, conjuring up a Cuban festival combining the latest valved brass instruments from Paris and primitive Caribbean drums, traditional European strings and Spanish folk instruments ... blend[ing] Parisian elegance with American democracy.[26]

OPERA

As suggested in Chapter 2 (see pp. 32–33), although the "lavish, costly, and aristocratic Baroque opera" of Europe had no place in early America, less elaborate musical-theater pieces did, especially ballad operas and English comic operas. Such plays with music continued in unbroken tradition through the period, in addition to other kinds of musical theater as vernacular entertainment with few pretensions to being "fine art." However, as one pathbreaking scholar has put it,

> Music was a normal and important part of all dramatic productions. ... A standard theatrical bill of fare from either the late eighteenth or the early nineteenth century consisted of an instrumental overture (often from an opera), a full-length dramatic piece with added songs and dances (either interpolated into the action or performed between the acts), and an afterpiece (a farce, burletta, one-act opera, dance, pantomime, or masque) that often was musical in nature. In addition, dances or musical compositions were frequently performed before and after either the dramatic work or the afterpiece.[27]

By the 1860s the ballad opera as such was virtually nonexistent, supplanted by transformations such as *The Black Crook* of 1866 (an extravagant mixture of Frenchy ballet and Germanic melodrama, to an American variation on the plot of Weber's *Der Freischütz*) or by operatic parodies such as those of the blackface minstrel shows (see p. 32 f). Central European operas also gained a foothold in America during the period, however—at first only in abbreviated versions, their texts translated into English—through a number of small, itinerant British troupes headlined by one or two vocal stars. (A perennial favorite of these, from 1831 on, was the adaptation, as *Cinderella*, by M. Rophino Lacy of Rossini's *La Cenerentola*.) By the mid-1850s these tiny troupes had disappeared almost entirely, having been replaced by opera companies (English, French, and Italian), with varying numbers of performers. And by that time, also, the first "grand operas" by American composers were produced.

[26] As quoted in S. Frederick Starr, *Bamboula! The Life and Times of Louis Moreau Gottschalk* (New York: Oxford University Press, 1995), 285. The complicated history of *La Nuit des tropiques* is well told by Richard Jackson in his notes for NW CD 80208 (which includes the work in a two-piano arrangement).

[27] Katherine K. Preston, *Opera on the Road: Traveling Opera Troupes in the United States, 1825–60* (Urbana: University of Illinois Press, 1993), 1–2.

The most lively, as well as the earliest, operatic center was New Orleans, where a cultivated French contingent of the cosmopolitan population had maintained support for French opera from 1796, when the theater on St. Peter Street produced Grétry's one-act comic opera *Silvain*. In the 1805–6 season alone, the St. Peter Theatre produced sixteen operas by nine composers, among them Monsigny, Grétry, Dalayrac, Boieldieu, Méhul, and Paisiello—and all these for a town of only twelve thousand people. With the establishment of a permanent opera company at the Orleans Theater, New Orleans was unrivalled as the operatic center of America. Several northern cities—Boston, Philadelphia, Baltimore—heard their first grand opera when the New Orleans company toured during the seven summers from 1827 to 1833, and New York admitted that the southern troupe was "fully equal to that we imported from foreigners,"[28] referring to Manuel García's Italian Opera Company, which had given New York its first foreign-language opera in 1825–26.

García's repertory favored Rossini—*Il barbiere di Siviglia* (the company's first production), *La Cenerentola, Semiramide, Tancredi,* and *Il Turco in Italia*—and Mozart's *Don Giovanni*. Later troupes discovered a substantial opera audience in New York, especially for Italian works—not only by Mozart and Rossini but even more especially by Bellini, Donizetti, and early Verdi. This vogue culminated in the construction and opening in New York of the Astor Place Opera House in 1847 and, in 1854, the Academy of Music (with 4,600 seats the largest theater in the United States). Opening night at the Astor Place featured Verdi's *Ernani*; at the Academy of Music, Bellini's *Norma*. German opera gained a foothold only after the wave of German immigration after 1848; in the 1862–63 season, however, New Yorkers heard sixty-five performances of German operas, the favorites being Weber's *Der Freischütz*, Beethoven's *Fidelio*, and Mozart's *Die Zauberflöte* and *Die Entführung aus dem Serail*.

As with orchestral music in New York, the American names to reckon with in opera of the period are those of Fry and Bristow. Fry's early life was spent in Philadelphia, and it was at the Chestnut Street Theatre on June 4, 1845, that Fry's *Leonora*, a full-scale three-act work on a libretto derived by his brother from Bulwer-Lytton's *The Lady of Lyons*, was first heard. Presented in an unusually lavish production for the time, at the hands of the English company of Anne Childe Seguin and Arthur Seguin with an orchestra of sixty and a chorus of eighty, *Leonora* had a successful run of sixteen performances. Its fashionably Romantic plot and Belliniesque music must have made it seem very up-to-date. Fry composed three other operas, only one of which, *Notre Dame de Paris*, was produced (in 1854).

[28] Quoted by Henry Kmen, *Music in New Orleans* (Baton Rouge: Louisiana State University Press, 1966),125, from the New York *American* as cited in the New Orleans *L'Argus* of August 24, 1827.

Fry was perhaps less gifted as a composer than as a journalist. As such he was a belligerent and articulate champion of the rights of American composers to be heard in America. Ironically, however, it was not Fry who turned to American subjects; it was his friend George Bristow. Bristow's *Rip Van Winkle* (1855; revised 1878–82), first produced at Niblo's Garden in New York by the Pyne and Harrison English Opera Company, was a modest success, with eighteen performances; his *Columbus* was never finished. *Rip Van Winkle* is less derivative from Italian opera than Fry's *Leonora*; indeed, it has been said to be "filled with music that would be incomprehensible to Donizetti or Bellini, music that evokes mid-century America, the musical language of the parlor ballad and the Protestant hymn."[29] It also reveals Bristow's solid grounding in German instrumental music of his time, although he seldom successfully bridges the gap between his fluid, chromatic harmony and his square-cut phrase structure.

BIBLIOGRAPHICAL NOTES

A useful source (to 1990) is James R. Heintze, ed., *American Music before 1865 in Print and on Records: a biblio-discography* (*ISAMm* 30 [1990]); Heintze also edited an anthology of ten essays, *American Musical Life in Context and Practice to 1865* (New York: Garland Publishing, 1994).

Arthur Rich's *Lowell Mason* (Chapel Hill: University of North Carolina Press, 1946) is complemented and partially superseded by Carol Ann Pemberton's dissertation-based *Lowell Mason: His Life and Work* (Ann Arbor: UMI Research Press, 1985); Michael Broyles also has much to say about Mason in his *"Music of the Highest Class": Elitism and Populism in Antebellum Boston* (cited in note 1). Mason's own *Musical Letters from Abroad* (1853) have been reprinted (New York: Da Capo Press, 1967).

Richard Crawford writes about musical education in "Musical Learning in Nineteenth-Century America," *AM* 1/1 (Spring 1983): 1–11. Besides Allen Britton's article cited in note 3, see his later, more comprehensive historical survey "Musical Education in the United States of America," *Bulletin of Historical Research in Music Education*, 3/2 (July 1982): 91–102.

We still lack a comprehensive survey of American song, though Charles Hamm's *Yesterdays* covers much of the early-nineteenth-century repertory (when the lines between popular song and art song were blurred), and Nicholas Tawa's *Sweet Songs for Gentle Americans: The Parlor Song in America*, 1790–1860 (Bowling Green, OH: Bowling Green Popular Press, 1980) is a broad study of that repertory. Grace D. Yerbury's *Song in America, from Early Times to about 1850* (Metuchen, NJ: Scarecrow Press, 1971) is complemented in part by Jon W. Finson's *The Voices That Are Gone: Themes in 19th-Century American Popular Song* (New York: Oxford University Press, 1994), which concentrates (as his subtitle implies) on song texts.

[29] Steven Ledbetter, introduction to Bristow's *Rip Van Winkle* (*EAM* 25), xi. See also Preston, *Opera on the Road*, 265.

J. T. Howard's *Stephen Foster, America's Troubadour* (New York: Thomas Y. Crowell, 1934; rev. eds. 1953, 1962) is still valuable, but even more detailed, especially in historical context, is Ken Emerson's enthusiastic *Doo-dah! Stephen Foster and the Rise of American Popular Culture* (New York: Simon & Schuster, 1997; repr. New York: Da Capo Press, 1998). William W. Austin's *Susanna, Jeanie, and The Old Folks at Home* (New York: Macmillan, 1975) inquires perceptively into the remarkable durability of Foster's songs in American culture. Twenty-two of Foster's household songs are reprinted in *EAM* 12; other valuable anthologies (also facsimile reprints) are Richard Jackson's *Popular Songs of Nineteenth-Century America* (New York: Dover, 1976) and Richard Crawford's *The Civil War Songbook* (New York: Dover, 1977). *The Music of Stephen C. Foster: A Critical Edition*, ed. Steven Saunders and Deane L. Root (Washington, DC: Smithsonian Institution Press, 1990), is definitive.

George Frederick Root's *Story of My Musical Life. An Autobiography* (1891) has been reprinted by Da Capo Press (New York, 1970). The publishing firm of Root & Cady is authoritatively chronicled by Dena Epstein in *Music Publishing in Chicago Before 1871: The Firm of Root & Cady, 1858–1871* (Detroit: Information Coordinators, 1969). A volume of thirty-nine songs by Henry Clay Work is reprinted as *EAM* 19. The temperance play *Ten Nights in a Bar Room* (1858), with his *"Come Home, Father!"*, *Yankee Doodle* set to a temperance text, and other musical insertions, is edited by Dale Cockrell (with an 1890 version of the script) in the anthology *Nineteenth-Century American Musical Theater*, ed. Deane L. Root (New York: Garland Music, 1994), vol. 8.

The chapters on the United States in Loesser's *Men, Women and Pianos* (see note 9) make fascinating reading. Both Richard Hoffman and William Mason wrote memoirs, devoting the most space to their European years; see Hoffman, *Some Musical Recollections of Fifty Years* (New York: Scribner's, 1910), and Mason, *Memories of a Musical Life* (New York: Century Co., 1902). S. Frederick Starr's massive biography of Gottschalk is cited in note 26; Jeanne Behrend's edition of Gottschalk's *Notes of a Pianist* (cited in note 16) supplements it nicely. John G. Doyle's *Louis Moreau Gottschalk 1829–1869: A Bibliographical Study and Catalog of Works* (Detroit: Information Coordinators, 1983) is definitive but not easy to use; see my review in *Fontes artis musicae*, 30/3 (July–September 1983): 168–70. All Gottschalk's works for piano, reprinted in facsimile from early editions, are included in *The Piano Works of Louis Moreau Gottschalk* (New York: Arno Press and The New York Times, 1969).

Philip Hart's *Orpheus in the New World: The Symphony Orchestra as an American Cultural Institution* (New York: W. W. Norton, 1972) is valuable. Jullien's flamboyant life is chronicled by Adam Carse in *The Life of Jullien* (Cambridge: W. Heffer & Sons, 1951). *Theodore Thomas: A Musical Autobiography*, ed. George P. Upton (Chicago: A. C. McClurg, 1905; repr. with added material New York: Da Capo Press, 1964); the basic biography is Ezra Schabas's *Theodore Thomas: America's Conductor and Builder of Orchestras, 1835–1905* (Urbana: University of Illinois Press, 1989)—to be read, however, in light of the brilliant critical review of it by Joseph Horowitz in *19th-Century Music* 14/3 (Spring 1991): 296–302. Howard

Shanet authoritatively zeroes in on *Philharmonic: A History of New York's Orchestra* (New York: Doubleday, 1975). A broader and voluminously detailed look at New York's mid-ninteenth-century concert life is Vera Brodsky Lawrence's *Strong on Music: The New York Music Scene in the Days of George Templeton Strong, 1836–1875*, vol. 1 (*Resonances, 1836–1850*) (New York: Oxford University Press, 1988), and vol. 2 (*Reverberations, 1850–1856*) (Chicago: University of Chicago Press, 1995).

Facsimile publications of music by Heinrich include, besides *The Dawning of Music in Kentucky* and *The Western Minstrel* (both in *EAM* 10), the similarly diverse collection *The Sylviad: or Minstrelsy of Nature in the Wilds of North America*, comp. J. Bunker Clark (Greenleaf, WI: Connors Publications, 1996). The only biography in English remains that of W. T. Upton (cited in note 14). Upton is also the unique biographer of *William Henry Fry, American Journalist and Composer-Critic* (New York: Thomas Y. Crowell, 1954, repr. 1974), but, for more lively accounts of his complicated personality, see Vera Brodsky Lawrence's "William Henry Fry's Messianic Yearnings: The Eleven Lectures, 1852–53," *AM* 7/4 (Winter 1989): 382–411, and Betty E. Chmaj's "Fry versus Dwight: American Music's Debate over Nationality," *AM* 3/1 (Spring 1985): 63–84.

3Centuries includes, in vol. 9, full scores of Fry's *Santa Claus: Christmas Symphony* (1853), pp. 229–321, and Bristow's *Rip Van Winkle Overture* (1852–53), pp. 323–73, with preliminary essays and documentation on each.

Katherine K. Preston's *Opera on the Road ... 1825–60* (cited in note 27) will not soon be superseded. For opera in New Orleans to 1841, see H. A. Kmen's *Music in New Orleans* (cited in note 28); in New York, Julius Mattfeld's *A Hundred Years of Grand Opera in New York* (New York: New York Public Library, 1927). The title of John Dizike's *Opera in America: A Cultural History* (New Haven: Yale University Press, 1993), which might have specified "1800–1977," promises much; but, for a carefully considered and critically blistering review, see Tom Kaufman's in *AM* 13/1 (Spring 1995): 104–6. *Nineteenth-Century American Musical Theater* includes, as vol. 3 (New York: Garland Publishing, 1994), M. Rophino Lacy's adaptation of Rossini's *La Cenerentola* as *Cinderella*, ed. John Graziano, with photocopies of the libretto and the piano-vocal score. *EAM* 25 includes the vocal score of the revised version of Bristow's *Rip Van Winkle* (G. Schirmer, 1882), edited by Steven Ledbetter, together with a complete libretto.

FIVE

THE VERNACULAR TRADITION, 1820–1920

Having considered the development of the cultivated tradition through the Civil War, let us go back to the early nineteenth century to consider vernacular-tradition music, carrying forward the discussion to the end of World War I and treating religious music, especially that of revival and gospel hymnody, and black spirituals; the music of the minstrel show, a new kind of popular lyric theater; dance music; the development of bands and music for them; and ragtime, at first a music of limited use among black Americans but by the turn of the twentieth century a music of national popularity.

SPIRITUAL FOLK SONGS, REVIVAL AND GOSPEL HYMNODY, AND BLACK SPIRITUALS

We have noted in the foregoing chapter the rejection of the music of the First New England School in the very area that had spawned it. Under the influence of the composers of "scientific" church music led by Lowell Mason and Thomas Hastings, the singing-school music of the Yankee tunesmiths was gradually eliminated from the churches of New England and the Middle Atlantic states. The imaginative shape-note notation of Smith and Little's *Easy Instructor* and its imitators was equally rejected in the North as being no more than "dunce notes" (Hastings's epithet). By 1853, as we have seen (p. 57), Nathaniel Gould, a Boston historian of American church music, believed that shape-note tunebooks and their music, "if used at all, have been crowded to the far west, mostly out of sight and hearing."[1]

He was wrong. Shape-notes and the music of the New Englanders were still within "sight and hearing" of many Americans. They had indeed been crowded out of the Northeast and Middle East cities, but they were flourishing in the Upland South and the Deep South, as well as in the "far west" (by which Gould probably meant any land west of the Appalachians). Spurned by the urban arbiters of cultivated taste in music, the tunesmiths' pieces had become essentially a rural music in the sparsely settled South and toward the frontier. There they were to join with several other kinds of religious song to form the basis of a vernacular music tradition that is still alive today. These other kinds of song are our immediate concern: folk hymns and revival hymns of the camp meetings, gospel hymns of the "city revivals" of the 1870s and later, and spirituals of American blacks.

The beginnings of the migration to the South of the shape-note tunebooks are reflected in several Pennsylvania publications of the first two decades of the nineteenth century. For the English-speaking population, there appeared such imitations of *The Easy Instructor* as the 1807 edition of *Philadelphia Harmony* (9th edition), *Ecclesiae Harmonia* (1807), and *The Musical Instructor* (1808). German-speaking Pennsylvanians first learned shape-note singing from Joseph Doll's *Der leichte Unterricht* of 1810 (its title a literal translation of *The Easy Instructor*'s) and Johannes Rothbaust's *Die Franklin Harmonie* (1821). The last two mentioned were published by a Harrisburg printer, John Wyeth (1770–1858), who also issued English-language tunebooks, among them *Repository of Sacred Music* (1810) and *Repository of Sacred Music, Part Second* (1813). The latter proved to be "the first really influential anthology of what the late George Pullen Jackson dubbed spiritual folksong."[2]

Spiritual folk songs are just what the term implies: religious songs set to folk melodies, whether secular song melodies, patriotic airs, or popular dance tunes. Three types of spiritual folk songs may be distinguished: religious ballads, folk hymns, and revival spiritual songs. Wyeth's collection of religious songs, in two, three, and four voice parts, included both ballads and hymns, besides many tunes from earlier New England collections (Billings, Jenks, Law, Chapin) and thirteen by Elkanah Dare (1782–1826), who seems

---

[1] Nathaniel Gould, *Church Music in America* (Boston: A. N. Johnson, 1853), 55. Some exceptional compilations of earlier psalmody were, however, published as interesting "antique" music; *The Stoughton Collection* (Boston, 1829) was followed by others such as *The Billings and Holden Collection* (Boston, 1836) and Simeon Cheney's *The American Singing Book* (Boston, 1879; reprinted as *EAM* 17).

[2] Irving Lowens, *Music and Musicians in Early America* (New York: W. W. Norton, 1964), 134. The reference is to Jackson's *Spiritual Folk-Songs of Early America* (1937; 3rd ed., 1965).

to have been Wyeth's musical adviser. *Heavenly Union*, for example, is a ballad in some ten strophes, which begins with the balladeer's typical invitation to listen to a story:

> Come, saints and sinners, hear me tell
> The wonders of Emmanuel,
> Who saved me from a burning hell,
> And brought my soul with him to dwell,
>   And gave me heav'nly union.

The tale goes on in a characteristically folkish, colloquial way:

> When Christ the Saviour from on high
> Beheld my soul in ruins lie,
> He look'd on me with pitying eye,
> And said to me as he pass'd by,
>   "With God you have no union."

The folk hymns are briefer, nonnarrative pieces; many are new settings of old favorite texts by Watts or Wesley to anonymous tunes. *Hallelujah* (Example 5–1 [a]) is one of three settings of the popular text of Robert Robinson, eighteenth-century English hymnodist, "Come thou fount of ev'ry blessing"; the tune, which was to be resecularized to the text "Tell Aunt Rhody," appears in print for the first time in Wyeth's *Repository* as an anonymous and presumably well-known folk tune; a later, gospel-hymn version shows how decades of popular usage reshaped the tune into the form known best today (Example 5–1 [b]).

As one can hear in *Hallelujah*, with early-nineteenth-century folk hymnody we are back again in the musical world of the Yankee tunesmiths: the parallel fifths of measures 2–3 and 4; the implied modal harmony; the gapped-scale melody, which makes the tune seem fundamentally pentatonic; the simple, sturdy rhythm. These old-style characteristics are maintained, indeed emphasized, in Wyeth's shape-note hymn collection, which was to be the model for later tunebooks in the developing tradition of Southern spiritual folk songs.

"Spiritual folk song" suggests the better-known term "spiritual." And in fact songs such as *Hallelujah* have been termed "white spirituals" by historians beginning with Jackson, who coined the term for his book *White Spirituals in the Southern Uplands* (1933). The complex relationships between such white spirituals and the spirituals of blacks are not yet wholly clear, though it seems certain that the black spirituals, which were hardly ever discussed in print (nor their melodies transcribed) before the Reconstruction period after the Civil War, arose out of the evangelical songs of the great revivals

EXAMPLE 5–1. (*a*) *Hallelujah, Repository of Sacred Music, Part Second*, 2nd ed. (Harrisburg, PA: J. Wyeth, 1820), 112; (*b*) *Come, Thou Fount*, attributed to John Wyeth in *Gospel Hymns. Nos. 1 to 6 Complete* (New York: Biglow & Main Co., 1894), No. 633 (soprano part only).

in the American South and West in the period after 1800.[3] These began with the Great Revival of 1800 in Kentucky, which set off a wave of religious revivalism, led by the aggressive Methodists, Presbyterians, and Baptists, that soon swept across Georgia, the Carolinas, Pennsylvania, Tennessee, and Ohio. The typical locale of the revivals was the camp meeting—a gathering of worshippers who brought tents, bedding, and food for several-day (and - night) marathons of preaching, praying, and singing. Attendance could run in the thousands: at Cane Ridge, Kentucky, in 1801, more than thirty ministers preached to a crowd estimated variously to be between 10,000 and 20,000. With meetings of such size, a new kind of religious song appeared: the revival hymn—musically simpler than traditional hymns and with the text repetitions or verse-and-refrain structure found in many folk cultures. This kind of song was often termed a "spiritual song," as in the title of John C. Totten's pocket-sized book of hymn texts, *A Collection of the Most Admired Hymns and Spiritual Songs, with the choruses affixed, as usually sung at camp-meetings* (New York, 1809). At least one critic of camp-meeting revivalism believed that the repetitive choral refrains of the new type of hymn derived from the practice of blacks: John F. Watson, in a tract of 1819 lamenting what he called *Methodist Error*, spoke of one

> most exceptionable error, which has the tolerance at least of the rulers of our camp meetings. In the blacks' quarter [of the camp ground], the coloured people get together, and sing for hours ... short scraps of disjoined affirmations, pledges, or prayers, lengthened out with repetition choruses. These are all sung in the merry chorus-manner of the southern harvest-field, or husking-frolic method, of the slave blacks.

Watson complained that "the example has already visibly affected the religious manners of some whites":

> From this cause, I have known in some camp meetings, from 50 to 60 people crowd into one tent, after the public devotions had closed, and there continue the whole night, singing tune after tune ... scarce one of which were in our hymnbooks. Some of these from their nature (having very long repetition choruses and short scraps of [text] matter) are actually composed as sung, and are indeed almost endless.[4]

"Short scraps" of verse, interspersed with "repetition choruses," sung in a "merry chorus-manner," often "actually composed as sung"—this is as good

---

[3] See Bruno Nettl and Gerard Béhague, *Folk and Traditional Music of the Western Continents*, 3rd ed. (Upper Saddle River, NJ: Prentice Hall, 1990), 230–32. The various claims and counterclaims regarding the origins of American spirituals are summarized in section *II*(2)—"African and European Sources"—of the article "Spiritual" in *AmeriGrove*; Dena Epstein argues persuasively in "A White Origin for the Black Spiritual? An Invalid Theory and How It Grew," *AM* 1/2 (Summer 1983): 53–59.

[4] Quoted in Don Yoder, *Pennsylvania Spirituals* (Lancaster: Pennsylvania Folklife Society, 1961), 27–28.

a definition as any of the typical revival hymn. It first appeared in print in pocket songsters, without the music but often with a separate section of "choruses" that could be added to or interpolated in the song leader's chanting of the verses. Wyeth's *Repository ... Part Second* contained no such revival hymns, but the later Southern tunebooks, which otherwise borrowed so much from Wyeth (Yankee fuging tunes and other pieces, religious ballads, and folk hymns), added revival hymns as well. The most successful such tunebooks—all with shape-note notation—were Ananias Davisson's *Kentucky Harmony* (1816) and its *Supplement* (1820); Allen Carden's *Missouri Harmony* (1820); the *Columbian Harmony* (1825) of William Moore from Wilson County, Tennessee; William Caldwell's *Union Harmony* (Maryville, Tennessee, 1837); and John Jackson's *Knoxville Harmony* (1838). Especially notable, because so lastingly popular, are *The Southern Harmony* of William Walker and *The Sacred Harp* of B. F. White and E. J. King.

"Singin' Billy" Walker (1809–75) of Spartanburg, South Carolina, published *The Southern Harmony* in 1835. In the Preface to his *Christian Harmony* (1866), he claimed to have sold 600,000 copies of the earlier work, and he is known to have added proudly to his signature the initials A.S.H. ("author *Southern Harmony* "). The Index to the 1854 edition, the last and largest, names 334 pieces, including many new tunes "suitable for revival occasions." Walker's name is attached to forty of the compositions; in his Preface to the first edition, he explains that in addition to having "composed several tunes wholly," he also "composed the [accompanying] parts to a great many good airs (which I could not find in any publication, nor in manuscript), and assigned my name as the author." Thus was a popular tune turned into a spiritual folk song. One such tune was *Auld lang syne*, which appears with the title *Plenary* as a setting of Watts's hymn "Hark! from the tombs a doleful sound." Another, attributed in *The Southern Harmony* to a David Walker, is *The Hebrew Children*, an infectious hexatonic tune that is known also as a black spiritual ("Wonder where is good ole Daniel?"), an Ozark Mountains play-party song ("Where, O where is pretty little Susie?") and, of later vintage, a college song ("Where, O where are the pea-green freshmen?").[5] The thrice-asked question of each stanza, "Where are the Hebrew children?" ("... the twelve apostles?" "... the holy Christians?" etc.), is answered by the refrain, "Safe [or: Safe at last] in the promised land," in a characteristic form of the verse-with-refrain revival hymn.

Typical of the compilers of southern shape-note tunebooks, Walker drew tunes that pleased him from no matter what source, transforming them

---

[5] Walker's *The Hebrew Children* is No. 97 in *Music in America: An Anthology ... 1620–1865* (New York: W. W. Norton, 1964)—now regrettably out of print—along with the first stanza of the black version, apparently taken from R. Nathaniel Dett, *Religious Folk-Songs of the Negro as Sung at Hampton Institute* (Hampton, VA: Hampton Institute Press, 1927), 73. The play-party version is in *Ozark Folk Songs*, ed. Vance Randolph (Columbia, MO: State Historical Society, 1946–50), 3/364. The college version is part of my own experience as an undergraduate at Dartmouth College.

into the rugged, sonorous shape-note style by the addition of two or three sur-rounding parts. Thus, we find in *The Southern Harmony* not only borrowings from the eighteenth-century Yankee composers, newly composed pieces by Walker and others, but even Lowell Mason's *Missionary Hymn* and the pa-triotic song *Hail! Columbia*. The Scottish folk song *Braes o' Balquhidder* is made over into *Lone Pilgrim*, and both *Thorny Desert* and *Something New* sound like folk-hymn variants of Scotch-Irish reels.

Even more lastingly popular than *The Southern Harmony* was *The Sacred Harp* (1844) of Benjamin Franklin White (1800–1879) and his lesser-known cocompiler E. J. King (d. 1844). This shape-note tunebook went through many editions; J. S. James's of 1911, affirmatively retitled *The Original Sacred Harp*, was edited by the Alabama singing-school master S. M. Denson (1854–1936), who added alto parts to those of the 600-odd tunes that were set in only three parts (about half of them). Denson's own revision of 1936 was still being published, in a revised edition containing no fewer than 554 hymns, as late as 1991. The twentieth-century *Sacred Harp* pre-serves the "dispersed harmony" (wide spacing of the upper voices, as op-posed to the "close harmony" of other religious song), the four-shape notation (*fa* ◁ , *sol* ○, *la* □, *mi* ◇), and the traditional introduction on "The Rudiments of Music." Even the basic "Old Time" style is fairly well pre-served. Example 5–2 shows the beginning of the moving folk hymn *Wondrous Love* in the three-part setting common to both *The Southern Harmony* (in the second edition of which [1840] it first appeared in print) and the first edition of *The Sacred Harp*, with Denson's alto part added in cue-sized notes. (Occasionally the "modern" full triad sound is created by Denson's adding a third to the original's open fifth.)

I spoke previously of this music as belonging to a "vernacular music tradition that is still alive today." Indeed it is—in the rural South and south-ern Midwest, where hundreds of "singings" from shape-note tunebooks take place every year. One such singing is well represented on *NW CD 80205*, recorded in 1959 at a weekend meeting of the Alabama Sacred Harp Con-vention in Fyffe, Alabama. Folk hymns such as *Wondrous Love* are includ-ed, as are others attributed to the shape-note tunebook compilers, such as William Walker's *Hallelujah* and White's *The Morning Trumpet* (of which a black variant—or perhaps the black original—is known, with the chorus "You may bury me in the East, / You may bury me in the West, / But I'll hear that trumpet sound in the morning!"); so too are pieces from the First New Eng-land School, such as the fuging tunes *Sherburne* (by Daniel Read), *Northfield* (by Jeremiah Ingalls), and the miniature anthem *David's Lamentation* (by William Billings).

Traditionally, shape-note singers seat themselves in a hollow square, sopranos on one side, tenors on another, and so on. For each hymn, gener-ally, an elder or a well-recognized singer rises to call for a piece, set its pitch, and conduct it in a rather solemn, simple, strong way. Almost always, a hymn is first sung through just to the "fasola" syllables, then repeated to the text.

EXAMPLE 5–2.   The folk hymn *Wondrous Love*, measures 1–8. Soprano, tenor, and bass parts from W. Walker, *The Southern Harmony* (New Haven, 1835), 1854 ed., 252. Alto part composed by S. M. Denson for "Denson Revision" (1936) of *The Sacred Harp* (Philadelphia, 1844); *Sacred Harp* version is a whole tone lower in original.

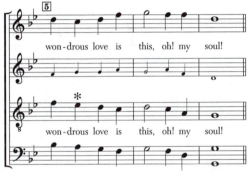

° Although early printed sources consistently give this note as E♭, shape-note singers sing it, just as consistently, as E♮ (thus turning the tune into Dorian mode [transposed up a fourth] and making the entire last phrase unroll in parallel fifths between tenor and bass).

And always men and women alike sing the treble and the tenor parts (and sometimes the alto), to make for a greatly enriched sonority. The rhythm is powerful, and usually some singers stomp as they sing. "Singings" are a matter of infectious enthusiasm and warmth—also of fellowship and spiritual exaltation. One imagines that the singing schools of an earlier time must have been very much like this.

    One of the best-known American spiritual folk songs, *Wayfaring Stranger*, appeared in print for the first time in the 1844 *Sacred Harp*. Its poignant text and mournful pentatonic tune tend to disguise the revival-hymn refrain of the final couplet (Example 5–3a; *NW* CD 80294 has an affecting unaccompanied performance by a fine Ozark singer). More characteristic of the lusty vigor of most revival songs is *The Old Ship of Zion* (Example 5–3b), a tune known in several variants including Negro ones, that of *The Sacred Harp* identified by William Hauser in his tunebook *The Olive Leaf* (see next paragraph) as a "North Carolina Version."

EXAMPLE 5–3.   Two revival hymns from *The Sacred Harp* (1844).
(*a*) *Wayfaring Stranger* (p. 457 of Denson Revision; tenor part only).
(*b*) *The Old Ship of Zion* (p. 79 of Denson Revision; tenor part only).

Besides the tunebooks previously cited, which used the four-shape notation of Smith and Little's *Easy Instructor* based on a *fa, sol, la, mi* solmization system, others appeared in a seven-shape notation that re-flected pressures (from the "scientific" school of musical thought) to adopt the European *do, re, me, fa, sol, si* (or *ti*) system. The first of these was

The Christian Minstrel (Philadelphia, 1846), compiled by Jesse Aikin (1808–1900). Aikin, who showed his respect for Lowell Mason by including eighteen of Mason's hymns in the work, used the same four shapes as *The Easy Instructor* and *The Sacred Harp* but added three others of his own invention. (Other seven-shape tunebook compilers, imagining that Aikin had patented *his* new shapes, invented yet others; hence the occasional application of the name "patent notes" to shape-notation.) Another seven-shape book, destined to be almost as long-lived as *The Sacred Harp*, was the eastern Tennessee tunebook *The Harp of Columbia* (Knoxville, 1848); present-day singers from this book call themselves "Old Harp Singers" as opposed to the "Sacred Harp Singers." One of the last shape-note tune-books in the traditional style of spiritual folk song, and one that used Aikin's seven shapes, was *The Olive Leaf* (1878), printed at Wadley, Georgia, by William Hauser (1812–80). But this book also reveals the impact of a new style in American vernacular hymnody, that of the gospel hymn.

The gospel hymn, like the earlier revival hymn, was the product of a revival movement. However, unlike the earlier nineteenth-century revival hymn, which arose mainly in the back country and on the frontier, the gospel hymn of the last half of the century was urban. Its musical background was the correct, bland style of Mason and Hastings, but its harmony tended to be more chromatically engorged, its texts more sentimentally swollen. From the earlier revival hymnodists, the gospel-hymn writers, equally intent on engaging large masses in cathartic songfests, took the idea of repeated refrain-choruses. As one scholar puts it, "the verse-and-refrain pattern of the revival song joins with Sweet Adeline harmonies to make the gospel song"; another remarks perceptively on the influence of German secular *Volkslieder* (as they might have become known in the American imitations of the *Männerchöre*).[6]

William B. Bradbury, whom we have met as the composer of *The Lament of the Blind Orphan Girl* (see p. 73), foreshadowed the gospel-song style in his *Woodworth* of 1849 (best known as sung to the text beginning "Just as I am, without one plea"; NW LP 224 has a performance recorded in 1959 by a choir organized for an "Australian Crusade" of the evangelist Billy Graham). However, the biggest sellers among gospel-hymn collections (and the "show-biz" connotation of that terminology is not inappropriate considering the polished publicity and commercial enterprise of the urban revivals) were those of Philip P. Bliss (1838–76), Ira D. Sankey (1840–1908), and a somewhat lesser light, Rev. Robert Lowry (1826–99). Lowry's *Beautiful River* ("Shall we gather at the river?") appeared in *The Olive Leaf*; its skipping rhythms entranced generations of Americans and were incorporated in instrumental works by Charles Ives (such as his Violin Sonata No. 4 ["Children's Day at the Camp Meeting"]) and Virgil Thomson (his *Variations on Sunday School Tunes* for organ). Sankey, after a two-year

---

[6] Robert Stevenson, *Protestant Church Music in America* (New York: W. W. Norton, 1966), 90 n; Edwin H. Pierce, "Gospel Hymns," *MQ* 26 (1940): 355–64.

revival tour of Great Britain (1873–75), became organist and song leader for the spellbinding evangelist Dwight L. Moody in Moody's revival meetings in Brooklyn, New York. There Sankey directed a choir of 250 and played the organ; he also found time to see into print a conflation of Bliss's *Gospel Songs* (1874) and his own *Gospel Hymns and Sacred Songs* (Cincinnati, 1875). After Bliss's death, Sankey and other collaborators continued to issue enlargements through a sixth cumulative volume, *Gospel Hymns Nos. 1 to 6 Complete* (1894; reprinted as *EAM* 5).

The gospel hymns of Bliss and Sankey have been denigrated as a "slough of sentimental music-hall sloppiness … flabby and futile," as a British observer has put it—but the same writer, shifting critical gears, views them rightly when he admits that "at its best this music is honestly flamboyant and redolent of the buoyancy of the civilization that created New York and Pittsburgh and Chicago."[7] Bliss's *Pull for the Shore* may have a text as metaphorically exaggerated as a seventeenth-century Italian opera aria and as artfully homespun as the worst poetaster's doggerel, but its chorus is an almost irresistible march, perfectly suited to its soul-stirring evangelistic purposes (Example 5–4).

EXAMPLE 5–4.　P. Bliss, *Pull for the Shore*, No. 51 of *Gospel Hymns Nos. 1 to 6 Complete* (New York: Biglow & Main, 1894), Chorus only.

---

[7] Erik Routley, *The Music of Christian Hymnody* (London: Independent Press, 1957), 166.

The universality of some gospel-hymn tunes and text phrases is undeniable. The tune many now know as "How dry I am!" can be found as "O happy day that fixed my choice / On Thee, my Saviour and my God." Bliss's *Hallelujah, 'tis Done* became the irreverent parody "Hallelujah, I'm a bum." Snatches of gospel-hymn texts have become commonplaces in the American vernacular: "Sweet by-and-by," "Arise and shine," "Throw out the lifeline," "Hold the fort," "The old, old story," "Where is my wand'ring boy tonight?" and many others.

The same post–Civil War period that saw the rise of urban gospel hymnody saw the dissemination of black spirituals and their rise in the national consciousness as a music of popular appeal and familiarity. The publication in 1867 of the first collection of songs of black Americans—*Slave Songs of the United States*, gathered and compiled by William Allen, Charles Ware, and Lucy McKim Garrison—was a symbolic step in this development.

Much more important, in terms of the eventual dissemination of black spirituals, was the formation—at the newly founded Fisk University in Nashville, Tennessee—of a group of black student musicians, billed as the Fisk Jubilee Singers, who toured the United States regularly, beginning in 1872, and Europe in the mid-1870s. With heartfelt—and polished—performances of spirituals in four-part harmony (besides other types of song), they introduced this music to audiences far and wide. Their success sparked the formation of other groups of "jubilee" singers and the transcription into music notation of their songs, resulting in the publication, eventually, of some thirty-five volumes containing black spirituals and related songs.

BLACKFACE MINSTRELSY

Early in 1854, when Jullien's orchestra was in New York offering "monster concerts for the masses," when the St. Charles Theatre in the Bowery had been presenting German opera for several months, when an Italian opera company producing works by Donizetti and Bellini was struggling to survive, and when Fry and Bristow were complaining of the New York Philharmonic's neglect of American composers, *Putnam's Monthly* for February called attention to another kind of musical entertainment:

> The only places of Amusement where the entertainments are indigenous are the African Opera Houses, where native American vocalists, with blackened faces, sing national songs, and utter none but native witticisms. These native theatricals ... are among the best frequented and most profitable places of amusement in New York. While [the] attempt to establish an Italian Opera here, though originating with the wealthiest and best educated classes, has resulted in bankruptcy, the Ethiopian Opera has flourished like a green bay tree.

This report pinpoints nicely the high point of the blackface minstrel show, a kind of American vernacular lyric-theater genre that was perhaps rejected by the "wealthiest and best educated classes" but embraced by all the others. A few months earlier the *Musical World* (October 8, 1853) had noted that "Ethiopian Minstrelsy is on the increase. We now have, in New York, six companies of Minstrels in full blast." The "native theatrical" of blackface minstrelsy was in full flower.

The American minstrel show crystallized as a form of public entertainment in the early 1840s. Like many other facets of early-nineteenth-century American culture, it had British antecedents. In the 1700s, British dramas often included black characters and so-called Negro songs. Some British comedians blackened their faces and impersonated blacks; some of these came to America, among them Charles Mathews. He was fascinated by American blacks, especially their dialect and their humor. In New York, at the blacks' own theater, he is said to have noted their performance of *Hamlet*; in Philadelphia, he tried to reproduce on paper the dialect of a black revivalist preacher; he collected "scraps of songs and malaprops." Mathews's skits, mock lectures, and dialect songs were among the huge numbers of blackface performances in America between 1751 and the early 1840s, estimated at more than twenty thousand by one scholar.[8]

Other northern comedians sketched blacks in the 1820s and 1830s. One was George Washington Dixon (1801?–61), to whom myth has attributed the infectious, danceable song *Zip Coon* (published in 1834) and who was perhaps the composer of *Coal Black Rose* (1829?; in *3Centuries* 1, 84–86). Another was Thomas Dartmouth Rice (1808–60), who, according to legend, created around 1830 the stage character of Jim Crow, legendarily based on a black stable groom and destined to become an internationally famous blackface hero. Such comedians as Dixon and Rice helped to crystallize two Negro stereotypes. Like the other two early American comic heroes—the shrewd, taciturn Yankee peddler and the lusty, bragging backwoodsman—they were oversimplified exaggerations of real life. One was the plantation hand, a tatterdemalion of low estate but high spirits; the other was the urban dandy with affectedly modish ways and a fashionable "long-tailed blue" dress coat—Jim Crow or Gumbo Chaff ("Weel about, and turn about, and do jis so; / Eb'ry time I weel about, I jump Jim Crow"; in *3Centuries*, 95–97); Zip Coon or Dandy Jim ("O ole Zip Coon he is a larned skolar / Sings possum up a gum tree an coony in a holler"; in *3Centuries* 1, 117–19).

Bit by bit such comedians, with faces blackened by burnt cork, enlarged their repertory of skits, songs, and dances; organized themselves into small troupes; and began to develop the format for a whole program. One important milestone was the formation of a minstrel band of instruments associated with blacks (fiddle, banjo, bones, and tambourine) by four star comedians in New York—Dan Emmett, Frank Brower, Billy Whitlock, and Dick Pelham. They announced their premiere performance as a group—set

[8] Dale Cockrell, *Demons of Disorder: Early Blackface Minstrels and Their World* (Cambridge: Cambridge University Press, 1997), 15.

for February 6, 1843, in the Bowery Amphitheatre (along with circus entertainment)—through an advertisement in the *New York Herald*:

> First Night of the novel, grotesque, original, and surprisingly melodious
> Ethiopian band, entitled the Virginia Minstrels, being an exclusively musical
> entertainment combining the banjo, violin, bone castanets, and tambourine,
> and entirely exempt from the vulgarities and other objectionable features which
> have hitherto characterized negro extravaganzas.

Successful in New York, the four Virginia Minstrels enlarged their act into a
full evening's entertainment of songs, dances, and a parody "lecture on lo-
comotives" and opened with it at the Masonic Temple in Boston on March
7; they called it an "Ethiopian Concert." It was the first real minstrel show.
    Following the success of the Virginia Minstrels, other troupes were
formed, and the ones already in existence enlarged their shows; soon Christy's
Minstrels, Bryant's Minstrels, The Sable Harmonists, The Kentucky Rat-
tlers, The Ethiopian Serenaders, and dozens of others were touring across the
country. Dialect solo songs; satirical stump speeches and dialogues; burlesques; instrumental numbers and dances, either solo or group; and "walk-
arounds" (small-scale vernacular-music acts combining solo song, choral song,
and dancing to instrumental "symphonies")—these became the staples of
the minstrel shows, as the craze for them rose to a peak in the 1850s. Through
them all, at this period, ran a strain of mild caricature of the black, who was
portrayed both as jokester and as butt of jokes, as comedian and as (less often)
tragedian. Even if by today's standards the stereotypes and the heavy dialect
of the early blackface minstrels are offensive, they did present the black as a
comic hero—if, however, one to be laughed at as well as with.[9] The minstrel
shows had their villains, but they were of other kinds.
    Standing up for American popular culture, the minstrels lashed out in
stinging parodies and burlesques at the arty and pretentious, the foreign and
imported. In the 1850s the "Tyrolean business," mocking the vogue of singing
families such as the Hutchinsons and the Rainer family, was often to be
heard, with such titles as "Tyrolean Solo, displaying a flexibility and volume
of voice astonishing and inimitable" and "We Come from the Hills, burlesque
à la Rainer family." Italian opera was a favorite target: Donizetti's *Lucia di
Lammermoor* was burlesqued as "Lucy Did Lam a Moor." The *New York
Clipper* of January 21, 1854, crowed over the Christy Minstrels' satire on
Jullien's monster concerts. The violin virtuosity of the visiting Norwegian
Ole Bull and of the fabled Italian, Nicolò Paganini, was deprecated by the
minstrels, who claimed that

[9] See Constance Rourke, *American Humor* (New York: Harcourt, Brace, 1931), chap. 3, and
her *Roots of American Culture* (New York: Harcourt, Brace, 1942; repr. Tallahassee: Florida State
University Press, 1986), 262–74, as well as the excellent notes by Robert B. Winans for *NW* CD 80338
(*The Early Minstrel Show*), which includes authentic recorded reconstructions of early minstrel-
show music.

> Loud de banjo talked away,
> An' beat Ole Bull from de Norway;
>   We'll take de shine from Paganini,
>   We're de boys from ole Virginny.

This was an echo of T. D. Rice's Jim Crow, who had boasted around 1828 that

> I'm a rorer on de fiddle,
>   And down in ole Virginny
> Dey say I play de skientific
>   Like massa Pagganninny.

Sometimes the minstrels portrayed the black as the same kind of swaggering superman as the frontiersman heroes:

> My mama was a wolf
>   My daddy was a tiger,
> I am what you call
>   De Ole Virginny Nigger:
> Half fire, half smoke,
>   A little touch of thunder,
> I am what you call
>   De eighth wonder.

And sometimes, in transparent disguise, he was shown as a clever black outsmarting an authority figure:

> A bullfrog dressed in soger's close
> Went in de field to shoot some crows,
>   De crows smell powder an' fly away,
>   De bullfrog mighty mad dat day.

The music of the minstrel shows was a mélange of well-known popular songs (even some of the sentimental household type), of adaptations from other sources (even of British and Italian opera airs), of dance tunes and dialect songs. These last were the mainstays of the shows and had the most remarkable music.

The typical minstrel band of the 1840s was that established by the Virginia Minstrels: violin, banjo, tambourine, and bone castanets, with perhaps also an accordion, a triangle, or a second banjo. All these except the accordion were instruments associated with southern blacks, particularly the banjo, which in fact had African origins. A British minister and lexicographer who had spent many years in Maryland and Virginia wrote,

> The favourite and almost only instrument in use among the slaves there was a
> *bandore*; or, as they pronounced the word, *banjer*. Its body was a large hollow

gourd, with a long handle attached to it, strung with catgut, and played on with the fingers.[10]

In the minstrel shows, a singer often accompanied himself on the banjo, tapping his foot in a steady metronomic beat and varying his sung melody on the instrument. Thus *The Boatmen's Dance* (NW CD 80338; see Example 5–5 [a]), claimed by Dan Emmett as his own song but known at least in part on the Ohio River in the 1820s and 1830s, might have been played as shown in Example 5–5 (b). The variation style of short, even running notes is not new: we have met it in the dance music, under English influence, of the late eighteenth and early nineteenth centuries (see Example 2–7).

EXAMPLE 5–5. (*a*) Dan Emmett(?), *De Boatmen's Dance* (Boston: C. H. Keith, 1843), measures 13–16 (air only). (*b*) *The Boatman's Dance*, as printed in *Frank B. Converse's Banjo Instructor* (New York, 1865), measures 1–4. After Hans Nathan, *Dan Emmett and the Rise of Early Negro Minstrelsy*, 192–93. Copyright 1962 by the University of Oklahoma Press.

Much more novel, indeed so fresh as to be a source for the indigenous American rhythms of ragtime and early jazz, are the banjo "jigs" of the minstrel-show dances. Hans Nathan, who first called attention to these remarkable tunes, describes them thus:

> The motion ... is animated by many irregular stresses: hectic offbeat accentuations projected against the relentless, metrical background of the accompanying taps [of the feet], which change $\frac{2}{4}$ into $\frac{6}{8}$. A large number of accentuations result from sudden, brief rests on one of the four beats in the measure.[11]

---

[10] Jonathan Boucher, *Boucher's Glossary of Archaic and Provincial Words ...* (London: Black, Young and Young, 1832), xlix, BAN, as quoted in Dena Epstein, *Sinful Tunes and Spirituals: Black Folk Music to the Civil War* (Urbana: University of Illinois Press, 1977), 34.

[11] *Dan Emmett and the Rise of Early Negro Minstrelsy* (Norman: University of Oklahoma Press, 1962), 195.

A fine example is *Pea-Patch Jig*, one of forty-eight banjo tunes in an early manuscript compiled by Dan Emmett; surprisingly, it also appeared in print in *Kendall's Clarinet Instruction Book* (Boston, 1845). The combinations of triplets and duplets and of even and uneven rhythms in running passages, the repeated notes, and above all the frequent accentuated rests on strong beats contribute to the propulsive, "swinging" character of the music (Example 5–6; the jig is recorded on *NW CD 80338*).

EXAMPLE 5–6. *Pea-Patch Jig*, first (and closing) strain only. From Hans Nathan, *Dan Emmett and the Rise of Early Negro Minstrelsy*, 344. Copyright 1962 by the University of Oklahoma Press.

Evidence suggests that, although the ultimate source of this style lay in British, especially Scottish and Irish, folk-dance music, the concentration of offbeat accents and other rhythmic shifts derived from the manner in which such music was played by American blacks, who provided the models for northern minstrel-show banjoists. The banjo-jig idiom was imitated on other instruments: it crops up not only in Kendall's *Clarinet Instruction Book* but also in violin, fife, and flute manuals; and the piano music of early ragtime is clearly indebted to it.

Mark Twain set the vernacular tradition's banjo tunes against the cultivated tradition's parlor piano pieces in inimitable prose:

> The piano may do for love-sick girls who lace themselves to be skeletons, and lunch on chalk, pickles, and slate pencils. But give me the banjo. . . . When you want *genuine* music—music that will come right home to you like a bad quarter, suffuse your system like strychnine whisky . . . and break out on your hide like the pin-feather pimples on a pickled goose,—when you want all this, just smash your piano, and invoke the glory-beaming banjo![12]

Something of the same buoyant, swingy, chattering spirit as the banjo jigs informs the dialect songs and the music for walk-arounds of the minstrel

---

[12] "Enthusiastic Eloquence," *The Works of Mark Twain*, ed. E. M. Branch and R. H. Hirst, vol. 2 (Berkeley and Los Angeles: University of California Press, 1981), 235; quoted in Ken Emerson, *Doo-Dah! Stephen Foster and the Rise of American Popular Culture* (New York: Simon & Schuster, 1997; repr. New York: Da Capo Press, 1998), 92.

shows. The two outstanding composers were Daniel Decatur Emmett (1815–1904) and Stephen Foster. Emmett was the more versatile: banjoist, fiddler, singer, and comedian; author of lyrics, stump speeches, plays for the minstrel stage, and instruction manuals for both fife and drum. He also composed, in addition to banjo tunes, many songs for the minstrel shows; about seventy were published. By far the most famous is *Dixie* (in *3Centuries* 1, 92–94; on NW CD 80202), originally presented by Bryant's Minstrels on April 4, 1859, and announced on the playbill as "Mr. Dan Emmett's new and original song and dance, *Dixie's Land*, introducing the whole troupe in the festival dance." Nathan's description of *Dixie*, which was virtually appropriated by the Confederacy as *its* song during the Civil War, cannot be improved upon:

> The tune is characterized by a heavy, nonchalant, inelegant strut. . . . If music, lyrics, and dance style are taken as an entity, there emerges a special kind of humor that mixes grotesqueness with lustiness and down-to-earth contentment—comparable, to overstate the case, to a blend of Brueghel and Mickey Mouse. . . . "Dixie" indeed is no polite genteel tune. It has a considerable measure of toughness.[13]

Like others of Emmett's walk-arounds, *Dixie* derived from various sources: its "song" and "chorus" melodies can be related to English and Scottish dance tunes as well as to *Gumbo Chaff*, a minstrel song of the 1830s; its closing instrumental "dance" was published in Emmett's *Fife Instructor* with the title "Albany Beef" and is a jig of Irish-Scottish ancestry. Nevertheless, like the best of Emmett's other songs and walk-arounds, *Dixie* integrates these raw materials in a new synthesis. Its rhythmic jolts, related to the banjo-jig syncopations, and its ridiculous homespun humor, common to the minstrel show but originating on the American frontier, make for "a very characteristically national music," as the songs of American minstrelsy were described in a Scottish encyclopedia of 1864.

Essentially, although it appeared on the minstrel-show stages of northern cities, the early minstrel song's earthiness, lustiness, lack of sentimentality, and sinewy vigor came from the world of the frontiersman and the boatman, when the frontier was just over the next range of hills and when rivers and canals were the highways of America. This connection with "primitive" America was certainly one reason why the genteel society of the cities—"the wealthiest and best educated classes," to recall the phrase of *Putnam's Monthly*—looked down their collective noses at the minstrel show and its music.

And this is why the other outstanding composer of minstrel-show song, Stephen Foster, had to justify with a fine but defensive show of resolution his decision to move wholeheartedly into the field of minstrel-song

---

[13] Nathan, *Dan Emmett*, 247–48, 250.

composition. In a letter of 1852 to E. P. Christy, leader of Christy's Minstrels, Foster declared, "I have concluded ... to pursue the Ethiopian business without fear or shame and ... to establish my name as the best Ethiopian songwriter."[14] By 1852 Foster was a well-known songwriter, both of household songs and of minstrel-show songs. His comment to Christy shows, however, the lingering doubts he must have had about the propriety and gentility of identifying himself unreservedly with the latter. (He had an economic reason, however, for overcoming those doubts, for his biggest hit, *Old Folks at Home*, had been published under Christy's name as composer; Foster rationalized in the same letter to Christy that "I find I cannot write at all unless I write for the public approbation and get credit for what I write.")

Foster's first songs for the minstrels, four published between 1847 and 1848, were already in the full-fledged indigenous style of the minstrel music of the earlier 1840s. In *Lou'siana Belle*, the banjo twang on the afterbeats of the accompaniment, and the strumming, rattling rhythm of *Away Down South* (Example 5–7) made those songs immediate successes, and *Uncle Ned* as well. But of the four early songs, it was *Oh! Susanna* that was to prove indestructibly vital. *Oh! Susanna* was probably derived in part from the earlier, anonymous *Gwine 'long Down* (1844), just as Foster's later *Nelly Bly* (1849) seems to have come from *Clare de Kitchen* (late 1830s; in *3Centuries* 1/82–83) and his *Camptown Races* (1850) from *Picayune Butler* (1847).

EXAMPLE 5–7. S. Foster, early minstrel songs. (*a*) *Lou'siana Belle* (Louisville & Cincinnati: Peters, 1847), measures 9–12. (*b*) *Away Down South* (Louisville & Cincinnati: Peters, 1848), measures 9–16.

---

[14] The entire text of this interesting letter is printed in Emerson, *Doo-dah!*, 183.

But, like Emmett's *Dixie, Oh! Susanna* was a transcendent synthesis of varied elements, not only because of the fine swinging movement of its solo verses and the solid stomp of its five-part chorus (with a potent rhythmic jolt on the last two syllables of "Oh! Su-*sán-ná*"), but also because of the deadpan nonsense humor of its text:

> It rained all night the day I left,
> The weather it was dry,
> The sun so hot I frose to death,
> Susanna don't you cry.

Between the summers of 1849 and 1850, Foster published nine songs for the minstrel shows, as compared with five for the parlor. Among them were *Nelly Bly*, with its "dulcem melody" rocking along in a heavy-footed two-step rhythm, and *Camptown Races*, with its perfect matching of text and music and its irresistible verve (Example 5–8). Its chorus bears a striking resemblance to that of *Lord, Remember Me*, first printed in the significant 1867 collection of black songs, *Slave Songs of the United States*—which suggests the interesting probability of some black songs' being indebted to the ubiquitously popular songs of Foster (a much more likely route of influence than the opposite, despite common misconceptions about Foster's debt to black music sources). Also a product of this period was *Nelly Was a Lady*, its text unusually sympathetic and sweet:

> Nelly was a lady—
> Last night she died;
> Toll de bell for Lubly Nell,
> My dark Virginny bride.

EXAMPLE 5–8. S. Foster, *Camptown Races* (Baltimore: Benteen, 1850), measures 8–15.

In the summer of 1851 appeared the song that would be most completely identified with Foster's name, despite its publication under Christy's: *Old Folks at Home*. Wilfrid Mellers was the first to point out[15] that with this song Foster introduced into the minstrel-show context the nostalgia that pervades his household songs:

> All up and down the whole creation,
>   Sadly I roam,
> Still longing for the old plantation,
>   And for de old folks at home.
>
> One little hut among de bushes,
>   One dat I love,
> Still sadly to my mem'ry rushes,
>   No matter where I rove.

The same note is heard in the other, later "best-loved" Foster songs issued as "plantation melodies": *My Old Kentucky Home, Good Night* (1853), and *Old Black Joe* (1860). Interestingly, as if conscious of having blurred the distinction between household and minstrel songs, Foster published these two without any black dialect spellings.

The reaction of the cultivated-tradition establishment to the fantastic popularity of *Old Folks at Home* was predictable. In its issue of October 2, 1852, *Dwight's Journal of Music* reported with perplexed incredulity on the universal appeal of the song:

> *Old Folks at Home* ... is on everybody's tongue, and consequently in everybody's mouth. Pianos and guitars groan with it, night and day; sentimental young ladies sing it; sentimental young gentlemen warble it in midnight serenades; volatile young "bucks" hum it in the midst of their business and pleasures; boatmen roar it out ... all the bands play it.

More than a year later (November 19, 1853), *Dwight's* was forced to an all-out attack—the cultivated against the vernacular tradition:

> We wish to say that such tunes ... become catching, idle habits, and are not popular in the sense of musically inspiring, but that such and such a melody breaks out every now and then, like a morbid irritation of the skin.

We can see now that Dwight's criticism was silly—like downgrading daisies because they are not orchids. It was also futile: blackface minstrelsy and its "morbid irritations" were on the rise in the 1850s. The genre was to continue through the 1860s as the most vital kind of "native theatrical," with some thirty established nontouring companies and many other traveling ones. From the 1870s on, however, the character of the minstrel show began to change:

[15] *Music in a New Found Land* (New York: Knopf, 1965), 249.

it tended to become more and more a variety show, foreshadowing vaude-ville and burlesque; its integrity was diluted by the introduction of nonblack characters and sketches; its format was inflated in a trend to gigantism re-flected in the names of such troupes as Haverly's Mastodons, Cleveland's Colossals, and Leavitt's Giganteans.

One irony of the minstrel show's declining years was the appearance on the minstrel stage of actual blacks, sometimes even in blackface makeup. (Ironic, yes, but also a significant step toward broader acceptance of blacks as professionals in the American theatrical world.) One such performer, and one of the few notable composers of the later period of minstrelsy, was James A. Bland (1854–1911), who began his theatrical career as a singer and ban-joist with the Original Black Diamonds of Boston and became a star in Haver-ly's Genuine Colored Minstrels. (He later paid homage to his old partners in Haverly's troupe in the song *De Golden Wedding* [1880; on *NW* CD 80265].) Bland probably did not write the six-hundred or seven-hundred songs some-times claimed for him (only forty were deposited for copyright), but he did produce some exceptionally popular ones, including *Carry Me Back to Old Virginny* (1878), *Oh, Dem Golden Slippers* (1879; in *3Centuries* 2, 285–88), and *In the Evening by the Moonlight* (1880). Another successful black com-poser of songs for the minstrel shows, though not as celebrated a performer, was Gussie Lord Davis (1863–99), whose *In the Baggage Coach Ahead* (1896) was an early hit of the dawning Tin Pan Alley age of the sheet-music indus-try, selling more than a million copies in a short time.

DANCES AND DANCE MUSIC

American social dances underwent major changes in the 1820–1920 period, largely as a result of the shifting patterns of immigration, which brought new dances—and appropriate music for them—from central and eastern Europe; by the end of the era, dance styles originating with American blacks had also had a considerable impact.

The English country dances and their French derivative, cotillions, which I discussed earlier as the most popular dances of the Federal era (see pp. 43–46), continued in popularity well into the Jacksonian era. "Long-ways" dancing, however, in which men and women lined up in two rows opposite each other, tended to give way to dancing in "squares," each square being made up of four couples. Whereas early in the century dancers memorized the various patterns of such dances, in the 1840s it became increasingly com-mon to have a "caller" prompt the participants. Moreover, in the urban cen-ters other dances wrested popularity from the older dances, which thus became identified with rural areas and with country folk, and also with im-provised music based on traditional tunes. (As such, these "square dances" and their music are preserved to the present day, not only as normal vernacular expressions in rural areas, but also as pleasant nostalgic diversions for urbanites, suburbanites, and exurbanites.)

Not many publications of cotillions postdate the 1818–19 issues by the Philadelphia publisher George Willig of eight "setts"—each with a dozen different dance patterns (and music for them)—by the leading dance bandleader in Philadelphia, the black-American cornetist, violinist, and composer Francis ("Frank") Johnson (1792–1844); publishers were more ready to issue the more fashionable offshoot of cotillions: quadrilles. (An abbreviated version of Johnson's *"La Sonnambula" Quadrille Number Two*, based in part on arias from Bellini's opera, is recorded on *NW CD 80293*.) By the mid-1850s, when Stephen Foster published a collection of instrumental solos, duets, trios, and quartets for chamber ensemble (*The Social Orchestra*, 1854; reprinted as *EAM* 13), he included no cotillions, but among the quartets, we find three sets of quadrilles: *Old Folks Quadrilles, Village Festival*, and [*Five*] *French Quadrille*[*s*]. (The first of these sets begins with a lively arrangement of *Old Folks at Home* and continues with separate quadrilles based on the tunes of the songs *Oh, boys, carry me 'long, Nelly Bly*, and *Farewell, my Lilly dear*, then ends with a brief original, *Plantation Jig*.)

The cotillion developed in two different directions. Out of it came not only the very highly structured quadrille, with its many patterns and great length, but also the "german," similarly lengthy but not so systematically patterned. Both these dances submitted to the influence of the newer "round" dances, for individual couples, emphasizing turning movements. Of these the waltz had been the first to gain popularity: as we have seen, it was introduced to America in the late eighteenth century, but it really became popular only in the 1820s and 1830s—and it remained popular throughout the entire century, and beyond, in a variety of forms—all, however, based on the idea of a couple dancing, in an embrace, to swooping music in $\frac{3}{4}$ meter. From the 1830s on, the galop, a fast $\frac{2}{4}$ dance for couples that often served as the finale of a quadrille, was popular; a later, slightly slower version of the galop, the two-step, superseded the waltz in the 1890s as the most popular round dance of all; it was danced to a marchlike music in $\frac{2}{4}$ or $\frac{4}{4}$. (One of John Philip Sousa's marches, *The Washington Post*, was identified with the two-step, and in England the two-step was for a long time referred to as the "Washington Post.")

In the mid-1840s the polka was introduced in America; it was one of the first dances to reflect the immigration of significant numbers of central Europeans. Slightly later came the similar but slower schottisch—not really "Scottish" but Germanic, though perhaps influenced by the steps and heel-taps of the Scots' reel. Also from central Europe came several dances related to the waltz but considered as "fancy dances"—the mazurka, the *redowá*, and the *varsovienne*.

The dance styles of American blacks had hardly any direct influence on white Americans until well after Emancipation. The way was prepared, however, by black dancers employed as entertainers in low-life nightspots in Northern cities, such as Almacks, a bar and brothel in the infamous Five Points slum district of New York. Charles Dickens, the celebrated British author, visited Almacks in 1842 and wrote vividly of his experience:

> ... A dance? It shall be done directly, sir: "a regular break-down."
>
> The corpulent black fiddler, and his friend who plays the tambourine, stamp upon the boarding ... and play a lively measure. Five or six couples come upon the floor, marshalled by a lively young negro, who is the wit of the assembly, and the greatest dancer known. ...
>
> The dance commences. Every gentleman sets as long as he likes to the opposite lady, and the opposite lady to him ... when suddenly the lively hero dashes in to the rescue. Instantly the fiddler grins, and goes at it tooth and nail; there is new energy in the tambourine; new laughter in the dancers; ... new brightness in the very candles. Single shuffle, double shuffle, cut and cross-cut; snapping his fingers, rolling his eyes, turning in his knees, presenting the backs of his legs in front, spinning about on his toes and heels like nothing but the man's fingers on the tambourine; dancing with two left legs, two right legs, two wooden legs, two wire legs, two spring legs— all sorts of legs and no legs. ... Having danced his partner off her feet, and himself too, he finishes by leaping gloriously on the bar-counter, and calling for something to drink, with the chuckle of a million counterfeit Jim Crows, in one inimitable sound![16]

Such dancers provided models for the Northern blackface minstrel shows, which soon included loose-limbed, pseudo-spontaneous duple-meter dances and, in walk-arounds, the prancing, strutting, turning, and bowing movements that were to characterize the later cakewalk. When all-black minstrel troupes came into existence after the Civil War, "essence" dances and soft-shoe numbers came with them, as did the cakewalk itself. The latter became a staple also in vaudeville and burlesque, as well as in the black musicals of the 1890s, such as *Clorindy, or the Origin of the Cakewalk* (1898) by Will Marion Cook (1869–1944), who was also chief composer for the collaborative shows of the comedians Bert Williams and George Walker—among them, *The Sons of Ham* (1900), *In Dahomey* (1902), and *In Bandanna Land* (1908). One characteristic common to all the dances of black origin was their basis in duple-meter music, which could serve, of course, for other dances as well, as is suggested by the subtitle (in the sheet-music version; *3Centuries* 4, 441–44)) of the best-known cakewalk song, Kerry Mills's *At a Georgia*

---

[16] Dickens, "New York" (chap. 6), *American Notes for General Circulation* (London: Chapman & Hall, 1842), quoted in *Writing New York: A Literary Anthology*, ed. Phillip Lopate (New York: Library of America, 1998), 51–64 (the passage quoted, 62–63).

Camp Meeting (1897): "a characteristic march which can be used effectively as a two-step, polka or cake walk." (A version recorded in 1908 by the Sousa Band is on *NW* LP 282.)

BANDS AND BAND MUSIC

The wind band was the vernacular tradition's equivalent of the cultivated tradition's strings-centered symphony orchestra. By the early twentieth century hardly any American hamlet was without its village band; hardly any public occasion passed without the sound of the brasses, woodwinds, drums, and cymbals of a band; hardly anyone in the Western world was ignorant of at least one American band composer: John Philip Sousa.

The American band developed out of the pre-Revolution British Army regimental bands. Early American bands were often attached to units of the local militia; as well as playing for parades and drills, they sometimes gave concerts. Two early bands whose rosters were exclusively filled with militiamen were the Massachusetts Band, organized in 1783, and the U.S. Marine Band (1798). In 1800 the Marine Band was made up of two oboes, two clarinets, two horns, a bassoon, and a drum; thus its constitution differed from that of a chamber orchestra only in its lack of stringed instruments. With the invention in Germany about 1815 of valves for cornets, trumpets, and horns, these instruments (admirably suited to the band's outdoor requirements of portability and plenty of sound) gained a new flexibility, hence new popularity. As the bands added brasses to their complements, the woodwinds were first forced out entirely (as, for instance, from New York's City Brass Band, reorganized in 1834 by Thomas Dodworth as an exclusively brass-instrument ensemble) only to be reintroduced, about the middle of the century, in even greater numbers to balance the noisier brass.

Band concerts up to the Civil War, like other concerts, were potpourris inevitably alternating solos by "guest vocal performers" with pieces by the band. Each item was carefully numbered in the printed programs of the day (perhaps the source of the colloquial use of "number" for a musical composition). The staples of the mid-century band repertory were quicksteps and other marches; dances, especially the popular waltz and polka, with usually a fast $\frac{2}{4}$ galop in conclusion; an occasional overture; and almost always a solo for keyed bugle or the novel valve cornet to amaze the audience with the newly won agility of such brass instruments. The high-brass soloists were the stars, and often the conductors, of American bands; one of the most celebrated early ones was Edward ("Ned") Kendall (1808–61), who formed the Boston Brass Band in 1835 and was noted for his performances of such virtuoso display pieces as John Holloway's *Wood Up Quick Step* (1835). Example 5–9 shows the third strain of *Wood Up* as published in 1839, in an unusual arrangement by Holloway himself that reproduces Kendall's agile

EXAMPLE 5–9.   J. Holloway, *Wood Up. A Quick Step* (Boston: Oliver Ditson, 1839), measures 25–32 (3rd strain).

embellishments. As was common in the period, the music is printed in keyboard short score rather than full score: since there was no standard instrumentation for bands, each band usually made its own arrangements. There were important exceptions, both in score publications—such as *Keith's Collection of Instrumental Music* (Boston, 1844)—and in publications of parts—such as G. W. E. Friedrich's 1854 compilation of twenty-four pieces, *Brass Band Journal*, with parts for a twelve-piece band composed of two E♭ soprano saxhorns (or cornets); two B♭ alto saxhorns (or cornets); one E♭ trumpet; two E♭ tenor saxhorns; one baritone horn; two bass horns; and two drums, one "small" and the other "bass."

Besides Kendall, prominent among the mid-century bandleaders were several members of the Dodworth family, connected with a band of that name based in New York and renowned from the mid-1830s through the 1870s. Even more celebrated, eventually, were several bands directed by Patrick S. Gilmore (1829–92), who had come from his native Ireland to the United States in 1849, already a cornet virtuoso as a laddie of nineteen. After directing several bands in the Boston area, Gilmore resigned from the leadership of the Salem Brass Band in 1858 to establish his own band—a professional concert-giving, dance-playing, and public-occasion-enhancing ensemble of thirty-two members known as Gilmore's Grand Boston Band.

During the Civil War, Gilmore was for a time in New Orleans, where he organized the first of the gargantuan concerts he became noted for.

Like Berlioz, Gottschalk, Jullien, and others, Gilmore dreamed of a monster concert to end all monster concerts. Back in Boston after the war, he began organizing such an affair on an unheard-of scale, a National Peace Jubilee to be held in 1869 and to surpass by far the chorus of 5,000 and band of 500 (plus supplementary drum and bugle corps) that he had mustered in New Orleans. Support for the idea was not easy to come by: Dwight, the Handel and Haydn Society, and other Boston Brahmans were shocked at the Barnumesque plan. However, Gilmore cleverly gained the backing of first one, then both of the rival directors of the Boston and New England conservatories (each newly established in 1867); launched a careful publicity campaign; found building funds for a three-and-a-half-acre Coliseum to house the festival; issued periodic rehearsal orders like a battlefield general to 100 choral organizations totaling 10,296 singers; inveigled the great Ole Bull into being concertmaster of 525 orchestra players; commandeered a band of 486 wind and percussion players; and on June 15, 1869, the Jubilee was on. It lasted five days, with a grand opening concert, a second day's "symphony and oratorio" concert, a fourth's "classical" concert, and a final "Children's Day." The third day's concert was called "People's Day"; it featured three overtures, several national and religious songs, a trumpet solo, and two marches; its climax was the "Anvil Chorus" from Verdi's *Il Trovatore* for the entire massed ensemble plus electrically operated city bells and a dozen cannon, with "the Anvil part performed by One Hundred Members of the Boston Fire Department."

Pleased with the popular (and financial) success of the National Peace Jubilee, Gilmore aimed to outdo it. Termination of the Franco-Prussian War gave him an excuse to try, and in 1872, in a new Coliseum holding an audience of 50,000, he staged a World's Peace Jubilee. A chorus of 20,000 (some from points as remote from Boston as Milwaukee, St. Louis, Iowa City, and San Francisco) and an instrumental assemblage of almost 2,000 proved, not surprisingly, unmanageable; the second Jubilee was a monumental failure, although somehow all ten days' concerts were presented.[17]

Gilmore attempted no more musical gigantism. Nevertheless, having associated himself in 1873 with the 22nd Regiment of New York, he enlarged its band to sixty-six players, and for almost two decades this new Gilmore Band was the foremost professional band in the country. Gilmore took it on successful and influential tours (to the West Coast in 1876, to Europe in 1878, then across the United States every fall and spring in the 1880s); and it kept growing in size until eventually its roster numbered one hundred.

---

[17] A historical footnote: concluding the fifth day's program, with the audience requested to sing the last two verses, was the venerable hymn *Coronation* (1793) by the eighteenth-century singing master Oliver Holden.

Gilmore died in 1892, on tour and playing at the St. Louis Exposition. His band settled on a new leader a year later, the Irish-born cellist and composer Victor Herbert (1859–1924); Herbert was to remain director of the 22nd Regiment Band for seven years. Meanwhile, another bandmaster was rising to prominence: John Philip Sousa (1854–1932).

As a bandmaster, Sousa became internationally renowned. Appointed in 1880 leader of the Marine Band, he made it into a balanced ensemble, which by 1891 included forty-nine players (twenty-six reeds, twenty brass, three percussion). Sousa organized his own band in 1892 and with it toured the United States, Canada, Europe, and (in 1910–11) the world. He hired the most spectacular virtuosos as soloists—such as the cornetists Bohumir Kryl, Alessandro Liberati, and Herbert L. Clarke; the clarinetist Herman Bellstedt; the trombonist Arthur Pryor; and the sopranos Estelle Liebling and Marjorie Moody. He also increased the size of his band, until in the 1920s it averaged seventy players, with about forty reed, twenty-five brass, and five percussion instruments. It became, quite simply, the most celebrated band in history.

Long-lived, Sousa is the first musician we have encountered in this study to have lived into the radio-and-recording era and to have helped enlarge the popular audience through the new technology of the twentieth century. Ironically, however, he delegated various members of the Sousa Band—notably Pryor, until 1903, when he left Sousa to form his own band—to conduct recording sessions, since Sousa believed that "canned music"—a term he coined—was a menace to musical culture, on several counts.[18]

As the last sentence implies, Sousa had larger concerns than just those of directing a commercial band. He was an active fighter for composers' rights, an important advocate of copyright reform, and one of the founders in 1914 of the American Society of Composers, Authors and Publishers (ASCAP). This, the first performing-rights organization in the United States, licenses to commercial establishments the rights to perform copyrighted musical compositions; collects royalties on such performances; and distributes the royalties to composers, lyricists, and publishers.

As a composer, Sousa essayed many kinds of popular music, notably songs and operettas; the well-known march *El Capitan* was fashioned from two of the songs in an operetta of 1896 with that title. But it was as a composer of wind-band marches that Sousa triumphed. He lived at a time when the march was especially popular: not only was it the foundation of the repertory of military and parade bands and of the ubiquitous village bands; it also provided the music for many ballroom dances (for example, the two-step of the 1890s, mentioned on p. 129), as well as songs and hymns. The marches

---

[18] Sousa's article "The Menace of Mechanical Music," first published in *Appleton's Magazine* 8/3 (September 1906): 278–84, is reprinted (slightly abridged) with some of Frederick Strothman's amusing drawings for it in *ISAM Newsletter* 16/2 (May 1987), passim.

of Sousa were so keenly attuned to his time's temper, so finely honed, such perfect exemplars that Sousa understandably came to be known as "The March King."

The typical Sousa march is a fairly brief work in, of course, duple meter—an even-pulsed $\frac{2}{4}$ or $\frac{2}{2}$, or a galloping $\frac{6}{8}$—with a number of 16- or 32-measure strains preceded by a 4- or 8-measure introduction. Within this conventional framework Sousa was able to achieve remarkable flexibility and variety, particularly in the harmony, which is by no means predictable and is often surprisingly wide-ranging, given the narrow confines of the march form. Sousa's most famous march, *The Stars and Stripes Forever* (1897), is constructed this way: introduction (4 measures); first (16) and second (16) strains, each repeated; Trio (32); "break" or "dogfight" (24)—unstable, dramatic, and suspensive—leading to a repetition of the Trio, louder and with new piccolo countermelody; repetition of the "break," leading again to the Trio, with yet another countermelody in trombones added (see Example 5–10). Typically, although the march begins in E♭, the Trio is in the subdominant A♭, and the piece ends in that key.

EXAMPLE 5–10. J. P. Sousa, *The Stars and Stripes Forever* (1897), after a photostat of the autograph manuscript, Music Division, New York Public Library. (*a*) Introduction and first-strain theme. (*b*) Second-strain theme. (*c*) Trio theme. (*d*) "Break," beginning.

   Sousa composed about 140 marches between *The Revival* of 1876 (which appropriately uses for its Trio theme the gospel hymn *In the Sweet By-and-By*) and *The Kansas Wildcats* of 1931. About half are in the skittish $\frac{6}{8}$ meter, including some of the best known: *Semper Fidelis* (1888), *The Washington Post* (1889), and *The Liberty Bell* (1893). *El Capitan* alternates $\frac{6}{8}$ and $\frac{2}{4}$, as do several other marches derived from operetta airs. Richard Franko Goldman (1910–80), like his father Edwin Franko Goldman (1878–1956) a prominent bandmaster, especially admired such lesser-known but "magnificent examples as *The Fairest of the Fair* (1908), *Hands Across the Sea* (1899), *The Invincible Eagle* (1901; full score in *3Centuries* 12, 291–314), [and] *The Gallant Seventh* (1922)."[19] Like the earlier favorites, these live up to Sousa's own ideal of a band march: "It must be as free from padding as a marble statue. Every line must be carved with unerring skill. Once padded, it ceases to be a march." Having thus spoken as an artist, Sousa spoke also for the free-and-easy eclecticism of the vernacular tradition:

> The composer must, to be sure, follow accepted harmonization; but that is not enough. He must be gifted with the ability to pick and choose here and there, to throw off the domination of any one tendency. If he is a so-called purist in music, that tendency will rule his marches and will limit their appeal.[20]

Sousa saw himself as a highly skilled and tasteful purveyor of entertainment: true to the vernacular tradition, he was not concerned with elevating his audience but with pleasing it. He unconsciously but sharply distinguished

---

[19] "John Philip Sousa," *HiFi/Stereo Review* 19/1 (July 1967): 35–47; reprinted in R. F. Goldman, *Essays and Reviews 1948–1968*, ed. Dorothy Klotzman (*ISAMm* 13 [1980]), 208–24.

[20] *Marching Along* (1928), rev. & annotated, ed. Paul Bierley (Westerville, OH: Integrity Press, 1994), 359.

between the thought of the cultivated and vernacular traditions in a reflection made after spending an afternoon with Theodore Thomas:

> Thomas had a highly organized symphony orchestra ... I a highly organized wind band. ... Each of us was reaching an end, but through different methods. He gave Wagner, Liszt, and Tchaikowsky, in the belief that he was educating his public; I gave Wagner, Liszt, and Tchaikowsky with the hope that I was entertaining my public.[21]

Mechanical Instruments

A note on mechanical instruments is appropriate here. American technology of the nineteenth century led to a wide variety of them, the so-called nickelodeons of public places and the player pianos of American living rooms. The former, cheaper in the long run for barrooms, poolrooms, brothels, restaurants, and ballrooms than live musicians, came in all shapes, sizes, and degrees of complexity. The Automatic Harp of the Rudolph Wurlitzer Co. was advertised as "especially desirable where a piano cannot be used, on account of its being too loud." The Violano-Virtuoso of the Mills Novelty Co. was a coin-operated, mechanically played violin with piano accompaniment. The Banjorchestra, when fed a nickel, would produce music from an automatic banjo, with support from piano, triangle, drums, tambourine, and castanets. Orchestrions, basically mechanical pipe organs with extras, ranged in size and cost up to the two behemoths of the Wurlitzer instrument-making firm, the Paganini Violin Orchestra and the Pian-Orchestra. The Seeburg Company's catalogue described the "KT Special" orchestrion as "piano, xylophone, mandolin attachment, bass drum, snare drums, tympani, cymbal, triangle, castanets, tambourines, Chinese block," all encased in a head-high glass-fronted cabinet of rich bird's-eye maple.

Mechanically operated player pianos or "pianolas" (the name reflecting the great success of the Aeolian Company's Pianola model, invented in 1895) were the domestic counterpart of nickelodeons. Activated by foot pedals or electricity, bellows-operated, and fed with perforated music rolls, player pianos were fabulously popular from the 1890s through the 1920s, when radio, phonorecordings, and ultimately the Great Depression spelled their demise. A later connoisseur and collector, Lewis Graham, claimed that "between 1895 and 1912 there were more player pianos in the United States than bathtubs,"[22] and according to U.S. Department of Commerce statistics, 205,556 of the 347,589 pianos sold in 1923 were player pianos (it was the peak year of their manufacture).

[21] Ibid., 132. A number of Sousa's lesser-known marches, with others by his contemporaries, are recorded on *NW* LP 226; *NW* LP 282 ("The Sousa and Pryor Bands") reissues the original recordings of 1901–26.

[22] *New York Times*, November 3, 1966.

RAGTIME

In 1899 the writer and musical enthusiast Rupert Hughes (1872–1956) commented,

> If Negro music has its "Go down, Moses" … so it had also its hilarious banjo-plucking and its characteristic dances. It is the latter mood that is having a strong renascence and is sweeping the country like a plague of clog-hopping locusts.[23]

Hughes was speaking of the craze for ragtime, which indeed swept the country in the 1890s through the media of piano players, player pianos, dance bands, and commercial sheet music (both songs and piano pieces). In the diluted form of the cakewalk march, it was played by Sousa's and other concert bands here and in Europe, where according to a publisher's blurb "the native bands have taken up this peculiar style of distinctly American music, even going so far as to play the *Marseillaise* [France's national anthem] in rag time."

Many threads of earlier American music came together to form the fabric of the ragtime of the 1890s. Earliest, perhaps, was an emphatic use of syncopation by American blacks, partly derived from African drumming, partly from Afro-Caribbean dance rhythms. Among the few reports we have on American secular slave music, several mention the practice of "patting Juba." (Typically, slaves were forbidden to use drums, which perhaps led to substitutions such as hand-clapping and "patting Juba"—patting with their hands other parts of their bodies.) The practice apparently involved intricate rhythmic patterns played off against a regular beat—syncopation, in short, but of a consistent, insistent kind. Thus, a correspondent of Edgar Allan Poe's, likening irregularities in poetic meters to "clapping Juba," described the latter for Poe in a letter of 1835:

> There is no attempt to keep time to all the notes, but then it comes so pat & so distinct that the cadence is never lost. p Such irregularities are like rests and grace notes. They must be so managed as neither to hasten or retard the beat. The time of the bar must be the same, no matter how many notes are in it.[24]

One source couples the Negro dance-name "Juba" with the English dance-name "jig" and speaks of "patting" as an intricate rhythmic accompaniment to such a "jig"; another, a Mississippi planter discussing in 1851 how to manage a plantation, tells of his slaves' Saturday night dance music: "Charley's fiddle is always accompanied with Ihurod on the triangle and Sam to 'pat.'"[25]

---

[23] "A Eulogy of Rag-Time," *Musical Record* (Boston), no. 447 (April 1, 1899): 157–59.

[24] *The Complete Works of Edgar Allan Poe*, ed. James A. Harrison (New York: Thomas Y. Crowell, 1902), 17/22.

[25] Both comments quoted in Epstein, *Sinful Tunes and Spirituals*, 142 and 154.

A particular kind of syncopated rhythm, conceivably one essence of "patting Juba," shows up in two disparate sources of the late 1850s. Gottschalk's *Souvenir de Porto Rico* of 1857 (see Example 4–10) opposes a typical $\frac{2}{4}$ bass rhythm of the Caribbean *danza* and a strongly syncopated upper part, emphasizing ♪♪♪ and ♪♪♪♪ patterns. In 1859, James Hungerford, of Maryland, published an autobiographical novel, *The Old Plantation*, and in it reproduced a "corn song" one of his slaves had sung on an outing in 1832. Prominent in an otherwise regularly accented $\frac{4}{4}$ meter are the syncopes ♪♪♪ and, one level higher, ♪♪♪. Even before the 1850s, however, such patterns were well known and were identified with blacks: they are commonplaces in the songs of the minstrel shows of the 1840s (see Example 5–8; also the choruses of *Oh! Susanna* and *Dixie*), particularly the walk-arounds, the dancing for which, in later minstrelsy, was the cakewalk, with its prancing kick-steps, bows back and forward, and salutes to the spectators. These particular mild syncopes became in fact the hallmarks of the cakewalk two-steps played by the Northern bands of the 1890s. Compare, for example, the excerpts in Example 5–11 from the "corn song" transcribed in 1859 by Hungerford and from the "Cake Walk-Two Step" *Bunch o' Blackberries* of 1899, as played by Sousa's band.

EXAMPLE 5–11. Negro slave song and cakewalk rhythms. (*a*) *Roun' de Corn, Sally!* as transcribed in James Hungerford, *The Old Plantation, and What I Gathered There in an Autumn Month* (New York: Harper & Brothers, 1859), 191 (excerpts). (*b*) Abe Holzmann, *Bunch o' Blackberries* (New York: Feist & Frankenthaler, 1899), Trio (treble melody only), measures 1–8.

Ragtime included the simple syncopations just cited, plus others. Perhaps the earliest American music to suggest the intricate and fanciful rhythms of ragtime is that of the banjo dances of the early minstrel shows (see pp. 121–22). Again, we can relate at least one aspect of these—accentuated rests—to "patting Juba." The poet and musician Sidney Lanier (1842–81) observed that every one who has noticed a Southern negro's "patting" will have been apt to hear an effect p produced by omitting the stroke, of foot or of hand, which the hearer expects to fall on the accented note at the first of the bar, thus:

and similar forms.[26]

The minstrel-show banjo tunes were generally called jigs. So was early ragtime: until about 1897, when the terms *rag* and *ragtime* gained currency, a pianist or a band that played in the ragtime style was occasionally called a *jig pianist* or a *jig band*. (Here we see, perhaps, the origin of the malodorous equation of the term "jig" with "black.") Thus, in its rhythmic aspects, ragtime derived from the banjo dance-tune style, which may itself be related to "patting Juba."

Ragtime typically involves two layers of rhythmic activity: a regularly accented, even bass and a strongly cross-accented treble. Against the bass, which normally stomps along with a heavy two-beat (♩ ♩) or prances in the bandlike oom-pah oom-pah rhythm of ♪♩ ♪♩ , the treble is "ragg'd" by throwing accents onto other, sub-beats. Melodic phrasing of even sixteenths can do it: ♫♫♫ ♫♫♫ or, more common, ♫♫♫ ♫♫♫ (the relationship of the first pattern to the Caribbean *danza*'s ♫♩♫ is worth noting). Variants of these, throwing an accent on the fourth sixteenth (the bass would come down on the fifth), are common in the early printed rags: ♫♫♩ , ♫♫♪ , ♫♫♫ , and ♫♫♫♫ all begin the same way. The phrase may run along evenly but bump into an offbeat accent— ♫♫♫♫ , ♫♫♫♫ —or be drily articulated: ♫♩♪ . Accentuating the final sixteenth in a measure, usually by anticipating the note on the downbeat of the next and holding that note over the barline, is also common (♫ ♫♫ |♩), especially in patterns borrowing the cakewalk motif (♫♫♫ |♩ or ♫♫♫♫ |♩). In Scott Joplin's *Stoptime Rag* (1910), the old banjo-tune technique of accentuated rests is expanded: the composer instructs that "the pianist should stamp the heel of one foot heavily upon the

---

[26] *The Science of English Verse* (New York: Scribner's, 1880), 189; Lanier's comment and his music excerpt are reproduced in facsimile in Epstein, *Sinful Tunes and Spirituals*, 142. Lanier was a flutist and composer (as well as poet); his extraordinarily virtuosic *Wind-Song* (1874) for unaccompanied flute, composed to play for an audition with the New York conductor Leopold Damrosch, heads the scores in *The Sidney Lanier Collection*, ed. Patricia Harper and Paula Robison (Vienna: Universal Edition [U.S. distributor: European American Music Distributors Corporation], 1997).

floor, whenever the word 'stomp' appears in the music" (which it does on *rests* appearing on normally accented beats).

The formal design and the basic meter and tempo of ragtime, as it was first published in the 1890s, came from Euro-American dances (quadrilles, polkas, schottisches) and especially post–Civil War marches, with their several strains, each repeated (and one or two dipping into the subdominant key), and their heavy two-beat meter. Joplin's celebrated *Maple Leaf Rag* (1899), the best-known early piano rag to be published, is in $\frac{2}{4}$, marked "Tempo di Marcia"; Joplin elsewhere indicated "Slow March Tempo" and even cautioned performers, "Notice! Don't play this piece fast. It is never right to play 'Ragtime' fast." The form of *Maple Leaf Rag* is basically that of a Sousa march: first strain (16 measures, repeated); second strain (16, repeated); first strain again; "Trio," so named and consisting of a third strain (16, repeated) in the subdominant; and a fourth strain (16, repeated) back in the tonic.

The earliest appearance of the word "rag" in connection with a musical work seems to have been in the sheet music of Ernest Hogan's song *All Coons Look Alike to Me* (1896), which has an optional syncopated accompaniment cited as a "Negro Rag." And indeed, although later ragtime revivals (in the 1950s and especially the 1970s) tended to concentrate on *instrumental* rags, ragtime was originally as much a vocal music as instrumental, its principal vehicle being the so-called *coon song* ("coon" being a term used by Americans—blacks as well as whites, and often mockingly—to refer to blacks). As with the music of the earlier minstrel shows, coon songs were initially written and performed by whites, on the newly popular vaudeville stage; one celebrated "coon shouter" was May Irwin (1862–1938), perhaps best known for her delivery of Charles E. Trevathan's *Bully Song* (1896; on *NW* CD 80221). Some blacks, however, were leading composers of the genre, notably Will Marion Cook, who composed the music for the lyrics of *Darktown Is Out Tonight* (1902; on *NW* CD 80265) by Paul Dunbar (1872–1906)—both of whom collaborated on the important black musical *In Dahomey*. Bob Cole (1863–1911), in collaboration with the Johnson brothers (James Weldon Johnson [1871–1938] and J. Rosamund Johnson [1873–1954]), opposed the coon-song conventions; one of the most successful of their many joint songs, and one that characteristically treats its subjects with some dignity, was the winsome *Under the Bamboo Tree* (1902; in *3Centuries* 2, 293–96); the beginning of its "Chorus" (refrain) is given as Example 5–12.

The first published instrumental rag so titled, *The Mississippi Rag* (January 1897), was composed by William Krell, a white bandmaster in Chicago. Soon to be acknowledged as "The King of Ragtime," however, was the black pianist and composer Scott Joplin (1867/68–1917). Joplin grew up in Texarkana, Texas, and began his career as an itinerant pianist, playing in honky-tonks and brothels. He went to Chicago briefly in 1893 to try his luck

EXAMPLE 5–12.   B. Cole, J. W. Johnson, and J. R. Johnson, *Under the Bamboo Tree* (New York: Jos. W. Stern. & Co., 1902), measures 1–10 of Chorus.

in the entertainment halls that had sprung up around the World's Columbian Exposition of that year; by 1896, after more restless wandering (he never really settled down), he was in Sedalia, Missouri. His first published piano rag, *Original Rags*, came out in March 1899; later the same year appeared *Maple Leaf Rag*, named for a club of that name in Sedalia (or the other way around, the club being named after the rag). The piece was eventually a resounding success and became the most famous of all piano rags. By the time of his death, Joplin had published more than thirty original rags and other piano pieces, songs, and arrangements as well.

Joplin had even larger aims. In 1899 in Sedalia he staged a ballet called *The Ragtime Dance*, and in 1903 in East St. Louis an opera, *A Guest of Honor* (unpublished and now apparently lost); in 1911 he published another opera, *Treemonisha*. The artistic success of these larger works is debatable, but that of Joplin's piano rags is not; they can only be described as elegant, varied, often subtle, and as sharply incised as a cameo. They are the precise American equivalent, in terms of a native style of dance music, of minuets by Mozart, mazurkas by Chopin, or waltzes by Brahms. They can be both lovely and powerful, infectious and moving—depending, of course, on the skill and stylishness of the pianist, for they are not easy music technically and they demand a clean but "swinging" performance. Joplin wrote poignantly of the genre in a brief manual of ragtime exercises that he published in 1908:

> That all publications masquerading under the name of ragtime are not the genuine article will be better known when these exercises are studied. That real ragtime of the higher class is rather difficult to play is a painful truth which most pianists have discovered. Syncopations are no indication of light and trashy music.[27]

The earliest published piano rags were a mature kind of music that had merely lacked crystallization in print. They were also a music of metrical precision, despite all their cross-accents and rhythmic jolts, music that could adequately and accurately be reproduced on the popular player pianos of the time—which they were, and the wide dissemination of the piano roll undoubtedly stimulated ragtime's acceptance and popularity. Ragtime on player-piano rolls is thus the very earliest American music we can actually hear in contemporaneous performances.

One such performance is Joplin's of his own *Weeping Willow* (1903), recorded for Connorized player-piano roll No. 10277 (transferred to tape in 1956; reissued on Riverside LP RLP-12–110, later on Biograph CD BCD-101). Like that of most early rags, the form of *Weeping Willow* is built on four different strains plus introduction, played in the order Intro–1–2–1–3–4; in Joplin's recorded performance the repetition of each strain finds the treble thrown up an octave to provide new color (Example 5–13). In some later rags—for example, the harmonically adventuresome *Euphonic Sounds* (1909)—Joplin turned to a clear-cut rondolike form, whereas in the darkly colored, dense-textured *Magnetic Rag* (1914) the form is a rounded Intro–1–2–3–4–1–Coda.

---

[27] *The School of Ragtime*, reprinted in *The Collected Works of Scott Joplin*, ed. Vera Brodsky Lawrence (New York: New York Public Library, 1971), 1/283. Some of the comments in this paragraph are adapted from my review (in *Stereo Review* 26/4 [April 1971]: 84) of Joshua Rifkin's recording *Scott Joplin: Piano Rags* (Nonesuch H-71248), which helped to pioneer a major ragtime revival in the early 1970s.

EXAMPLE 5–13. S. Joplin, *Weeping Willow* (St. Louis: Val A. Reis Music Co., 1903). (*a*) First strain, beginning. (*b*) Second strain, beginning. (*c*) Third strain, beginning. (*d*) Fourth strain, beginning.

Other ragtime composer-performers modified still other aspects. The New Orleans pianist Ferdinand "Jelly Roll" Morton (1890?–1941) exemplified the Crescent City's style of fairly slow rags, with swingier rhythms than the St. Louis manner of Joplin and with melodic "walking" basses, as in Morton's *King Porter Stomp* (1906; *SCCJ* CD 1[recorded by Morton himself in 1939]). Elements of Negro blues (see p. 223), both formal structure and "blue notes," crept into rags from the time of *Memphis Blues* (1912; on *NW* LP 269) by W. C. Handy (1873–1958), in fact subtitled "A Southern Rag"; its publication preceded by two years that of Handy's most celebrated and universally known blues, *St. Louis Blues* (*SCCJ* CD 1 [as recorded by Bessie Smith in 1925]) . The New York "stride" piano style, exemplified by the music of James P. Johnson (1894–1955), marked the turn from ragtime to jazz: in works like *Carolina Shout* (ca. 1917; *SCCJ* CD 1 [as recorded in 1921 by

Johnson]), *Caprice Rag* (1917), and *Harlem Strut* (1921), Johnson's striding left hand emphasizes the offbeats and transforms the older two-beat meter into a jazzy four, while his right-hand style dissolves the classic ragtime syncopes into long-breathed runs of even eighths (not quite even, in actual performance) and triplets (Example 5–14). Another master stride pianist, and one who in fact studied with Johnson, was Thomas "Fats" Waller (1904–43); many of his recordings leave ragtime far behind stylistically, but others, such as the dazzlingly virtuosic *Handful of Keys* of 1929, are clearly in the ragtime tradition.

EXAMPLE 5–14. *Caprice Rag*, measures 5–8, by James P. Johnson. Copyright © 1963 by Mills Music, Inc.

This shift in style, however, marked the end—temporarily, at least—of the short, happy public career of ragtime and the beginning of the era of jazz and urban blues (at least in the public consciousness of Americans).

BIBLIOGRAPHICAL NOTES

Paul C. Echols's "Hymnody" in *AmeriGrove* is a fine overview, with a rich bibliography. On the shape-note tradition, George Pullen Jackson's books, beginning with *White Spirituals in the Southern Uplands* (Chapel Hill: University of North Carolina Press, 1933), are basic; later research is reflected in the text and bibliography of *AmeriGrove*'s "Shape-note hymnody," by Harry Eskew and James C. Downey. The 1991 edition of *The Sacred Harp* was revised by the Sacred Harp Music Committee (Bremen, GA: Sacred Harp Publishing Co.); Buell E. Cobb Jr.'s important history, *The Sacred Harp: A Tradition and Its Music* (Athens: Brown Thrasher Books, University of Georgia Press, 1989), is illuminatingly reviewed by Ron Pen in *AM* 12/1 (Spring 1994): 93–98. Wallace White writes engagingly about the "Big Singing" (from *The Southern Harmony*) in Benton, Kentucky, in *The New Yorker* of January 19, 1987, 78–85.

Eileen Southern's seminal history *The Music of Black Americans* has reached a 3rd edition (New York: W. W. Norton, 1997). Dena J. Epstein's research on black music is brought together in the superb *Sinful Tunes and Spirituals: Black Folk Music to the Civil War* (Urbana: University of Illinois Press, 1977); later valuable studies by her include "Black Spirituals: Their Emergence into Public Knowledge," *Black Music Research Newsletter* 8/2 (Spring 1986): 5–9, and "The Story of the Jubilee Singers: An Introduction to Its Bibliographic History," in *New Perspectives on Music: Essays in Honor of Eileen Southern* (Warren, MI: Harmonie Park Press, 1992), 151–62. The pioneer song anthology by Allen, Ware, and Garrison, *Slave Songs of the United States* (1867), has been reprinted several times, most recently (1992) by the Clearfield Company of Baltimore. Irene V. Jackson has made a helpful bibliographical contribution with *Afro-American Religious Music: A Bibliography and a Catalogue of Gospel Music* (Westport, CT: Greenwood Press, 1979).

Dale Cockrell's *Demons of Disorder* of 1997 (cited in note 8) is the first *musicological* study of early (1829–43) blackface minstrelsy; Robert B. Winans's "Early Minstrel Show Music, 1843–1852," in *Musical Theatre in America*, ed. Glenn Loney (Westport, CT: Greenwood Press, 1984), 71–97, is strong on a later decade. Both were preceded by Hans Nathan's excellent monograph on *Dan Emmett and the Rise of Early Negro Minstrelsy* (cited in note 11). Robert C. Toll's *Blacking Up: The Minstrel Show in Nineteenth-Century America* (New York: Oxford University Press, 1974) and Eric Lott's *Love and Theft: Blackface Minstrelsy and the American Working Class* (New York: Oxford University Press, 1993) deal more with socioeconomic and political aspects of the later minstrel shows.

Pauline Norton's major article "Dance" in *AmeriGrove* and Thornton Hagert's lengthy liner notes for *NW* CD 293 (... *Instrumental Dance Music, 1780's–1920's*) are both illuminating. See also, in *Chronicles of the American Dance*, ed. Paul Magriel (New York: Henry Holt, 1948), Lillian Moore's "John Durang—The First American Dancer" (15–37) and Rosetta O'Neill's "The Dodworth Family and Ballroom Dancing in New York" (81–100). Thomas Riis's essay on, and edition of, the scripts and music for *In Dahomey* (1903) are contained in *RRAM* 25 (= *MUSA* 5).

The periodical *Journal of Band Research* (1964/65–) is a good source on American bands and band music; for the period dealt with in this chapter, Frank Cipolla's "Annotated Guide for the Study and Performance of Nineteenth Century Band Music in the United States" (14/1 [Fall 1978]: 22–40) is helpful. Jon Newsom's "The American Brass Band Movement," *Quarterly Journal of the Library of Congress* 36/2 (Spring 1979): 114–39, is especially well illustrated and documented; an even more comprehensive and colorful history is Margaret and Robert Hazen's *The Music Men: An Illustrated History of the Brass Band in America, 1800–1920* (Washington, DC: Smithsonian Institution Press, 1987). *3Centuries* 12 includes, from *Keith's Collection of Instrumental Music*, the score of Simon Knaebel's *Rockaway Quick Step* (105–6) and, from G. W. E. Friedrich's *Brass Band Journal*, those of *Lilly Bell Quick Step* (152–54) and *Prima Donna Waltz* (155–59).

A fine beginning to studies of Patrick Gilmore is that of Frank Cipolla, "... Gilmore: The Boston Years," *AM* 6/3 (Fall 1988): 281–92. Sousa has been admirably served in several books by Paul Bierley, including *John Philip Sousa, American Phenomenon* (New York: Meredith Corporation, 1973), and *The Works of John Philip Sousa* (Columbus, OH: Integrity Press, 1984). The source of the music of the march *El Capitan*, Sousa's operetta of the same title, is edited by Bierley as vol. 14 of *Nineteenth-Century American Musical Theater* (New York: Garland Publishing, 1994), with facsimiles of the printed libretto, a fascinating manuscript stage manager's guide, and the piano-vocal score (London, 1896).

Frank W. Holland's "Player Piano" in *AmeriGrove* is a good summary; that in *The New Grove Dictionary of Musical Instruments* (London: Macmillan, 1984), also by him, is virtually the same but includes illustrations.

Edward Berlin's *Ragtime: A Cultural and Musical History* (Berkeley and Los Angeles: University of California Press, 1980) remains the most authoritative account; it is complemented by the useful (if uneven) anthology *Ragtime: Its History, Composers, and Music*, ed. John Hasse (New York: Schirmer Books, 1985). Berlin's *King of Ragtime: Scott Joplin and His Era* (New York: Oxford University Press, 1994) is unmatched (and will probably remain so). Vera Brodsky Lawrence revised her facsimile reprints of *The Collected Works of Scott Joplin* (1971) in 1981 as *The Complete Works* ... (New York Public Library, 1981).

SIX

THE CULTIVATED TRADITION, 1865–1920

American music of the cultivated tradition from the end of the Civil War to the end of World War I was dominated largely by the attitudes, the ideals, and the modes of expression of nineteenth-century Europe, particularly Austria and Germany. Virtually all our leading composers were initiated into music by Americans who had emigrated from Europe; they were trained professionally during sojourns in Europe; and when they came back their music was played by ensembles, choruses, and orchestras led either by Europeans or by Americans trained in Europe. Some of their music was even published first in Europe, by Breitkopf & Härtel in Leipzig or by the Leipzig branch of the Boston firm of Arthur P. Schmidt (1846–1921), who in grateful return for an American career (he was German-born but emigrated to the United States in 1866) made it a point of conscience to publish American music. In Chapter 3 we examined the sources of this Germanophilia; in Chapter 4 we saw evidences of its rising tide up to the Civil War; in the present chapter we see its high-water mark. However, toward the turn of the twentieth century, the work of a few composers reflected other currents: a new interest in American folklore, in developments in French and Russian music, and in topical subject matter related to the American scene.

INSTITUTIONAL FOUNDATIONS

It was during the 1860–1920 period that the institutional foundations of the cultivated tradition were firmly consolidated. Music conservatories were founded, among them some still considered preeminent: in 1857 the Peabody Conservatory in Baltimore (but instruction there was delayed by the Civil War and other problems until 1868); in 1865 the Oberlin Conservatory in Ohio; in 1867 the New England Conservatory in Boston as well as the Cincinnati Conservatory and the Chicago Academy of Music (later renamed the Chicago Musical College); in New York City, the New York College of Music in 1878, the National Conservatory in 1885, the Institute of Musical Art in 1905 (merged in 1926 with another conservatory to become the Juilliard School of Music), and the Mannes College of Music in 1916; in San Francisco, the Community Music Center in 1919.

Thanks to Lowell Mason's efforts of the 1830s, music was a part of school curricula across the land. After the Civil War it entered the colleges and universities as well: Vassar College, the University of Pennsylvania, and Harvard University established music professorships in the 1870s, and they were followed soon by Yale, Columbia, and other universities and colleges. The Music Teachers National Association was founded in 1876, and the Music Educators National Conference in 1907 (under the name of Music Supervisors National Conference).

The first American copyright act, that of 1790, had not mentioned musical compositions (though some collections of music categorized as "books" were protected), but a revision of 1831 did; a third revision in 1909 provided performing-rights protection for musical works presented "for profit" but left unmentioned the important technological developments of player-piano rolls and sound recordings. Composers, lyricists, and music publishers alike were benefited by the establishment in 1914 of ASCAP, the American Society of Composers, Authors and Publishers (see p. 134). Musicians had organized sporadically in protective associations ever since the founding of the Musical Fund Society of Philadelphia in 1820; by the end of the nineteenth century, the AFM (American Federation of Musicians) was their principal union (with a membership by 1913 of 64,000 in 636 locals).

With monies provided not by government but by groups of private citizens spearheaded by individual philanthropists, major concert halls were built: Philadelphia's Academy of Music (1857), Cincinnati's Music Hall (1878), the Auditorium in Chicago (1889), Carnegie Hall in New York (1891), Boston's Symphony Hall (1900). The Metropolitan Opera House in New York was inaugurated in 1882 (razed in 1966 in favor of a brand-new house).

During the entire period, the performance center of the cultivated tradition was New York City. But the ideological center was undoubtedly Boston, where John Sullivan Dwight (1813–93) reigned through his *Journal of Music* as chief spokesperson for the tradition. A Harvardian who had trained for the ministry, Dwight began his career as the first really significant and broadly influential American music critic and arbiter of taste with more than one hundred articles in *The Harbinger*, journal of the Transcendentalist community at Brook Farm from 1845 to 1849. A bit later, he began *Dwight's Journal of Music*, which ran through 1,051 issues in nearly thirty years of publication (1852–81) and was the most substantial and long-lived music periodical America had known, despite a comparatively small subscription list. It included critical reviews, analyses, reports on concert life in both Europe and the United States, essays on music history and theory, and translations from German and French music treatises, biographies, and journals. Throughout its existence, it was informed with Dwight's unshakably high-minded belief in music—art-music, at least—as the language of feeling and, indeed, faith, whose purpose was "to hallow pleasure, and to naturalize religion" (as he expressed it in an address to the Harvard Musical Association as early as 1841). In announcing his *Journal*, Dwight promised that "it will insist much on the claims of 'Classical' music ... because the enduring needs always to be held up in contrast with the ephemeral."[1] The *Journal* did so insist, with Dwight of course determining what was to be considered "the enduring."

Among the contributors to *Dwight's Journal* who might appropriately be mentioned in this summary of the "institutional foundations" of the cultivated tradition were (besides Dwight as our first major music critic) America's first musicologist and the first historian of America's music: the former was Alexander Wheelock Thayer (1817–97), whose *Ludwig van Beethovens Leben* (1866–79, completed by Hermann Dieters and Hugo Riemann; English versions published in 1921 and 1964) is still valuable; the latter was Frédéric Louis Ritter (1824–91), born in Alsace and emigrant to America in 1856. Ritter's *Music in America* (1883) was the first attempt at a comprehensive survey. Ritter relieved himself, however, of any responsibility to treat the vernacular or folk traditions by saying flatly, as he began a last chapter on "The Cultivation of Popular Music," that "the people's song ... is not to be found among the American people"!

THE SECOND NEW ENGLAND SCHOOL

If Dwight and contributors to his journal such as Thayer and Ritter were the literary voices of the art-music of the age, a group of New England composers constituted the musical voice. I call them the Second New England School, grouping them together by virtue of their common inheritance, attitudes, and general style much as I grouped the late-eighteenth-century composers of the First New England School.

---

[1] Quoted in George Willis Cooke, *John Sullivan Dwight* (Boston: Small, Maynard & Co., 1898), 147.

Oldest of the group, and teacher of several of the younger ones, was John Knowles Paine (1839–1906). His first musical studies were with Hermann Kotzschmar, who had come to America in 1848 with the Saxonia Band, an ensemble similar to the Germania Musical Society (see p. 94), and had settled in Paine's hometown of Portland, Maine. Aiming to become a church organist, Paine went to Germany in 1858 and stayed nearly four years, studying with the Berlin organist Karl August Haupt (as did almost forty younger Americans) and others. Back in America in 1861, he got a post as organist in a Boston church. The next year he was appointed instructor at Harvard, to teach a non-credit music course and serve as university organist. By the mid-1870s the university was convinced of the validity of a music curriculum, and the 1875–76 academic year began with Paine as Harvard's first professor of music.[2] He was to remain at Harvard for thirty years, until his retirement in 1905. As Kenneth Roberts has written perceptively (in the entry on Paine in *AmeriGrove*),

> By his ... serious concern with music in a liberal arts college he awakened a regard for music among many generations of Harvard [students]. ... he made Cambridge a center of musical America [and] pioneered not only in the setting up of a collegiate department of music, but in being a 'composer-in-residence,' in contrast to the nature of appointments in contemporary European universities.

Paine's work as a composer ranged from piano and organ pieces and chamber music to incidental music for plays, overtures, symphonic poems, and two symphonies; from songs, hymns, and choral cantatas to an oratorio, a Mass, and a grand opera. Most of it cannot be faulted in workmanship, none of it in seriousness of purpose: Paine took very seriously music's mission to "hallow pleasure," and if his music seems somewhat overaspiring to profundity, hardly daring to relax or smile, this should be ascribed not to incompetence but to his aesthetic attitude and to the difficulty of attempting to emulate the masterworks of Europe's mature cultivated tradition from a base in a still-New World.

Stylistically, most of Paine's music falls within the orbit of the Viennese Classicists and the early German Romantics; he also held J. S. Bach in high esteem, was one of the first American organists to perform Bach's works regularly, and developed considerable contrapuntal craft. Mendelssohn is the strongest influence on choral works such as the *Centennial Hymn* (1876; text by Whittier), the cantata *Realm of Fancy* (1882; after Keats), and the oratorio *St. Peter* (1872; piano-vocal score in *3Centuries* 7, 108–282). Earlier than these works is the extraordinary Mass in D (first performed in Berlin in 1867, with Paine conducting)—a work of "grandeur and haunting beauty" (as described by Gunther Schuller, who exhumed the work in 1972 and conducts

---

[2] Not the first in the United States, as is often claimed: Ritter, at Vassar College, preceded Paine in holding a professorial chair in music, as did Hugh A. Clarke at the University of Pennsylvania.

it on *NW* CD 80262) and the first major concert composition by an American to be performed in Europe. Beethoven's earlier symphonies, especially the Fifth, are the major models for Paine's First Symphony (1875; premiered in Boston by the Theodore Thomas Orchestra); Schumann's four, for Paine's Second ("Im Frühling," 1879; *NW* CD 80350).

Paine spoke in 1872 in favor of "adherence to the historical forms, as developed by Bach, Handel, Mozart, and Beethoven" as a "healthy reaction" to the "extremely involved and complicated technics of music, like Wagner, Liszt, and their adherents."[3] However, his own style eventually reflected the music of the latter group. An orchestral prelude, part of Paine's incidental music for Sophocles' *Oedipus Tyrannus*, Op. 35 (1881), is quite Lisztian in its design and its thematic transformations (Example 6–1). And Paine admitted that in his opera *Azara* (1900; libretto by Paine on the medieval legend of Aucassin and Nicolette) he had "followed throughout the connected orchestral rhythmical flow, and truth of dramatic expression char-

EXAMPLE 6–1. Thematic transformations in J. Paine, *Oedipus Tyrannus*, Op. 35 (Boston: Arthur P. Schmidt, 1881), Prelude, measures 26–29, 54–57, 78–80.

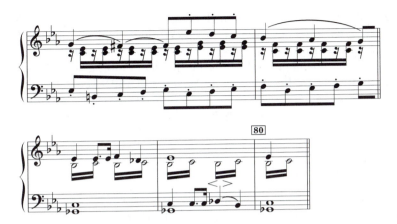

acteristic of Wagner."[4] Nevertheless, Paine's basic musical attitude was conservative; on one of the very few occasions when he permitted himself to turn to a bit of light Americana for source material, he used it as the subject of *Fuga Giocosa* (ca. 1882–84; on *NW LP 206* and reprinted in *EAM 27*), given as Example 6–2—a fugue remarkably dry, considering its musical theme (sung colloquially to the phrase "Over the fence is out, boys!").

EXAMPLE 6–2.   J. Paine, *Fuga Giocosa*, *3 Piano Pieces*, Op. 41 (Boston: Arthur P. Schmidt, 1884), No. 3, measures 1–2.

After Paine as members of the Second New England School came a group of composers about a generation younger; the major figures—at least, those who began to enjoy a modest revival, in live performances and on recordings, beginning in the 1970s—were George Chadwick, Horatio Parker, Arthur Foote, and Amy Cheney Beach. Of these, Chadwick and Parker emerge as the strongest, if not necessarily the most gifted, musical personalities.

George Whitefield Chadwick (1854–1931) is notable among the group for his sympathy—reflected unevenly, however, in his works—for the American vernacular tradition's music; for his achievement in approaching a natural declamation in the setting of English texts; and for an earthy humor (occasionally joined to a social consciousness) not common to his rather aristocratic, more isolated peers. A prolific composer, productive from his student days in Leipzig (*Rip Van Winkle* overture, 1879) until the 1920s, he was the most versatile of the New Englanders. His Symphony No. 2 (1885;

[4] Letter to Henry T. Finck, May 27, 1900; quoted in Kenneth C. Roberts, Jr., "John Knowles Paine" (Master's thesis, University of Michigan, 1962), 2–3.

NW CD 80339; reprinted as *EAM* 4) includes melodies prophetic of the folk-ish themes of Dvořák's much-discussed "New World" Symphony; and a folk-like pentatonicism crops up in works of varied character, as in the opening measures of a *Sinfonietta in D* (1904) or the "Jubilee" movement of his best-known orchestral work, the *Symphonic Sketches* of 1895–1904 (Example 6–3). Such "American" references are sometimes well assimilated; often, however, they are lodged in a lushly harmonized and orchestrated matrix that contradicts their very nature.

EXAMPLE 6–3.   Folklike themes of Chadwick. (*a*) Symphony No. 2 (Boston: Arthur P. Schmidt, 1888), second movement, measures 5–8 and rehearsal-letter "M" (accompaniment omitted from both). (*b*) *Sinfonietta in D* (New York: G. Schirmer, Inc., 1906), first movement, measures 4–13 (violin part only). (*c*) *Symphonic Sketches* (New York: G. Schirmer, Inc., 1907), "Jubilee," measures 58–61 (string parts omitted).

One specialist in Chadwick's music has emphasized that the later works, from about 1907 to 1920, reveal "a gradual discard of the German conservatory style [and] a more mature musical language, combining pentatonic melody, subdominant-modal harmony and syncopated rhythmic elements."[5] The "syncopation" is generally limited to the short-long pattern common to English two-syllable words (cf. "wítching" and "éxile" in Example 6–5; "slúmber" and the related "lamentátion" in Example 6–6), but even so, Chadwick's use of such natural speech rhythms, long a commonplace in songs of the vernacular tradition, sets him apart from Paine, Parker, and others of the Second New England School, who tended to set English as if it were German or Latin. Chadwick transfers this rhythmic motif to instrumental music as well, as in the phrase endings of the "Scherzino" of the *Sinfonietta* (Example 6–4, measures 24 and 27).

EXAMPLE 6–4. G. Chadwick, *Sinfonietta in D* (New York: G. Schirmer, Inc., 1906), "Scherzino," measures 21–28.

A song such as "Adversity," one of more than a hundred by Chadwick, is in the slow waltz tempo often heard in late-nineteenth-century American ballrooms and even approaches popular song style—transcending it, however, in a sensitive darkening of the harmony in the last measures (Example 6–5).

[5] Victor Yellin, "The Life and Operatic Works of George Whitefield Chadwick" (Ph.D. diss., Harvard University, 1957), 291.

EXAMPLE 6–5.   G. Chadwick, "Adversity," *Six Songs for Mezzo-Soprano or Baritone* (New York: G. Schirmer, Inc., 1902), No. 3, measures 1–11, 28–38.

Chadwick's stage works, seven operas and operettas, range in mood and manner from the playful pasticcio *Tabasco* (1894)—a "burlesque opera" (really an operetta) containing galops, marches (one on *NW CD 80266*), hymn tunes, waltzes, jigs, and a "plantation ballad,"—to the sobriety, drenched in a Saint-Saëns–like lyricism and laced with Wagnerian leitmotifs, of *Judith* (1901; see Example 6–6). Perhaps least deserving of its neglect is *The Padrone* (1912–13; refused by the Metropolitan Opera Company). This is a lone example of American turn-of-the-century *verismo*, its subject the exploitation of Italian immigrants in Boston by their dockside guarantors and landlords, the "padroni."

EXAMPLE 6–6. G. Chadwick, *Judith* (New York: G. Schirmer, Inc., 1901), Act I, scene 5 ("The Vision of Judith"), measures 54–62.

Chadwick, like Paine, became an academic, joining the faculty of the New England Conservatory in 1882 and serving as its director from 1897 until 1930. Horatio Parker (1863–1919) did likewise, becoming a professor at Yale University in 1894, after a musical apprenticeship under Chadwick and, from 1882 to 1885, Josef Rheinberger in Munich. Parker's most illustrious student said of him: "I had and have great respect and admiration for Parker and most of his music. It was seldom trivial." Charles Ives then went on to pinpoint Parker's strengths and weaknesses:

His choral works have a dignity and depth that many of [his] contemporaries, especially in the [field of] religious and choral compositions, did not have. Parker had ideals that carried him higher than the popular, but he was governed too much by the German rule. . . . Parker was a bright man, a good technician, but apparently willing to be limited by what Rheinberger et al and the German tradition had taught him.[6]

---

[6] Quoted in Charles E. Ives, *Memos*, ed. John Kirkpatrick (New York: W. W. Norton, 1972), 49, 115–116.

The major part of Parker's creative output was music for chorus, on medieval or religious subjects, all serious in tone. They range from *a cappella* Latin motets (*Adstant Angelorum Chori*, 1899; text by Thomas à Kempis) through occasional pieces (*Hymnos Andron*, ode on a Greek text for the bicentennial of Yale, 1901; *The Spirit of Beauty*, ode for the dedication of the Albright Art Gallery in Buffalo, 1905) to epitomes of the Victorian cantata (*The Dream King and His Love*, 1891) and oratorio for soloists, chorus(es), and orchestra (*The Legend of St. Christopher* [1897] and *Hora Novissima* [1893]). The last-named is considered Parker's masterpiece: an hour-long choral cantata in eleven movements, it is a setting of a portion (describing the glories of Heaven) of a twelfth-century Latin poem. The spacious work is all the more impressive for its disguise of the rigid tercets of the poem ("Hora novissima / tempora pessima / sunt, vigilemus") through long, leisurely, wide-ranging harmonic sequences, extensive fugues on expansive subjects, and masterly handling of the choral-orchestral medium. In one aria (No. 3, "Spe modo vivitur"), $\frac{4}{4}$ and $\frac{3}{4}$ measures in alternation—a "modern" novelty for the time—hide the metrical rigidity of the verses. Though its solo movements suggest Italo-French influence, the main atmosphere of *Hora Novissima*, true also of other choral works by Parker, is that of a German-American hymnic grandeur, rich in sound and powerfully stable in rhythm; this may be suggested by the several fugue subjects given in Example 6–7 or the very impressive organ Fugue in C minor, Op. 36, No. 3 (1893; *NW CD 80280*).

Arthur Foote (1853–1937) was unusual among the Second New England School composers in being trained exclusively in the United States: he studied with the influential Boston musician B. J. Lang (1837–1909) and with Paine at Harvard (where he was awarded in 1875 the first American M.A. degree in music). Though an organist (like most of his Bostonian colleagues), he wrote a polished, Brahmsian chamber music, and his most highly acclaimed compositions are for strings: the Suite in E for string orchestra (1907)—published by Arthur P. Schmidt in 1909 as *Suite in E dur für Streich-Orchester* (reprinted in *EAM 24*)—and *A Night Piece* (1922) for flute and strings.

Amy Marcy Cheney (1867–1944) conformed to the convention of her time and referred to herself as Mrs. H. H. A. Beach after her marriage to a socially prominent Boston physician. She did not conform to convention, however, in remaining merely a dilettante in music: both as a pianist and as a composer, she worked at truly professional levels and was unarguably the foremost American woman composer of her time; indeed, she was probably the most talented of the Second New England School. Her output is dominated by piano works—of great fluidity, facility, and frequent virtuosity—but it also includes a number of beguiling chamber compositions (notably a Quintet for Piano and Strings of 1907), an impressive symphony, the "Gaelic," of 1894–96 (full score in *3Centuries* 10, 191–411), and a piano concerto (each of the last two works the first of its kind by an American woman).

EXAMPLE 6–7. Fugue subjects by Horatio Parker. (*a*) *Hora Novissima* (London: Novello, Ewer and Co., 1893): (1) No. 4, measures 27–31; (2) No. 10, measures 1–5; (3) No. 11, measures 41–44. (*b*) *Adstant Angelorum Chori* (New York: G. Schirmer, Inc., 1899), measures 88–92. (*c*) *The Legend of St. Christopher* (London: Novello, Ewer and Co., 1898), p. 134 (Act III, scene 2).

Beach's songs number about 120; they were regularly performed by international recitalists such as the celebrated sopranos Emma Eames and the German-born Johanna Gadski (whose performance of *The Year's at the Spring*, from the *Three Browning Songs*, Op. 44 [1900], is on *NW LP 247*).

Yet another New Englander, though not a member of the circle of Bostonians we have been considering, achieved considerable renown in the late nineteenth century—the Connecticut-born Dudley Buck (1839–1909), who worked in Hartford, Chicago, and Boston as an organist and choir director but finally settled in Brooklyn. Buck's expansive choral works impressed audiences at Patrick Gilmore's World's Peace Jubilee of 1872 (*Festival Hymn*), the Third Triennial Festival of Boston's Handel and Haydn Society in 1874 (*The Forty-Sixth Psalm*), and the U.S. Centennial Celebration in Philadelphia in 1876 (*The Centennial Meditation of Columbia*; piano-vocal score in *3Centuries* 7, 283–319). Buck also seems to have been the first American to compose a full-scale organ sonata—the Grand Sonata in E♭ (1866; on *NW* CD 80280)—its last movement a climactic fugue and fantasy based on the tune of *Hail! Columbia*.

The composers of the Second New England School have been called "the Boston academics" (by Rupert Hughes, writing in 1900) and "the Boston classicists" (by Benjamin Lambord in 1915 and by Gilbert Chase in *America's Music*—in its first and second editions [1955 and 1966]; in the third, he termed them, along with some other contemporaries, "Conservative Eclectics"). But not all of them were academicians; nor, if the term "academic" is one of disparagement, were they all or always hidebound; nor were they all eclectics. And none of them was a "classicist" except in the sense that Brahms was a classicist: they belong to that wing of Romanticism that maintained a belief in the viability of the abstract instrumental forms. Like Brahms, and like Beethoven, Schubert, Schumann, and Mendelssohn before him, they wrote symphonies, sonatas, and chamber music; like Brahms, and like Handel, Bach, Mozart, and Beethoven before him, they wrote fugues and contrapuntal choruses. To the late nineteenth century such composers as Paine, Chadwick, Parker, Foote, Beach, and Buck might have seemed "classicists"; our perspective should let us rather see them in context as a group of Romantics of a particular persuasion.

EDWARD MACDOWELL

To another wing of Romanticism belonged Edward MacDowell (1860–1908). Not for him the abstract traditional forms of symphony and string quartet or the semiabstract forms of orchestral overture or choral cantata. In the tradition of the "New German School" of Liszt and Wagner, MacDowell saw himself as a "tone-poet," trusting in the evocative power of richly colored harmony (especially when the response was directed by a suggestive programmatic title) and narrative, ongoing forms rather than the problem-solving constructivism of imitative counterpoint or the balanced logic of sonata form. MacDowell believed that Bach was "one of the world's mightiest tone-poets [who, however,] accomplished his mission, not by means of the contrapuntal fashion of his age, but in spite of it," and, for MacDowell, Mozart's instrumental sonatas were "entirely unworthy of the author of *The Magic Flute*."[7] In the climate of aesthetic opinion in the later nineteenth century, these attitudes must have seemed truly progressive, truly Romantic, untinged by a "classicistic" bent. Not surprisingly, MacDowell was viewed, about the turn of the twentieth century, as America's foremost modern composer by those who shared his aesthetic—which is to say, all but a few.

Of Scotch-Irish descent, MacDowell was born in New York. In 1876 he was enrolled in the Paris Conservatory, but, dissatisfied, he moved to Frankfurt in 1878 for two more years of study as a pianist and composer; a powerful influence on him there was the conservatory's director, the composer Joachim Raff. Except for one trip to America to get married, MacDowell remained in Germany teaching, composing, and playing piano concerts until 1888, twelve years after leaving the United States. He then lived in Boston until 1896, when he accepted an appointment as the first professor of music at Columbia University. In 1904, after some unfortunately public wrangling with the university administration, MacDowell resigned. Mental illness, exacerbated by a horse-cab accident, prevented his composing any more; he declined more or less steadily until his death.

MacDowell's works were all composed between about 1880 (*Erste moderne Suite* for piano; First Piano Concerto) and 1902 (*Summer Wind* for women's chorus; *New England Idyls* for piano). They consist mainly of sixteen collections of "character-pieces" for piano, plus four suggestively titled sonatas and two concertos; forty-two songs for solo voice and more than twenty works for chorus; four symphonic poems; and two orchestral suites. All the favorite themes and images of Romanticism are explored: landscapes and seascapes (*Woodland Sketches*; *New England Idyls*; *Sea Pieces*), medieval romances (the symphonic poem *Lancelot and Elaine*; Piano Sonata No. 2 ["Eroica"], on the Arthurian legend); exoticism (Second ["Indian"] Suite for orchestra; *Les Orientales* for piano), and reminiscences of childhood (the piano pieces "From Uncle Remus" in *Woodland Sketches* and "Of Br'er Rabbit" in *Fireside Tales*). Shakespeare inspired a symphonic poem in two parts, *Hamlet and Ophelia*; Romantic poets are interpreted pianistically in *Six Idyls after Goethe* and *Six Poems after Heine*. In the latter collections, MacDowell printed the poems at the head of the music; to many others, he similarly added verses of his own to suggest the "programs" of individual pieces.

Considering the brevity of the composer's creative life (comparable to Foster's or Gottschalk's), a lack of stylistic development should not surprise us. More surprising, in view of MacDowell's extraordinary reputation about 1900 (the Columbia University trustees who hired MacDowell announced that he was "the greatest musical genius America has produced"), is the fact that having begun boldly as a composer of piano concertos of truly Lisztian sweep and breadth, he then tended to produce ever smaller, more rarefied

---

[7] MacDowell, *Critical and Historical Essays* (Boston: Arthur P. Schmidt, 1912; repr. New York: Da Capo Press, 1968), 265, 194.

works. After the Second Suite (1891–95), he wrote no more orchestral music. He never attempted opera. Of the later works, only the Third ("Norse") and Fourth ("Keltic") piano sonatas approach large-scale forms, described by MacDowell as "'bardic' rhapsodies" on their subjects. MacDowell ended up as a composer of concise, evocative genre pieces, surprisingly terse even when their subject matter is grandiose ("To the Sea," "From a German Forest"); basically very economical and clean of line, even fragile sometimes ("To a Wild Rose," "To a Water Lily," both among the *Woodland Sketches*); and very precisely fashioned and clearly projected.

MacDowell was himself a competent concert pianist, and some of his most successful piano music demands a virtuoso technique, such as the "Scherzo" of the Second Piano Concerto and various études, notably "March Wind" among the *Twelve Virtuoso Studies*, Op. 46 (1893–94; all twelve on *NW* CD 80206 and reprinted in *EAM* 29). More of it, however, is relatively easy to play and reveals MacDowell to be a late-nineteenth-century composer of "household music." He has also in common with that earlier American music a considerable nostalgia: Mellers has remarked trenchantly that MacDowell's best pieces "are a boy's view of the American past, looked back to from a premature middle age,"[8] as in the song collection *From an Old Garden*, "From an Indian Lodge" and "A Deserted Farm" in *Woodland Sketches*, and "From a Log Cabin" and "From Puritan Days" in *New England Idyls*.

The composer's vocabulary, which has often been likened to that of Edvard Grieg (whom MacDowell admired and to whom he dedicated the Third and Fourth piano sonatas), shares with Grieg's a remarkable integrity, homogeneity, and identifiability. The most characteristic features of MacDowell's style are its Wagnerian chromatic harmony, full of enharmonic modulations, appoggiatura dissonances, and inversions of triads, seventh chords, and ninth chords; its texture, which tends to be thick and fat and, although ranging freely over the entire keyboard, seems to emphasize the lower registers; and its ebb and flow of rhythmic activity and dynamic contour, both in a state of constant flux. Example 6–8, from "In Mid-Ocean" of the *Sea Pieces*, reported by MacDowell's first biographer to be one of the composer's own favorites,[9] shows most of these hallmarks of his style. In another vein, however, are many works that derive, no matter how indirectly, from dance meters, including Mendelssohnian scherzos. These are lighter in texture, "snappy" in rhythmic shape (often literally so: MacDowell's Scottish background was strong and "Scotch snap" iambs appear regularly), and less chromatic in harmony, though never wholly diatonic. Of this stamp are the "Uncle Remus" pieces of *Woodland Sketches* and *Fireside Tales*; the fifth of the Goethe *Idyls*; the third of the Heine *Poems*; "Humoreske" and "March" in the Four Pieces, Op. 24; also the "Love Song" and "In War-Time" movements of the "Indian" Suite for orchestra. To this genre also belongs "To a Wild Rose" (MacDowell's best-

[8] Wilfrid Mellers, *Music in a New Found Land* (New York: Knopf, 1965), 27.

[9] Lawrence Gilman, *Edward MacDowell, A Study* (New York: John Lane Co., 1909; repr. New York: Da Capo Press, 1969), 70–71.

EXAMPLE 6–8.   E. MacDowell, "In Mid-Ocean," *Sea Pieces*, Op. 55 (Boston: Arthur P. Schmidt, 1899), No. 8, measures 1–8.

known single work), although it is often mistaken for a "poetic" and sentimental piece, played with rubato not even hinted at in the score and at a tempo considerably slower than that indicated by the composer. Faintly reminiscent of Schumann's "Träumerei" in its design, it moves "with simple tenderness" through a long up-down dynamic arch to a final, strategically placed climax (though gentle and *pianissimo*) and a lone, conclusive iamb (Example 6–9).

OTHER CURRENTS

Inevitably, a reaction against the predominantly Germanic cast of post–Civil War art-music took place. It took two forms: some composers sought to refresh American music with an infusion of folkloristic elements; others turned enthusiastically to the new modes of expression emanating from Russia and France or to even more exotic sources.

Folklorism was hardly unknown to the European Romantics. A fascination with "primitive" peasant culture or with traditional anonymous folk forms was one manifestation of the Romantics' infatuation with the untram-

EXAMPLE 6–9.   E. MacDowell, "To a Wild Rose," *Woodland Sketches* (1896), Op. 51 (Boston: Arthur P. Schmidt, 1899), No. 1, measures 43–51 (conclusion).

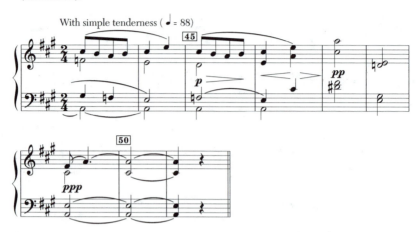

meled expression of innocent childhood, the "folk" being viewed as national or regional or even racial children. Ultimately, some American composers came to share this aspect of Romantic thought. The problem for them was: what was American musical folklore? A few men had given tentative hints of *their* answer to the question: MacDowell, Chadwick, even old Father Heinrich. Others now followed the hint: all too simplistically, they looked to the most "primitive" kinds of music in the nation, the music of American Indians and blacks. That there might be other "folkish" music in their past and under their very noses, that the vernacular tradition of popular music might provide a usable stock of invigorating source materials, seems not to have occurred to most of these composers. But then, had not Frédéric Ritter claimed that America had no "people's song"? Had not the great composer Antonín Dvořák (then in New York as director of the National Conservatory) suggested, in articles in both the *New York Herald* (December 15, 1893, one day before the premiere performance of his symphony "From the New World") and *Harper's New Monthly Magazine* (February 1895), that "inspiration for truly national [American] music might be derived from the negro melodies or Indian chants"? (Note that Dvořák did not recommend *borrowing* tunes from them, as is often wrongly claimed; only getting "inspiration" from them.)

Besides their (perhaps unconscious) Romantic interest in "folk" materials, some American composers of the late nineteenth century saw them as a nationalistic instrument as well, as had some Europeans earlier—the Russian "Mighty Five," for example. For to the degree that a nation's composers could borrow from indigenous musical sources, they were assured a certain national identity; their music would be different from that of other regions or nations. In late-nineteenth-century America, and indeed through the first three decades of the twentieth century, this aspect of folklorism exerted a strong pull on many composers, who yearned to free themselves from a European musical yoke, hoping to be somehow recognizably "American."

Aggressive steps in this direction were first taken by the Middle Westerner Arthur Farwell (1872–1952). He turned to Indian music in a number of arrangements, such as *Impressions of the Wa-Wan Ceremony of the Omahas* (1905) and *Three Indian Songs* (1908; *NW CD* 80463), and also original works based on Indian melodies, such as his *Navajo War Dance* for piano of 1905 (later, in 1937, arranged for unaccompanied chorus; both versions recorded on *NW LP* 213) or his String Quartet "The Hako" (1922).

Perhaps even more significant was Farwell's enthusiastic championing of new currents in American music through publication by the Wa-Wan Press, which he established in 1901. Looking about him, Farwell saw a "quantity of compositions ... and my own work, all blocked as to publication." He determined to "combine my work with that of these others—we were all in the same boat—and launch a progressive movement for American music, including a definite acceptance of Dvořák's challenge to go after our folk music."[10] When the Wa-Wan Press was sold to the firm of G. Schirmer in 1912, it had published works by thirty-seven composers. Among them were a number with folkloristic interests, especially in Indian and Negro music.

Matching Farwell's preoccupation with Indian music was the interest in black music of Henry F. B. Gilbert (1868–1928), composer of *Comedy Overture on Negro Themes* (ca. 1906; full score in *3Centuries* 11, 7–59) and *The Dance in Place Congo* (ca. 1908, revised 1916; on *NW CD* 80228). Other composers published by Wa-Wan Press who had less self-consciously "Americanist" aims were such composers as Arthur Shepherd (1880–1958) and Edward Burlingame Hill (1872–1960). Hill, who had been a pupil of both Paine and Chadwick, was one of the first Americans to feel the lure of the new French music of the 1890s, reflecting it in his own works and passing on a taste for it to his students at Harvard, among them Walter Piston and Virgil Thomson. In fact, Boston, long the ideological center of American music's Germanophilia, was at last beginning to rebel, beginning to see in the more or less individual styles of Camille Saint-Saëns, Vincent D'Indy, Gabriel Fauré, Claude Debussy, and Maurice Ravel a refreshing change. *The Musical Record* (issue of December 1890) quoted approvingly from the *Boston Home Journal*:

A plea for more French music and less German is demanded. ... We grope about in German mists ... and say it is purer and healthier than clear air and a blue sky. We pay American money for the privilege of submitting to German dictation.

---

[10] Quoted in Edward Waters, "The Wa-Wan Press: An Adventure in Musical Idealism," *A Birthday Offering to Carl Engel*, ed. Gustave Reese (New York: G. Schirmer, 1943), 214–33. "Wa-Wan" is an Omaha Indian word identified with a ceremony of peace, fellowship, and song.

Another composer trained at Harvard, John Alden Carpenter (1876–1951), shared Hill's partiality toward French music and showed it in the song cycle *Gitanjali* of 1913 (two songs on *NW* LP 247), the orchestral suite *Adventures in a Perambulator* (1914), and a Concertino for piano and orchestra (1915).

Charles Martin Loeffler (1861–1935) was a composer so hospitable to French poetry and the *raffinement* of the modern French musical style at the turn of the century that he has often been called a French-American. Actually, although perhaps born in Alsace, he came of German stock, and his formative years were spent successively in Russia, Berlin, and Paris. Trained as a violinist, he came to New York in 1881 but was snatched off to Boston by Major Henry Lee Higginson, patron of the brand-new Boston Symphony Orchestra. Loeffler sat at the first desk of the orchestra's violin section until 1903, when he resigned to devote himself to composition. An exquisite craftsman, almost obsessively revising his scores again and again, Loeffler published comparatively little; the music he did allow into print is of high polish and a kind of fin-de-siècle fastidiousness. Among his orchestral works, *A Pagan Poem* (1906) has proved durable. Many works combine voices and instruments; of these, perhaps the most perfectly realized is a setting of St. Francis of Assisi's *Canticum Fratris Solis* for soprano and chamber ensemble, commissioned for the first concert sponsored by the Elizabeth Sprague Coolidge Foundation at the Library of Congress (October 28, 1925). Typifying Loeffler's interest in unusual instruments and instrumentation are *La mort de Tintagiles* (1897; *NW* CD 80332), for full orchestra with solo viola d'amore, and two delicate chamber Rhapsodies for oboe, viola, and piano (1901); the latter are derived from a pair of songs that, like a number of others by Loeffler, add a string instrument (viola or violin) to the conventional piano accompaniment.

Another composer who was susceptible not only to the new French music but also to Russian, particularly that of Scriabin, was Charles T. Griffes (1884–1920). Considering that he spent four years in Germany (1903–7), it is not surprising that early works were Germanic; among them are some strong songs of 1909, to poems by Heine, Lenau, Eichendorff, and others. But Griffes must have considered these works as preliminary to his real beginnings; he later commented, "When I began to write [more maturely,] I wrote in the vein of Debussy and Stravinsky; those particular wide-intervalled disonances are the natural medium of the composer who writes today's music."[11] In a number of songs of 1912 to poems by Oscar Wilde, including *Symphony in Yellow* and *La Fuite de la lune*, Debussyesque harmony predominates, with however a rather firm, chiseled melodic line close to Ravel's (Example 6–10). Related in style are the *Roman Sketches* for piano (1915–16), which include the best known of Griffes's works, *The White Peacock* (*NW* CD 80310), later to be orchestrated delicately by the composer.

---

[11] Quoted in Edward Maisel, *Charles T. Griffes* (New York: Knopf, 1943, repr. with additions 1984), 112.

EXAMPLE 6–10. C. Griffes, *Symphony in Yellow*, Op. 3, No. 2 (New York: G. Schirmer, Inc., 1915), measures 1–8.

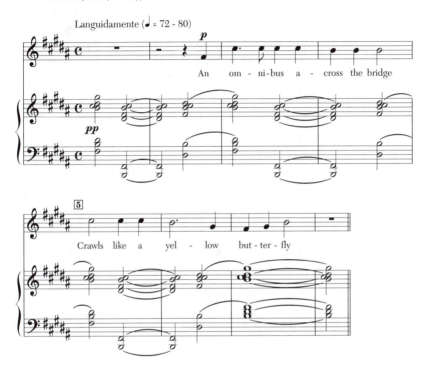

An interest in oriental music shows up in Griffes's *Pleasure Dome of Kubla Khan* (piano version 1912, revised and orchestrated 1917; on *NW* CD 80273). Oriental flavor is pervasive in a group of songs on pentatonic and hexatonic scales, *Five Poems of Ancient China and Japan*; and, for a pantomime titled *Sho-Jo* (1917), Griffes composed a unique score on Japanese themes, with orchestration

> as Japanese as possible: thin and delicate, and the muted string points d'orgue serve as neutral-tinted background, like the empty spaces in a Japanese print. The whole thematic material is given to the flute, clarinet, and oboe—akin to the Japanese reed instruments: the harp suggests the koto.[12]

Sho-Jo was never published; another unique dance-drama of the same year, *The Kairn of Koridwen*, scored for a chamber ensemble of flute, two clarinets, two horns, celesta, harp, and piano, had to wait for its publication until 1993. These works, related in their novel instrumentation to Schoenberg's *Pierrot Lunaire* (1912) and Stravinsky's *Histoire du soldat* (1918), must have been considered too exotic to be publishable.

---

[12] Ibid., 206

Near the end of his brief life, Griffes renounced the delicate shades of the French style and the Orient and produced several works of power, even ferocity, that suggest he was approaching a mature synthesis of the several styles in which he had successively immersed himself. Such works as the Piano Sonata (*NW CD 80310*—its conclusion given here as Example 6–11), a *Notturno* for orchestra, the *Poem* for flute and orchestra, and a group of *Three Poems* to texts by Fiona MacLeod, including the shattering song *The Lament of Ian the Proud* (all three on *NW CD 80273*), reveal Griffes as an American composer on the brink of greatness. The promise of these works was not to be realized, however: Griffes died at the age of thirty-five after a creative career of fewer than fifteen years.

EXAMPLE 6–11.   C. Griffes, Piano Sonata (New York: G. Schirmer, Inc., 1921), concluding measures.

BIBLIOGRAPHICAL NOTES

The following entries in *AmeriGrove* are helpful on the "institutional foundations" of cultivated-tradition music, 1865–1920: "Education in Music"; "Copyright"; "American Society of Composers, Authors and Publishers"; and "Unions, musicians'." The complete run of *Dwight's Journal* was issued in facsimile (New York: Arno Press, 1968); its predecessors and successors are discussed and comprehensively listed in the entry "Periodicals" in *AmeriGrove*.

The only substantial study of the Second New England School as a whole is Nicholas E. Tawa's *The Coming of Age of American Art Music: New England's Classical Romanticists* (New York: Greenwood Press, 1991). Published works on individuals include John C. Schmidt's *Life and Works of John Knowles Paine* (Ann Arbor: UMI Research Press, 1980), Victor Fell Yellin's *Chadwick, Yankee Composer* (Washington, DC: Smithsonian Institution Press, 1990), William Kearns's *Horatio Parker 1863–1919: His Life, Music, and Ideas* (Metuchen, NJ: Scarecrow Press, 1990), and Adrienne Fried Block's *Amy Beach: Passionate Victorian* (New York: Oxford University Press, 1998). Emphasizing the Boston context, Gunther Schuller's extensive liner notes for *NW* CD 80262 (Paine's Mass in D) are valuable, as are Herbert A. Kenny's notes for *NW* LP 268 (violin sonatas by Amy Beach and Arthur Foote). Wilma Reid Cipolla has published a useful catalogue of the works of Foote (Detroit: Information Coordinators, 1980).

RRAM includes, by Paine, three of his five chamber works, ed. John C. Schmidt (*RRAM* 17; recorded on Northeastern CD NR 219–CD); by Foote, *Music for Cello and Piano*, ed. Douglas B. Moore (*RRAM* 8); and by Loeffler, *[Ten] Selected Songs with Chamber Accompaniment*, ed. Ellen Knight (*RRAM* 16). *EAM* includes reprints of the scores of Paine's First Symphony (*EAM* 1) and his complete piano music (*EAM* 27); Chadwick's Second Symphony (*EAM* 4), *Judith* (*EAM* 3; regrettably, only a piano-vocal score), and songs to poems by Arlo Blake (*EAM* 16); Parker's *Hora Novissima* (EAM 2); and string-orchestra music by Foote (*EAM* 24) and his Piano Quintet (*EAM* 26).

MacDowell's *Critical and Historical Essays* (cited in note 7) reveal his attitudes clearly. Lawrence Gilman's study of 1908 (cited in note 9) remains the most extensive survey, but a most valuable overview is that of Irving Lowens in *High Fidelity/Stereo Review* 19/6 (1967): 61–72. Richard Crawford offers a revisionist view in "Edward MacDowell: Musical Nationalism and an American Tone Poet," *JAMS* 49/3 (Fall 1996): 528–60. Dolores Pesce has published valuable articles: on the symphonic poems (*AM* 4/4 [Winter 1986]: 369–89), the Lisztian legacy of the "Eroica" piano sonata (*The Music Review* 48/1 [February 1988]: 169–89), and the *Sea Pieces* (*AM* 10/4 [Winter 1992]: 411–40). Pesce is also author of the entry on MacDowell in the revised edition of *The New Grove*. Four collections of piano pieces are reprinted in *EAM* 8, five sets of the later songs in *EAM* 7; *EAM* 29 includes twenty-five études and two sets of *Technical Exercises*, all for piano.

Dvořák's incitements to American composers are discussed in two well-conceived anthologies: John C. Tibbetts, ed., *Dvořák in America* (Portland, OR: Amadeus Press, 1993), and Michael Beckerman, ed., *Dvořák and His World* (Princeton: Princeton University Press, 1993). Self-explanatory is Tara Browner's title "'Breathing the Indian Spirit': Thoughts on Musical Borrowing and the 'Indianist' Movement in American Music," *AM* 15/2 (Summer 1997): 265–84. Farwell is well introduced by Evelyn Davis Culbertson in "Arthur Farwell's Early Efforts on Behalf of American Music, 1889–1921," *AM* 5/2 (Summer 1987): 156–75. The entire output of Farwell's Wa-Wan Press is reprinted in facsimile, with a fine introductory essay by Gilbert Chase (New York: Arno Press, 1970).

Ellen Knight's *Charles Martin Loeffler: A Life Apart in American Music* (Urbana: University of Illinois Press, 1993) is unimpeachable and a valuable portrayal of the art-music scene on the East Coast, 1880–1930. Donna K. Anderson's biography *Charles T. Griffes: A Life in Music* (Washington, DC: Smithsonian Institution Press, 1993) is authoritative, based in part on her catalogue of his works (Detroit: Information Coordinators, 1977); she also wrote the notes for a generous group of works by Griffes recorded on *NW* CD 80273. (Songs by him are recorded on *NW* CD 80463, his complete piano works on *NW* CD 80310).

SEVEN

CHARLES IVES

The most extraordinary and significant American composer of the late nineteenth and early twentieth centuries was Charles Edward Ives (1874–1954). Because of serious physical (and probably psychological) problems, Ives composed very little after about 1921. It was only after he had stopped intensive composing and "cleaned house," as he put it—by having printed (at his own expense) the Second ("Concord") Piano Sonata (1920), a small book titled *Essays Before a Sonata* (1920), and a volume of *114 Songs* (1922)—that his music began to be known at all. Acceptance was slow even then: not until the 1940s were many works by Ives performed. After World War II, however, the number of performances, publications, and phonorecordings grew steadily, as did Ives's influence on other composers' thought. By the mid-1970s there were few who would have differed with the first sentence of this paragraph: Ives had become a kind of national hero musically, especially among the collegians of the nation. The first American society dedicated to an American composer was the Charles Ives Society (activated in 1973); and the first international conference organized around an American composer was the Charles Ives Centennial Festival-Conference (1974), cosponsored by Brooklyn College's Institute for Studies in American Music and Yale University's School of Music.

IVES'S LIFE AND CREATIVE CAREER

Ives grew up in Danbury, Connecticut. In later years he emphasized the importance of his father in shaping his musical thinking. George Ives (1845–94) was in some ways a typical late-nineteenth-century provincial American musician: leader of the Connecticut Heavy Artillery First Brigade Band during the siege of Richmond, he returned after the Civil War to Danbury, where he played the piano for dances and the organ for church services, gave music lessons, organized the Danbury Band, and was in general a musical jack-of-all-trades. He knew academic music theory and was a practical music arranger (but not a composer). Where he differed from other such town musicians was in his passionate curiosity about sound, his experimental attitude, and his open-mindedness; all these were to be reflected concretely in his son's music and musical thought. From the age of five, Charles Ives was taught by his father: "Bach and the best of the classical music, and the study of harmony and counterpoint etc., and musical history [and] the use of the ears ... and the mind to think for themselves and be more independent—in other words, not to be too dependent upon customs and habits."[1] Ives was thus exposed, through his father's diverse musical occupations, to the American vernacular musical tradition; his father initiated his training in music of the cultivated tradition; and he was encouraged toward an open-minded independence of musical thought that could encompass both traditions.

Ives's formal music study was completed at Yale (1894–98) under Horatio Parker, for whom he had a qualified respect (see p. 157) and from whom he got a rigorous training in advanced harmony, counterpoint, and "free" composition in the larger forms of the Classic-Romantic European tradition. Upon graduation, already aware that his music was "impractical" and sharing his father's view that "a man could keep his music-interest stronger, cleaner, bigger, and freer, if he didn't try to make a living out of it" (*Memos*, 131), Ives decided on a business career in life insurance. He pursued it with great success from 1898 until his retirement in 1930. He had been a paid professional organist since 1884, and, even after going into business, he continued to serve for a time (1898–1902) as a practicing musician—first as organist and choirmaster at the First Presbyterian Church in Bloomfield, New Jersey, then at Central Presbyterian Church in Manhattan. From 1902 on, howev-

---

[1] *Charles E. Ives: Memos*, ed. and with many appendixes by John Kirkpatrick (New York: W. W. Norton, 1972), 115.

My quotations of statements by Ives in this chapter come mainly from three sources: Ives's *Memos*, written in the early 1930s "to answer questions from people curious about his music" (as Kirkpatrick puts it); Charles Ives, *Essays Before a Sonata and Other Writings*, ed. Howard Boatwright (New York: W. W. Norton, 1962; revised as *Essays Before a Sonata, The Majority, and Other Writings*, 1970); and John Kirkpatrick, *A Temporary Mimeographed Catalogue of the Music Manuscripts and Related Materials of Charles Edward Ives 1874–1954* (New Haven: School of Music Library, Yale University, 1960). I shall refer to these hereafter as *Memos*, *Essays*, and *KirkCat*.

er, he limited himself to business, and his composing was done—furiously, at white heat—only during evenings, weekends, and vacations.

One can distinguish six periods of his life as a composer. The period of his *youth* in Danbury (to 1894) and that of his *apprenticeship* at Yale and his first four years in New York (1894–1902) were succeeded by a period of *innovation and synthesis* (1902–8). There followed ten years of *maturity* (1908–18) "following his marriage to Harmony Twichell, who reinforced in Ives the idealism, literary interests, and sense of the American past that were the subjects of much of his greatest music"; declining productivity in the period of his *last works* (1918–27); and an autumnal period of *revising* (1927–54), when, "in failing health, he began no new works and restricted his activities to editing and revising music already written."[2]

In all but the first and (most of) the last of these six periods, Ives lived a double life, to which some have attributed his debilitating illnesses: as (public) businessman and (private) composer. He claimed not to regret it; in a well-known statement, he said,

> The fabric of existence weaves itself whole. You cannot set art off in the corner and hope for it to have vitality, reality and substance. There can be nothing *"exclusive"* about a substantial art. It comes directly out of the heart of experience of life and thinking about life and living life. My work in music helped my business and my work in business helped my music."[3]

The demands on his time of business, the nonacceptance of his music, and the lack of direct involvement with the professional music world freed, or forced, the mature Ives to develop his own aesthetic. It was a unique one, and we must understand it if we are to view his music in proper perspective.

IVES'S MUSICAL THOUGHT

Ives prized what he called "substance" rather than "manner" in both music and its performance. "Manner" for Ives approached what others might call "technique," on the part of either composer or performer. "Substance ... is practically indescribable," he admitted, but it "suggests the body of a conviction which has its birth in the spiritual consciousness, whose youth is nourished in the moral consciousness, and whose maturity as a result of all this growth is then represented in a mental image" (*Essays*, 75). Common notions of beauty have nothing to do with it; it "has something to do with

---

[2] The periodization of Ives's life given here, and the quotations, are from J. Peter Burkholder, *All Made of Tunes: Charles Ives and the Uses of Musical Borrowing* (New Haven: Yale University Press, 1995), 6.

[3] Quoted first in Henry Bellamann, "Charles Ives: The Man and His Music," *MQ* 19/1 (January 1933): 45–58; partially reprinted in *Charles Ives and His World*, ed. J. Peter Burkholder (Princeton: Princeton University Press, 1996), 373–75.

character.... The substance of a tune comes from somewhere near the soul, and the manner comes from—God knows where" (*Essays*, 77). On this philosophical ground Ives based some startling concrete ideas. If substance has nothing to do with beauty or manner, then the very sound of music may be insignificant compared with the spirit in which it is produced. The roots of this idea are apparent in an anecdote about Ives's father:

> Once a nice young man ... said to Father, "How can you stand it to hear old John Bell (the best stone-mason in town) sing?" (as he used to at Camp Meetings)[.] Father said, "He is a supreme musician." The young man ... was horrified—"Why, he sings off the key, the wrong notes and everything ... and he bellows out and hits notes no one else does—it's awful!" Father said, "... Look into his face and hear the music of the ages. Don't pay too much attention to the sounds—for if you do, you may miss the music." (*Memos*, 132)

The music, the *real* music, resided in the humanity of its producer and in the spirit of its performer. This is why Ives could cry out passionately, "My God! What has sound got to do with music!" (*Essays*, 84). This is why, in recalling revivalist camp meetings, he could speak with affection of the aberrations in the hymn singing and of

> the great waves of sound ... when things like *Beulah Land, Woodworth, Nearer My God to Thee, The Shining Shore, Nettleton, In the Sweet Bye and Bye* and the like were sung by thousands of 'let out' souls.... If they threw the poet or the composer around a bit, so much the better for the poetry and the music. There was power and exaltation in these great conclaves of sound from humanity." (*Memos*, 132–33)

This is why he could even drive the argument to its logical conclusion and say, "That music must be heard is not essential—what it sounds like may not be what it is" (*Essays*, 84). And this in turn helps to explain a puzzling statement in the so-called postface to his *114 Songs*: "Some of the songs in this book ... cannot be sung,—and if they could perhaps might prefer, if they had a say, to remain as they are,—that is, 'in the leaf.' ... A song has a few rights the same as other ordinary citizens."

Ives's music often shares the variety, the apparent disorder, the coexistence of seemingly unrelated things of life itself; characteristic is a planar, heterophonic polyphony occasionally so dense that the ear simply cannot distinguish the separate strands. Ives analogized between such coexistent but independent ideas in his music and a game of tennis doubles—"Having four nice different men playing tennis together doesn't always destroy personality" (*Memos*, 50)—or the participants in the unstructured discussion and argument of a New England town meeting. In a sketch for the Second String Quartet (its movements titled "Discussions," "Arguments," and "The Call of the Mountains"), Ives described the work as a "S[tring] Q[uartet] for 4 men—who converse, argue (in re 'Politics'), fight, shake hands[,] shut up—then walk up the mountain side to view the firmament."

Ives seemed sometimes to view musical texture as a microcosm in which the coexistence of disparate elements does not threaten order any more than, say, in a forest the coexistence of different trees, rocks, mosses, flowers, animals, and insects threatens order; "order," in this instance, is an irrelevant concept, or one too narrowly conceived. Traditional devices for "ordering" musical form (repetitions, periodic phrase structure, classical tonality, and the like), although common enough in Ives's music, are not by any means always present. Ives could scoff at such devices, questioning for instance "how far repetition is an essential part of clarity and coherence.... If nature is not enthusiastic about explanation, why should Tschaikowsky be?" (*Essays*, 99). Ives admired quite another order-principle, which he expressed most clearly in his essay on Emerson:

> His underlying plan of work seems based on the large unity of a series of particular aspects of a subject rather than on the continuity of its expression. As thoughts surge to his mind, he fills the heavens with them, crowds them in, if necessary, but seldom arranges them along the ground first. (*Essays*, 22)

This is a fair description of the tumultuous congeries of materials, and their apparent lack of continuity, in many of Ives's works.

The subject matter of Ives's music was often life itself, or "a series of particular aspects" of it. The pages of his manuscripts are studded with verbal comments that particularize the diary-like outpourings of his musical mind. One of the most illuminating examples is found in a manuscript copy of the first movement of the First Piano Sonata:

> What is it all about—Dan S. asks. Mostly about the outdoor life in Conn[ecticut] villages in the '80s and '90s—impressions, remembrances, & reflections, of country farmers in Conn. farmland.
>
> On page 14 back, Fred's Daddy got so excited that he shouted when Fred hit a home run & the school won the baseball game. But Aunt Sarah was always humming *Where Is My Wandering Boy*, after Fred an' John left for a job in Bridgeport. There was usually a sadness—but not at the Barn Dances, with their jigs, foot jumping, & reels, mostly on winter nights.

In the summer times, the hymns were sung outdoors. Folks sang (as *Old Black Joe*)—& the Bethel Band (quickstep street marches)—& the people like[d to say] things as they wanted to say, and to do things as they wanted to, in their own way—and many old times … there were feelings, and of spiritual fervency! (*Memos*, 75)

Thus viewing some of his music as reminiscences, or re-creations in sound, of life experiences, many of which included actual music or were easily associable with specific kinds of music, Ives constantly used preexistent music in his works: most often it is not just baldly "quoted" (as has often been said) but instead is the very basis of the musical fabric, the preexistent material being reshaped, reformulated, reordered into a new, genuinely Ivesian music.[4] Traditional American hymn tunes, marches, patriotic songs, and bits of ragtime are the most commonly referred to, but material from other composers also appears, from Handel, Haydn, Beethoven, and Tchaikovsky to Foster, Mason, Bradbury, and Sankey. Such borrowings had nothing to do with nationalism, folklorism, or mere "local color"; they bespoke, rather, an acceptance of the validity, even divinity, of all things under God that Ives had known, felt strongly, and believed to have vitality and "substance." Without naming names, but perhaps referring to Arthur Farwell or Henry Gilbert, Ives wrote that the composer born in America and "so interested in 'negro melodies' that he writes a symphony over them [cannot, if he] has not been interested in the 'cause of the Freedmen'," produce something with substance, only with "color." Yet, "if a man finds that the cadences of an Apache war-dance come nearest to his soul," he can use them "fervently, transcendentally, inevitably, furiously, in his symphonies, in his operas, in his whistlings on the way to work [and] his music will be true to itself and incidentally American" (*Essays*, 79–80).

Just as no kind of musical source material was excluded from the Ives grab bag, no kind of performance was either. Ives found the mix-ups and mistakes, the wrong notes and off-key playing of amateur musicians just as "substantial" and thus in his view as "musical" as polished perfection, perhaps more so. Some of his music was planned to include such "mistakes": in a score-sketch for *The Fourth of July*, third of his *Holidays* for orchestra, Ives twice warned his copyist, "Mr. Price: Please don't try to make things nice! All the wrong notes are right. Just copy as I have—I want it that way…. Mr. Price: Band stuff—they didn't always play right & together & it was as good either way" (*KirkCat*, 11). Ives wanted performances of his music to have a sense of involvement in action, of spontaneity and vitality. When *Three Places in New England* was first played in New York (1931) and conductor Nicolas Slonimsky

---

[4] Ives's uses of preexistent music have been widely discussed, most thoroughly and perceptively by J. Peter Burkholder in *All Made of Tunes*.

apologized for a ragged performance, Ives reassured him, "Just like a town meeting—every man for himself. Wonderful how it came out!"[5] In some of his scores, Ives offers choices to the performer: a passage in the Second Sonata for violin and piano may be repeated "2 or 3 times *decr[escendo]* and *rit[ardando]* gradually," and a cadenza in the *Scherzo: Over the Pavements* is "to play or not to play! if played, to be played as not a nice one—but evenly, precise & unmusical as possible!" At the dramatic climax of the song *Charlie Rutlage* (about a cowboy whose horse "turned and fell with him"—and killed him), Ives tells the pianist, "In these measures, the notes are indicated only approximately; the action, of course, is the main point."

Among Ives's manuscripts is a *"take-off"*—a parody—of the Andante of Haydn's "Surprise" Symphony, marked "nice little easy sugar plum sounds"; and beneath some harmonically knotty measures of his *Robert Browning Overture* Ives wrote, "Browning was too big a man to rest in one nice little key ... he walked on the mountains not down a nice proper little aisle." "Nice" meant to Ives something weak, lily-livered, conventional, effetely genteel. He felt that people's ears and minds could encompass much more than they thought possible. He equated harmonic complexity with strength; remembering Thanksgiving as a holiday celebrating the early American colonists, he noted on one of the sketches for the *Thanksgiving and Forefathers' Day* movement of *Holidays* that "our forefathers were stronger men than can be represented by 'triads' only—these are too easy sounding" (*KirkCat*, 13).

Persons of a "nice" conformist gentility were epitomized by Ives with the name "Rollo," borrowed from a mid-nineteenth-century series of children's books about a boy insufferably priggish, proper, and perfect. About "Rollo," Ives made many sarcastic marginal comments in his manuscripts: in the Second String Quartet, "too hard to play—so it just can't be good music—Rollo"; in the *Browning Overture*, "R. B[rowning]'s mental workmanship is as sound logical & strong as easier plans [that] Rollo likes."

The other side of that ideological coin was Ives's own willingness to try anything musically, his rejection of dogmatic and exclusive musical concepts, and the embodiment of his theoretical speculations not in verbal tracts but in musical works. In the one essay that comes closer to being a rounded theoretical statement than anything else he wrote—"Some 'Quarter-tone' Impressions" (1925; reprinted in *Essays*)—Ives's open-mindedness is trenchantly expressed in two sentences: "Why tonality as such should be thrown out for good, I can't see. Why it should be always present, I can't see" (*Essays*, 117).

---

[5] Henry Cowell and Sidney Cowell, *Charles Ives and His Music* (New York: Oxford University Press, 1955; rev. 1969), 106. This was the first book-length biography of Ives, by a younger composer who was one of his earliest admirers (and wrote the passages on music in the book) and his wife, Sidney, who actually wrote most of it.

In sum, Ives believed in substance over manner, in spirit over technique; he believed in music as a re-creation in sound of life itself; he felt that passionate, honest self-expression, by composer or performer—no matter how unusually organized or "unmusically" handled—could create a unity far more significant than traditional order-principles; he could accept as source material any sort of musical idea, his own or others', cultivated or vernacular; he identified difficulty with strength; he abhorred the "nice," the easy-sounding, and the genteel; and he was willing to try anything. He had a streak of Transcendentalism in him—maybe more than a streak—but J. Peter Burkholder has argued persuasively that Transcendentalist thought was not a constant, let alone a lifelong persuasion, with Ives (contrary to almost every earlier writer on him); rather, that it crystallized briefly only toward the end of his creative life, as is reflected in the "Concord" Sonata and the book of *Essays Before a Sonata* of 1920, which, after all, were both—sonata and book—*about* a group of Transcendentalist thinkers and writers.[6]

IVES'S MUSIC

Ives was a fairly prolific composer, especially considering that his creative life was not particularly long (from 1886 to 1926) and that during most of it (from 1898 on) he had a full-time job apart from music. His works fall into five major categories:[7]

1. *Orchestral music*
    a. Large orchestra: Four numbered symphonies plus the four-movement *New England Holidays* (or simply *Holidays*) and the unfinished *Universe Symphony* for multiple orchestras; two three-movement "sets," the first one best known by its subtitle, *Three Places in New England*; the twenty-minute-long *Robert Browning Overture*; and various incomplete works.
    b. Small orchestra (chamber or "theater" orchestra): Youthful popular-entertainment pieces such as *Holiday Quickstep*, *"Country Band" March*, and *Overture and March "1776"*; "songs with or without voice" such as *The Pond, The Rainbow*, and the last movement ("In the Night") of the *Set for Theatre Orchestra*; a pair of "contemplations" (*The Unanswered Question* and *Central Park in the Dark*); and the *Scherzo: Over the Pavements*; plus other, slighter works.

---

[6] J. Peter Burkholder, *Charles Ives: The Ideas Behind the Music* (New Haven: Yale University Press, 1985), especially chap. 3 ("Ives and Transcendentalism: A Second Look").

[7] Summarized here after *KirkCat* and James B. Sinclair's recent, definitive *Descriptive Catalogue of the Music of Charles Ives* (New Haven: Yale University Press, 1999). The datings of works by Ives cited in this chapter—a matter of considerable discussion among scholars and critics—conform to those in Sinclair's catalogue.

2. *Chamber music*

About fifteen complete compositions, including four violin-and-piano sonatas; two string quartets; a trio for violin, cello, and piano; and other sets and single movements, the best-known being *From the Steeples and the Mountains*, for trumpet, trombone, and four sets of eight bells each, and *Hallowe'en*, for string quartet, piano, and optional drum.

3. *Keyboard music*

About forty works, mostly for piano, although two well-known ones are for organ: *"Adeste Fideles" in an Organ Prelude* and *Variations on "America."* Of the two major piano sonatas, the second ("Concord, Mass., 1840–1860") is probably Ives's most famous work; a third sonata, briefer but very original in shape, is called *Three-Page Sonata*. Besides a series of single-movement experimental "studies," there are three unusual larger late works: *The Celestial Railroad*, *Varied Air and Variations*, and, for two pianos tuned a quarter tone apart, *Three Quarter-Tone Pieces*.

4. *Choral music*

   a. Sacred works, notably a series of short anthems and psalm settings (from the early *Psalm 67* to the late *Psalm 90*), the semisacred *Three Harvest Home Chorales*, and the sprawling Victorian concert cantata *The Celestial Country*; many other choral compositions for church use that are lost.

   b. Glees and other part-songs, only a few of which, from the Yale years, survive (such as *A Song of Mory's* and *The Bells of Yale*).

   c. Other secular works for unison chorus (sometimes *divisi*) and varied instrumental ensembles, the best-known of which are *He Is There!*, *Lincoln, the Great Commoner*, and *Majority* or *The Masses*.

5. *Solo songs*

Composed throughout Ives's career, from *Slow March* (ca. 1887 or 1888) to *Sunrise* (1926, Ives's last newly composed work; on *NW* CD 80463), they total about 150, plus some 30 revised with different texts.

The extraordinary diversity of Ives's music is well seen in his songs. Some sense of the amazement with which other composers greeted the book of *114 Songs* is conveyed in Aaron Copland's breathless summary:

Almost every kind of song imaginable can be found—delicate lyrics, dramatic poems, sentimental ballads, German, French, and Italian songs, war songs, songs of religious sentiment, street songs, humorous songs, hymn tunes, folk tunes, encore songs; songs adapted from orchestral scores, piano works, and violin sonatas; intimate songs, cowboy songs, and mass songs. Songs of every character and description, songs bristling with dissonances, tone clusters, and "elbow chords" next to songs of the most elementary harmonic simplicity.[8]

Clearly, one cannot hope to describe briefly such an oeuvre. A close look at one or two songs can, however, suggest some aspects of them, and of Ives's mature music in general.

[8] "One Hundred and Fourteen Songs," *Modern Music* 11 (January–February 1934): 59–64; reprinted in *Charles Ives and His World*, 307–12.

Two Little Flowers (1921; *CRI* CD 675) is superficially simple, sweet, uncomplicated. The text, written by Ives and his wife (Harmony Twichell Ives), tells of "two little flowers" seen in the backyard on sunny days; other blossoms may be beautiful, but "fairest, rarest of them all are Edith and Susanna" (young Edith Ives and her playmate). The atmosphere of both text and setting is that of the nineteenth-century sentimental household song, and initially the melody moves predictably in smooth contours of pitch and rhythm (Example 7–1 [a]). Suddenly, however, three tiny rhythmic jolts occur, at "one in green," "passing fair," and "ever rare"; they point up, in a subtle way, the syntactical divisions of the verses, and they prepare for the wholly original melodic climax with its downward vaulting of an octave and a third (unless the singer can't make it; and Ives offers a simpler alternative) and its suspensive pause on "all" (surprisingly climactic, since it *is* pitched low) (Example 7–1 [b]).

EXAMPLE 7–1.   C. Ives, *Two Little Flowers*. Copyright 1935 Merion Music, Inc.; used by permission. (*a*) Measures 1–10. (*b*) Measures 23–27.

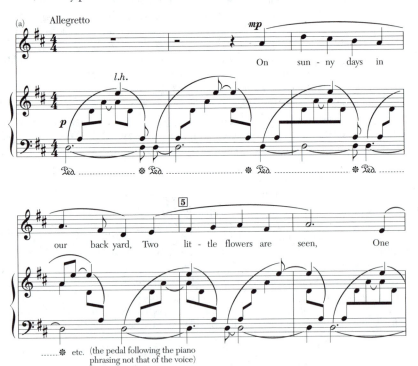

The accompaniment of *Two Little Flowers* has its subtleties, too: initially sounding like a commonplace arpeggiated vamp, it turns out to revolve in groups of seven (not eight) eighth notes, and rather than outlining a conventional triadic harmony it is quintal, spanning the intervals D–A–E. The D–E whole-tone interval is the basis for the harmonic events through two-thirds of the song, as each of these notes moves outward in whole-tone motion: D–E, C–F♯, A♯–G♯. Approaching the end, Ives shifts to a V-of-ii, V-of-V, I$^6_4$ pattern, full of harmonic energy (measures 23–24) but returns to the whole-tone idea at the climax: superimposed on the surprising, dark chord at the word "all" is an even more surprising C–E third high in the piano, as if the B♭–D interval (implied in the voice part in measure 24) were going to move upward (through C–E and D–F♯) to the piano's E–G of the next measure but couldn't wait. The song ends with chords that sound like ii–V–I, but each contains the critical whole-tone interval: E–D, A–B, D–E.

Even this brief analysis makes the music seem more complicated than it sounds: the total effect of the song is that of simplicity and "familiarity"; yet, the commonplace is everywhere avoided, and we recognize a work in which the familiar is transcended.

Less traditional by far in melody, harmony, and rhythm is *Cradle Song* (1919), given in its entirety as Example 7–2, although within its tiny nine-measure span it speaks just as evocatively and directly as *Two Little Flowers*. Each of the three phrases of the vocal line comes to rest on G♯, establishing that pitch class as one tonal center, although the scale basis of the melody might suggest F♯. The accompaniment is less certain about its tonality, finally settling on A (but G♯ appears here, too, linking voice with accompaniment). No systematic harmony is present, except an avoidance of simple triads: there are Debussyesque bichords (measures 1, 9), added-sixth chords (1, 2, 9), Wagner's "*Tristan* chord" with complications (5), and other simultaneities inexplicable as single sonorities without taking into account linear aspects (e.g., the high F♯ of measure 4, part of a treble line beginning in measure 3 and moving C♯–E–F♯–G♯). Harmonically, the song seems to "float" in a void, an effect consonant with the text. The rhythm of the piece confirms this effect, as it sways gently between $^2_4$ and $^6_8$, the $^2_4 \, \mathord{\scalebox{1}{$\downarrow$}} = {}^6_8 \, \mathord{\scalebox{1}{$\downarrow$}}$ prescription precluding any sense of regular meter at all and allowing the rhythm to float, unmoored to a metric anchor. In measure 8, voice and accompaniment are really in different meters, the voice part ending on a disguised $\frac{3}{4}$ measure, the accompaniment continuing in its broad $\frac{6}{8}$.

EXAMPLE 7–2. C. Ives, *Cradle Song*. Copyright 1935 Merion Music, Inc.; used by permission.

Notes: End song on $\frown$; This chord may be repeated very quietly at the end of verse sung last.
*It will be observed that a ♩ of the $\frac{2}{4}$ measure is a ♩ of the $\frac{6}{8}$ and not a ♩.

One of the lengthiest and most powerful songs, *General William Booth Enters into Heaven* (1914; revised ca. 1933; *CRI* CD 675), based on a poem by Vachel Lindsay, exemplifies Ives's use of "imitative dissonance" and of musical borrowing. The hectic, militant atmosphere of the text, which celebrates the fanatic revivalism of the first commanding general of the Salvation Army, leads Ives to begin the song in the piano with a typical marching band's drumbeat: the whack of the snare drums and the thud of the bass drum (lagging a bit behind) are projected in dissonant clusters (Example 7–3 [a]). Where Lindsay's poem quotes parenthetically (from a Salvation Army hymn, "Are you washed in the blood of the Lamb?"), so does Ives, though he uses the revival hymn tune *Cleansing Fountain* ("There is a fountain filled with blood"), and his equivalent of parenthesizing it is to present it in a key far removed from the tonal sphere of the context. This melody, redolent of American gospel hymnody in general, is developed in all kinds of ways in the course of the song; other borrowed melodies are the introduction to James A. Bland's minstrel-show song *Oh, Dem Golden Slippers* (at the mention of a banjo; measures 52–55, piano part) and trumpet calls (at the mention of trumpets, measures 69–72, and of marching, measures 103–5). One of the most moving passages of the song (Example 7–3 [b]) finds the singer circling "round and round" on a three-note figure, the pianist's right hand circling similarly but in a two-note cycle, while in the middle of the accompaniment, strangely askew, the *Cleansing Fountain* melody winds its tranquil way. *General William Booth* ends with a haunting, parenthetically off-key statement of *Cleansing Fountain* set to hymnbook harmony; then the drumbeats, lower pitched as if in the distance, fade —"as a band marching away," wrote Ives in the manuscript.

EXAMPLE 7–3.   C. Ives, *General William Booth Enters into Heaven.* Copyright 1935 Merion Music, Inc.; used by permission. (*a*) Measures 1–10. (*b*) Measures 82–91.

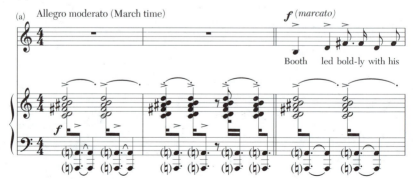

big bass drum (Are you washed in the blood of the Lamb? Are you

washed in the blood of the Lamb, of the Lamb?)

(b) Adagio

Je - sus came from the court-house door,— Stretched his hands

a - bove the pass - ing poor.— Booth saw

Other notable songs by Ives include *Charlie Rutlage* (1920 or 1921), a cowboy ballad in which (in addition to the crashing piano climax I cited above) Ives turns to unpitched rhythmic declamation; *The Circus Band* (originally for piano, 1894?; the song adaptation 1899? or later), with much prancing band music and a striking, subtle text by Ives; *Serenity* (1919?; *CRI* CD 675), to a tranquil poem by Whittier in which a virtually monotonous chantlike vocal line is spun out against an otherwordly, "floating" harmonic oscillation; *Walking* (ca. 1902–7; *CRI* CD 675), in which the diffuse, cloudy overtones of church bells are captured subtly, and also the giddy syncopations of ragtime. In *Majority* (originally for chorus and orchestra, ca. 1915–16; the solo-song arrangement 1921), with its perfervid Whitmanesque text (by Ives), there is an equation between "the Masses" of the poem and massive chords (as many as fifteen notes) built in clusters of massed seconds; these must be played either with the forearm or a board or with the help of a second pianist. *Soliloquy* (1913?; revised ca. 1933) is subtitled "a study in 7ths and other things" and systematically explores nontraditional harmonies and retrograde motion.

The bulk of Ives's choral music was for the church: some forty sacred choruses remain. Best-known among these is a setting of *Psalm 67* (ca. 1898), not bitonal (as often claimed) but based on a most unconventional harmonic plan. Most awesome is an eleven-minute setting of *Psalm 90* (reconstructed, or recomposed, by Ives in 1923–24) for choir, organ, and bells, underscored throughout by a low C in the organ. A number of the choral works are, in effect, compositional études; they reveal the experimental vein of Ives's thought, akin to Darius Milhaud's studies in bichords and Béla Bartók's in scales and intervals. Among these are *Psalm 24* (ca. 1900; revised ca. 1914–15), which is based on mirror-image counterpoint and systematic interval expansion (Example 7–4 [a]) and the *Processional "Let There Be Light"* (ca. 1902–3; revised ca. 1907 and the late 1930s), whose harmonies are based on consistently changing structural intervals; Example 7–4 (b) shows the harmonic plan of its core passage (P = perfect; A = augmented; M = major; m = minor). Devout, but not conventionally so, are *Three Harvest Home Chorales* (ca. 1902 in part; revised and completed 1912?–16) for chorus, brass ensemble, and organ—"a kind of outdoor music," said Ives, in which the tangled yet harmonious coexistence of "the trees, rocks, and men of the mountains in days before machinery" is expressed through radically independent counterpoint among the three sound components.[9] *Lincoln, the Great Commoner* (ca. 1920–21), for (mostly unison) chorus, orchestra, and piano, exceeds even the *Chorales* in density of texture and heterophonic polyphony; quotations from *The Battle Hymn of the Republic, Hail! Columbia, The Red, White & Blue* ("O Columbia, the gem of the ocean"), *The Star-Spangled Banner, America,* and *The Battle Cry of Freedom* appear in almost cinematic collage, and more than once the voices split into a tumult of shouted tone clusters, a kind of choral noise of overwhelming power.

The shorter instrumental works of Ives, like the songs, are remarkable for their diversity and individuality: each seems to create its own expressive world; taken together, they cover an immense range of affective ends, achieved by an equally broad spectrum of technical means.

Among the shorter piano pieces are various Studies (1907?–14?), part of an incomplete series of twenty-seven (perhaps after Chopin's 27 *Études*), including *Some South-Paw Pitching* (No. [21]; *CRI* CD 811), a showpiece for the left hand under right-hand variants of Foster's *Massa's in de cold ground* and *The Anti-Abolitionist Riots in the 1830's and 1840's* (No. [9]; *CRI* CD 810, 811). Interesting for its relationship to Schoenberg's twelve-tone

---

[9] The quotations are from a letter of May 18, 1937, from Ives to Lehman Engel (conductor of the Madrigal Singers in New York) as published in Gertrude Norman and Miriam Lubell Shrifte, eds., *Letters of Composers* (New York: Grosset & Dunlap, 1946), 345–46.

EXAMPLE 7–4. "Compositional études" of Ives. (*a*) *Psalm 24* (Bryn Mawr, PA: Mercury Music Corp., 1955), measures 1–6; used by permission. (*b*) *Processional "Let There Be Light"* (New York: Peer International, 1955), harmonic plan of measures 9–18; used by permission.

row technique (of which Ives knew nothing) is the theme of the *Varied Air and Variations* (ca. 1914–19 and ca. 1923–29): likened by Ives in the manuscript to "the old stone wall around the orchard—none of those stone eggs are the same size," it is made up of four interlocked, rowlike chromatic series. (Ives may have intended the title of this piece as reading secretly *Very Darin' Variations*.) The *Three-Page Sonata* (ca. 1907–14, rev. ca. 1923; *CRI* CD 811), actually a substantial eight-minute work, compresses the traditional four-movement form into a dramatic first section, a lyrical slow section, and a last section alternating clangorous march motifs and jerky ragtime rhythms. Another large one among the "shorter" piano pieces is *The Celestial Railroad* (ca. 1919–23), a perfect example of Ives's reworking material into varied forms and media: titled after a short story by Nathaniel Hawthorne, it is an expansion of the "Hawthorne" movement of the "Concord" Piano Sonata, which itself borrows from Ives's *"Country Band" March*; and Ives later orchestrated *The Celestial Railroad* as the second movement of his Symphony No. 4.

Free from the necessity to accommodate his music to conventional performance media, Ives wrote works for an astonishing variety of small instrumental ensembles, from the aforementioned *Three Pieces* for two pianos tuned a quarter tone apart (1923–24) to the combination of brass and bells of *From the Steeples and the Mountains* (ca. 1901–7). Many of the chamber works derived from, or were rebuilt into, other pieces. Among those originally conceived for small orchestra ("theater orchestra") are two well-known works of 1906 often performed separately but considered by Ives as a pair—*The Unanswered Question* and *Central Park in the Dark*—the first "A Contemplation of a Serious Matter," the second "A Contemplation of Nothing Serious." *The Unanswered Question*, for trumpet, four flutes, and strings, has an elaborate metaphysical program explaining the three sound components: the strings represent "the silence of the druids," the trumpet asks "the perennial question of existence," to which the flutes—"Fighting Answerers"—attempt (unsuccessfully) to find a satisfactory response. But no questions, answered or not, need be asked about the exquisitely delicate balance in which the three components are independently suspended: the strings move slowly and placidly in spacious, diatonic harmony from beginning to end; the trumpet periodically sounds a disturbing, not-quite-repetitive atonal phrase from another musical world; and the flutes, increasingly raucous and agitated, provide a dynamic arc for the whole structure.[10] Few works by Ives so immediately and movingly bring us in touch with his faith in the harmonious coexistence of disparate elements. *Central Park in the Dark* is for a totally different ensemble (piccolo, flute, oboe, clarinet, bassoon, trumpet, trombone, percussion, two pianos, and strings) but similarly juxtaposes quiet sounds (this time atonal) with what Ives called "off tunes and sounds" (diatonic and based on ragtime and popular-song sources, especially the well-known coon song *Hello, Ma Baby* [1899]).

Ives was capable of musical contemplation not only of cosmically serious matters but also of earthly comic ones. *Hallowe'en* (ca. 1911), for string quartet and piano with drum ad lib., is a cacophonic spoof combining the humorous surprise of April Fools' Day jokes with the crude pranks of Hallowe'en. The first violin plays in the key of C, the second in B, the viola in Db, the cello in D; the piano is atonal. Seldom do accents coincide. Only eighteen measures long, the piece is to be repeated three or four times, omitting or altering various parts each time until the last, when, with a drum adding

[10] The "atonal" trumpet phrase was not always thus. For its history, including Ives's revision of it before the work's first publication (1953), see H. Wiley Hitchcock and Noel Zahler, "Just What Is Ives's Unanswered Question?" *[MLA] Notes* 44/3 (March 1988): 437–43; a different "answer" is proposed, with a revelation of the source of the work's title, by Wayne D. Shirley in "Once More Through *The Unanswered Question*," *ISAM Newsletter* 18/2 (May 1989): 8–9, 13. The revised Ives Society critical edition (New York: Peer International, 1985) includes both the original (1906) and the later "atonalized" trumpet parts.

to the general din, the tempo is to be "as fast as possible without disabling any player or instrument." Hardly apparent, as the work rushes by in a blur, is the rigorous contrapuntal texture of the string parts—"canonic," said Ives, "not only in tones, but in phrases, accents, and durations or spaces" (*Memos*, 91). The *Scherzo: Over the Pavements* (1906–13)—with the cadenza "to play or not to play"—is for piccolo, clarinet, bassoon, trumpet, three trombones, cymbal, drum, and piano. It grew out of a work called *Rube Trying to Walk 2 to 3!!*, which suggests its emphasis on polyrhythmic counterpoint; this reaches a knotty climax (Example 7–5) in the second section of the A B C–[cadenza]–C′ B′ A′ form. Ives has the last laugh on the struggling performers in a comic ending, which sees them all together in an oom-pah, oom-pah vamp on a simple C major triad—a mocking concession to "Rollo."

EXAMPLE 7–5.   C. Ives, *Scherzo: Over the Pavements*, measures 59–61. Copyright 1954 by Peer International Corporation. Used by permission.

Ives combined several groups of chamber pieces into "sets," with several pieces in each. One such set, a three-movement group of which the second is lost, he called *Tone Roads* (1915?). No. 3, for woodwinds, brass, strings, piano, and chimes, is interesting for its repetitions of sections at varied tempos; its use of quarter-tone inflections; and the "tone road" of the chimes, which approximates a twelve-tone row and is treated at the beginning like a medieval isorhythmic-motet *color*, its pitch pattern repeated, but in a varied rhythmic pattern (see "X" in Example 7–6).

In more conventional media, and somewhat more conventional forms, are the sonatas for piano and for violin and piano, and the symphonies.

Besides the *Three-Page Sonata*, Ives composed two numbered piano sonatas and began a third, now lost. The Piano Sonata No. 1 ("Concord") (ca. 1913–19; *NW* CD 80378; *CRI* CD 810 [parts performed by Ives]) is a big four-movement work reflecting Ives's admiration for some of the American literary giants of the mid–nineteenth century. Howard Boatwright writes, in

EXAMPLE 7–6.   C. Ives, *Tone Roads*, No. 3 (chimes part only), measures 1–12. Copyright 1952 by Peer International Corporation. Used by permission.

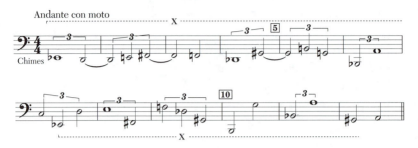

his edition of the *Essays Before a Sonata* (which Ives wrote in conjunction with the music):

> For some composers, one work, more than any other, may become a channel through which the streams of philosophical concept, musical technique, and style flow in singular unity. For Charles Ives, the Concord Sonata was such a work. It … is representative of Ives' highest achievements in richness of harmony and freedom of rhythm. (*Essays*, xiii)

Ives himself spoke of the work (*Essays*, xxv) more diffidently, saying it was "a group of four pieces, called a sonata for want of a more exact name, as the form, perhaps substance, does not justify it." He described the four movements as "impressionistic pictures of Emerson and Thoreau, a sketch of the Alcotts, and a scherzo supposed to reflect a lighter quality which is often found in the fantastic side of Hawthorne." The first movement, "Emerson," is a musical portrait of immense power and density; although based on a sonata-form idea, it reminds one of Ives's view of Emerson's own "plan of work" (see p. 175). The scherzo, "Hawthorne,"—closely related to that author's tale "The Celestial Rail-Road"—rushes by in a blur, except for one quiet, slow passage colored by two-octave-wide cluster-chords vibrating sympathetically high in the treble, and a couple of other passages in which Simeon Marsh's hymn *Martyn* appears in hushed, halting, hymnbook harmony. "The Alcotts" evokes a gentle variant of *Martyn* (its tune related to the opening motif of Beethoven's Fifth Symphony, which appears throughout the "Concord" Sonata) and several "old Scotch airs," one of them related (coincidentally?) to the minstrel-show song *Stop That Knocking at My Door* (1843). The final movement, "Thoreau," is deceptively calm in spirit; it builds to a single climax, then unwinds in a long denouement synthesizing materials from earlier movements and closes with a hauntingly tentative final gesture. Said Ives of the "Concord" Sonata,

Every time I play it or turn to it, [it] seems unfinished.... Some of the passages now played haven't been written out ... and I don't know as I ever shall write them out, as it may take away the daily pleasure of playing this music and seeing it grow and feeling that it is not finished. (*Memos*, 79–80)

Besides a "Pre-First" Violin Sonata, Ives wrote four sonatas for violin and piano between about 1907 and 1916. More than any similar group of Ives's works, these all seem interrelated, citizens of the same musical world. All are in three movements; all end with hymn-tune finales, each in a "cumulative setting" (to use Peter Burkholder's term for a form in which a piece begins with "development" of fragments of a borrowed tune and gradually works toward a close in which the tune is revealed in its simple entirety); and all are characteristically "easy" pieces (by Ives's standards). Sonatas Nos. 1 and 3 are abstract; Sonata No. 2 offers portraits of "Autumn" and a square dance ("In the Barn"), plus a nostalgic view of the mounting intensity of a camp meeting ("The Revival"). Sonata No. 4, entirely based on hymn tunes, is called "Children's Day at the Camp Meeting."

"The Revival" movement of Sonata No. 2 is an ingeniously worked piece, a sort of freely unfolding stream of variations on the old hymn tune *Nettleton* (or *Hallelujah*; see p. 109). The ingenuity and integrity with which Ives "recomposed" such borrowed material can be suggested by comparing a passage from "The Revival" (Example 7–7 [a]) with the opening of the third movement of String Quartet No. 1 (Example 7–7 [b]). In the former, Ives sets the tune as a bitonal canon at the tritone over cloudy pedal points on the tonic and the dominant of the respective keys; in the latter, he invents a new ending and sets the tune to a cross between Schubertian and barbershop harmony.

The First String Quartet (1896) is an assemblage from earlier organ pieces composed for Center Church on the New Haven "Green" (where Ives served as organist during his years at Yale). The first movement is a fugue—on Lowell Mason's *Missionary Hymn* (see p. 68), soon combined contrapuntally with Oliver Holden's *Coronation* (see p. 133 n)—which Ives had written as an assignment for Horatio Parker. (Ives later adapted the quartet movement to form the slow movement of the Fourth Symphony.) The Second String Quartet of ca. 1907–14 (see p. 175) is a thoroughly mature and "tough" work, one of the most striking examples of Ives's involving the performers in "Discussions" and "Arguments" (the titles of the first two movements). The third movement ("The Call of the Mountains") finds the arguments resolved and the participants "viewing the firmament," to material based on the hymn tunes *Nettleton* and *Bethany* (Mason's "Nearer, my God, to thee") and the change-ringing carillon melody *Westminster Chimes*.

In his symphonies (as in his violin sonatas), Ives seems to have been mindful of traditional broad, formal procedures, and indeed in many ways these demonstrate clearly Ives's relation to, and respect for, the Classic-Romantic

EXAMPLE 7–7.   Two uses of the hymn tune *Nettleton* by Ives. (*a*) Sonata No. 2 for violin and piano (New York: G. Schirmer, Inc, 1951), third movement, measures 22–23. (*b*) String Quartet No. 1, third movement, measures 1–4. Copyright 1961 and 1963 by Peer International Corporation. Used by permission.

art-music tradition. The early First Symphony (ca. 1898–ca. 1902), in four movements, is unmistakably modeled on Dvořák's "New World" Symphony (1893); Ives was consciously displaying his mastery of the tradition. The Second Symphony (ca. 1902–7, rev. ca. 1909), in five movements, introduces American vernacular tunes, which are borrowed for every one of its main themes; Ives turns to European sources and idioms (from Bach, Brahms, and Wagner) only in transitional passages. The symphony's last movement is the most "Ivesian," with pileups of borrowed tunes (*Camptown Races*, another more lyric melody reminiscent of *Old Black Joe*, country-fiddle-style counterpoints, *The Red, White & Blue*, and the wake-up trumpet-call *Reveille*). Ives made the conclusion all the more "Ivesian"—in a dubiously tasteful change introduced late in his life—by changing the very last chord from a tonic F major triad to a raucous eleven-note squawk. As Burkholder has put it, however, the Second Symphony is "both a pinnacle and a turning point, Ives's most successful attempt to integrate American melody into European forms."[11]

The Third Symphony (ca. 1907–11), slighter in scoring and scope but more original in form and feeling, is characterized by its subtitle, "The Camp Meeting"; it is a hymnic three-movement work in which both first and last movements, based on American hymn tunes, are powerful, persuasive cumulative settings.

Between the Third Symphony and the completion of the Fourth, Ives wrote three other works of symphonic proportions. The work originally entitled *A Symphony: New England Holidays* (ca. 1913–23) is a gathering of four separate orchestral movements into a kind of American *Four Seasons* (recalling the spirit, though by no means the style, of Antonio Vivaldi's *Le quattro stagioni* concertos): *Washington's Birthday, Decoration Day, The Fourth of July*, and *Thanksgiving and Forefathers' Day*. The First Orchestral Set (*Three Places in New England* [1908–23]) is cast in one of Ives's favorite multimovement orders: slow-fast-slow. Its first movement, *The 'St. Gaudens' in Boston Common*, is a brooding piece, with some of Ives's most subtle, highly developed use of older melodies. Inspired by the monument of Augustus Saint-Gaudens commemorating Colonel Robert Shaw and the regiment of black Americans he led during the Civil War, Ives based his music on Foster's *Old Black Joe*, Root's *Battle Cry of Freedom*, and Work's *Marching Through Georgia*. Example 7–8 shows one moment when Ives finds a common denominator ([a] in the example) between the phrase "I'm coming" in Foster's song and "[Hur]rah! hurrah!" in Work's, combines that material with the chorus ("The Union forever, Hurrah boys, Hurrah!") of *The Battle Cry of Freedom* (b), fashions an ostinato bass (c_1) from a pentatonic motive (c_2) common to the two Civil War songs, and underscores the whole with a traditional military band's drumbeat (d). The second movement of *Three Places—Putnam's Camp*—combines the gay, brassy music of a late-nineteenth-century Fourth of July picnic at a Revolutionary War campsite (complete with the village brass band) and a child's fantasizing about the apparition nearby of figures from the Revolution; the middle section finds the drumbeat of Example 7–8 (d) going along at two different speeds in the proportion $o = d.$ in a famous example of polytempo. The movement is full of hilarious gaiety and ends in a fine Independence Day burst of pyrotechnical pandemonium and a rather besotted blast of *The Star-Spangled Banner*. The last movement of *Three Places* begins in murmuring tranquility, with an autumnal evocation of hymn singing heard across a New England river: *The Housatonic at Stockbridge*.

[11] *All Made of Tunes*, 135.

EXAMPLE 7–8.   C. Ives, *Three Places in New England,* first movement ("The 'St. Gaudens' in Boston Common"), measures 66–69. Quoted by permission of Mercury Music Corporation.

Ives's Second Orchestral Set (1912–15) is also in three movements (again slow-fast-slow): *An Elegy to Our Forefathers, The Rockstrewn Hills Join in the People's Outdoor Meeting,* and *From Hanover Square North, at the End of a Tragic Day, the Voice of the People Again Arose.* The last movement, largely built around the gospel hymn *In the Sweet By-and-By,* builds to perhaps the most spine-tingling climax in all of Ives's work. A Third Orchestral Set and a visionary *Universe Symphony* (see *Memos,* 106–8) were left unfinished.

Ives labored off and on between about 1916 and 1923 at his Fourth Symphony, one of the most grandly conceived works in the history of American music. Scored for a big orchestra and chorus plus a "distant choir" of strings and harps and a special "battery unit" of percussion, it had to wait until April 26, 1965, for its premiere performance (under Leopold Stokowski, assisted by two other conductors). Two movements had been performed in 1927, and program notes for that performance were written by Henry Bellamann, obviously from information supplied by Ives:

> This symphony … consists of four movements,—a prelude, a majestic fugue, a third movement in comedy vein, and a finale of transcendent spiritual content. [The order of the second and third movements was later reversed.] The aesthetic program of the work is … the searching questions of What? and Why? which the spirit of man asks of life. This is particularly the sense of the prelude. The three succeeding movements are the diverse answers in which existence replies. … The fugue … is an expression of the reaction of life into formalism and ritualism. The succeeding movement [i.e., the movement ultimately made the second] … is a comedy in the sense that Hawthorne's Celestial Railroad is a comedy.[12]

Ives added to Bellamann's notes a word on the last movement: it is "an apotheosis of the preceding content, in terms that have something to do with the reality of existence and its religious experience."[13]

The four movements of the Fourth Symphony resolve into two pairs. The Prelude, with its choral plea ("Watchman, tell us of the night / What the signs of promise are"), leads to the "comedy" movement (the scherzo), in which nostalgic song passages are constantly interrupted by strident marches, rags, square-dance tunes, and patriotic ditties—not just separately but sometimes all at once. The third-movement fugue (derived from the First String Quartet's first movement)—stately, hymnic, suffused with 16- and 32-foot organ pedal color—serves as preparation for the last movement, which is even more complex in texture than the second, but a tapestry of murmurs rather than shouts. It begins mysteriously, like a distant march, with a complex percussion pattern that never ceases, is wholly independent of the rest of the movement's music, and, lingering after the orchestra (with wordless voices) dissolves, fades off finally in the distance. For all its growing, then ebbing, complexity, the movement breathes a spirit of utter tranquility. Ives wrote no more profoundly conceived and perfectly realized music than this.

---

[12] Quoted in John Kirkpatrick's extensive preface to the score published in 1965 (New York: Associated Music Publishers), viii. (A revised Ives Society critical edition is forthcoming.) Kirkpatrick's preface includes a detailed account of the background of the symphony and identification of its many musical borrowings.

[13] First published in Ives's lengthy "Conductor's Note" to the second movement of the Fourth Symphony, as printed in Henry Cowell's *New Music* 2/2 (January 1929); repr. in the 1965 edition cited in note 12; Ives's comment is also in *Memos*, 66.

Seen against the background of a nineteenth-century American musical culture sharply divided between cultivated and vernacular traditions, Ives's historical position is a unique one. Alone among his contemporaries, he embraced both traditions without reservation: his works emphatically declared that in its vernacular tradition American music had an artistically usable past; they also embodied the highest aspirations of, and mastery over, the Euro-American cultivated tradition. Moreover, Ives's open-mindedness and freshness of musical imagination were to be a continuing challenge to American composers after 1920. Ives is seen by many as the fountainhead of a new tradition in American music, a basically experimental, pathfinding one. In a few sentences that are rather Ivesian in their bluntness and humor, Virgil Thomson, commenting on "the composer who lives by non-musical work," remarked,

> [He] makes up his music out of whole cloth at home. He invents his own aesthetic. When his work turns out to be not unplayable technically, it often gives a useful kick in the pants to the professional tradition. The music of...Charles Ives did that very vigorously indeed.[14]

BIBLIOGRAPHICAL NOTES

The literature on Ives mushroomed immensely after the mid-1980s; even the useful, extensive bibliography in *AmeriGrove* (1986) is, at the end of the twentieth century, only a beginning. Cited here are mostly works published since the mid-1980s that seem especially significant and potentially durable.

To the basic documentary works on Ives cited in note 1 must be added James B. Sinclair's superlative *Descriptive Catalogue of the Music of Charles Ives* (cited in note 7); also Vivian Perlis's register of *The Charles Ives Papers* (New Haven: Yale University Music Library, 1983), a detailed listing of the all-important Ives Collection at Yale University. Neither replaces, but both complement, Kirkpatrick's *Temporary...Catalogue* (see note 1). Other important book-length studies include Perlis's compilation of reminiscences, *Charles Ives Remembered: An Oral History* (New Haven: Yale University Press, 1974); Frank R. Rossiter's well-documented *Charles Ives and His America* (New York: Liveright, 1975); J. Peter Burkholder's *Charles Ives: The Ideas Behind the Music* (cited in note 6), Stuart Feder's "psychoanalytic biography" *Charles Ives: "My Father's Song"* (New Haven: Yale University Press, 1992), and Jan Swafford's lengthy biography *Charles Ives: A Life with Music* (New York: W. W. Norton, 1996).

Among studies of Ives's music, two that complement each other are *Charles Ives and the Classical Edition*, ed. Geoffrey Block and J. Peter Burkholder (New Haven: Yale University Press, 1996)—emphasizing Ives's roots in the Euro-American

[14] *The State of Music*, 2nd ed. (New York: Vintage Books, 1962), 85. In his *American Music Since 1910* (New York: Holt, Rinehart & Winston, 1971), 22–30, Thomson discusses "The Ives Case" rather less charitably.

Classic-Romantic tradition—and Philip Lambert's *The Music of Charles Ives* (New Haven: Yale University Press, 1997)—emphasizing, and essentially limited to, post-tonal analysis of Ives's "experimental" music. Larry Starr's *A Union of Diversities: Style in the Music of Charles Ives* (New York: Schirmer Books, 1992) finds a common stylistic denominator in Ives's musically inclusive eclecticism. Geoffrey Block's *Ives: Concord Sonata* (Cambridge: Cambridge University Press, 1996) is a useful approach to a major work; another is William Brooks's "A Drummer-Boy Looks Back: Percussion in Ives's *Fourth Symphony*," *Percussive Notes* 22/6 (September 1984): 4–45. My own *Ives* (Oxford, 1977) was reprinted (with a few additions) under the more helpful title *Ives: A Survey of the Music* (ISAMm 19 [1983]).

Especially valuable as analytic studies are (in chronological order of publication): William Brooks's "Unity and Diversity in [the first movement of] Charles Ives's Fourth Symphony," *Yearbook for Inter-American Musical Research* 10 (1974): 5–49; J. Peter Burkholder's "The Critique of Tonality in the Early Experimental Music of Charles Ives," *Music Theory Spectrum* 12 (Fall 1990): 203–23; and composer Larry Austin's discussion of his "Realization and First Performance of Ives's *Universe Symphony*," in *Ives Studies*, ed. Philip Lambert (Cambridge: Cambridge University Press, 1997), 179–232; the last-named book includes other valuable essays, two of which are cited below.

Diverse approaches to Ives and his music include such works as Maynard Solomon's "Charles Ives: Some Questions of Veracity," *JAMS* 40/3 (Fall 1987): 443–70 (a provocative challenge to Ives's datings of his works and to traditional claims of his "modernity"); Judith Tick's "Charles Ives and Gender Ideology," in *Musicology and Difference: Gender and Sexuality in Music Scholarship*, ed. Ruth A. Solie (Berkeley and Los Angeles: University of California Press, 1993), 83–106; Thomas Brodhead's revelatory redating of the Fourth Symphony's second movement, "Ives's *Celestial Railroad* and His Fourth Symphony," *AM* 12/4 (Winter 1994): 389–424; J. Peter Burkholder's *All Made of Tunes* (cited in note 2); Gayle Sherwood, "Redating Ives's Choral Sources," in *Ives Studies*, 77–101 (prelude to a book dating all Ives's works); Philip Lambert's "Ives's *Universe*," in *Ives Studies*, 233–59 (exploring Ives's position, philosophically as well as musically, in the "timeless tradition of universal contemplation and cosmological speculation"); H. Wiley Hitchcock, "'A Grand and Glorious Noise!': Charles Ives as Lyricist," *AM* 15/1 (Spring 1997): 26–44 (on Ives's song texts, not only his own but also those of others as "edited" into lyrics by him); and Hitchcock, "Charles Ives's *114 [+15] Songs* and What He Thought of Them," *JAMS* 52/1 (Spring 1999): 97–144.

part three

Between the World Wars (1920–1945)

EIGHT

THE 1920s

REACTIONS TO THE CLASSIC-ROMANTIC TRADITION

The period surrounding World War I, roughly from 1910 to the mid-1920s, was a critical one for Western music in general and for American music as part of the larger scene. Many young European composers felt that the main Classic-Romantic tradition had reached a crisis and that means had to be found to renovate it. Various reactions to the tradition, more or less violent, became apparent during this period, which was one of the most turbulent aesthetically and stylistically in the history of Western music. Paris, especially, was a cauldron of ferment; but so was Vienna, for so long a center of the tradition. Composers of other nationalities shared the same sense of crisis, partly out of a nationalistic urge for musical independence from central European domination.

In some works, barbs of satire and ridicule were aimed at the hyper-expressivity and bombast of the tradition. Thus Claude Debussy slyly quoted Wagner's *Tristan und Isolde* in "Gollywog's Cakewalk," the slightest piece in his *Children's Corner* suite (1906–8), with a tongue-in-cheek instruction to the pianist to play "avec une grande émotion." Erik Satie became virtually a professional musical satirist. The young Darius Milhaud reacted against the inordinate length and grandiloquence of the post-Romantic symphonies and operas with three-minute symphonies (1917) and *opéras minutes* (1927).

Another kind of reaction was that of an outright rejection of the tradition and an attempt to revolutionize musical expression, especially through media related to the machine age: this was the aim of the Futurist group of artists and intellectuals, at first centered in Italy (where not many musicians were involved), then in Paris, where concerts of noise instruments—hissers, exploders, cracklers, buzzers, screamers, and the like—were given.

Older, established composers such as Ralph Vaughan Williams, Richard Strauss, Gabriel Fauré, and Jean Sibelius, not sharing the sense of crisis of their younger colleagues, more or less unconsciously extended the tradition. But the group of composers in Vienna around Arnold Schoenberg sought *consciously* to extend it beyond past limits, particularly its element of chromaticism. Considering Classic-Romantic tonality a procrustean bed ill fitted to the increasingly chromatic vocabulary of melody and harmony, they wrote an ultrachromatic music that avoided traditional tonality and approached a free atonality. In another sort of evolutionary extension of the tradition, the Czech composer Alois Hába began working with microtones, intervals smaller than the traditional semitones of the twelve-note tempered scale.

Finally, an immense number of works of the period suggest attempts to revitalize and enlarge the tradition by exotic and atavistic borrowings from musical cultures distant in space, spirit, or time. Thus the primitivistic manner of Igor Stravinsky's *Le Sacre du printemps* (1913) and *Les Noces* (1917–23); the delving into the heart of folk music of Béla Bartók; and the popular-music idioms of urban cafés in Milhaud's *Le Boeuf sur le toit* (1920), Arthur Honegger's Concertino for piano and orchestra (1925), and Francis Poulenc's Sonata for piano duet (1918). Related in impulse to these works, which looked to primitive, folk, and popular music for a fresh note, were others that looked back, beyond the Romantic era, to the Classical, Baroque, and even earlier periods in Western music for inspiration: Sergei Prokofiev's "Classical" Symphony (1916–17); Stravinsky's *Pulcinella* (1920) and Octet for wind instruments (1923); Schoenberg's chamber *Serenade*, Op. 24 (1923), and neo-Classic *Suite* for piano, Op. 25 (1924); Maurice Ravel's *Le Tombeau de Couperin* (1914–17); Ottorino Respighi's *Antiche arie e danze* (1916–31) and *Concerto gregoriano* (1922).

In sum, the atmosphere of European music just before and after World War I was charged with various currents and crosscurrents of progressivism: "New Music" and "Modern [or "Modernist"] Music" marched under a variety of banners. This atmosphere was characteristic also of the United States, slightly later, between the end of World War I and the economic collapse of 1929. An era of unprecedented prosperity in the United States, the 1920s were notable in American music as years when progressive currents could flourish, and did; years when youthful composers could afford to spurn the achievements of the generation that preceded them, and did.

The older generation, composers in their forties and fifties in the decade after World War I, continued to write in an essentially nineteenth-century manner, to get performances and continued respect. Chadwick, Hill, Frederick Converse (1871–1940), Rubin Goldmark (1872–1936), and Daniel Gregory Mason (1873–1953) carried forward the traditionalism, the solid craft if not notable inventiveness, of the Second New England School. Converse, who studied with Paine and Chadwick and returned to Boston after completing his training in Munich with Rheinberger, saw his opera *The Pipe of Desire* produced by the Metropolitan Opera in 1910, the first by an American to be performed there (full score in *3Centuries* 6, 107–326); his symphonic poem *The Mystic Trumpeter* (1904) has maintained its early reputation as his best work (nominally, if not given many performances). Goldmark came to be best known as a teacher: among his students were George Gershwin and Aaron Copland, and in 1924 he was named head of the composition department of the Juilliard School of Music. Mason, grandson of Lowell Mason, achieved a considerable success with his overture *Chanticleer* (1926; *NW* CD 80321) but wielded more influence as a writer on music for the general public—not necessarily a positive influence, since he was both an arch-conservative and a rather unpleasantly anti-Semitic one in an era when Jewish patrons, impresarios, performers, and composers (of both concert and popular music) were becoming increasingly significant in American music circles.

Some slightly younger composers were gaining reputations as the inheritors of the American cultivated-tradition ideal of a music of serious import and large-scale edification—"Americans who work along more or less conservative lines and make no attempt to write anything departing from general types of European music."[1] Among those who were to maintain some prominence during and after the decade of the 1920s was Howard Hanson (1896–1981), a composer of big rhetorical works such as the choral cantata *The Lament for Beowulf* (1925), the Second ("Romantic") Symphony (1930), and the opera *Merry Mount* (1933; after Hawthorne; one scena for baritone solo recorded on *NW* LP 241). Hanson was also immensely influential as the director of the Eastman School of Music in Rochester, New York, from 1924 to 1964 and as an officer of many national music organizations. Others in this group were Leo Sowerby (1895–1968), an organist-composer who provided much viable music for his instrument, and Randall Thompson (1899–1984), who became strongly identified with works for chorus—notably the witty, satirical settings of texts from H. L. Mencken's *American Mercury* entitled *Americana* (1932; *NW* CD 80219), the cantata *The Peacable Kingdom* (1936), and a very widely performed, unaccompanied *Alleluia* (1940).

[1] Henry Cowell, introducing his anthology *American Composers on American Music* (1933; 2nd ed. New York: Frederick Ungar, 1962), 9. It is interesting to compare Cowell's "grouping of composers according to accomplishments and ideals" with Aaron Copland's earlier grouping of "America's Young Men of Promise," *Modern Music* 3/3 (March–April 1926): 13–20.

A few other composers leavened their academic heritage with sprinklings of folk- or popular-music idioms. Charles Wakefield Cadman (1881–1946), interested in the lore of native Americans, published a set of *Four American Indian Songs* in 1909 (*NW CD 80463*); one of them, *From the Land of the Sky-Blue Water*, achieved great popularity. His opera *Shanewis, or the Robin Woman*, based on the life of an Indian woman with whom he had given lecture-recitals, was enough of a success at the Metropolitan in 1918 that the company produced the work again the next year; it was the first American opera so honored. John Powell (1882–1963) delved in Anglo-American and black-American folk song, as in his most successful work, the *Rhapsodie Nègre* (1918; *NW CD 80228*); Emerson Whithorne (1884–1958) and Henry Eichheim (1870–1942), in oriental music. Eichheim made no fewer than five trips to the Far East; his *Oriental Impressions* (1918–22), in piano, chamber, and orchestral versions, was widely performed during the 1920s, and later compositions by him, such as *Java* (1929) and *Bali* (1933), were among the first by an American to include Asian instruments in their scoring. John Alden Carpenter's ballet scores *Krazy Kat* (a "jazz pantomime" of 1921; *NW CD 80228*) and *Skyscrapers* (1923–24) were indebted to some rhythmic aspects of American dance music. The strains of the pseudojazz of white America's ballrooms and dance halls were useful for Louis Gruenberg (1884–1964) in a number of works that were highly thought of during the period, among them *The Daniel Jazz* (1924) for tenor and chamber ensemble, *Jazz-Suite* (1925) for orchestra, *Jazzettes* (ca. 1925) for violin and piano, and *Jazzberries* (1925?) for piano solo. Gruenberg's best dramatic work in this vein was the opera *The Emperor Jones*, produced at the Metropolitan in 1933. (The aria *Standin' in the Need of Prayer*, sung by Lawrence Tibbett, who created the opera's title role, is on *NW LP 241*.)

More notable than these, however, more characteristic of the era of the "Roaring '20's," were younger composers grappling with the new ideas, the new materials, the new approaches to organizing sound that had been proposed by the European leaders of "New Music" (Stravinsky, Schoenberg, the sassy young French composers, the Futurists) and by the new American "urban folk music" of jazz. As Aaron Copland, along with George Gershwin the most prominent young composer of the decade, wrote, "Contemporary music as an organized movement in the U.S.A. was born at the end of the First World War."[2]

NADIA BOULANGER; AARON COPLAND

Copland (1900–1990) was one of a large group of American composers to become the student, in Fontainebleau and Paris, of the remarkable musician and teacher Nadia Boulanger (1887–1979). Boulanger's unique combination

---

[2] *Our New Music* (New York: McGraw-Hill, 1941), 137.

of exacting severity and liberating encouragement (the latter given in exquisitely precise proportion to the pupil's efforts) was to be a magnet for several generations of young Americans; in the 1920s, as one of her pupils of that decade has commented, "What endeared [her] most to Americans was her conviction that American music was about to 'take off,' just as Russian music had done eighty years before."[3] She was capable of training young composers without dictating one exclusive style: the measure of her phenomenal gifts as a teacher was the variety of personal styles developed in her atelier. Nevertheless, the example of Stravinsky was most often set before her students, and certainly Copland's work in the 1920s reveals the impact of Stravinsky more than that of any other composer. It also reveals a preoccupation with "Americanism"—with a national identity. The models of Farwell and Gilbert, who had turned to black- and Native American materials, seemed irrelevant, perhaps especially to Copland, a Brooklyn-born Jew; that of Ives was as yet unknown. Besides, as Copland recalled later,

> Our concern was not with the quotable hymn or spiritual: we wanted to find a music that would speak of universal things in a vernacular of American speech rhythms. We wanted to write music on a level that left popular music far behind—music with a largeness of utterance wholly representative of the country that Whitman had envisaged.[4]

In a few works written after his return from three years (1921–24) in Paris under "Mademoiselle," Copland seemed to have imagined that the jazzy rhythms and blue notes of contemporary dance music would provide sources for the music he sought to write. The first of these works was *Music for the Theatre* (1925), a twenty-minute suite for small orchestra in five symmetrically ordered movements with a "motto" theme appearing in each (Example 8–1). The scale of the work, its chamber medium, its orderly structure, and its crisp unsentimental tone all reflect the precise anti-Romanticism of Copland's French experience. Its crackling sonorities, bichordal harmonies, and jerky motoric rhythms suggest Stravinsky and the younger French composers. Its declamatory "motto" (Example 8–1 [a]), on the other hand, has been related to Copland's Jewish backgrounds; and the rhythmic and pitch inflections especially of the second ("Dance") and fourth ("Burlesque") movements relate to dance music of the 1920s such as the Charleston (Example 8–1 [c]). Rather similar in manner but larger in conception is a Concerto for piano and orchestra of 1926–27. In later works of the 1920s, Copland gave up the limited expressive range of dance music and turned to a more abstract, less self-consciously "American" manner—but one equally hard, lean, and rhythmically

[3] Virgil Thomson, *Virgil Thomson* (New York: Knopf, 1966), 54.
[4] *Music and Imagination: The Charles Eliot Norton Lectures, 1951–1952* (Cambridge: Harvard University Press, 1952), 111.

EXAMPLE 8–1.   A. Copland, *Music for the Theatre* (1925). (*a*) "Motto," first movement, measures 2–5 (trumpet part only). (*b*) First movement, measures 14–17. (*c*) Second movement, measures 1–7 (bassoon part only). © Copyright 1932 by The Aaron Copland Fund for Music, Inc. Copyright Renewed. Reprinted by permission of Boosey & Hawkes, Inc., Sole Licensee.

knotty—in a *Dance Symphony* (1929; three movements adapted from the earlier ballet *Grohg*); a trio, *Vitebsk* (1929); a *Symphonic Ode* (1927–29); and a set of *Piano Variations* (1930).

For many, the *Piano Variations* mark the summit of Copland's achievement (even acknowledging such better-known later works as *Appalachian Spring* or *Fanfare for the Common Man*). Based on a theme that has a certain hard-edged grandeur (Example 8–2 [a]), the work, from the

outset, treats the piano anti-Romantically as a basically percussive instrument, with hammers (which of course it is). The continuous set of twenty
close-knit, mainly clangorous variations culminates in an overwhelmingly

EXAMPLE 8–2. A. Copland, *Piano Variations* (1930). (*a*) Theme, measures
1–11. (*b*) Variation 2, measures 21–24. © Copyright 1932 by The Aaron Copland
Fund for Music, Inc. Copyright Renewed. Reprinted by permission of Boosey &
Hawkes, Inc., Sole Licensee.

resonant coda. Certain variations suggest that Copland had by this time absorbed the principle of Schoenberg's tone-row technique, perhaps unconsciously, into his own lucid, often brittle, and generally rhythm-dominated style (Example 8–2 [b]). The *Piano Variations* seem to mark a synthesis by Copland of his American background, his French training, and a range of expression and means of tonal organization related to the Viennese School; they come very close to achieving Copland's ideal in the 1920s of a music that would "speak of universal things ... with a largeness of utterance wholly representative of the country." (Copland's own masterly performances of the *Piano Variations*, as recorded in 1945, and his *Four Piano Blues*, begun in the 1920s, are on *NW LP 277*.)

Many other young composers hied themselves to Boulanger's studio in the 1920s: Virgil Thomson, Roy Harris, Walter Piston, Elliott Carter, Robert Russell Bennett, Marc Blitzstein, and others. These, however, did not gain the early prominence of Copland; their works belong more to the story of American music after the 1920s, and I shall refer to them in later chapters.

EDGARD VARÈSE

The "organized movement" in contemporary music in the 1920s spoken of by Copland was reflected in the many groups founded to give concerts of new music, such as the series produced between 1928 and 1931 by Copland and Roger Sessions; in the contributions of some major conductors who performed new works, notably Serge Koussevitzky (1874–1951), conductor of the Boston Symphony Orchestra from 1924 to 1949, and Leopold Stokowski (1882–1977), conductor of the Philadelphia Orchestra from 1912 to 1938; and in the formation of composers' groups, especially the League of Composers (which sponsored the important journal *Modern Music*, 1924–46), the International Composers' Guild (1921–27), and the Pan American Association of Composers (1928–34).

Founder of both the Guild and the P.A.A.C., and prominent as a leader of the vanguard of American music in the 1920s (and again in the 1950s), was the Paris-born composer Edgard Varèse (1883–1965), who came permanently to New York City late in 1915. In the 1920s Varèse founded no school of composers, but with his first American work, *Amériques* (1918–22)—a screaming, squalling, earthshaking and earthquaking orchestral tumult—he offered a challenge to musical tradition that was reiterated with each of his important compositions of the 1920s (*Offrandes, Hyperprism, Octandre, Intégrales, Arcana*) and the celebrated all-percussion piece *Ionisation* (1930–31).

Varèse's name has sometimes been linked with the Futurists. He stood alone, however: he was uninterested in a revolutionary "noise music" or "machine music," but he did believe in the legitimacy of *any* sound as a vehicle for musical expression, and (as he put it in a lecture at Princeton University,

September 4, 1959) he became "a sort of diabolic Parsifal looking not for a Holy Grail but for a bomb that would blow wide open the musical world and let in sound—all sounds, [including those] at that time, and sometimes even today, called 'noise.'" As early as 1917 he was writing of a "dream of instruments obedient to my thought, which with their contribution of a blossoming of unsuspected timbres will... bend to the demands of my inner rhythm."[5]

That dream was to be realized, but only in the electronic era of the 1950s; in the 1920s Varèse had to content himself with conventional instruments—assembled, however, in unusual groupings and supplemented with a large number of so-called percussion instruments, some not so conventional. Important among the latter were sirens, whose arching curves of sound embodied and projected one of Varèse's most important concepts: that of music as a spatial art, as "moving bodies of sound in space." Sirens are employed not only in *Amériques* but in *Hyperprism* (1922) and *Ionisation* as well. Their use, and that of an immense variety of drums, cymbals, gongs, tam-tams, bells, chimes, wood blocks and castanets, slapsticks and rattles, chains and anvils, bespoke Varèse's definition of music simply as "organized sound," limited in no way to traditional notions of "musical tone" as opposed to "noise."

Varèse's music of the 1920s is marked especially by an emphasis on sheer sonority, often unconventional—by writing at the extremes of an instrument's range, for example, or by dispersing "chords" through a huge registral spectrum. Stridency of expression is characteristic: the performance-indication *"hurlant"* (yelling, howling, roaring) is not uncommon. Traditional harmonies are unusual, yet the music is not organized by anything like Schoenberg's chromatic tone rows. Individual sounds, pulsating with a life of varied intensities and changing timbres, are important, as at the opening of *Hyperprism*, where a C♯ introduced by a trombone is variously mutated, first by different attacks and approaches; then by coloration in horn, then by dynamic, timbral, and articulative shifts among three horns (Example 8–3 [a]). That single note and the D–C♯ interval formed when the bass trombone enters with a low *D* are examples of what Varèse called "sound-masses":

> There is an idea, the basis of an internal structure, expanded and split into different shapes or groups of sound, constantly changing in shape, direction, and speed, attracted and repulsed by various forces. The form of the work is the consequence of this interaction. (Princeton lecture)

Varèse likened such "an idea, the basis of an internal structure," to a crystal—restricted in internal form but able to be combined with others into limitless external forms. In *Hyperprism* the most important such "crystal" would seem to be the major seventh interval (or its inversion, a semitone):

[5] My translation (from the French), in *391*, No. 5 (New York, June 1917).

EXAMPLE 8–3. E. Varèse, *Hyperprism* (1922). (*a*) Measures 1–6 (percussion parts omitted). (*b*) Measures 11–13 (percussion parts omitted). © Copyright 1924 by Casa Ricordi/BMG Ricordi S.p.a. Copyright Renewed. Reprinted by permission of Hendon Music, Inc., a Boosey & Hawkes company, U.S. Agent of Casa Ricordi/BMG Ricordi S.p.a.

this interval appears in innumerable aggregates. The sonority of measures 12–13, for instance, is a "splitting" of the C♯ sound (measure 11) into a four-note aggregate composed of two pairs of sevenths: flute C and clarinet D♭, and trumpet C♯ and trombone C♮ (Example 8–3 [b]). These sevenths relate back, of course, to the first interval heard in the work, the D–C♯ of measure 5 (see Example 8–3 [a]); and the final sonority of the entire piece is a nine-note aggregate made up of the following transpositions of that interval: C–B, B♭–A, G–F♯, E♮–E♭, F♯–F♮.

"Themes" in a traditional sense are not characteristic of Varèse's music: "sound-masses," based on pitch, timbre, or rhythm, replace them. These are then varied, developed, interlocked, or superimposed somewhat the way themes might be. Ironically, in view of the incredulous reactions to *Ionisation*, it has a very important idea (in the *tambour militaire*, measures 8–13) that approximates the periodic organization of a "theme," its midpoint signaled by an isolated *sforzando* bang (Example 8–4). To follow this idea through the entire work, in which there is no melody or harmony in the traditional sense, only rhythms and an extraordinary variety of timbres produced by thirteen players on about forty instruments, is a fruitful approach to Varèse's concept of musical crystals, the variety of external forms they may assume, and their "attraction and repulsion" by various forces.[6]

EXAMPLE 8–4. E. Varèse, *Ionisation* (1930–31), measures 8–13 (tambour militaire part only). © Copyright 1934 by Casa Ricordi/BMG Ricordi S.p.a. Copyright renewed. Reprinted by permission of Hendon Music, Inc., a Boosey & Hawkes company, U.S. Agent of Casa Ricordi/BMG Ricordi S.p.a.

HENRY COWELL AND HIS NEW MUSIC

Another composer who embodied the progressivism of American music of the 1920s in his own music, his energetic and generous support of new trends, and his piano recitals, lectures, and writings was Henry Cowell (1897–1965).

---

[6] An authoritative approach to analyses of two works is made by Chou Wen-chung in "*Ionisation*: The Function of Timbre in Its Formal and Temporal Organization," in *The New Worlds of Edgard Varèse*, ed. Sherman Van Solkema (*ISAMm* 11 [1979]), 26–74, and the section on *Intégrales* in "Varèse: A Sketch of the Man and His Music," *MQ* 52 (1966): 151–70. Leo Kraft discusses Varèse's famous solo flute piece, *Density 21.5* (1936), in his analytic guidebook *Gradus* (New York: W. W. Norton, 1976), Book II, Part 1, 143–44.

Cowell was a Californian, a significant fact in its suggestion of the end of the American frontier and the broadening of America's musical base to encompass the entire continent—also in its reminder that though American composers had traditionally looked eastward across the Atlantic to European cultural models, they could also look westward across the Pacific to Asia. In a long career as gadfly of American new music, Cowell sought to find a context in world music for that of America, interesting himself in traditional and folk music of the entire world's peoples.

In the 1920s Cowell became notorious for novel uses of the pianoforte, including *tone clusters* (masses of contiguous pitches); for extensions of the rhythmic range of music; and for many other explorations into *New Musical Resources*, as the title of his 1919 book (published 1930) put it. (The book has been said to provide "a new and visionary basis for musical exploration based in the unalterable facts of acoustics, a basis so broad that it opened up room for ... compositional systems that have not even been conceived yet [in 1997]."[7] While still in his teens, Cowell amazed San Francisco music-club audiences with such pieces as *The Tides of Manaunaun* (1917?), which superimposes folkish melodic material on deep oceanic roars—tone clusters produced by playing the lowest notes of the piano with the flat of the left hand or with the forearm. *Advertisement* (1917) finds fistfuls of tone clusters cascading frantically from top to bottom of the keyboard, in a satiric evocation of the repetitious raucousness of advertisers. Besides his use of tone clusters of massed seconds on the keyboard, Cowell achieved other new sonorities by playing directly on the piano strings. In *The Banshee* (1925) the lower bass strings (which are wrapped in metal coils) are stroked along their length; this produces sounds four octaves above the keyboard tones, with a curious and even terrifying wailing effect. In *Sinister Resonance* (1930) Cowell applied to the piano strings various techniques—of stopping, muting at the bridge, and producing harmonics—that had previously been used only on such stringed instruments as violins. (Several of these piano works are recorded on *NW* CD 80203).

Cowell also made music with textures fashioned of melodic strands in extremely independent rhythms: the piano piece *Fabric* (1920), for instance, begins with a three-voice texture in which the relationship of beats between the voices in the first measure is as 8 to 6 to 5, in the second measure 9 to 7 to 5, and so on, throughout the piece. Believing that human limitations precluded realization of the full range of polyrhythms that he envisioned, Cowell developed (in cooperation with the musical-instrument inventor Leon Theremin) the *rhythmicon*, an instrument capable of producing very complex combinations of beat patterns; it was combined with orchestra in a work

---

[7] Kyle Gann, "Subversive Prophet: Henry Cowell as Theorist and Critic," in *The Whole World of Music: A Henry Cowell Symposium*," ed. David Nicholls (Amsterdam: Harwood, 1997), 171–222; the passage quoted, 172.

of 1931 entitled *Rhythmicana* (retitled later Concerto for Rhythmicon and Orchestra), which had to wait, however, until 1971 for its premiere, in a version in which the rhythmicon part was realized with the help of a computer.

Other works reflecting Cowell's originality of thought and his preoccupation—one among many—with expanded rhythmic usage include the "rhythm-harmony" quartets, *Quartet Romantic* (1917; NW LP 285) for two flutes, violin, and viola, and *Quartet Euphometric* (1919; NW CD 80453) for string quartet. In these works rhythmic structure is inextricably linked with harmonic structure (for example: two notes creating a perfect fifth harmonically, with their vibration rates in the ratio 3:2, are rhythmically related to that harmony by Cowell as three pulses sounding together with two in the same period of time); both quartets are virtually atonal, being written in the "dissonant counterpoint" that Cowell favored in this period. A later work of similar though less rigid rhythmic complexity, with a sort of "wheels-within-wheels" quality like that of intricate clockwork, is *Ostinato Pianissimo* (1934), for eight percussion players. Cowell went on, over a long creative career that lasted right up to his death, to become the most prolific American composer since Charles Grobe—and a more versatile and free-thinking one.

Cowell was a fighter for others' new music as well as his own. In 1927 he founded a quarterly publication of innovative scores, *New Music* (which survived until 1958). In an introductory note to Volume I, Number 1, he commented on the dilemma of progressive composers, even in an era of "modernism":

> There are very few opportunities at present for the modern American composer to publish his works, as publishers cannot afford to risk losing money in such publications, with the result that many of the finest works ever written in America remain unpublished. When modern works are published in America, few copies are sold. The work is therefore not distributed, and the composer gains no financial profit.

As editor of *New Music* until 1936 (when he was imprisoned on a flimsy morals charge, though paroled in 1940 and fully pardoned in 1942), Cowell bravely and selflessly sought to change that situation. The first issue (October 1927) consisted of a piece for small orchestra, *Men and Mountains* (CRI CD 715), by Carl Ruggles (1876–1971), an older New England composer similar to Charles Ives in his disdain for popular success, his alternation of composing and nonmusical activity (painting, in Ruggles's case), and his forging of a unique personal style. By no means a prolific composer (his complete music was recorded on two long-playing records, in CBS Masterworks album M2–34591, released in 1980), Ruggles produced a handful of tough, dense-textured contrapuntal works of an uncompromising integrity and a very high incidence of secundal dissonance. (On his studio wall hung the motto "Dissonant chords should have talismanic ecstasy.") Ruggles's major composition is the sixteen-minute symphonic work *Sun-Treader*, begun in

1926 and completed in 1931; other important ones are *Angels*, originally (1920–21) for six trumpets; *Portals* (1925) for thirteen strings; *Evocations* for piano (1937/43; *NW* CD 80402), revised later for orchestra; and *Organum* for full orchestra (1944–47; *CRI* CD 715).

Cowell helped many other composers, too, by publishing their works in *New Music*. Ives was one: the unprecedentedly complex score of his Fourth Symphony's second movement was published in 1929, the *Set for Theatre or Chamber Orchestra* in 1932, and collections of *34 Songs* and *19 Songs* a bit later. (Ives was the principal—but undeclared—financial supporter of Cowell's publishing and recording ventures.) Other composers who seemed poised on the leading edge of musical practice during the later 1920s and who were helped by Cowell included George Antheil, John J. Becker, Ruth Crawford (known also by her married name of Seeger), Colin McPhee, Wallingford Riegger, and Adolph Weiss.

George Antheil (1900–1959), who liked to think of himself as a "bad boy of music" (as he titled his autobiography of 1945), had a patchy career that climaxed early with the extraordinary score of *Ballet mécanique*, initially written for sixteen player pianos and elaborate percussion but first performed publicly in Paris in 1926 in a reduced version for one amplified player piano, two ordinary pianos, three xylophones, electric bells, airplane propellers, siren, and percussion.

John J. Becker (1886–1961) remained largely unappreciated, especially after he turned to a dissonant modernist manner with the *Symphonia brevis* of 1929 and wrote such pieces as *The Abongo*, subtitled "A Primitive Dance" (1933; *NW* CD 80285); its primitivism was surprisingly tame, though its scoring, for an all-percussion ensemble, was certainly unconventional. He later was claimed (perhaps overgenerously) as one of an "American Five" (by analogy with the "Mighty Five" Russian nationalists of the nineteenth century); the others were identified as Cowell, Ives, Riegger, and Ruggles.

The early promise of Ruth Crawford (1901–53), well deserved (and well exemplified in the two-movement *Music for Small Orchestra* of 1926), climaxed in such works as *Four Diaphonic Suites* for differing chamber combinations (1930; the suite for solo oboe on *CRI* CD 658); the pianistically demanding (and aurally challenging) *Piano Study in Mixed Accents* (1930, published 1932; *CRI* CD 658); *Three Songs* to texts by Carl Sandburg (1930–32; on *CRI* CD 658); and especially the unique, uncommonly advanced *String Quartet 1931*, which came to be viewed as her most enduring and important work. But her promise, as a composer, was perhaps never fully realized: after a year in Berlin on a Guggenheim Fellowship (the first woman composer to be awarded one) and marriage in 1932 to the composer/theorist/ethnomusicologist Charles Seeger, she deflected her creative activity into "composing babies" (as she put it wryly) and arranging folk songs, especially for children. (She was a gifted and dedicated teacher.)

Colin McPhee (1900–1964) eventually was known perhaps better as an ethnomusicologist than as a composer: he lived in Bali from 1931 to 1938 and wrote affectionately about it in *A House in Bali* (1946), penetratingly about its music in *Music in Bali* (posthumous, 1966). Cowell saw in him a promising composer and published in *New Music* McPhee's neo-Classic *Concerto for Piano, with Wind Octette Accompaniment* (1928); later he lauded (in *MQ* 34 [1948]: 412) McPhee's orchestral masterpiece—the glittering, gamelan-inspired symphony *Tabuh-Tabuhan* (1936)—as "an important landmark" in its exploration and integration of musical materials from more than a single culture.

Wallingford Riegger (1885–1961) was initially a loser: his progressive early scores—the finest of which are *Study in Sonority* (1927), for ten violins or any multiple thereof, and *Dichotomy* (1931–32) for chamber orchestra—earned him respect from fellow composers but boos and hisses from audiences. From the 1930s on, however, dancers much admired and used his music; and still later, after World War II, he gained critical respect and a modicum of success as a composer of concert music, notably for his Symphony No. 3 (1946–47; *CRI* CD 572), a fine example of his individual application of Schoenberg's method of "composition with twelve tones related only to each other."

Adolph Weiss (1891–1971) was the first American to study with Schoenberg (in Berlin, in 1926), the first to adopt Schoenberg's newly developed twelve-tone method, and the first to teach twelve-tone techniques to other Americans. (In 1933, John Cage was one of his pupils.) He never quite took off as a composer, though he had a distinguished career as a bassoonist.

POPULAR MUSIC AND MUSICAL COMEDY

The 1920s also saw major developments in popular music. Some of the most important were technological: the establishment of commercial radio stations and the development of the electrical recording process (with disc recordings as its product), the public-address system, and the sound track for film. All used the microphone and the sound amplifier, with significant impact on the nature of orchestration and popular vocal style, hence on the ideas of performers, arrangers, and even songwriters. All tended to broaden the audience for popular music—in a sense to nationalize it—but at the same time to make it a more passive audience, an audience of listeners rather than participants. This tended to heighten the importance of professionalism and sophistication among both performers and arrangers; it also tended to increase commercialism in the transmission (the "distribution") of popular music to its audience. Thus a new era of the American popular-music industry was born—an inevitable concomitant of the electronic age's "mass media" (though the term was yet uncoined).

New York City was the power center of the popular-music industry during the 1920s: it had Broadway and Shubert Alley, center of American popular lyric theater (the declining operetta and the developing musical comedy), and it had the so-called Tin Pan Alley, center of the songwriting business and the still-powerful sheet-music publishers. ("So-called" because the term was simply a metaphor for that part of the city most heavily populated by popular-music publishers; the "Alley" moved, first in the 1890s from East 14th Street to West 28th Street; then between the world wars to the Brill Building and others near it, on Broadway at about 50th Street.) The recording studios and the radio networks were also based in New York. But recordings and radio opened up possibilities for a striking new development: they made available, to any who cared to listen, kinds of popular music heard previously only in limited geographical areas or by specific ethnic and social groups—especially the blues, gospel songs, and jazz of black Americans (at whom a subsection of the recording industry aimed so-called race records), as well as the traditional music of the southern Appalachians and other rural areas of the South and West ("hillbilly music," as a term coined in this period defined it). The hillbillies' country music was not to affect the mainstream of American popular music until much later, but black-American secular styles began to influence American popular music in general in many ways in the 1920s; the novelist Scott Fitzgerald could even call the era "The Jazz Age"—which, although an exaggeration (since genuine black jazz, as opposed to a watered-down white version, was largely unknown), reflected the emergent impact of black-American musical influence on the consciousness of the nation at large.

Out of the popular mania for ragtime at the turn of the century had come an American craze for dancing. By the second decade, the older waltz, two-step, and cakewalk had given way—especially under the influence of the smooth, elegant models of Irene and Vernon Castle, the foremost dance team of the time—to a brisk but modest $\frac{4}{4}$ dance for couples: the fox-trot. With many variants, it was to be the basic step in "ballroom dancing" for decades, relieved occasionally by more exotic ones such as the tango, the rumba, and the maxixe. But another dance is even more strongly identified with the 1920s (and especially with the New American Woman of the 1920s, now a legal voter and thought to be emancipated in various other ways over her Victorian mother and grandmother). This was the athletic Charleston, which despite its name and its anything but langorous tempo, probably derived musically from Latin sources: its basic rhythm ($\frac{4}{4}$ ♩. ♩ 𝄽 | ♩. ♩ 𝄽 |), like that of the tango, was related to the Spanish *habanera*. (Music for each of the dances mentioned in this paragraph is recorded on NW CD 80293; excellent notes are provided by Thorton Hagert.)

Responding to the new popularity of dancing two by two (and also, as Irving Berlin's song of 1935 put it, *Cheek to Cheek*), dance bands proliferated in the 1920s. But in retrospect the period seems more notable for an explosion of songs and songwriters than for instrumental music and composers of it (except in jazz). Individual songs were published in great numbers; some were immensely popular, such as *Star Dust* by Hoagy Carmichael (1899–1981), a ballad (a term connoting, in popular music, not a storytelling song but a slow, often introspective love song). (*Star Dust* originated in 1927 as a piano piece but was furnished with memorable lyrics by Mitchell Parish [sung—and whistled—by the composer on *NW* LP 272].) But the most successful songs, in every sense, came out of the newly popular form of American lyric theater, the musical comedy (or just "musical").

The combination of a play with interpolated songs and dances was not new: as we have seen, it had been part of the American tradition from the eighteenth century on, and, after the minstrel-show interlude, had regained popularity, in the form of operetta, late in the nineteenth. But the musicals of the 1920s had a different style and feeling from those of operetta: they tended to avoid the sentimentality and the slightly aristocratic tone (which came out of Viennese operetta); they were more brash and brassy, lively and spicy, colloquial and earthy; they incorporated more identifiably American elements of dance and music; and they mirrored faithfully the optimism and hedonism, the motoric energy, and the devil-may-care attitudes of the post–World War I boom era.

The American musical has been likened to a latter-day ballad opera, but the balance and interrelationship of its components are vastly different. The ballad opera had been basically a play dotted with occasional songs; the musical, at least that of the 1920s, was essentially a garland of songs and dances strung on a thin plot line, with occasional spectacular "production numbers" planned at strategic points. Least important, perhaps, in a musical comedy of the period was the "comedy"—the drama. The success of a musical depended essentially on three things: the quality of the actor-singers and dancers (and of the director who guided them), the quality of the songs themselves, and a delicate balance between the music and the other components of the whole work. It was the necessity for that balance, perhaps more than anything else, that resulted in the inevitable out-of-town tryouts (i.e., in other places than New York) during which songs were shuffled about, rewritten, replaced, or dropped entirely until, it was hoped, a "hit" was assured.

The ad hoc and ad hominem/feminam attitudes that went into the making of a musical, whereby its components were all separable from one another, ready to be reassembled into various shapes and orders, meant that never was a work subject to the single-minded vision or the unique control of one individual; all kinds of "specialists" were involved—producer, director, author, lyricist, composer, music arranger, orchestrator, conductor, choreographer, and various associates and assistants (not to mention those performers who would actually project the work across the footlights). This splintering of authority over a musico-dramatic work, even greater than in the mounting of an opera, was and remains one of the greatest problems of the American musical.[8]

---

[8] A fascinating account is Don Dunn's *The Making of No, No, Nanette* (New York: Dell Pub. Co., Inc., 1972), a chronicle of the 1970 revival of a 1925 musical with a score by Vincent Youmans.

The songwriters of the 1920s who dominated the field of the musical were Jerome Kern, Irving Berlin, Richard Rodgers, and George Gershwin.

Jerome Kern (1885–1945) began as a composer of songs interpolated in American adaptations of British operettas and musical comedies; his first hit was *How'd You Like to Spoon with Me?* (1905; NW LP 221), written to go into the British show *The Earl and the Girl*. He turned to a more colloquial, popular American manner at about age thirty; more than one critic of American popular song dates the shift as 1914, with the poignant *They Didn't Believe Me*, written for the New York version of the British show *The Girl from Utah*.[9] Over a long career, with about a thousand songs in more than one hundred stage works to his credit, Kern achieved many hits with a song style that tended to be gentle, lyrical, and virtually untouched by elements of blues or jazz. In fact, many of his songs border on an operetta-like theatricality (*Ol' Man River* and *Bill*, from *Show Boat* of 1927, the musical considered by many to be Kern's masterpiece) or "artiness" (*Yesterdays* and *Smoke Gets in Your Eyes*, from *Roberta* of 1933; *All the Things You Are*, from *Very Warm for May* of 1939, his last musical). The harmonic scheme of the refrain of *All the Things You Are* (Example 8–5) suggests how rapidly American pop-

EXAMPLE 8–5.   Basic melodic and harmonic design of *All the Things You Are*, "Burthen" (= Chorus) only. Lyrics by Oscar Hammerstein II, music by Jerome Kern. Copyright © 1939 PolyGram International Publishing, Inc. Copyright Renewed. International Copyright Secured. All Rights Reserved.

[9] See Alec Wilder, *American Popular Song: The Great Innovators, 1900–1950* (New York: Oxford University Press, 1972), 32, 34–36, and Charles Hamm, *Yesterdays* (New York: W. W. Norton, 1979), 341 ff.

ular songwriters had developed in sophistication of harmonic thought. In less than a half-century, a basic vocabulary of little more than tonic, dominant, and subdominant chords, seldom in any but the tonic key, had increased immensely, to include major sevenths as consonances (measures 4, 12), enharmonic changes (23–24), sudden changes of mode (8–9), and altered chords (30); and tonal sensibility had been refined to allow for such uncertain, floating tonality as we hear in this song—until it ends declaratively in A♭, we cannot be certain whether it is in the key of F minor, A♭ major, C major, C minor, E♭ major, G major, or E major.[10]

Irving Berlin (1888–1989) survived several major shifts in American popular musical taste and until the rock revolution, at least, went on writing songs at an incredible pace, for a total that has been estimated at fifteen hundred. Berlin's first great popular hit was *Alexander's Ragtime Band* (1911), which has little to do with ragtime rhythms but, with its black protagonists ("Come on and hear … Alexander's ragtime band, … That's just the bestest band what am, honey lamb"), it was a coon song and thus identified with ragtime. In the 1920s Berlin was associated with Flo Ziegfeld, the extraordinary producer of super-spectacular "revues," and wrote songs for a number of the periodic *Ziegfeld Follies*, beginning with that of 1919 (which included Berlin's *A Pretty Girl Is Like a Melody*). Later, his knack for pouring essentially old familiar musical wine into slightly different bottles and having it come out seeming fresh and beguiling led to some apparently timeless songs: a few are *Say It with Music* (1921), *Always* (1925), *Blue Skies* (1927), *How Deep Is the Ocean?* (1932), and *The Girl That I Marry* and *I Got the Sun in the Morning* (both from the musical *Annie Get Your Gun* of 1946). In a special class altogether are two other songs by Berlin—*White Christmas* (from the 1942 film *Holiday Inn*), which with its yearning lyrics matched by a surprisingly sensuous chromatic vocal line has become virtually a popular hymn, and *God Bless America* (instantly popularized by singer Kate Smith in 1938, although it had lain unused since 1918), which has become a sort of unofficial national anthem.

A few extremely effective collaborations between musical-comedy songwriters and lyricists arose in the 1920s. Among them was the team of Richard Rodgers (1902–79) and Lorenz Hart (1895–1943), who worked together from 1919 (when Rodgers was only sixteen) until 1940. Most of Rodgers's more than 250 songs were composed for the stage; an unusual number of them became hits. More than either Kern or Berlin, Rodgers picked up from popular dance music rhythmic devices derived from jazz; they appear in the opening "verse" and following "chorus" of both *The Blue Room* (from the very successful musical *The Girl Friend*, 1926) and *Thou Swell* (1927; from *A Connecticut Yankee*). Less colloquial, more "arty," are others, such as the top hit of 1929 by Rodgers and Hart, *With a Song in My Heart*.

---

[10] For an extensive, subtle analysis of this song, see Allen Forte, *The American Popular Ballad of the Golden Era 1924–1950* (Princeton: Princeton University Press, 1995), 73–79.

Almost all these songs—and this can be said of the overwhelming majority of American popular songs for a quarter-century after about 1925—share certain formal characteristics. An opening "verse," apt to be somewhat tentative and suspensive musically, and frequently declamatory in vocal style, is followed by a "chorus" (by which the entire song is generally identified, at least by all but pop-song connoisseurs). The "chorus" is more shapely and memorable from the musical standpoint; it is typically thirty-two measures long, in eight-measure phrases, in an A A B A form (or variants of it). The B phrase is called for no good reason whatsoever the "release"—a real misnomer, for it usually wanders afield harmonically and the tensions thus created are *not* "released" until the return of the A material. The overall bipartite form (verse/chorus) resembles, and may have ultimately derived from, the recitative/aria form of opera and operetta.[11]

Another brilliant collaboration of the 1920s was that between George Gershwin (1898–1937) and his brother Ira (1896–1983). Together they wrote some of the merriest musical-comedy scores of the decade, especially *Lady, Be Good* (1924), *Oh, Kay!* (1926), and *Funny Face* (1927), all seeming in retrospect to be preparation for the political satire *Of Thee I Sing* (1931), the first musical to weld together so firmly plot, dialogue, and music that it received the Pulitzer Prize for drama. (A Pulitzer Prize for a musical composition as such was not awarded until 1943.) Gershwin's later *Porgy and Bess* (1935), which he characterized as "folk opera—opera for the [popular] theatre, with drama, humor, song, and dance," was a more pretentious but perhaps not more artistically successful contribution. It relied mainly on some memorable songs (*Summertime; I Got Plenty o' Nuttin'; It Ain't Necessarily So; Bess, You Is My Woman Now*) that displayed the same special characteristics as Gershwin's earlier show songs: beguiling rhythms (as in *Fascinating Rhythm*, 1924, and *I Got Rhythm*, 1930); unusual form (*Embraceable You*, 1930); a relaxed, jazzy swing (*'s Wonderful*, 1927; *Nice Work If You Can Get It*, 1937); and harmonic materials richer than those of most American popular songs (*The Man I Love*, 1927; *Liza*, 1929; *So Are You!*, 1929). *Porgy and Bess* has had a checkered career, both in the variety of its productions (many cut savagely, others badly cast, still others wavering uncertainly between Broadway-musical and grand-opera approaches) and in its critical reception. One evenhanded historian concludes, however:

> Opera critics have objected to arias that sound too much like Broadway songs and to the score's lack of organic symphonic integration. Black critics have found Gershwin's evocations of their music inauthentic. [But, despite] all of these criticisms, and others, *Porgy and Bess* is full of moments that show Gershwin at his most convincing.[12]

---

[11] Hamm's *Yesterdays*, 293–94 and 358–61, includes a valuable discussion of the verse/chorus form and the thirty-two-bar chorus structure of Tin Pan Alley songs.

[12] Richard Crawford, in his entry on George Gershwin in *AmeriGrove*.

That the boundary between cultivated- and vernacular-tradition American music was becoming blurred once again is suggested not only by the sophistication and artistry, albeit on a small scale, of many of the songs mentioned in the preceding paragraphs, together with their undeniable popular mass appeal, but also by such a phenomenon as Gershwin's moving back and forth from popular to "serious" music, or the critical success of one of his musicals (*Of Thee I Sing*) alongside the popular success of his full-scale opera (*Porgy and Bess*). More than a decade before the latter work, in fact, Gershwin had successfully introduced the idioms of Tin Pan Alley into the concert hall, first with *Rhapsody in Blue* (1924), billed as a "jazz concerto" (for piano and dance band; later orchestrated more fully). Its unparalleled, and lasting, popularity seems to depend not only on its joyous, effervescent verve but also on its unique mélange of stylistic sources: the Afro-American music of melodic blues and rhythmic syncopation, the harmonic idiom and four- and eight-bar phrase-structures of Tin Pan Alley song, and the pianistic virtuosity and dimensions of Romantic-era concerto movements by such composers as Liszt and Grieg.

Belatedly, Gershwin conscientiously sought to learn more techniques of "classical" composition—the *Rhapsody* had been orchestrated not by the composer but by Ferde Grofé (1892–1972)—and produced several other concert works, among them a Concerto in F (1925) for piano and orchestra and *An American in Paris* (1928) for orchestra alone. Three Preludes for piano (1926), smaller in scale and better controlled than the orchestral works, are unpretentious but charming and perfectly honed trifles, among the very best "household music" of the 1920s.

CITY BLUES AND JAZZ

For many people, Americans and others alike, the most significant American music of the 1920s, the most indigenous and unprecedented, was jazz. Jazz had existed for decades before the 1920s, as had the special vocal styles and forms of blues, but only as a music of blacks and virtually unknown to the larger American community. What had been a music of and for southern blacks began to be diffused, through the earliest phonograph recordings (sporadically from 1917, then in greater numbers from 1923); World War I (which found black Americans, jazz performers among them, in Europe, not just North America);[13] commercial radio stations (from 1920); and the increased mobility of southern blacks, particularly toward the larger northern cities. In New York, especially, a huge influx of blacks and their concentration in the

---

[13] One important "ambassadorial" group was the black-American 369th Infantry regimental band, led by Lieutenant James Reese Europe (1881–1919) in France. Before the war, in New York, Europe had directed all-black dance bands (Europe's Society Orchestra) and concert groups such as the Clef Club Symphony Orchestra (100 to 150 strong); the former is heard on *NW* LP 269, the latter on *NW* LPs 260 and 269. For more on Europe, see Eileen Southern, *The Music of Black Americans: A History*, 3rd ed. (New York: W. W. Norton, 1983), passim.

Harlem area of upper Manhattan was important in the development of jazz and its diffusion to the white community. Harlem nightspots, with blues singers and jazz groups, were active interracial entertainment centers. A whole series of "black musicals" appeared "downtown," just off Broadway; important among them were the collaborations of Eubie Blake (1883–1983) and Noble Sissle (1889–1975) in such shows as *Shuffle Along* (1921), *The Chocolate Dandies* (1924), and *Shuffle Along of 1933*. The first *Shuffle Along* included the hit songs *Love Will Find a Way* and *I'm Just Wild About Harry* as well as Walter Donaldson's *How Ya' Gonna Keep 'Em Down on the Farm* (these and other songs recorded on *NW* LP 260).

The surest sign of the impact of jazz on America at large was the appearance in the popular entertainment world of jazz-influenced dance bands such as that of Paul Whiteman (1890–1967) and others, and the characterization (even if exaggerated) of the entire decade as "The Jazz Age." (It was Whiteman who commissioned *Rhapsody in Blue* from Gershwin and premiered it in a famous concert, "An Experiment in Modern Music," presented in New York on February 12, 1924. The polish and versatility of his dance band made it a powerful influence on American popular music of the 1920s.) The end of the decade saw jazz recognized as a national phenomenon, though centered in the black ghettoes of northern cities, notably Kansas City, Chicago, Detroit, and New York (besides, of course, southern centers such as New Orleans and Memphis). It saw the faithful emulation of black jazz musicians by whites, not just the diluted strains of Whiteman's "symphonic jazz"; it saw black musicians and combos enter the new subdivision of "race records" in the phonorecording business; it saw the beginnings of world interest in jazz as a new music; and it saw the first major shift in jazz style itself, from the small "combo" of early jazz to the "big band."

Early jazz was a synthesis of the march/dance beat and overlaid syncopations of ragtime; other kinds of syncopated dance rhythms of Afro-Caribbean origin; a rudimentary but dynamic harmony rooted in the Euro-American traditions of dance music and revival hymnody; and the expressive, flexible vocal style of various branches of American black song, such as the repetitive, chantlike, and usually responsorial work song, the solitary field holler, the religious spiritual, and (hardly different from the last-named in musical style) the secular blues.

In the formally standardized, instrumentally accompanied form of "city blues" (as opposed to the formally unstandardized and earlier "country blues"),[14] the blues was to become one of the two major foundations of 1920s jazz (the other being rags). City blues, as recorded by such classic female blues singers as Mamie Smith (1883–1946), Ma Rainey (1886–1939), Bessie

---

[14] Two valuable discussions of the latter are Alan Lomax's notes for *Roots of the Blues* (NW LP 252) and the section on "Origins" of Paul Oliver's entry "Blues" in *AmeriGrove*. Helpful on the distinctions between country and city blues is Charles Keil, *Urban Blues* (Chicago: University of Chicago Press, 1966), especially chap. 2 and appendix C.

Smith (1894–1937), and Ida Cox (1896–1967), tended to be strophic songs with a text typically based on two-line strophes (but with the first line of each strophe's text repeated, AAB) and a standard succession of harmonies underlying each strophe's melody. Jazz musicians appropriated the musical structure of such blues; from then on, the term *blues*, whether sung or not, connoted that structure. Basically, the most common structure of such blues was (and remains) one of a repeated twelve-measure pattern ("12–bar blues"), which is divided into three four-measure phrases accompanied by a standard basic harmonic progression, as indicated:

$$\begin{array}{c} 4 \\ 4 \end{array} \quad \overline{\begin{array}{cccc} 1 & 2 & 3 & 4 \end{array}} \quad \overline{\begin{array}{cccc} 5 & 6 & 7 & 8 \end{array}} \quad \overline{\begin{array}{cccc} 9 & 10 & 11 & 12 \end{array}}$$

$$\text{I} \underline{\hspace{3cm}} \text{IV} \underline{\hspace{0.5cm}} \text{I} \underline{\hspace{0.5cm}} \quad \text{V} \quad (\text{IV}) \quad \text{I} \underline{\hspace{1cm}}$$

Other lengths than twelve measures are found, and elaborations of the basic harmonies are legion; I have indicated (with parentheses in measure 10) one of the most common in the 1920s; after that time, the general tendency was to add more and more elaborate variants to the scheme of harmonies, preserving, however, the twelve-measure structure and the principal harmonic pillars.

In vocal blues, the three phrases of song per stanza are superimposed on this basic structure. Each of the singer's phrases typically lasts for about three measures of the four-measure unit, leaving a "hole" until the beginning of the next unit; this hole is filled, in a way perhaps going back to primordial call-and-response techniques, by some sort of instrumental or hummed or spoken response to the singer's phrase. The whole combination, then, might be suggested this way:

$$\begin{array}{ccc} \text{Singer} \;\; [\text{response}] & \text{Singer} \;\; [\text{response}] & \text{Singer} \;\; [\text{response}] \end{array}$$

$$\overline{\begin{array}{cccc} 1 & 2 & 3 & 4 \end{array}} \quad \overline{\begin{array}{cccc} 5 & 6 & 7 & 8 \end{array}} \quad \overline{\begin{array}{cccc} 9 & 10 & 11 & 12 \end{array}}$$

$$\text{I} \underline{\hspace{3cm}} \text{IV} \underline{\hspace{0.5cm}} \text{I} \underline{\hspace{0.5cm}} \quad \text{V} \quad (\text{IV}) \quad \text{I} \underline{\hspace{1cm}}$$

One particularly clear example (available in both a recording and a notated transcription)[15] among many that might be cited is the performance by Jelly Roll Morton of *Mamie's Blues*. In an introduction to the music, spoken as he begins to play, Morton explains that this is "no doubt the first blues I ever knew," which (if we can believe his memory) would place it about the turn of the century.

---

[15] *New Orleans Memories Plus Two* (Commodore Records LP XFL-14942); Alan Lomax, *Mister Jelly Lord*, 2nd ed. (Berkeley and Los Angeles: University of California Press, 1973), 269–71.

If blues contributed to jazz one of its most common formal structures, it contributed even more importantly to its instrumental style. Early blues vocal style was one of great variety and flexibility of intonation, mode of attack, tone color, vibrato, degree of nasality or gutturalism, and regular rhythm or rubato. These freedoms (from the viewpoint of a singer trained in the Euro-American cultivated tradition of art song or opera) were partly inherent in the folkish lack of "sophistication" of the country-blues singers, partly the result of vestiges of the primordial African style concepts of black Americans. Significant for jazz was the transfer from voice to instrument of this blues style: jazz instrumentalists, unbound by notions of "correct" performance on a trumpet, a trombone, a banjo or guitar, used instruments as substitutes for, or extensions of, the voice, bringing to them the same broad range of expression as that of the blues singer's voice. The various narrowly prescriptive attempts that have been made to categorize the "blue notes" of jazz (usually oversimplified as the flatted third and seventh of the major scale) arise from a preconception, dominated by the cultivated tradition's ideas of the musical scale and of instrumental performance technique, about what is and what is not "basic" or "natural" in musical structure and style.

Rags were the other major source of the repertory of jazz in the 1920s, thanks to the broad popularity of ragtime as a kind of marching and dancing music early in the century. The historic first recordings of jazz, made by the all-white, all-male performers of the New Orleans–based Original Dixieland Jazz Band (1917–18), included blues and rags in about equal measure, such as *Livery Stable Blues* or *Clarinet Marmalade Blues* and *Tiger Rag* or *Sensation Rag*; so did the musically more significant recordings, from the middle 1920s, of the bands of King Oliver (1885–1938), Louis Armstrong (ca. 1898–1971), and Jelly Roll Morton. Among these are the epochal 1923 recordings of Oliver's Creole Jazz Band, including *Dippermouth Blues* (on *SCCJ* CD 1) and *High Society Rag*; the 1925–27 recordings by Armstrong's Hot Five of *Big Butter and Egg Man from the West* or his Hot Seven of *Potato Head Blues* (both on *SCCJ* CD 1) and *Muskrat Ramble*, the latter a rag composed by the trombonist Kid Ory (1886–1973); and the 1926 recordings by Morton's Red Hot Peppers of *Dead Man Blues* and *Black Bottom Stomp* (both on *SCCJ* CD 1).

Jazz instrumentalists brought to the performance of ragtime the same flexible, vocalistic nuances of pitch and rhythm that they brought to the blues; thus, in performance style the two types of early jazz were equivalent. Within the frameworks of blues or ragtime forms, early jazz performances were built on a principle of improvisatory variation; in terms of the broad Euro-American Western tradition, the result was close to the Baroque era's "strophic variations," a chain of varied repetitions of a basic "tune." In jazz, the "tune" was more a matter of the underlying harmonies of an original piece than its melody, and virtually any music could become jazz, by adoption of its "tune" as the basis for improvisatorily varied repetitions in jazz style. (Jelly Roll Morton demonstrated to Alan Lomax, during Library of Congress interviews in the 1930s, that a French quadrille was the source of *Tiger Rag*.)

Most of the early jazz recordings were made by New Orleans musicians, and despite attempts to challenge the legendary primacy of the Crescent City as the sole birthplace of jazz, New Orleans—with its multicultural ethnic profile, its blacks, whites, and Creoles—was without question important as the first major center. The New Orleans jazz bands were typically small groups ("combos") often made up of clarinet, cornet, trombone, and drums (instruments common to the military and civic marching bands of the post–Civil War period). They played outdoors for parades and funerals and, seated in placarded wagons, for advertising; indoors, for dancing, in brothels, barrelhouses, and dance halls, with perhaps a piano and a banjo or guitar. The ensemble style, as heard typically in the first chorus (stanza) and the last, "ride-out" chorus(es) of a piece, was a rough-ly contrapuntal music with the powerful cornet projecting the main melodic voice, the clarinet weaving a treble countermelody, the trombone providing a solid but melodic bass, and the drums and other instruments supplying the basic beat against which raggy syncopations could work. (The degree to which such choruses constituted "collective improvisation" has been generally exaggerated.) Between first and last choruses, individual musicians would play one or more improvisatory solo choruses (with rhythmic background) in succession.

Example 8–6 shows the improvisatory melodic style of such New Orleans jazz, taken from a later recording (1947) by Louis Armstrong; the example is chosen partly to suggest the absorption by jazz, as the 1920s closed, of a third formal pattern in addition to those of ragtime and blues: that of the thirty-two-measure chorus, in AABA design, of the popular songs of Tin Pan Alley. In Example 8–6, (a) is the original melody of the pop song (*What Did I Do to Be So*) *Black and Blue* (1929), with its harmonies indicated("Am" = A minor chord; G^7 = G-7th chord; G^+ = G-augmented chord, etc.); first and second sections A A = measures 1–8, 9–16; section B = measures 17–24; last section A = measures 25–32. The transcription of Armstrong's cornet melody (b) does not attempt to show the nuances of pitch and tone quality in his solo; it does, though, attempt to show rhythmic nuances, as Armstrong plays slight-ly earlier (+) or later (−) the notes as given in the published song version.

Following the early successes of the Original Dixieland Jazz Band, other white musicians took up jazz in the 1920s. Early in the decade a group in Chicago centered on three musicians originally from New Orleans—trum-peter Paul Mares, clarinetist Leon Roppolo, and trombonist George Brunies—was formed as the New Orleans Rhythm Kings; later came the gifted cornetist Bix Beiderbecke (1903–31) and the Wolverines; and a group of Chicago musicians who, playing together from their school days, came to be known as the Austin High School gang. Among them were Bud Freeman (1906–91) and Frank Teschemacher (1906–32), both players of the saxo-phone, an instrument that although not always found in New Orleans jazz was to become indispensable in later jazz groups. Other instruments assuming new importance in jazz of the late 1920s were the trumpet, replacing the more mellow but less brazen cornet; the guitar, replacing the earlier banjo; and the string bass, replacing the tuba of the brass bands.

EXAMPLE 8–6.   (*What Did I Do to Be So*) *Black and Blue* by Andy Razaf,
Thomas Waller, and Harry Brooks. Copyright © 1929 by Mills Music, Inc.
Copyright renewed © 1957 by Mills Music, Inc. Used by Permission. (*a*) As
published. (*b*) As played by Louis Armstrong on the recording *Satchmo at
Symphony Hall* (Decca DL 8037; rel. 1951); my transcription.

Another important development in jazz of the 1920s was the formation of "big bands," rather than small combos. Any group larger than, say, a half-dozen players needed some kind of musical arrangement, a plan of action, whether sketched out in notation or worked out empirically through rehearsals; it could not rely on the so-called collective improvisation within the spare, linear contrapuntal texture of a small group. Early examples of such "arranged" jazz, which required a real composer or at least a dominant director and organizer, are the 1926 recordings of Jelly Roll Morton and his Red Hot Peppers. Even the earliest recordings by this band (which numbered seven or eight members)—including *Grandpa's Spells* (on *SCCJ* CD 1), *Smokehouse Blues*, and *The Pearls*—have been described (by Gunther Schuller, in his *AmeriGrove* article on Morton) as "a triumphant fusion of composition and improvisation," and Morton himself as "the first important jazz composer."

Three other pianists, each with a different orientation from Morton's (which was, of course, that of New Orleans jazz), proved equally skillful and even more progressive leaders of big-band jazz in the 1920s. One was Fletcher Henderson (1898–1952), who was born in Georgia but drifted into jazz only after he moved to New York in 1920 and absorbed the New York style of "stride" piano playing and other Harlem dance music. Henderson's music director and arranger was Don Redman; he developed an immensely satisfactory and influential technique of scoring, especially for the brass and reed sections of a big band: it gave the music the feeling of freedom, mobility, and relaxation of a small combo (for example, in the 1926 recording of *The Stampede*; on *SCCJ* CD 2). Redman treated each section of the band— reeds, brass, percussion—like a single voice; they alternated with one another in call-and-response fashion, or one backed up the other with repetitive, improvisatory phrases (later called "riffs"). Individual soloists—such as Louis Armstrong, who joined Henderson's band in 1924 and was a major influence in turning it into a propulsive "swinging" group—could still improvise freely over such cleverly arranged backgrounds. Famous recorded examples of the Henderson band's early style, featuring Armstrong as soloist, include *Copenhagen* (1924) and *Sugar Foot Stomp* (1925), the latter based on King Oliver's *Dippermouth Blues*. Henderson's ensemble went into a decline in the late 1920s, but in the mid-1930s, its best arrangements bought by Benny Goodman for his band and nationally popularized (see p. 252), it was to have a triumphant vindication.

Another pianist important in the development of successful big-band style was Bennie Moten (1894–1935), whose six-piece group became the most popular jazz combo in Kansas City in the early 1920s. Reflecting the Southwest origins and popularity of ragtime, Moten's band (as heard on recordings from 1923 on) played very differently from either the New Orleans or the New York schools: it emphasized a heavy beat, even eighth-note rhythms, and frequent tunes based on blues "changes" (harmonies). By 1926 Moten was recording with a ten-piece band and had developed both an earthy, rocking beat (*Kansas City Breakdown*, 1928; *Moten Swing*, 1932; on *SCCJ* CD 2) and a pushy rhythmic drive based on the motoric ostinato cycles, within a 12–bar blues form, of "boogie-woogie" piano (*New Tulsa Blues*, 1927). Out of this style was to develop the powerful "Kansas City" swing style of the 1930s.

The last of the three progressive big-band pianist-leaders of the 1920s to be cited here—and, quite simply, one of America's greatest composers— is Edward Kennedy "Duke" Ellington (1899–1974). Initially a leader of dance bands in Washington, D.C., Ellington moved to New York in 1923 and began working with his band, the Washingtonians, at the Hollywood Club (renamed in 1925 the Kentucky Club); from 1927 on, well into the 1930s, they embellished (and made famous) the Cotton Club in Harlem. Ellington cut his first electrical recordings in 1926, with a twelve-piece band. An important element in roughening and individualizing the otherwise rather sweet, "white dance-band" sound of the group was the plunger-mute technique and raspy "growling" of trumpeter James "Bubber" Miley and trombonist Joe "Tricky Sam" Nanton. Miley's original compositions and his ideas on arranging for the band were also important in the crystallization of the "Ellington sound," which, emphasizing at first so-called jungle effects, was documented in the three major early works the band recorded: *East St. Louis Toodle-Oo* (or *Toddle-O*) (on *SCCJ* CD 3), *Black and Tan Fantasy*, and *Creole Love Call* (late 1926–late 1927). The last of these broadened even further the group's sonorous palette by employing a wordless voice—that of Adelaide Hall—as an extra instrument (as does *The Mooche* of 1928).

Besides his "jungle" pieces, Ellington also explored new jazz sonorities in bluesy "mood" compositions like *Misty Mornin'* and *Awful Sad* (both recorded in 1928), which seem in retrospect to have been precursors of the most famous such composition, *Mood Indigo* (1930; on NW LP 272). Ellington also sought restlessly to expand and vary the conventional forms of jazz, which—at least on recordings—had been limited to the brief time span (about three minutes) of one side of a 10-inch, 78 revolutions-per-minute disc. This search culminated first with the two-side composition *Creole Rhapsody* (two versions completed by 1931, the first briefer than the second); the stage was set for the even larger and more complex works of later decades.

BIBLIOGRAPHICAL NOTES

A book that communicates vividly the sense of ferment in European music and the other arts at the turn of the twentieth century is Roger Shattuck's *The Banquet Years* (1958; rev. ed. New York: Vintage Books, 1968). The early chapters of Eric Salzman's *Twentieth-Century Music: An Introduction*, 3rd ed. (Upper Saddle River, NJ: Prentice Hall, 1988), Glenn Watkins's *Soundings: Music in the Twentieth Century* (New York: Schirmer Books, 1988), and Robert P. Morgan's *Twentieth-Century Music* (New York: W. W. Norton, 1991) are all valuable. Kyle Gann's *American Music in the Twentieth Century* (New York: Schirmer Books, 1997)— written, like Salzman's, from a composer's standpoint—is insightful on matters of musical style and thought.

Copland's autobiography, interlarded by his coauthor Vivian Perlis with remarks (derived from her oral-history interviews) by many of his contemporaries, is presented in *Copland: 1900 Through 1942* (1984) and *Copland Since 1943* (1989), both published by St. Martin's Press, New York. Nadia Boulanger's complex personality is well caught in Suzanne R. Hoover's "Nadia Boulanger," *The American Scholar* 46/4 (Autumn 1977): 496–502.

On the Copland-Sessions concerts, see Carol J. Oja, "The Copland-Sessions Concerts and Their Reception in the Contemporary Press," *MQ* 65 (1979): 212–29. An inside story of the League of Composers and especially its journal, *Modern Music*, is Minna Lederman's *The Life and Death of a Small Magazine* (ISAMm 18 [1983]); Wayne D. Shirley indexed the magazine (New York: AMS Press, 1976). On the International Composers' Guild, see R. Allen Lott, "'New Music for New Ears': The International Composers' Guild," *JAMS* 36 (1982): 266–86; on the Pan American Association of Composers, see Deane L. Root, "The Pan American Association of Composers (1928–1934)," *Yearbook for Inter-American Musical Research* 8 (1972): 49–70. (Both articles, as well as Oja's, give lists of the music performed in the concerts sponsored by the organizations they discuss.)

A Futurist manifesto of 1913, "The Art of Noise" by Luigi Russolo, is given in *Classic Essays on Twentieth-Century Music*, ed. Richard Kostelanetz and Joseph Darby (New York: Schirmer Books, 1996), 35–39. The same anthology (pp. 47–53) includes substantial portions of various writings and lectures by Varèse, including the 1939 Princeton lecture; for annotations on that by his former pupil Chou Wen-chung, see Chou's "The Liberation of Sound," *PNM* 5/1 (Fall–Winter 1966): 11–19. Varèse's early years (to 1928) are recounted by his wife, Louise, in *Varèse: A Looking-Glass Diary* (New York: W. W. Norton, 1972).

William Lichtenwanger's *The Music of Henry Cowell: A Descriptive Catalog* (*ISAMm* 23 [1986]) is definitive; Martha Manion's *Writings About Henry Cowell* (*ISAMm* 16 [1981]) is a copiously annotated bibliography. A full-scale biography of Cowell is promised by Joel Sachs; meanwhile, Rita Mead's *Henry Cowell's New Music, 1925–1936: The Society, the Music Editions, and the Recordings* (Ann Arbor: UMI Research Press, 1981) is rich in detail and comment on Cowell and the composers whose works he published in *New Music*. David Nicholls edited *The Whole World of Music* (cited in note 7), a valuable anthology of six essays by Cowell experts; he also introduced and annotated a facsimile reprint of Cowell's *New Musical Resources* (Cambridge: Cambridge University Press, 1996). Cowell's arrest, conviction, and San Quentin experience are documented by Michael Hicks in "The Imprisonment of Henry Cowell," *JAMS* 44/1 (Spring 1991): 92–119. Andrew Porter discusses the Romantic and Euphometric quartets very lucidly in his *Music of Three More Seasons: 1977–1980* (New York: Knopf, 1981), 184–88; I have explored *Ostinato Pianissimo* in *MQ* 70 (1984): 23–44, as has David Nicholls the *United Quartet* (1936) in *AM* 13/2 (Summer 1995): 195–217.

Ruth Crawford's life is chronicled brilliantly by Judith Tick in *Ruth Crawford Seeger: A Composer's Search for American Music* (New York: Oxford University Press, 1997), perceptively reviewed by Juanita Karpf in *[MLA] Notes* 55/2 (December 1998), 369–71.; Crawford's compositions, similarly, by Joseph N. Straus in *The Music of Ruth Crawford Seeger* (Cambridge: Cambridge University Press, 1995). Her *Music for Small Orchestra* (1926) and *Suite No. 2 for Four Strings and Piano* (1929) are published as *MUSA* 1 (= *RRAM* 19).

Carol Oja's title *Colin McPhee: Composer in Two Worlds* (Washington, DC: Smithsonian Institution Press, 1990) defines her biographical study accurately.

Cecil Smith's *Musical Comedy in America* (1950) has been updated by Glenn Litton, 2nd ed. (New York: Theatre Arts Books, 1981). Four books by Gerald Bordman (all published by Oxford University Press) add up to a virtually total account of the American popular lyric theater; most comprehensive is *American Musical Theatre: A Chronicle* (2nd ed., 1992). On the musical side, Charles Hamm's *Yesterdays* and Alec Wilder's *American Popular Song … 1900–1950* (both cited in note 9) complement each other nicely; on the lyrics' side, Philip Furia takes a broad look in *The Poets of Tin Pan Alley: A History of America's Great Lyricists* (New York: Oxford University Press, 1990).

Irving Berlin's complete output of songs from 1907 to 1914 (totaling about 200), is published as *MUSA* 2 (= *RRAM* 20) in a critical edition by Charles Hamm: *Irving Berlin: Early Songs*. Hamm expanded on its valuable introduction in *Irving Berlin, Songs from the Melting Pot: The Formative Years, 1907–1914* (New York: Oxford University Press, 1997).

An enthralling and illuminating account of no fewer than thirty-three productions of the Kern/Hammerstein masterpiece *Show Boat*, lavishly illustrated and meticulously documented, is Miles Kreuger's *Show Boat: The Story of a Classic American Musical* (New York: Oxford University Press, 1977). Dorothy Hart and Robert Kimball meticulously edited *The Complete Lyrics of Lorenz Hart* (New York: Knopf, 1986).

A documentary biography of George Gershwin is yet to be written; perhaps the best in print (though, as a semi-"authorized" work, it is somewhat slanted) is Edward Jablonski's *Gershwin* (New York: Doubleday, 1988; repr. with additions New York: Da Capo Press, 1998). Charles Hamm and David Schiff have both offered revisionist views of Gershwin as "crossover" composer: Hamm in "Towards a new reading of Gershwin" and "A blues for the ages," both reprinted in his *Putting popular music in its place* (Cambridge: Cambridge University Press, 1995), 306–24 and 325–35; Schiff in "Misunderstanding Gershwin," *The Atlantic Monthly* (October 1998), 100–105. (Schiff has also written concentratedly, and with a composer's perceptiveness, on *Gershwin: Rhapsody in Blue* [Cambridge: Cambridge University Press, 1997].) Besides his *AmeriGrove* entry on George Gershwin, see Richard Crawford's articles "It Ain't Necessarily Soul: Gershwin's 'Porgy and Bess' as Symbol," *Yearbook for Inter-American Musical Research* 8 (1972): 17–38, and "Gershwin's Reputation: A Note on *Porgy and Bess*," *MQ* 65 (1979): 257–64, as well as chap. 7 ("George Gershwin's 'I Got Rhythm' [1930],") of his book *The American Musical Landscape* (Berkeley and Los Angeles: University of California Press, 1993). For another, highly original view, see Ned Rorem's "Living with Gershwin" (1985), in his *Settling the Score* (New York: Harcourt Brace Jovanovich, 1988), 3–20. Ira Gershwin comments selflessly and informatively (on his craft as a lyricist) in *Lyrics on Several Occasions* (1959; repr. with additions New York: Viking, 1973, and Limelight Editions, 1997); his lyrics are collected in *The Complete Lyrics of Ira Gershwin*, ed. Robert Kimball (New York: Knopf, 1993), and brilliantly discussed in Philip Furia's *Ira Gershwin: The Art of the Lyricist* (New York: Oxford University Press, 1996).

Thomas Riis's *Just Before Jazz: Black Musical Theater in New York, 1890–1915* (Washington, DC: Smithsonian Institution Press, 1989) is a path-breaking study. Robert Kimball and William Bolcom treat the lives of two later black-musical collaborators in *Reminiscing with Sissle and Blake* (New York: Viking, 1973).

Paul Oliver's studies of blues (see the bibliography of his *AmeriGrove* article "Blues") are masterly, as is Robert Palmer's *Deep Blues* (New York: Viking, 1981).

Jazz origins outside New Orleans have been chronicled by Lawrence Gushee in "New Orleans–Area Musicians on the West Coast, 1908–1925," *Black Music Research Journal* 9/1 (Spring 1989): 1–18, and "How the Creole Band Came to

Be," *Black Music Research Journal* 8/1 (1988): 83–100. Unparalleled on the music of early jazz, with many transcriptions notated from recordings, is Gunther Schuller's *Early Jazz: Its Roots and Musical Development* (New York: Oxford University Press, 1968). The pianistic artistry of Jelly Roll Morton is documented, in transcriptions of his recordings, by James Dapogny, *Ferdinand "Jelly Roll" Morton: The Collected Piano Music* (Washington, DC: Smithsonian Institution Press, 1982). William Kenney's *Chicago Jazz... 1904–1930* (New York: Oxford University Press, 1993) is valuable. Mark Tucker's *Ellington: The Early Years* (Urbana: University of Illinois Press, 1991) is concerned with Ellington's life and works in Washington (1899–1923) and New York (1923–27). Tucker's huge, generously annotated anthology (covering Ellington's whole career) *The Duke Ellington Reader* (New York: Oxford University Press, 1993) is superb; one able reviewer (in *[MLA] Notes* 51 (1995): 954–56) said flatly that there is "no better reference work on Duke Ellington."

NINE

THE 1930s AND EARLY 1940s

The 1930s in American music were a complete contrast to the 1920s. The optimistic, progressive, strident voices of the 1920s were muted in the decade of the Great Depression. As Virgil Thomson wrote later in his autobiography, "The time was not for novelty." Aaron Copland, in a famous statement about the trend to simplicity in his own works of the 1930s, said,

> The old "special" public of the modern music concerts had fallen away, and the conventional concert public continued apathetic or indifferent to anything but the established classics. . . . I felt that it was worth the effort to see if I couldn't say what I had to say in the simplest possible terms.[1]

A characteristic gesture of the concert-music establishment was the Philadelphia Orchestra management's announcing just before the 1932 season opened that "debatable" new music would be avoided on the orchestra's programs. Even the lusty voice of jazz seemed stilled after the stock market crash of 1929; with a few notable exceptions, it was not widely heard again for about six years, and then it spoke differently from before. This musical atmosphere of conservatism, probably due in largest part to the impact of the Depression,

---

[1] Aaron Copland, *Our New Music* (New York: McGraw-Hill, 1941), 229.

seems not to have been broken until after the end of World War II (1946); thus "the 1930s" as an era in American musical history actually extended to the mid-1940s.

THEMES OF THE PERIOD

Even if the most characteristic atmosphere of the period was one of a broad conservatism, the music of the Depression era revealed several new and distinctive trends. Perhaps the strongest was a historical or regional Americanism. This was certainly related to the political and social thought of the era, its populist temperament and its tendency toward an American isolationism; the latter was reflected musically in a suspicious attitude toward the "Europe-ness" of the international new-music movement of the 1920s. One might speak of an "American Wave" among composers in the 1930s as art historians do of such painters as Charles Burchfield, Thomas Hart Benton, and Grant Wood—and recall the work of John Dos Passos and John Steinbeck.

Closely related to this trend was a new and persistent preoccupation of composers with their relationship to the broad musical community and to society at large. The century's new mass media of communication (radio, phonorecordings, sound films, and, beginning late in the 1930s, television) had created a vast new potential audience for music, but a different one from the concert audiences of the past; many composers saw these media as a challenge—and, for some, an opportunity—to communicate on a broad scale. At the same time, conflicting impulses of individualism and integrity beset them; the role of the composer in an industrial society, wishing both to serve and to be served by it, was an issue. As one major figure of American music of the 1930s, Roy Harris, put it, "How to serve society as a composer, how to become economically and socially recognized as a worth-contributing citizen, how to establish durable human contacts with individuals or groups is a harassing problem."[2]

One common American way to become "economically . . . recognized" in the 1930s was through trade-union organization; and in place of the idealistic and music-minded modern-music societies of the 1920s, composers of the 1930s banded together in hardheaded, economics-minded protective associations. In addition to the virtually monopolistic American Society of Composers, Authors and Publishers (ASCAP) as a performing-rights organization, the period saw the formation of the rival Broadcast Music, Inc. (BMI; organized 1939)—both organizations aiming to collect fees for the performance of works by their member-composers. The American Composers Alliance (ACA; organized 1938) also aimed to promote the interests of American composers and later (1977) sponsored the establishment of the American Com-

---

[2] "Problems of American Composers," in Henry Cowell, ed., *American Composers on American Music* (1933; 2nd ed. New York: Frederick Ungar, 1962), 149–66; the passage quoted, 164.

posers Orchestra for performance of their works. Performers too became more solidly organized: the American Federation of Musicians (organized 1896) became ever more aggressively protective under its president, James C. Petrillo; the American Guild of Musical Arts (AGMA), organized in 1936, watched over the fortunes of musicians, especially singers, and other artists in opera, oratorio, ballet, and concerts in general. Some aid to both composers and performers during the depths of the Depression was forthcoming from the government through the Federal Music Project of the Works Progress Administration. Created in 1935, by 1938 the project was providing work for about 10,000 people. Project-supported concerts, music lending libraries, and music education in rural and congested urban areas helped to broaden the American audience; programs of collecting folk and ethnic music stimulated interest in these fields. Composers were not, however, subsidized for free musical composition (as were painters under the Federal Art Project of the WPA); they were assigned other musical tasks of various sorts, and a few were asked to supply music for documentary films.

The major works of Aaron Copland during this 1930–45 period reflect the themes I have cited: a conservative trend, a historical or regional Americanism, and a search for a broader public. Copland replaced abstract music with the acidity and astringency of his *Piano Variations* or *Vitebsk*, both dating from the late 1920s, with gentler, smoother, and generally more accessible works, virtually all of them on regional or topical themes.[3] The orchestral tone poem *El Salón México* (1936) was based on popular-song material from south of the border. The ballet scores for *Billy the Kid* (1938) and *Rodeo* (1942) evoked the spirit of the Far West and included some skillfully recomposed cowboy tunes, whereas *Appalachian Spring* (1944) dealt with early-nineteenth-century Pennsylvania rural life, expressed in country-fiddle-style tunes and hymnlike cantilenas and climaxing with some lucid variations on the Shaker hymn tune *Simple Gifts* (subtly smoothed-out melodically by the composer). In a cheerfully utilitarian spirit, Copland wrote works for amateur and school ensembles, such as the high school play-opera *The Second Hurricane* (1937) and *An Outdoor Overture* (1938) for orchestra. For the new mass media he composed *Music for Radio* (1937; subtitled *A Saga of the Prairie*) and film scores for *The City* (1939), *Of Mice and Men* (1939), *Our Town* (1940), *The Red Pony* (1948), and others. The entry of the United States into World War II evoked several frankly patriotic works from him, among them *Lincoln Portrait* (1942), which mingled Stephen Foster song fragments and folk songs (notably *On Springfield Mountain*; see p. 30 and Example 2–1) with narrated excerpts from Lincoln's speeches; and *Fanfare for the Common Man* (1942). The latter—at least its opening, which was bought for commercial use in various media—became probably Copland's

---

[3] The exceptions that proved the rule were two abstract sonatas—for piano (1939–41) and for violin and piano (1942–43)—and *Statements* (1932–35), for orchestra, in which something of the harshness of the *Piano Variations* is to be heard.

most universally known work; its wide-intervalled, jagged diatonic theme typified his new melodic manner, one that somehow was inevitably associated with the broad plains and rugged mountains of the country, though it came from the pen of an urbane New York City composer (Example 9–1).

EXAMPLE 9–1.   A. Copland, *Fanfare for the Common Man* (1942), measures 1–16 (percussion omitted). © Copyright 1943 by The Aaron Copland Fund for Music, Inc. Copyright Renewed. Reprinted by permission of Boosey & Hawkes, Inc., Sole Licensee.

Most of such works—by others as well as Copland—not only were aimed at the broad new American audience but also drew from a wide spectrum of the American experience for subject matter and from the American past for musical materials. Indeed, the American musical past was generally viewed with new interest and reevaluation during the period. In 1931 appeared the first really comprehensive history of American cultivated-tradition music, *Our American Music*, by John Tasker Howard (1890–1964); by 1946, so much new research had been done that Howard had to revise the book completely. Especially notable was the rediscovery (perhaps it would be more accurate to say the "discovery") of the music of Charles Ives—pianist John Kirkpatrick's premiere public performance in 1939 of the "Concord" Sonata was a landmark—and of earlier American music, especially the eighteenth-century New England singing-school music and American folk music in general. These rediscoveries were reflected in the form of innumerable "Hoedowns," "Hayrides," "Square Dances," and the like, in a variety of media.

Ross Lee Finney (1906–97), a Middle Westerner trained under Nadia Boulanger and Alban Berg in Europe, found inspiration in American Colonial music for his choral work *Pilgrim Psalms* (1945), which drew on melodies from Ainsworth's psalter (see p. 3), and in Federal-era music for his orchestral *Hymn, Fuguing and Holiday* (1943), which went back to the Yankee tunesmiths, as did the *Prelude to a Hymn Tune (after William Billings)* (1937) of Otto Luening. Henry Cowell began a long series of works inspired by shapenote hymnody, most of them titled *Hymn and Fuguing Tune* (1944–64); as he put it, "I asked myself the question, What would have happened if this fine, serious early style had developed?"[4] William Schuman made use of a ubiquitous American children's cry (phoneticized by him as "wee-awk-eee") in *American Festival Overture* (1939); his *William Billings Overture* (1943) drew from three singing-school pieces of the early Boston composer.

THOMSON, HARRIS, AND BLITZSTEIN

Three composers who shared a common background of study in the 1920s with Boulanger and who participated in the musical "American Wave" were Virgil Thomson, Roy Harris, and Marc Blitzstein. The first two were interested in America's musical past, Blitzstein in certain aspects of the present. Of Harris and Thomson, both Middle Westerners, Harris was the more aggressively "Americanist," but Thomson's music suggested an equally profound immersion in, and sympathy for, the American musical heritage; and his uses of it, which went back to the late 1920s, antedated other composers'.

Thomson once wrote a quotably succinct autobiographical note:

> I was born November 25, 1896 in Kansas City, Missouri, grew up there and went to war from there. That was the other war. Then I was educated some more in Boston and Paris. In composition I was a pupil of Nadia Boulanger. While I was still young I taught music at Harvard and played the organ at King's Chapel, Boston. Then I returned to Paris and lived there for many years, till the Germans came, in fact. Now I live in New York, where I am Music Critic of the Herald Tribune [from which he resigned in 1954 but stayed in New York and lived on until 1989].[5]

Thomson called his *Sonata da Chiesa* (1926) for clarinet, trumpet, viola, horn, and trombone in three dissonant, neo-Baroque movements (Chorale, Tango, Fugue) a "bang-up graduation piece" from Boulanger's studio, but the inclusion of the dance rhythms of a tango suggests the impact of Satie and

---

[4] Quoted in Wayne D. Shirley, "The Hymns and Fuguing Tunes," in *The Whole World of Music: A Henry Cowell Symposium*, ed. David Nicholls (Amsterdam: Harwood Academic Publishers, 1997), 95–143 (the quotation, 96).

[5] Quoted in Peggy Glanville-Hicks, "Virgil Thomson," *MQ* 35 (1949): 210.

the younger French composers, as had those of the piano works *Two Senti-mental Tangos* (1923) and *Synthetic Waltzes* (1925). As early as 1926, how-ever, Thomson, a Protestant and an organist, began to turn to American hymnody. One important result was a *Symphony on a Hymn Tune* (two movements sketched 1926; completed 1928). At about the same time, he composed for organ the pointedly irreverent and very funny *Variations on Sunday School Tunes* (1927) and settings of texts by Gertrude Stein, who had accepted Thomson as an artistically fastidious, amusing, and courageous fellow expatriate in Paris (the song *Susie Asado*, 1926; the male-chorus piece *Capital Capitals*, 1927).

Thomson's Francophilia, his sophisticated, pseudo-innocent way with American hymnbook harmony, his respect for language, his wit, and his close relationship with Stein were to result in one of the most extraordinary works of American music: the opera *Four Saints in Three Acts* (1928), first pro-duced by the Friends and Enemies of Modern Music of Hartford, Con-necticut, in 1934. Stein's account of the genesis of the work goes this way:

> Virgil Thomson had asked Gertrude Stein to write an opera for him. Among the saints there were two saints whom she had always liked better than any others, Saint Theresa of Avila and Ignatius Loyola, and she said she would write him an opera about these two saints. She began this and worked very hard at it all that spring [1927] and finally finished Four Saints and gave it to Virgil Thomson to put to music. He did. And it is a completely interesting opera both as to words and music.[6]

Four Saints is a work of fantasy, liveliness, and inexplicable charm. Impossi-ble to interpret literally, equally impossible to dismiss as meaningless, it of-fers a childlike, surrealistic procession of tableaux about saints (many more than four) doing what we suppose saints do: receive visitors, pose for earth-ly reproductions, discuss human problems and saintly ones too, love Christ, rejoice. Thomson's setting is similarly childlike. He explained, "With mean-ings already abstracted, or absent, or so multiplied that choice among them was impossible ... you could make a setting for sound and syntax only, then add, if needed, an accompaniment equally functional";[7] and he composed de-ceptively simple music, which both supports discreetly and projects impec-cably Stein's verses. The original chamber orchestration of nineteen players is dominated by the sound of an accordion, which gives a pungent reediness to the successions of plain chords that characterize the harmony.

The very beginning of the Prologue of *Four Saints* establishes the tone of affected yet effective simplicity, with a waltz vamp underlying a metrical-ly variable exhortation by the chorus, in crystal-clear octaves, to "prepare for

---

[6] *The Autobiography of Alice B. Toklas* (New York: Harcourt, Brace, 1933), 281.
[7] *Virgil Thomson* (New York: Knopf, 1966; repr. New York: Da Capo Press, 1977), 90.

EXAMPLE 9–2. V. Thomson, *Four Saints in Three Acts* (1934), measures 1–8. Copyright © 1948 (Renewed) by G. Schirmer, Inc. (ASCAP). International Copyright Secured. All Rights Reserved. Reprinted by Permission.

[four?] saints" (Example 9–2). Saint Theresa is introduced with affectionate malice as one who pontificates repetitiously about the obvious ("There are a great many persons and places near together"); Thomson's music leads to a neo-Handelian climax marked "Grandioso (liberamente)." A celebrated Vision of the Holy Ghost ("Pigeons on the grass alas") begets strangely moving music. A Saints' Procession finds Thomson retiring almost completely into the background, allowing Stein's leaden processional ("In wed in dead / in dead wed led / in led wed dead") to plod solemnly across the stage, over sustained chords. Ultimately the work defies description and perhaps analysis; as John Cage wrote sensitively, "To enjoy it, one must leap into that irrational world from which it sprang, the world in which the matter-of-fact and the irrational are one, where mirth and metaphysics marry to beget comedy."[8]

---

[8] Kathleen Hoover and John Cage, *Virgil Thomson: His Life and Music* (New York: T. Yoseloff, 1959), 157.

Historically, *Four Saints* more than any other single work offered a model for the new simplicity in American music of the 1930s and suggested how the triadic harmony of the American past could be used with fresh incisiveness: as Thomson commented in his saucy survey of *The State of Music* in 1939, it had music that was "simple, melodic, and harmonious ... after twenty years of everybody's trying to make music just a little bit louder and more unmitigated and more complex than anybody else's." A similar artful simplicity pervades the later Stein-Thomson collaboration, *The Mother of Us All* (1947; *NW* CD 80288), an opera about political life in nineteenth-century America centered on the women's-rights activist Susan B. Anthony. Its music is wholly of Thomson's contrivance, but it has a warmly nostalgic atmosphere; he spoke of the work as

> a memory-book of Victorian play-games and passions ... with its gospel hymns and cocky marches, its sentimental ballads, waltzes, darned-fool ditties and intoned sermons ... a souvenir of all those sounds and kinds of tunes that were once the music of rural America.[9]

Thomson was the first major American composer of concert music to write for films. But he did not enter the highly specialized and, for a concert-music composer, infinitely frustrating musical wing of the Hollywood industry; he wrote instead scores for several government-sponsored documentary films: two directed by Pare Lorentz, *The Plow That Broke the Plains* (1936) and *The River* (1937), and a wartime propaganda film for the Office of War Information, *Tuesday in November* (1945). For Robert Flaherty's *Louisiana Story* (1948), similarly a documentary (but produced by the Standard Oil Company), Thomson wrote a score that provided music for almost sixty of the film's seventy-seven minutes; except for Thomson's operas, it was his longest composition. In all these films, Thomson's sympathy for American folk and vernacular-tradition music was apparent: *The Plow That Broke the Plains* borrows cowboy songs; *The River*, white spirituals from *The Southern Harmony* and *The Sacred Harp*; *Tuesday in November*, waltzes, hymns, and *Yankee Doodle*; *Louisiana Story*, the Acadian ("Cajun") songs and dances of the bayou country.

Roy Harris (1898–1979) was another of the early pupils of Boulanger, between 1926 and 1929. A prolific composer, by the early 1940s he had produced a vast number of works in almost all media except opera. Beginning with his Op. 1, a Piano Sonata (1928–29; *CRI* CD 818), Harris's style seemed firmly and idiosyncratically established: it was marked by expansive, rolling melodies, often modal but equally often chromatic; bichordal harmony of a personal and immediately recognizable sort; contrapuntal textures and devices of all kinds; and a sense of form that avoided the neo-Classic types popular in the 1930s with many composers, but favored neo-Baroque ideas such

---

[9] Quoted in the informative notes, by Robert Marx, for the recording cited.

as fugue, ostinato, and passacaglia. Harris displayed his American interests in works such as the Symphony No. 4 with chorus (*Folksong Symphony*; 1940); the orchestral piece *When Johnny Comes Marching Home* (1934; subtitled "An American Overture"), which Harris based on a Civil War song and planned precisely in length and form to fit the two sides of a 78–rpm recording; *Gettysburg Address Symphony*, No. 6 (1944); *Railroad Man's Ballad* (1941) for chorus and orchestra; and *American Ballads* (1942) for piano.

Many works by Harris, however, were musically abstract, such as the two that some still consider, at this writing six decades later, to be his most masterly: the Quintet for Piano and Strings (1936) and the Third Symphony in One Movement (1939). Characteristic of the long-breathed melodic line of Harris is the theme of the symphony's second ("lyric") section: very chromatic, uncertainly focused on any single tonic note; fluid in tempo, phrase length, meter, and dynamics but even-paced in rhythm, it seems boundless, a grand rhetorical proselike utterance (Example 9–3 [a]). In sharp contrast is the terse, motive-centered, energetic yet asymmetrical subject of the fugal section of the symphony; not identifiably related to anyone else's music, its internal cross-rhythms and ambiguous meter nevertheless stamp it as "Made in the U.S.A." (Example 9–3 [b]). The Third Symphony's "pastoral" section is justly famous for its "seemingly endless succession of spun-out melodies" (the phrase is Copland's); its basis is a bellowslike ostinato figure, expanding and contracting in the bass, and its carefully planned polychordal harmony gradually increases in density, resonance, and tension until it bursts into the resolute fugue. The Piano Quintet is less originally shaped; it represents the more retrospective, contrapuntal turn of Harris's mind with its three movements, Passacaglia, Cadenza, and (triple) Fugue.

EXAMPLE 9–3.   R. Harris, *Third Symphony in One Movement*. Copyright © 1939 (Renewed) by Associated Music Publishers, Inc. (BMI). International Copyright Secured. All Rights Reserved. Reprinted by Permission. (*a*) "Lyric" theme (measures 60–97). (*b*) "Fugue" subject (measures 416–21).

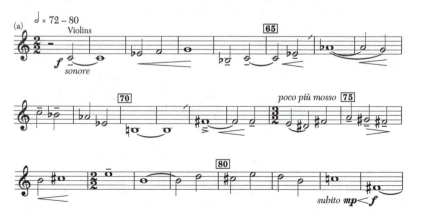

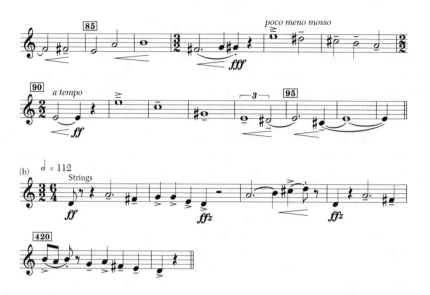

Harris's star declined rather precipitously after the 1940s; by the 1990s (and even during his centennial in 1998) he was virtually a forgotten composer.

If works like Thomson's *Hymn Tune Symphony* and Harris's *Folk-song Symphony* suggested a new rapprochement between concert music and the music of America's older vernacular and folk traditions, many works by Marc Blitzstein (1905–64)—for the lyric theater, the legitimate theater (incidental music), films, and radio—bespoke a similar rapprochement with contemporaneous popular music. In such operas, or "plays with music," as he preferred to call them, as *The Cradle Will Rock* (1936–37) and *No for an Answer* (1938–40), Blitzstein was strongly influenced by the music-theater works of Bertolt Brecht and Kurt Weill, particularly *Die Dreigroschenoper* (1928), which Blitzstein later translated and adapted as *The Threepenny Opera* (1952). His main achievement, one might claim, was to raise the style of the Broadway musical to an exquisitely calculated level of harsh refinement.

Both *The Cradle Will Rock* and *No for an Answer* were morality plays written from a leftist political and social viewpoint; both may be seen as modern ballad operas based on the style of the American pop song and the speech of the American streets; both were deceptively "easy" works; and neither could have been composed by anybody without the thorough training (both with Schoenberg in Berlin and with Boulanger in Paris) and high intelligence of Blitzstein. In these "plays with music," Blitzstein cunningly built up substantial scenes with a unique combination of spoken dialogue, precise rhythmic speech (notated musically), and song; take any of these elements away, and much of the peculiar power of their blend is lost. "Penny Candy," from *No for an Answer*, is a murderous satire on a do-gooder's morbid curiosity about addiction; without its preliminary monologue, spoken over a sparse, dry accompaniment, the song itself seems only silly. Yet even the briefest excerpt of "Honolulu," from *The Cradle Will Rock*, can suggest Blitzstein's subtle transformation of popular-song style: the clichés of the vocal line are cancelled out by the freshness of the accompaniment, with its irregular texture underlying the first four phrases; its hint of Hawaiian steel guitars under "-lulu" and "banned"; its offbeat accentuation of the bass under the raucous refrain; and its acrid inversion of a dominant-ninth chord under "isle" (Example 9–4).

EXAMPLE 9–4. M. Blitzstein, "Honolulu," *The Cradle Will Rock* (1937), measures 1–13. © 1938 Christopher Davis and Stephen E. Davis. Renewed. Quoted by permission of the Estate of Marc Blitzstein.

Blitzstein was committed to an ideal of moral persuasion in his art. One song's lyrics in *The Cradle Will Rock* summarize his scorn for other ideals:

> Art for Art's sake,
> It's smart, for Art's sake,
> To part, for Art's sake,
> With your mind, for Art's sake,
> Be blind, for Art's sake,
> And deaf, for Art's sake,
> And dumb, for Art's sake,
> Until, for Art's sake,
> They kill, for Art's sake,
> All the Art for Art's sake.[10]

This was a common point of view among socially conscious, leftist musical artists of the 1930s. A number among them were members of the Composers Collective of New York, which met regularly from 1931 to 1936 to discuss politics and assess newly composed "mass songs, dealing with immediate social issues ... to be sung at meetings, on parades, and on picket lines." (Thus did Blizstein, as secretary of the Collective, begin a list of the group's aims.) Other members, who often wrote such songs under pseudonyms, included Henry Cowell (apparently only briefly); the émigrés Hanns Eisler and Stefan Wolpe; Ruth Crawford's husband, Charles Seeger ("Carl Sands"); Elie Siegmeister ("L. E. Swift"); and Earl Robinson, whose *I Dreamed I Saw Joe Hill* became a staple of the "folk revival" of the 1950s and later, especially with the performance of Joan Baez at Woodstock in 1969. Both Aaron Copland and Roy Harris, though not members, were sympathetic; Copland's setting of Alfred Hayes's "Into the Streets May First" even won a Composers Collective competition for the best new song for May Day 1934 and was published in the second *Workers' Songbook* (1935).

Nevertheless, periodic revivals of Blitzstein's *The Cradle Will Rock* as well as his later (and more elaborate) opera *Regina* (1949) and his powerful adaptation of *The Threepenny Opera* (the first run of which, in New York in 1954–61, lasted for more than 2,500 performances) suggest that it was not so much the message as the music that was significant in his art.

IN THE GROVES OF ACADEME

Reflecting a new approach to the education of professional musicians (and confirming the fact that few composers of concert music could make a living by composing alone), many of the most highly esteemed composers of the period occupied professorial chairs in American colleges and universities.

---

[10] © 1938 Christopher Davis and Stephen E. Davis. Renewed. Quoted by permission of the Estate of Marc Blitzstein.

Roger Sessions (1896–1985) taught at several institutions before settling first at Princeton University (1935–44), going to the University of California at Berkeley (1944–53), then returning to Princeton until his retirement in 1965 (after which, however, he taught for years at the Juilliard School of Music). Sessions's early studies at Harvard and Yale linked him with the academic tradition of the Second New England School (as did his later long residence, 1926–33, in Europe), but more significant in his development were years of study and association with the Swiss-American composer Ernest Bloch (1880–1959). In the 1930–45 period, Sessions's style was moving from the diatonic neo-Classicism of his First Symphony (1927; *CRI* CD 573) and First Piano Sonata (1930), through the more chromatic and expressionistic manner of a Violin Concerto (1935; *CRI* CD 676) and a First String Quartet (1936), to the highly chromatic, long-lined, and dense-textured Second Piano Sonata and Second Symphony (both 1946). His largest work is the opera *Montezuma* (1963); one of his few public successes was the forty-minute choral cantata *When Lilacs Last in the Dooryard Bloom'd* (1970; *NW* LP 296), setting Walt Whitman's response to the death of Abraham Lincoln; composer John Harbison—a former Sessions student—called it (in his entry on Sessions in *AmeriGrove*) unparalleled in its "natural and inevitable flow," with its "big, asymmetrical phrases springing forward like Whitman's sprawling, irrepressible poetic lines."

Walter Piston (1894–1976) returned in 1926 from study in Paris with Boulanger to Harvard University (where he had trained in the first place) and remained on the faculty there until his retirement in 1960. His music is of an elegant neo-Classic sort, beautifully crafted and mostly limited to abstract, traditional instrumental genres. A perfect example is the Symphony No. 6 (1955; *NW* LP 286), composed for the Boston Symphony Orchestra, which Piston, as a Boston-area resident, knew intimately. It is twenty-four minutes long in four movements. An influential teacher, Piston reinterpreted Boulanger's French scholastic pedagogy in several influential textbooks: *Principles of Harmonic Analysis* (1933), *Harmony* (1941), *Counterpoint* (1947), and *Orchestration* (1955). (That *Harmony* could be reprinted, even with revisions, in a fifth edition [1987] more than forty-five years after its first publication may say as much about the conservatism of academic education in music theory as about the excellence of Piston's pedagogy.)

Quincy Porter (1897–1966) taught at Vassar College and the New England Conservatory in Boston, then in 1946 returned to Yale University, where he had begun as a pupil of Horatio Parker. He was emphatically a composer of chamber music—for example, nine string quartets, in an international style. Douglas Moore (1893–1969) was at Columbia University and well into a career emphasizing operas on American subjects: *The Headless Horseman* (1936) and *The Devil and Daniel Webster* (1938) were followed after World War II by the highly successful, musically nostalgic opera *The Ballad of Baby Doe* (1956) and another, *Carry Nation* (1966). William Schuman was at Sarah Lawrence College (later at the Juilliard School of Music);

Ross Lee Finney, at Smith College (later to move to the University of Michigan). Roy Harris moved from institution to institution.

The presence on college and university campuses of these and other eminent composers reflected the fact that especially in institutions to the south and west beyond the northeastern seaboard, the professional training of young musicians—formerly limited typically, as in Europe, to music conservatories—was being taken up by academic institutions. The major conservatories in the United States, such as the Juilliard School in New York, Peabody Conservatory in Baltimore, Curtis Institute in Philadelphia, and New England Conservatory in Boston, still offered the most thorough professional training for performers. More and more, however, the colleges and universities, better endowed than the smaller conservatories, also became training grounds for workday musicians. This was to have broad ramifications in the post–World War II years in the development of college instrumental ensembles and opera workshops of remarkably high caliber, and the establishment of professional performing groups, soloists, and first-rank composers "in residence" (if also required to do some teaching). But before the war, the picture was dominated by the composer-professors, attempting to maintain their integrity as composers while employed as full-time professors.[11]

To many colleges and universities in the 1930s, furthermore, came refugees from Europe during the Nazi and Fascist regimes. The 1940s opened with such composers in America as Stravinsky, Schoenberg, Bartók, Milhaud, Weill, Paul Hindemith, Ernest Krenek, Bohuslav Martinů, and Stefan Wolpe, and most of them were soon attached to college-level music departments. Their very presence contributed to a breakdown of the American tendency, during this period, to a musical isolationism, and ultimately to a new role for the United States after World War II as international leader of progressive trends in Western music.

Scholar-musicians, too, were among the European émigrés to arrive in the United States; they provided a stimulus for the establishment of musicology as an accepted discipline in American universities. Although a chair of musicology had been created at Cornell University in 1930 for Otto Kinkeldey (1878–1966), it was really the impact of such newly arrived European musicologists of the stature of Hans T. David, Alfred Einstein, Karl Geiringer, Curt Sachs, Leo Schrade, and others that led to a rapid development of musicological curricula in American universities and to the consolidation of the American Musicological Society (established 1934) and the Music Library Association (1931).

---

[11] Sessions offered some sober speculations on the composer as professor in a "Conversation with Roger Sessions," *PNM* 4/2 (Spring–Summer 1966): 29–46. Twenty-three American composers confronted the matter, in as many essays, in "The Composer in Academia: Reflections on a Theme of Stravinsky," *College Music Symposium* 10 (1970): 55–98.

YOUNGER COMPOSERS OF THE PERIOD

If the composer-professors typified the basic conservatism of the 1930–45 period, so did the rise to prominence of fundamentally conservative young composers as opposed to vanguardists. The acknowledged young leaders were probably Samuel Barber, Gian Carlo Menotti, William Schuman, and an "Eastman School group."

Samuel Barber (1910–81) demonstrated a conservative lyricism in his earliest works: songs and choral pieces and an impassioned setting for voice and string quartet of Matthew Arnold's *Dover Beach* (1931; Barber's own performance of 1935, with the Curtis Quartet, is on *NW* LP 229). Tending to write single, masterly examples in each instrumental genre, he applied an easy, cantabile vocal line to works such as the Sonata for Violoncello and Piano (1932) and to two orchestral pieces that achieved a *succès d'estime* when, alone among American compositions, they were performed by the ultraconservative conductor Arturo Toscanini and his NBC Symphony Orchestra: the (first) *Essay for Orchestra* (1937) and an *Adagio for Strings* (1938, adapted from the slow movement of the 1936 String Quartet). Despite some absorption of Stravinskyan textures in a work such as the ingratiating *Capricorn Concerto* (1944) and of Schoenbergian chromaticism in a big Piano Sonata (1949), Barber's style continued along a neo-Romantic, "expressive" path. One of the most poignant exemplars of that style, partly because of the warm nostalgia of its text by James Agee, is *Knoxville: Summer of 1915* (1948) for voice and orchestra, in a characteristically accessible rondolike form. Barber's ill-starred opera *Antony and Cleopatra*, a failure when in 1966 it opened the Metropolitan Opera Company's new house at Lincoln Center in New York, was better received as revised later (1974; *NW* CD 80322).

A close associate of Barber's from their days together as students at the Curtis Institute was Gian Carlo Menotti (he was to be the librettist for Barber's elaborately Victorian grand opera *Vanessa* [1958] and his ten-minute chamber opera *A Hand of Bridge* [1959]). By the mid-1940s Menotti (b. 1911 in Italy; to America 1927) had successfully bridged the gap between the opera house and Broadway: after modest successes with *Amelia al Ballo* (produced in 1937 in English translation as *Amelia Goes to the Ball*) and *The Old Maid and the Thief* (1939), his intense and spooky short opera *The Medium* (1946), preceded by a clever curtain-raising skit, *The Telephone*, began in 1947 a durable career as competitor to the spoken dramas of the Broadway playhouses. Menotti combined the theatrical sense of a popular playwright and a Pucciniesque musical vocabulary with an Italianate love of liquid language and a humane interest in characters as real human beings; the result was opera more accessible than anyone else's at the time. Writing his own librettos, Menotti had a knack for choosing timeless themes of human conflict in topical settings.

Two other operas by Menotti that are cannily full of *coups de théâtre* are *The Consul* (1950), based on the frustrations of life under a bureaucracy (its powerful, moving climactic scena, "To this we've come: / That men withhold the world from men," is on NW LP 241), and an hour-long Christmastide fantasy, *Amahl and the Night Visitors* (1951), the first opera commissioned for production on television. Both became even greater popular successes than *The Medium*. The full-scale opera *The Saint of Bleecker Street* (1954), poised on the razor's edge of the human conflict between spiritual and physical desires, won several prizes and had many productions; Menotti's later works, however, were less successful—even the inventive *Help, Help, the Globolinks!* (1968), with its electronic music haloing invaders from outer space.

William Schuman (1910–92) was mentioned earlier (p. 237) as a participant in the "American Wave" of the 1930s. *American Festival Overture* was followed by other works on American themes, such as *New England Triptych* (1956) for orchestra (built on William Billings's *Be Glad Then, America; When Jesus Wept* (see p. 11); and *Chester*); a baseball opera, *The Mighty Casey* (1953); and a cantata after Walt Whitman, *A Free Song* (1942). Schuman also wrote several big works for wind band, among them *Newsreel (in Five Shots)* (1941) and *George Washington Bridge* (1950). These were a response to the immense proliferation of bands in schools and colleges across the land. The marching band, most often in evidence between the halves of intercollegiate football games, had once again become a major voice of American vernacular-tradition music. This revival of the band's popularity was accompanied, however, by cultivated-tradition ideals of polished performance. An old problem of bands, their uncertain instrumentation, was disappearing as a more or less standardized instrumentation emerged (as suggested in an informative table by Raoul Camus in his entry "Bands" in *AmeriGrove*). After the football season the marching bands, often retitled "symphonic wind ensembles," became concert-giving organizations. Good contemporary music was needed for them. Schuman was not alone in helping to fill the demand: among others, Thomson contributed *A Solemn Music* and *At the Beach* (both 1949); Harris, the overture *Cimarron* (1941), *Take the Sun and Keep the Stars* (1944), and *Fruit of Gold* (1949); Barber, a *Commando March* (1943).

More important in Schuman's output were orchestral symphonies, string quartets, and choral works. A pupil of Harris, Schuman shared with him a fondness for rhapsodic or ostinato forms, long chromatic slow themes, and polychordal harmony. Schuman's rhythms, however, tended to be more nervously athletic than Harris's, more clearly related to pop-music origins, and his orchestration brighter, more sharp-edged with brass and metal-percussion instruments. Two excerpts from his *Symphony for Strings* (1943; effectively his Fifth Symphony), the first used also in one movement of his *Three-Score Set* for piano (1943), can suggest, respectively, Schuman's resonant bichordal harmony and his energetic, stuttering fast-movement rhythms

EXAMPLE 9–5. W. Schuman, *Symphony for Strings.* Copyright © 1943 (Renewed) by Associated Music Publishers, Inc. (BMI). International Copyright Secured. All Rights Reserved. Reprinted by Permission. (*a*) Second movement, measures 1–4 (piano score reduction). (*b*) Third movement, measures 1–11 (First Violin part only).

(Example 9–5). The Symphony No. 3 (1941) joined Copland's Third and Harris's Third as a modern classic; the three works were occasionally programmed together. Critical opinion, however, rated even higher the secular cantata to a text by Whitman *A Free Song* (1942), which won the first Pulitzer Prize in music, and the Sixth Symphony (1948), considered by some to be Schuman's masterpiece. Other important scores, by a composer convinced of the power and potential of modern dance, and one for whom the orchestra was the most natural as well as the most important vehicle of his thought, were for dance; for Martha Graham, Schuman wrote a number of scores, including *Undertow* (1945; *NW LP 253*) and the Graham masterpiece *Night Journey* (1947; *CRI CD 791*).

Several other younger composers of promise in the late 1930s and early 1940s were graduates of the Eastman School of Music at the University of Rochester, under Howard Hanson's administration; they had studied either with Hanson or with Bernard Rogers (1893–1968). This "Eastman Group" included Robert Palmer (b. 1915), Robert Ward (b. 1917), William Bergsma (1921–94), and Peter Mennin (1923–83). All shared the relatively conservative, evolutionary attitudes of their mentors; all seemed to share an aim to write the Great American Symphony by way of the Depression-Era Overture—a one-movement piece ten minutes in length or less, with at least one section of broadly arching, wide-intervalled, mostly diatonic melody supported by slow-moving, rich harmony. The harmony, although functional and directive, avoided structures such as dominant sevenths or ninths and diminished-seventh chords; nontertial sonorities replaced them, as did sometimes triads or added-tone chords derived from diatonic (but not usually major) modes.

Also related to the Eastman School (if only as a sometime student there) was David Diamond (b. 1915), whose first major orchestral work, *Symphony in One Movement* (1931), was premiered at Eastman while he was a special student of violin there. Diamond left the school after a year's study with Rogers (1933–34) to seek a more progressive atmosphere. He worked with both Sessions and Boulanger and lived for many years in Florence, Italy (1953–65). A prolific, professional composer with nine symphonies, ten string quartets, and many other works in all media to his credit, Diamond had many performances of works such as *Psalm* (1936) for orchestra, *Elegy in Memory of Maurice Ravel* (1938–39), *Rounds* (1944) for string orchestra, and an orchestral suite from incidental music for *Romeo and Juliet* (1947), perhaps his most frequently performed piece—all in a lyrical, but intense and finely crafted personal style.

The only strong avant-garde impulse during the period was felt on the West Coast: there, carrying on where Cowell had begun, younger composers such as John Cage and Lou Harrison (b. 1917) interested themselves in percussion music, non-Western scales, and new means of formal organization. An older one, Harry Partch (1901–74), pursued a lonely path to a whole new theory of music based on division of the octave into forty-three tones. Partch codified his theory in detail in the book *Genesis of a New Music* (1949) and, in order to have his music performed according to the theory, invented and built more than two dozen extraordinary (and exceptionally beautiful) instruments. They admirably supported his ideal of a vital, corporeal, theatrical musical experience, projected in such "dramatic" works (some unstaged) as *Barstow* (1941; revised versions to 1968; *CRI* CD 752), originally for solo voice and three of Partch's instruments (Adapted Guitar, Chromelodeon, and Kithara), its text eight hitchhiker's inscriptions that Partch found on a highway railing outside Barstow, California. Others of Partch's highly idiosyncratic works are *The Bewitched* (1955; *CRI* CD 754), subtitled *A Ballet Satire*—"a seeking for release—through satire, whimsy, magic, ribaldry—from the catharsis of tragedy," for female voice and twelve instruments; and *Castor and Pollux* (*A Dance for the Twin Rhythms of Gemini*) (1952; *CRI* CD 751), for six dancers and six instruments (Kithara, Surrogate Kithara, Harmonic Canon, Cloud-Chamber Bowls, Diamond Marimba, and Bass Marimba).

John Cage (1912–92) studied with both Cowell and Schoenberg. In a foreword to a catalogue of his works, he summarized "the various paths my musical thought has taken"; those of the period before World War II were based on

> ... chromatic composition dealing with the problem of keeping repetitions of individual tones as far apart as possible (1933–34); composition with fixed rhythmic patterns or tone-row fragments (1935–38); composition for the dance, film and theatre (1935–); composition within rhythmic structures (the whole having as many parts as each unit has small parts, and these, large and small, in the same proportion) (1939–56); [and] intentionally expressive composition (1938–51).[12]

Few people in the period were aware of Cage as an early exponent of Schoenberg's tone-row technique or a composer who applied rather similar principles to the organization of rhythm. Many more were familiar with Cage's "prepared piano." "Preparation" meant the alteration of the instrument's tonal quality by inserting between the strings various bits of material; the preparation varied depending on the expressive aim. The sonic result, totally unlike the usual sound of a piano, is like a tiny version of an Indonesian gamelan orchestra of chimes, gongs, and delicate percussion instruments. This ingenious adaptation of the instrument arose out of Cage's work with modern dancers (from 1938 on, first as accompanist for a group in Seattle, where he met the dancer and choreographer Merce Cunningham and they began a long collaboration). "The need to change the sound of the instrument arose through the desire to make an accompaniment, without employing percussion instruments, suitable for the dance ... for which it was to be composed" was Cage's comment on the first prepared-piano piece, *Bacchanale* (1940). His most extended work for prepared piano, the seventy-minute *Sonatas and Interludes* (1946–48; *CRI* CD 700, partially on *NW* LP 203), aims to express the various "permanent emotions" of the Indian subcontinent's tradition. (His interest in Asia, later to be decisive in his musical thought, was already apparent.) Two movements for prepared piano flank two all-percussion trios in *Amores* (1943); and Cage's interest in what Varèse had called "sound—any sound" led him to write a number of all-percussion pieces, adding to the more or less conventional instruments such new sound sources as phonorecording-playbacks of constant and variable speeds, sound-generator whines, and other mechanical and electronic devices (*Imaginary Landscape* No. 1 [1939] and *Imaginary Landscape* Nos. 2 and 3 [1942]).

---

[12] *John Cage* (New York: Henmar Press, 1962), 5; the "comment" by Cage in the following paragraph, 15.

JAZZ: SWING

Jazz of the 1930s underwent a major change in style from that of the 1920s. For most of the pre–World War II period, in fact, the very term "jazz" implied the earlier style, the "hot jazz" of the 1920s. The newer style was called "swing," a term emblemized by a 1932 recording of Duke Ellington's band with singer Ivie Anderson (1905–49): *It Don't Mean a Thing If It Ain't Got That Swing.* The swing style was materializing in the late 1920s and early 1930s, but most Americans did not hear it until about 1935. In the intervening years, between the financial crash and the mid-1930s, the strident, earthy music of New Orleans jazz was out of fashion; America in crisis seemed to want rather to be lulled by the soothing sounds of radio crooners, such as Rudy Vallee (1901–86) and Bing Crosby (1904–77), and of nonjazz dance bands such as that of Guy Lombardo (1902–77). Some bands, however, found a way to compromise between the large, euphonious, popular dance band and the improvisatory, "swinging" manner of jazz, and their new jazz style reached the ears of the public (partly through several popular late-evening radio programs such as "Let's Dance" and "The Camel Caravan," the former sponsored by a cracker-manufacturing corporation, the latter by a cigarette company).

The main vehicle for swing was the big band—even bigger than those developed in the later 1920s. As Benny Goodman (1909–86), the virtuoso clarinetist whose band more than any other helped to popularize swing, explains in his autobiography, "It was about this time [1934], or maybe just a little earlier, that large bands became standardized with five brass, four saxes, and four rhythm. ... Ten men ... used to be considered the limit of even a large dance orchestra.[13] In the new big-band style, the individual voices of earlier jazz combos were replaced by the three "sections" mentioned by Goodman (and forecast by Don Redman's arrangements [see p. 228])—one of brass (trumpets and trombones), one of reeds (saxes, doubling occasionally on clarinets), and one of rhythm instruments (typically guitar, double bass, piano, and drums). Too unwieldy to permit either the casual approach to form or the pseudo-improvisation of early jazz, the big swing band of the 1930s relied on written arrangements. Increasingly, jazz improvisation became a matter of solos set off against an arranged background music. Models for such arrangements were found in the earlier work of Fletcher Henderson and Duke Ellington and in the arrangements for Jimmy Lunceford's band made by Sy Oliver (1910–88) between 1933 and 1939. These men could simulate an improvisatory style in their written-out, repetitive "riffs" for full band, or their antiphonal call-and-response dialogues of reeds against brass sections. Moreover, the musicians did not play the notes exactly as written: through many rehearsals, they shaped the written arrangements into an even more

---

[13] *The Kingdom of Swing* (Harrisburg, PA: Stackpole Sons, 1939), 138.

improvisatory, swinging style.[14] Partly because of the new necessity to be able to read music, partly because of the richly harmonized ensemble arrangements, and partly because the swing band had to play not only the older jazz "standards" but also the harmonically more sophisticated new popular songs, the chordal vocabulary of jazz musicians expanded. This was reflected in more adventurously chromatic solo improvisations.

The rhythmic basis of swing was a strong, even $\frac{4}{4}$ ("solid" was a favorite adjective of the period), as opposed to the tendency of earlier jazz to march along in $\frac{2}{2}$. Swing drummers typically overlaid the regular thumping four-beats-to-the-measure of the bass drum with a slight emphasis on beats 2 and 4 through a conventional pattern (♩ ♪♫ ♩ ♪♫ ♩) played with drumstick or wire brush on a hi-hat cymbal, with totally different effect from that produced by early jazz's accents on beats 1 and 3. One of the first drummers to establish this convention was Chick Webb (1902–39), but it was more closely identified with the Kansas City style of jazz as played by the bands of Bennie Moten (see p. 228) and his successor, William "Count" Basie (1904–84). Basie's band, along with Ellington's, was probably the most influential of all in establishing the swing style, but nationally the style was diffused by the bands of such white leaders as Goodman, Tommy Dorsey (1905–56), Artie Shaw (b. 1910), and Glenn Miller (1904–44), mainly because discriminatory practices made it difficult for the black bands to get the same degree of exposure to a mass audience.

The swing era seemed to breed virtuosos. Some were dazzling soloists, such as the peerless pianist Art Tatum (1910–56). From 1933 on, Tatum made more than six hundred recordings (some with small combos) that display his Harlem-stride-based style, enriched with harmonic elaborations, rhythmic and contrapuntal complications, and an almost unbelievable fleetness of hand (see/hear his solo performances of *Willow Weep for Me* and *Too Marvelous for Words* on *SCCJ* CD 2). Another soloistic virtuoso was the tenor saxophonist Coleman Hawkins (1904–69), noted especially for his "harmonic improvisation"—improvisation on the chords underlying the melody, as in his celebrated treatment, in 1939, of Johnny Green's *Body and Soul* (*SCCJ* CD 2).[15] Virtuosic, too, were a few legendary singers. One was Ella Fitzgerald (1918–96), who began a very long career with beguiling songs such as *A-Tisket, a-Tasket* (1938) backed up by Chick Webb's band (which Fitzgerald joined in 1935) and with "scat singing" (of wordless vocalises) with

---

[14] The use of "square" as a term of contempt was common during the era; it was a precise description of the way swing was *not* to be played. To the degree that soloists and even whole sections did not round off notated rhythms and pitches in an improvisatory, feelingful way, they were "square."

[15] Gunther Schuller transcribes Hawkins's entire solo in his *The Swing Era* (New York: Oxford University Press, 1989), 442–43; Lewis Porter, its first chorus (differently) in Porter and Michael Ullman, *Jazz from Its Origins to the Present* (Upper Saddle River, NJ: Prentice Hall, 1993), 174. See also the extended discussion of the solo in Scott DeVeaux, *The Birth of Bebop* (Berkeley and Los Angeles: University of California Press, 1997), 98–104.

an immense range of timbres and pitch (from d to c^3); another was Billie Holiday (ca. 1912–59), whose singing between about 1936 and 1944, a fresh synthesis based on that of Bessie Smith's blues and Louis Armstrong's improvisatory style, justified claims for her as the preeminent jazz singer of the period. Holiday had a special empathetic musical relationship with Count Basie's tenor saxophonist Lester Young (1909–59); among her most celebrated recordings are ones in which they worked together (as in *He's Funny That Way* or *All of Me*, on *SCCJ* CD 2, and *I Can't Get Started with You*, on *NW* LP 295).

Other jazz performers rose to virtuoso status as star soloists who improvised brilliantly over the background riffs of the big bands' "sidemen." Some of the misplaced values of any star system were evident in this development of the swing era, as the star performers seemed to be trying to play as fast or as high, or both, as possible. One thinks of several musicians associated with the Benny Goodman band during this period: the trumpeter Harry James (1916–83), who was celebrated for machine-gun-like velocity in such pieces as *The Flight of the Bumblebee*, and whose high notes were to be exceeded only later by the stratospheric "screech trumpet" of Maynard Ferguson (b. 1928), star soloist with the huge, colorful band of Stan Kenton (1911–79); the drummer Gene Krupa (1909–73), whose sweat-drenched head and body, behind a blizzardlike flurry of drumsticks flailing an ever larger battery of instruments, became a familiar swing-era photo image; and the vibraphonist Lionel Hampton (b. 1909), whose natural taste and invention were often left behind in response to his public's demands for sheer virtuosity. Hampton, along with another black, the pianist Teddy Wilson (1912–86), was employed by Goodman to play in small groups that alternated with the big band (and made recordings of their own), thus initiating a breakdown of "segregated" jazz.[16]

One could claim a special kind of virtuosity for Duke Ellington in the late 1930s and 1940s in his role as a *composer* in the jazz world. Improvisation, as we have seen, remained crucial to jazz expression (and it continued to be crucial in the Ellington band's work, with the help of such fine improvisers as alto saxophonist Johnny Hodges [1907–70], trumpeter Cootie Williams [1910–85], and tenor saxophonist Ben Webster [1909–73]); and composerly skills were required, as we have also seen, in preparing the necessary arrangements for the big bands. But no one before Ellington, and few after him, had such a farsighted vision of the jazz orchestra (his was a fifteen-piece ensemble by 1940, with six brass, five reeds, and four rhythm) as a challenging, malleable "instrument" with a huge potential for sonic variety; no one had Ellington's gifts for conceptual creativity; and no one had Elling-

---

[16] A good example of the crowd-pleasing, blazing virtuosity discussed here is *Flying Home*, a riff-based showcase for soloists Sid Robin, Benny Goodman, and Lionel Hampton, as recorded in 1942 by Hampton and his own orchestra (*NW* LP 261); note especially the concluding dialogues between Hampton on vibes and the screech trumpet of Joe Newman.

ton's capacity for molding his jazz conceptions into freshly shaped and convincing compositions. As Gunther Schuller summarized in his *AmeriGrove* article on Ellington,

> Ellington is generally regarded as the most important composer in jazz history. ... The exact number of his compositions is unknown, but is estimated at about 2000. [He] was one of the first musicians to concern himself with composition and musical form in jazz—as distinct from improvisation, tune writing, and arranging.

"Composition," in this context, has of course a special meaning: Ellington was celebrated for embodying his conceptions in arrangements that were worked out during rehearsals and not always fully written down and that were inspired by, and expressly intended for, the musicians of his orchestra. In the 1930s and early 1940s, these arrangements resulted in a unique jazz-orchestra sound, identified (as Mark Tucker puts it in his entry "Jazz" for the revised *New Grove Dictionary*) by its "signature muted brass sonorities, its thick, polyphonic textures, and its high level of dissonance," in such works as *Azure* (1937), *New East St. Louis Toodle-Oo* (1937; on *SCCJ* CD 3), *Concerto for Cootie* (1940; on *SCCJ* CD 3), *Ko-Ko* (1940; on *SCCJ* CD 3), or *Never No Lament* (*Don't Get Around Much Anymore*) (1940).

With such abundant virtuosity, of various sorts, on hand, and with a transcontinental popularity bred in radio stations, in recording studios, and on the stages of movie houses (where swing bands appeared increasingly "in person"), jazz began to be more than just a functional music to dance to or to drink to: it became a concert music as well. In 1938, Goodman's band appeared in concert at New York's Carnegie Hall; since that time, jazz as concert music has become commonplace and the balance between its use as utilitarian music and as art-music has swung increasingly toward the latter.

THE BROADWAY AND HOLLYWOOD MUSICAL; POPULAR SONG

With the rapid rise of sound films, during the 1930s, to a favored position among public entertainment media ("mass media"), the Broadway musical was threatened by the film musical of Hollywood, which could lavish more money on a single show and thus produce even more star-studded, eye-popping, mind-boggling spectaculars than Ziegfeld had offered in his Follies. Musically, however, the Hollywood musical offered nothing new. Nor did the theater musical of the 1930s immediately strike out on any new paths. Nevertheless, it tended to give increasing emphasis to the dramatic element and to span in its songs a greater range of emotional and psychological expression. And now and then, some of the social preoccupations of other American arts (and music) were visible in it, as in *Pins and Needles* (1937), with music and lyrics by Harold Rome (1908–93), the opening number of which (*Sing Me a Song of Social Significance*) ushered onstage a cast drawn entirely from theater classes of the International Ladies' Garment Workers Union. (It became a kind of theme song of the political left during the Depression years.)

Among the musical comedy figures to be lured to Hollywood were the Gershwins, who left New York for California after the opening of *Porgy and Bess* in 1935 (see p. 220). They seemed on the way to a series of successful film musicals (beginning with *Shall We Dance* and *A Damsel in Distress*; both 1937) when the composer died of a brain tumor at the age of thirty-eight. *The Goldwyn Follies*, for which Gershwin had planned to compose a full-scale ballet under the working title of *The Swing Symphony*, to be choreographed by George Balanchine, was released in 1938; it included four Gershwin songs, among them the ineffably sweet *Love Walked In* and the last collaboration of the Gershwin brothers, *Love Is Here to Stay*.

The other top musical comedy team, Rodgers and Hart, maintained their successful collaboration. They began the decade with a score for *Simple Simon* (1930), which included the poignant *Ten Cents a Dance*, about a dime-a-dance "hostess" in a Depression-era public ballroom. Later musicals by them that were outstanding for their songs were *Babes in Arms* (1937), *The Boys from Syracuse* (1983), and—outstanding also for its unwonted dramatic weight and development of character (that of a "perfect heel")—*Pal Joey* (1940).

The 1930–45 period saw the major successes in the lyric theater of Cole Porter (1891–1964). Unlike Gershwin or Rodgers, Porter wrote both the lyrics and the music of his songs. A Yale University graduate (and later a student of music at both Harvard and the Schola Cantorum in Paris), a homosexual (if also married to a beloved wife), and a *bon vivant* with an independent income and a fondness for residence in both Paris and Venice, Porter wrote songs with mordantly witty lyrics married to music of often brittle and always sophisticated charm. He was an ironic, sometimes caustic spokesman for pre-jet-set, *New Yorker*-reading, up-to-the-minute urbanites who knew a good double entendre when they heard one—whether verbal (*Let's Do It*, from the show *Paris* of 1928; *Katie Went to Haiti*, from *Du Barry Was a Lady* of 1939) or both verbal and musical (*But in the Morning, No*, also from *Du Barry*; the song is a gavotte, with a wicked quotation of a musical phrase from *The Star-Spangled Banner*). Blues inflections in Porter's earlier songs (*What Is This Thing Called Love?* of 1929) are cast in swing-style rhythms in the later ones (*It's De-Lovely*, from *Red, Hot and Blue* of 1936; *Most Gentlemen Don't Like Love*, from *Leave It to Me* of 1938).

Porter's thorough musical training shows up in various ways in his songs. To point only to his two most famous ones: in *Begin the Beguine* (from *Jubilee*, 1935) it allows him to control a song of extraordinary length (108 measures) and unique form; in *Night and Day* (from *Gay Divorce*, 1932) it lies behind the unusual chromaticism and tonal plan, the unconventional form, and the cleverly offset repeated-note monotony.[17] At another level, that of the musical as a whole, Porter was to reveal this thorough musical knowledge, along with an innately elegant and witty personality, in his later (and perhaps greatest) musical, *Kiss Me, Kate* (1948), based on Shakespeare's *The Taming of the Shrew*—even though its individual songs did not become classics of the popular genre.

A few other composers deserve mention here as writers of songs or musicals that are striking in one way or another. Harold Arlen (1905–86) is considered by some critics to be in every way the peer of Gershwin.[18] His *Stormy Weather* (1933) suggests the flexibility of Arlen's phrase lengths (in a field tyrannized by four-measure fragments); his *Over the Rainbow*, to lyrics by E. Y. "Yip" Harburg (1898–1981), seemed to be tailor-made for the wide-eyed yearning innocence of the young Judy Garland (in the 1939 film *The Wizard of Oz*); and his Depression-era *Brother, Can You Spare a Dime?* (1932), *Blues in the Night* (1941), and *That Old Black Magic* (1942) each have unique qualities. Vincent Youmans (1898–1946) proved to have remarkable staying power: his 1925 hit musical *No, No, Nanette* had a successful revival in the early 1970s (see p. 217 n); *Tea for Two* was its top song. Kurt Weill (1900–1950), who had come to the United States as a refugee in the mid-1930s, put his experience in German musical theater to good use in several Broadway musicals, most notably *Lady in the Dark* (1941) and the virtually operatic *Street Scene* (1946). But *Street Scene*—and, no less, a work such as Porter's *Kiss Me, Kate*—might never have been possible without a musical of 1943 that set a new standard for the genre. This was *Oklahoma!*, a collaboration between Richard Rodgers and his second partner, Oscar Hammerstein II, with excitingly original choreography by Agnes de Mille that synthesized ballet movement and square-dance figures. The artfully folkish work brought plot, music, and dance into such a tightly knit whole that some believed themselves witnessing a new form of American vernacular opera.

Another composer identified with musicals of the 1930s (and others earlier and later) must be mentioned here, although he never wrote one. This is Robert Russell Bennett (1894–1981), one of the early students of Nadia Boulanger. Bennett dominated the field of orchestrations for musicals from Kern's *Show Boat* (1927) through Lerner and Loewe's *Camelot* (1960); among no fewer than three hundred shows for which he provided adroit orchestrations between 1920 and 1975 were the Gershwins' *Of Thee I Sing*, Porter's *Kiss Me, Kate*, Rodgers and Hammerstein's *Oklahoma!* and *South Pacific*, and Lerner and Loewe's *My Fair Lady*.

---

[17] Pianist-composer Leo Smit noted the resemblance between the chorus theme of *Night and Day* and Schumann's song *Die Lotosblume* (and similar echoes of European art-music in other Porter songs) in "The Classic Cole Porter," *Saturday Review*, December 25, 1971 (quoted in part in William McBrien's *Cole Porter: A Biography* [New York: Knopf, 1998], 76).

[18] Alec Wilder, *American Popular Song ... 1900–1950* (New York Oxford University Press, 1972), 253–55 et seq.

BIBLIOGRAPHICAL NOTES

Eric Salzman's *"Modern Music* in Retrospect," *PNM* 2/2 (Spring–Summer 1964): 14–20, analyzes the American musical mood of 1924–46 as revealed in the pages of that lively magazine (see its citation on p. 229). Copland's *Our New Music* (New York: McGraw-Hill, 1941)—or the relevant chapters in its revision under the title *The New Music 1900–1960* (New York: W. W. Norton, 1968)—remains valuable as a view of things looking back from 1941; the anthology overseen by Cowell cited in note 2 is similarly valuable as a view looking forward from 1933. Thomson's *The State of Music* (1939; rev. ed. New York: Vintage Books, 1962) is concerned with the aesthetic and economic ways and means of the American composer.

Thomson's *Virgil Thomson* (cited in note 7) is a deliciously written autobiography; John Cage's incisive analysis of the music—the second half of *Virgil Thomson: His Life and Music* (cited in note 8)—remains a fine, attentive account. Superseding both in some ways is the candid, comprehensive biography by Anthony Tommasini, *Virgil Thomson: Composer on the Aisle* (New York: W. W. Norton, 1997). Thomson's *Symphony on a Hymn Tune* is discussed by Michael Meckna in "Sacred and Secular ...," *AM* 8/4 (Winter 1990): 465–76.

Dan Stehman's *Roy Harris: An American Pioneer* (Boston: Twayne Publishers, 1984) is regrettably uncritical; more objective and helpful is his *Roy Harris: A Bio-Bibliography* (New York: Greenwood Press, 1991). Marc Blitzstein's life is well served, his music not so convincingly, in Eric A. Gordon's *Mark the Music: The Life and Work of Marc Blitzstein* (New York: St. Martin's Press, 1989); Blitzstein's version of Weill's *Die Dreigroschenoper* is amply discussed (in chap. 4, "'The Threepenny Opera' in America" by Kim Kowalke, especially p. 101ff) in Stephen Hinton's anthology *Kurt Weill: The Threepenny Opera* (Cambridge: Cambridge University Press, 1990).

We still await major monographs on many of the composers cited in this chapter (among them Quincy Porter, Douglas Moore, William Schuman, and Ross Lee Finney); exceptions are Howard Pollack's *Walter Piston* (1982) and Andrea Olmstead's *Roger Sessions and His Music* (1985)—both from Ann Arbor: UMI Research Press—and Barbara Heyman's substantial *Samuel Barber: The Composer and His Music* (New York: Oxford University Press, 1992). Sessions's thoughtful and revealing essays on music have been edited by a sometime student and longtime colleague, Edward T. Cone, in *Roger Sessions on Music: Collected Essays* (Princeton: Princeton University Press, 1979).

Besides Harry Partch's own *Genesis of a Music* (Madison: University of Wisconsin Press, 1949; rev. and enl. New York: Da Capo Press, 1974), see Bob Gilmore's lengthy biography, *Harry Partch* (New Haven: Yale University Press, 1998). Thomas McGeary is helpful as editor of Partch's *Bitter Music: Collected Journals, Essays, Introductions, and Librettos* (Urbana: University of Illinois Press, 1991) and *The Music of Harry Partch: A Descriptive Catalogue* (*ISAMm* 31 [1991]). The literature on John Cage is enormous; his first book, *Silence* (Middletown, CT: Wesleyan University Press, 1961), includes writings from 1937 on. Valuable as the informed view of a serious observer is James Pritchett's *The Music of John Cage* (Cambridge: Cambridge University Press, 1993). Among a legion of anthologies, I would cite here only two: *Writings about John Cage*, ed. Richard Kostelanetz (Ann Arbor:

University of Michigan Press, 1993), drawn, as he says, from "the wealth of *critical literature* engendered by [Cage]" (emphasis mine), and *A John Cage Reader*, ed. Peter Gena, Jonathan Brent, and Don Gillespie (New York: C. F. Peters, 1982). The first chapters of the comprehensive monograph *Lou Harrison: Composing a World*, by Leta E. Miller and Fredric Lieberman (New York: Oxford University Press, 1998), take Harrison up to 1953.

Apart from the surveys of jazz cited in the bibliographical notes of Chapter 8, the literature on jazz of the 1930s and early 1940s, though vast, is very uneven. Magisterial, however, is Gunther Schuller's 920–page tome *The Swing Era . . . 1930–1945* (New York: Oxford University Press, 1989); even stronger on the cultural context of swing is David W. Stowe's *Swing Changes: Big-Band Jazz in New Deal America* (Cambridge: Harvard University Press, 1994). Lewis Porter's *Lester Young* (Boston: Twayne Publishers, 1985) is a fine style study; also useful are his *Lester Young Reader* (Washington, DC: Smithsonian Institution Press, 1991) and Ross Russell's *Jazz in Kansas City and the Southwest* (Berkeley and Los Angeles: University of California Press, 1971). On Ellington during 1930–45, see Mark Tucker's *Duke Ellington Reader* (cited on p. 232).

Richard Rodger's *Musical Stages* (New York: Random House, 1975) is a pleasant autobiography. Robert Kimball's *Cole* (New York: Holt, Rinehart & Winston, 1971), rich in photographs linked to authoritative commentary, is superseded in biographical depth (and candor) by the book of William McBrien cited in note 17. Kimball also scrupulously edited Porter's *Complete Lyrics* (New York: Knopf, 1983) and, with Dorothy Hart, those of Lorenz Hart (cited on p. 231). George Ferencz edited *The Broadway Sound: The Autobiography* [1971] *and Selected Essays of Robert Russell Bennett* (Rochester, NY: University of Rochester Press, 1998). A unique contribution to studies of American popular ballads of "the Golden Era 1924–1950" is Allen Forte's thoroughgoing—and convincing—Schenkerian analytic approach (cited in note 10 of Chapter 8).

part four

Since World War II

TEN

THE POSTWAR DECADES:
INTO THE 1960s

The period immediately following World War II, like that after World War I, was one of marked progressivism and rapid development in American music, due partly to a rising prosperity that increased the sources of patronage and the audience for music. With the introduction in 1948 of the "long-playing" ($33\frac{1}{3}$ rpm) microgroove recording, the cost of records diminished and sales boomed; the phonorecord became almost as important a medium for new music as the concert (more important, for some music), and assessment of a composer's "success" tended more and more to be based not on the number of his or her compositions that were published but on how many were record-ed. Giant philanthropic entities such as the Ford and Rockefeller founda-tions, and smaller music-oriented ones such as the Koussevitzky Foundation and the Martha Baird Rockefeller Fund, as well as municipal, county, state, and (by 1965) federal organizations in support of the arts, provided new money for composers' commissions and performance organizations. The au-dience for music grew spectacularly: a favorite statistic of the 1950s was one demonstrating that more Americans went to concerts than to baseball games.

By the early 1960s, arts centers were being constructed in city after city, the most extensive one being Lincoln Center for the Performing Arts in New York, a complex of buildings housing one major concert hall and several smaller ones; two theaters for drama, ballet, musical comedy, and some sorts of opera; a performing-arts branch of the New York Public Library; and a huge opera house (the new home of the Metropolitan Opera Company). Despite the advent of television, radio continued to appeal to a large audience, and a 1955 survey revealed that about 1,000 American radio stations broadcast a weekly total of 13,795 hours of "concert music" (i.e., neither pop music nor jazz), an average of almost 14 hours per week per station (an average that was to drop precipitously over the next decades). The number of composers increased dramatically. So did the number of performance organizations: one survey reported that whereas in 1939 there had been about 600 symphony orchestras in the United States, by 1967 there were 1,436, more than half of the world's 2,000 such orchestras; there were 918 opera-producing groups; there were, in American schools, some 68,000 instrumental music organizations (of which 50,000 were wind bands).[1]

This lively, developing scene in the musical culture at large was reflected in musical composition as well. The postwar period saw various trends of widely diverging character, in rapid evolution.

TWELVE-TONE COMPOSITION AND RELATED METHODS; ELLIOTT CARTER

One striking development was the widespread adoption by many composers of the twelve-tone technique of composition. Viewed before the war as the more or less private method of composers associated directly at one time or another with Arnold Schoenberg, the techniques of organizing music on the basis of a row or series of the twelve chromatic tones now came to be used by a majority of young American composers (as also by their European contemporaries). Some older ones as well, who before the war had not practiced row technique at all, began to do so in the late 1940s.

Reflecting this trend was the belated recognition of a composer such as Wallingford Riegger (see p. 215), who had long utilized serial technique but had to wait until its general adoption before gaining the esteem of the musical community, as embodied in the New York Music Critics Circle prize awarded for his Third Symphony (1948; *CRI* CD 572). Riegger was typical of the Americans who had grown into twelve-tone technique from other directions than direct tutelage by Schoenberg; his application of it, from his earliest examples (*Three Canons for Woodwinds*, 1931, and *Dichotomy*, 1931–32), was anything but doctrinaire. In the Third Symphony, a twelve-tone row is the main source of the first movement's thematic material (Example 10–1; the oboe theme—[b] in the example—exposes the entire row, its opening "motto" [a] notes 4–7; and compare the "quasi fugato" subject of the recapitulation [d]); the development section of the quasi-sonata structure, on the other hand, abandons the row, reverting to chromatic clusters of a

---

[1] *Concert Music USA, 1968* (New York: Broadcast Music, Inc., 1968).

EXAMPLE 10–1.   W. Riegger, Symphony No. 3, first-movement row-based
themes. Copyright © 1949 (Renewed) by Associated Music Publishers, Inc.
(BMI). International Copyright Secured. All Rights Reserved. Reprinted
by Permission. (*a*) "Motto," measures 1–4. (*b*) First-group theme, first
statement, measures 4–6. (*c*) First-group theme, climax, measures 64–68.
(*d*) Recapitulation, "Quasi fugato," measures 213–16.

sort found in many other works by Riegger (e.g., his *Music for Brass Choir*
[1948–49]; *CRI* CD 572). The second movement of the Third Symphony is
not row-based at all, and the last movement's passacaglia and fugue subjects
are both eight-tone themes, not twelve-tone (although they are ultrachromatic). A work such as the one-movement Woodwind Quintet, or to give it
its title as published in Germany, *Bläserquintett*, Op. 51 (1952; *NW* LP 285),
is so accessible in its peppery vigor and its perfectly idiomatic writing, full of
a telegraphic chatter especially congenial to wind players, that one hardly
notices that it is full of rather rigorous canons and serial chromaticism.

Two older European-born composers with twelve-tone experience
also rose to prominence shortly after World War II: Ernst Krenek
(1900–1991) and Stefan Wolpe (1902–72). Though Krenek was a prolific
composer, his impact on American music was felt more through his teaching
and his didactic works, especially the books *Music Here and Now* (originally
Über neue Musik; English translation published 1939) and *Studies in Counterpoint Based on the Twelve-Tone Technique* (1940). Wolpe, in America
from 1938, was to influence a number of young Americans through his music
per se, which proposed many new extensions of the tone-row technique. Like
that of Webern (with whom he had worked briefly in 1933), Wolpe's music
invited a new method of listening based on the perception of intervals rather

than melodic "themes" or harmonic "chords," let alone larger-dimension relationships between chords; a fairly brief work that is particularly rewarding along these lines is *Form*, for piano (1959; on *NW* CD 80308).

Among the mature Americans who gradually came to incorporate dodecaphonic principles in their music were Roger Sessions, Aaron Copland, Ross Lee Finney, a whole "Stravinsky school," and Hugo Weisgall.

Sessions's increasingly chromatic style of the 1930s and 1940s had led him to the brink of row usage. In the most natural way, he began viewing his ideas as susceptible to tone-row abstraction: "As a result of the fact that the opening theme [of the Sonata for Violin Solo, 1953] contained twelve different tones, and seemed to go naturally on that basis, I caught myself using the twelve-tone system."[2] Thus Sessions's twelve-tone music sounded hardly different from his pre-twelve-tone music. It retained the dense texture; the proliferation of contrapuntal filigree-work; the lengthy, nonrepetitive and usually nonsequential melodic line; and the traditional Classic-Romantic expressive gestures of his earlier music. It also retained a high seriousness, a loftiness, that proved generally forbidding to audiences and made Sessions more a composers' composer than anyone else of his generation. Perhaps most accessible among his later compositions are *The Idyll of Theocritus* (1954), for soprano and orchestra, and the work many consider his masterpiece, the cantata *When Lilacs Last in the Dooryard Bloom'd* (1970; *NW* CD 80296), setting Whitman's text that was a response to Abraham Lincoln's death. The critic Michael Steinberg wrote of this work (in notes for its recording), "Projecting the poetry now in simple chordal declamation, now in the long, high-arched melodies of which he is the master, [Sessions] conveys wonderfully the feel and variety of Whitman's lines."

Copland first essayed serial technique, tentatively and not without a certain stiffness of effect, in his Piano Quartet (1950), more masterfully in his Piano Fantasy (1952–57). In the Fantasy a ten-note row is the basis; the other two notes (E and G♯) are reserved for special use as a kind of cadence-interval. In fact, the work may be heard tonally as being in or about E major. Neither the Fantasy nor the Quartet, nor the later *Connotations* for orchestra (1962; *NW* CD 80368), makes use of folk or popular materials; even so, each is transparently the work of the composer of *Appalachian Spring* and *Rodeo*. In this connection, Copland had some sensible things to say about the impact (or lack of it) of twelve-tone usage on a composer's style and the expressive content of his music:

> To describe a composer as a twelve-toner these days is much too vague. ...
> Twelve-toneism is nothing more than an angle of vision. Like fugal treatment,
> it is a stimulus that enlivens musical thinking. ... It is a method, not a style.[3]

---

[2] Quoted in Edward T. Cone, "Conversation with Roger Sessions," *PNM* 4/2 (Spring–Summer 1966): 40.

[3] Quoted in "Fantasy for Piano," *New York Times*, October 20, 1957.

Finney had been, as mentioned earlier, a student not only of Boulanger (in 1927–28) but also (in 1931–32) of Berg (who, along with Schoenberg and Webern, had been one of the first twelve-tone composers); not until about 1950, however, did Finney interest himself in serial technique. I have already mentioned (see p. 237) his interest in the American musical past; this was expressed through a forceful, masculine style in a music distinctly tonal, rhythmically energetic, and neo-Classic in formal principles. With his String Quartet No. 6 (1950), however, Finney began to work with tone rows—with the explicit aim of reconciling them with larger plans of tonal organization, such as architectonic design of tonal centers and aspects of functional harmony. (A later example is his Concerto for Saxophone and Orchestra of 1974; *NW* CD 80211.) Another of his concerns in the 1950s was with arch forms and other symmetrical or circular plans, as in his Sixth and Seventh Quartets. The latter (1955) he thought of as resembling a figure eight:

> Like a skater, the first movement starts at the mid-point, then circles out, returning to the beginning, using the pitches in reverse order but making different music with them. The second (final) movement accomplishes figuratively the opposite sweep, and the quartet ends in the center with the theme.[4]

Such "spatial" visions of music, derived perhaps from the various reversible and invertible, horizontal (linear) and vertical (harmonic) projections of the tone row possible with twelve-tone techniques, were becoming increasingly common during the 1950s.

   Among other mature composers who, after many years of lack of interest in Schoenberg's method, adopted and absorbed it into their individual styles were some identified as a "Stravinsky school." These were mainly former pupils of Boulanger; they included Louise Talma (1906–96), Arthur Berger (b. 1912), Ingolf Dahl (1912–70), and Irving Fine (1914–62). At the same time that Stravinsky (influenced by Renaissance counterpoint) approached row composition in his *Cantata* (1952) and turned definitively to dodecaphony in the mid-1950s, these composers also began to espouse the twelve-tone idea. As with Sessions and Copland, its use by them hardly affected their personal idioms, although it distinctly reduced their tendency to borrow neo-Classical formal structures. The transparent elegance of Dahl's instrumental writing in such works as his *Concertino a tre* (1946; *NW* LP 281), the convincing if surprising contours and rhythms in Fine's *Childhood Fables for Grownups*, settings of witty poems by Gertrude Norman (1954–55; *NW* LP 300, *CRI* CD 574), and the biased, off-center rhythmic torque of

---

[4]The description is by the composer Leslie Bassett (b. 1923), a pupil (later a colleague) of Finney. (Program booklet for the University of Michigan School of Music's 1966 Festival of Contemporary Music.)

both men's music speaks clearly for their admiration and absorption of the "neo-Classic" Stravinsky.

Twelve-tone procedures and a style akin to the Viennese expressionists were heard in several operas of the 1950s and 1960s by Hugo Weisgall (1912–97), a former pupil of Sessions. A cultivated litterateur, Weisgall found libretto material in plays by Wedekind (*The Tenor*, 1950; *CRI* CD 757), Strindberg (*The Stronger*, 1952; *CRI* CD 757), Pirandello (*Six Characters in Search of an Author*, 1956; *NW* CD 80454), Yeats (*Purgatory*, 1958), and Racine (*Athaliah*, 1963). Musically, all are intense, densely packed works; *Six Characters*, leavened by wit and melodrama, has the most subtle and penetrating characterization, sensitive balancing of voices and orchestra, and theatrical presence.

Related to the intense, near-expressionist atmosphere of Weisgall's operas is the music of three other composers, all of whom felt the impact of Schoenberg's ideas or his music in significant ways. Leon Kirchner (b. 1919) studied with both Schoenberg and Sessions, and although he did not adopt the twelve-tone method, his music carries on their highly expressive, ultrachromatic manner. George Rochberg (b. 1918) tended to move stylistically with the vanguard: after works of the 1940s in various neotonal manners, the *Twelve Bagatelles* for piano (1952) were twelve-tone pieces; dedicated to Luigi Dallapiccola, they reflect that Italian composer's lyrical and finely ordered style. Ben Weber (1916–79) also wrote a music of lyric grace; characteristic is his *Symphony on Poems of William Blake* (1950), for baritone and orchestra, and his String Quartet No. 2 (1951; *CRI* CD 750). The work of all three composers during this period suggested that for them the anti-Romantic struggle was over, its issues dead. As Rochberg put it in 1963: "Now that the question arises on all sides: after abstractionism, what next? the answer rings out clearly: the 'new romanticism.'"[5] (As we shall see, this was a prophetic declaration, made a decade or so before the fact.)

By about 1960, the composer whose music, though not twelve-tone, seemed most sovereignly to embody these attitudes of an urgent expressivity, of careful, considered organization of highly chromatic pitch materials, and of high seriousness and even "monumentality" was Elliott Carter (b. 1908). Carter was a "second generation" pupil of Boulanger (from 1932 to 1935) after working under Piston at Harvard. The mastery of craft he owed to these master teachers is exemplified by his *a cappella* choral setting, dating from 1937, of the seventeenth-century poet Robert Herrick's *To Music* (1937; *NW* CD 80219), appropriately reminiscent of unaccompanied English-madrigal style. More important in his later development were his close association with

---

[5] Quoted in Alexander Ringer, "The Music of George Rochberg," *MQ* 52 (1966): 414.

Ives and Ives's music, certain procedures in Debussy's music with unusual modes of "musical logic" (change, process, evolution), and a single-minded insistence on music composition as an art of the heart *and* the mind.

Writing slowly and fastidiously, Carter first achieved in his Piano Sonata (1945–46) the sense of each work's being one of a kind that typified almost every composition by him for a long time. The sonata is in every way a work for a pianoforte; no transcription is imaginable, nor is any aspect of the piece derived from other instrumental idioms. Even the harmonic materials grow from the piano's special qualities of resonance and its sostenuto-pedal effects. Rhythmic complexities abound, and, in two big, subdivided movements, the Piano Sonata is ever developmental; various ideas announced in the introduction (Example 10–2)—the conflict between B and A♯, the material in thirds, the rising arpeggio figure—are re-presented, but in constant flux. The scope of the work sonorously and formally is very grand.

EXAMPLE 10–2. E. Carter, Piano Sonata (New York: Mercury Music Corporation, 1948), measures 1–7. Quoted by permission.

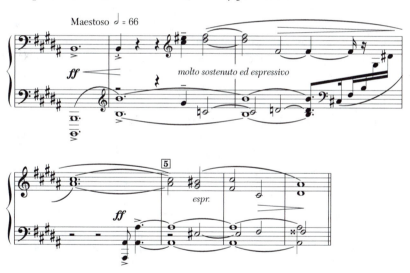

With each of his major works following the Piano Sonata, Carter's musical conception seemed to grow larger, his mode of expression more commanding. The Sonata for Cello and Piano (1948); five string quartets (the first three in 1951, 1959, and 1972); the Sonata for Flute, Oboe, Cello, and Harpsichord (1952); the Variations for Orchestra (1955–56); the Double Concerto for Piano and Harpsichord (1961); the Piano Concerto (1965)—all are "masterworks" in concept, aims, and realization. Carter usually took a long time to write a piece of music—there were no works premiered between the last two just mentioned, for instance—but each piece was a major event.

In this period, Carter's music was marked by an increasing richness of texture, an increasing "personalization" of instrumental voices, and an increasing complexity of rhythmic procedures. The Piano Concerto has passages with as many as seventy-two different parts proceeding simultaneously (a degree of density the composer referred to as "swamping"); what a leap from one movement in the earlier *Eight Etudes and a Fantasy* (1949), for woodwind quartet, which is written on one note only (although of course that was only a witty conceit).

Carter's personalization or personification of instruments reflects his view that his scores are "scenarios, auditory scenarios, for performers to act out with their instruments." In the Second Quartet, each instrument is

> like a character in an opera made up primarily of "quartets." The individuals of this group are related to each other in what might be metaphorically termed three forms of responsiveness: discipleship, companionship, and confrontation.

In the Piano Concerto, the solo piano "is in dialogue with the orchestral crowd, with seven mediators—a concertino of flute, English horn, bass clarinet, solo violin, viola, cello, and bass"—who serve as a kind of soothing Greek chorus between the sassy piano and the square orchestra.[6]

The increasing rhythmic complexity in Carter's mature works arose from his dissatisfaction with the limited range and modes of continuity in even the most "advanced" scores of Western music, and from his perception of the broader rhythmic repertory in various non-Western musics. While composing the Cello Sonata, Carter worked out a manner of evolving rhythms and tempos, a constant change of pulse, based on a technique that has come to be called metric modulation (though Carter prefers "tempo modulation")—"a means of going smoothly, but with complete accuracy, from one absolute metronomic speed to another, by lengthening or shortening the value of the basic note unit."[7] This technique ensures the most precise temporal controls over a music in rhythmic flux while permitting the greatest degree of independence among the separate voices in Carter's favored contrapuntal textures. Example 10–3, from the sixth variation of his Variations

---

[6] The quotations of Carter's words in this paragraph are from, respectively, his "Shop Talk by an American Composer," *MQ* 46 (1960): 189–201; jacket notes for the Composers Quartet recording of his First and Second string quartets (Nonesuch LP H-71249); and an essay in *The Orchestral Composer's Point of View*, ed. R. S. Hines (Norman: University of Oklahoma Press, 1970), 39–61.

[7] Richard Franko Goldman, "The Music of Elliott Carter," *MQ* 43 (1957): 161. Goldman was the first to use the term "metric modulation"; David Schiff, in his major study of *The Music of Elliott Carter* (New York: Da Capo Press, 1983), 26, points out that the term is "misleading, because the metre does not really change," which explains Carter's preference for "tempo modulation." (Schiff's book appeared in a revised edition in 1998 [Ithaca, NY: Cornell University Press].)

for Orchestra, shows one use of the technique. Each six-measure period accelerates gradually from ♩ = 80 to ♩ = 240: as the cello breaks into triplet eighth notes at measure 301, the viola begins the theme again in quarters, at the initial ♩ = 80 tempo. (Example 10–3 can also suggest the thoroughgoing

EXAMPLE 10–3. E. Carter, Variations for Orchestra, measures 295–307 (piano score reduction). Copyright © 1958 (Renewed) by Associated Music Publishers, Inc. (BMI). International Copyright Secured. All Rights Reserved. Reprinted by Permission.

chromaticism, not quite twelve-tone in organization, of Carter's mature style and its energetic, strongly directional melodic action, which contributes to the sense of dynamism and "expressivity" in his work.)

Carter's later works continued to extend the boundaries of rhythmic inventiveness, "harmonic" structure (in the sense of plans of structural intervals and more complex simultaneities), and form (breaking down boundaries in that realm—as in the interlocked duos of the String Quartet No. 3 of 1971). They also became seemingly more spontaneous and somewhat more accessible: the textures were more aerated, and with pieces such as the song cycle *A Mirror on Which to Dwell* (1975) and the settings of poetry by Robert Lowell *In Sleep, in Thunder* (1981), Carter returned to vocal music for the first time in many years. Bayan Northcott (in his 1986 *AmeriGrove* article on Carter) summarized the composer's chief achievements this way:

> His aim [has been] to complement the innovations of the earlier modern masters in the handling of pitch (Schoenberg), rhythm (Stravinsky), and texture (Varèse) with parallel developments in the domain of timing, through the large-scale integration of tempo relationships and harmonic backgrounds. ... [He displays] a grasp of dynamic form comparable, among 20th-century composers, only with Berg.

More than ten years later, just past Carter's ninetieth birthday in 1998, one might add other achievements, most important among them being, on the one hand, a Verdian old-age wit and élan (embodied in such works as the Clarinet Concerto of 1996–97, in six short sections adding up to about twenty minutes of music, or the tiny *Shard* of 1997, for solo guitar often made to sound like two, sparring); and, on the other hand, an unprecedented emotional and spiritual intensity that reached a culmination—comparable only to Ives's Fourth Symphony—in the fifty-minute, three-movement orchestral *Symphonia* (1993–98). What next? The nonagenarian composer may himself have answered the question in his first, and perhaps last, opera, a one-acter for the Berlin State Opera, titled in fact *What Next?* (1999).

SYSTEMATIC SERIAL COMPOSITION; MILTON BABBITT

Arnold Schoenberg's "method of composing with twelve tones which are related only with one another," as he called his serial technique of twelve-tone composition, was initially a substitute for the comprehensive principles of pitch organization of Classic-Romantic tonality, in which eleven of the twelve tones were related hierarchically to the other (the "tonic"). The twelve-tone method sought to acknowledge fully the chromatic vocabulary developed in Western music by ensuring a continued and total chromaticism in the organization of pitch. However, just as tonality had affected aspects of music other than pitch, so did the new "atonal" method. In a work such as Anton Webern's Symphony, Op. 21 (1928), for example, the structure of the pitch row affects aspects of rhythm, dynamics, phrase-structure, counterpoint, orchestration, and overall form; in the second movement, even the choice of transpositions of the tone row in each variation derives from the structure of the pitch row itself. This extension of the serial principle made Webern, not Schoenberg, the hero of a whole generation of composers after World War II: the "post-Webernites" of the 1950s, headed in Europe by the French composers Olivier Messiaen and Pierre Boulez and the German composer Karlheinz Stockhausen. However, even before these Europeans began working out the implications of Webern's later works, the American Milton Babbitt (b. 1916) was moving in a similar direction.

A trained mathematician, Babbitt saw not just a "method" in twelve-tone music but a real *system*, and in the pitch row not just a "series" but an ordered *set*, in the definitive mathematical sense. As early as the mid-1940s, Babbitt was using the serial principle to structure durational and other non-pitch components of his music. He was also addressing himself to control of the two dimensions of pitch, horizontal-linear and vertical-harmonic, in such a way that every note—or to use a newer and more precise terminology, every pitch class (C, E♭, etc., the register not specified)—was a member not only of an unfolding linear set but also of another, related set, governing and in fact creating the vertical dimension. This kind of thinking led him to a study of the structure of twelve-tone sets themselves and to an extension of a principle advanced first in Schoenberg's music, that of "combinatoriality" (as Babbitt termed it): the combining of various forms of a set without note duplication between simultaneous hexachords (six-note series or half rows)—or, in short, the production of twelve-tone *aggregates*.

Babbitt developed Schoenberg's combinatorial principle still further, formulating methods for constructing pitch sets that would be "semi-combinatorial" or "all-combinatorial." A semi-combinatorial set is so constructed that one of its transformations (besides its retrograde) can be transposed so that the first hexachord includes the same notes as the last hexachord of the original set; it can then be combined with that transposed version without destroying the ideal of total chromaticism. The all-combinatorial set is so constructed that *all* its transformations and one or more of its transpositions achieve the same end. These sorts of sets open up vast possibilities for contrapuntal techniques that still maintain total chromaticism.

The earliest works by Babbitt to be based on these ideas were *Three Compositions for Piano* (1947), *Composition for Four Instruments* (1948), and *Composition for Twelve Instruments* (1948; revised 1954). In the first of the *Three Compositions for Piano*—on which I shall concentrate in the next few paragraphs—the pitch set is all-combinatorial. Four forms only (and their

EXAMPLE 10–4.   Pitch-set forms used in M. Babbitt, *Three Compositions for Piano*, No. 1.

retrogrades) are used; as Example 10–4 shows, various pairs of these may be combined without duplicating the pitch content of corresponding hexachords (see any pairing of the A and B hexachords in the example). Constant rotation of the chromatic total in the music is ensured not only by consistent aggregate formations but also, in single voices, by following one set linearly with another whose first hexachord is the "opposite" of the one just completed: in the lower (bass) voice of measures 1–8, for instance (see Example 10–5), there appear successively the prime form of the set at the "zero" level (mm. 1–2: P-0; A–B hexachord order), then the retrograde inversion at the first transposition (mm. 3–4: RI-1; A–B order), then the inversion at the seventh transposition (mm. 5–6: I-7; A–B order), then the retrograde at the sixth transposition (mm. 7–8: R-6; A–B order). The order of successive set forms

EXAMPLE 10–5.   M. Babbitt, *Three Compositions for Piano* (Hillsdale, NY: Boelke-Bomart, Inc., 1957), No. 1, measures 1–8. Quoted by permission.

is constantly varied as the composition proceeds: in these eight measures, in the lower voice they are successively the P, RI, I, and R forms.

In addition to pitch, Babbitt "serializes" other components in this music: duration, dynamics, and the three-note chords characteristic of the composition.

The numerical series 5 1 4 2 (adding up to 12, or the number of sixteenth notes in a measure of $\frac{3}{4}$, which is the meter of the piece) is chosen as the prime form of a "duration set"; 2 4 1 5 is its retrograde, 1 5 2 4 its inversion, and 4 2 5 1 its retrograde inversion. The form of the movement, in six sections, is determined by the various uses of this set: in measures 1–8, it controls the grouping of even attacks (Example 10–6 [a]); in measures 9–18, the articulations between groups of even sixteenths (Example 10–6 [b]); in measures 20–28, accents and repeated notes (Example 10–6 [c]); in measures 29–48, temporal durations between attack points (Example 10–6 [d]). In measures 49–56 an effect of recapitulation is achieved by a return to the manner of measures 1–8. It will be noticed that the "duration set" forms parallel those of the pitch set: when, for example, an RI form of the pitch set appears, it is associated with the 4 2 5 1 (RI) form of the "duration set" (see Example 10–6 [c]).

Dynamics in the piece are also "serialized" in such a way as to reflect and confirm the serial ordering of pitch materials. The *mezzo piano* (*mp*) of measure 1 is associated with the prime form of the pitch set; *mezzo forte* (*mf*), with the retrograde; *forte* (*f*), with the inversion; and *piano* (*p*), with the retrograde inversion. This holds true up to the "recapitulation" of measures 49–56, when the "dynamics set" is "transposed."

Finally, the three-note chords—or better, simultaneities (since the very term *chord* implies earlier tonal music)—that appear frequently in the

EXAMPLE 10–6.   Use of the "duration set" in M. Babbitt, *Three Compositions for Piano* (Hillsdale, NY: Boelke-Bomart, Inc., 1957), No. 1. Quoted by permission.

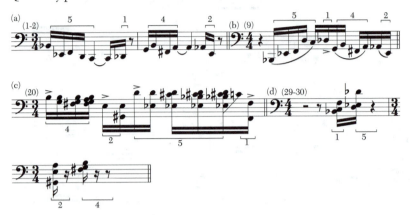

composition are ordered by a serial approach: the *register* chosen for the notes of each—that is, the particular pitch assigned to each of the row's pitch classes—is determined by the following scheme:

$$
P = \begin{array}{cccc} \uparrow 2 & 3 & \uparrow 8 & 9 \\ 1 & 4 & 7 & 10 \\ 0 & \downarrow 5 & 6 & \downarrow 11 \end{array}
\qquad
R = \begin{array}{cccc} \uparrow 9 & \uparrow 6 & 5 & 2 \\ 10 & 7 & 4 & 1 \\ 11 & 8 & \downarrow 3 & \downarrow 0 \end{array}
$$

$$
I = \begin{array}{cccc} 0 & \uparrow 5 & 6 & \uparrow 11 \\ 1 & 4 & 7 & 10 \\ \downarrow 2 & 3 & \downarrow 8 & 9 \end{array}
\qquad
RI = \begin{array}{cccc} 11 & 8 & \uparrow 3 & \uparrow 0 \\ 10 & 7 & 4 & 1 \\ \downarrow 9 & \downarrow 6 & 5 & 2 \end{array}
$$

Thus, in measure 11 (Example 10–7) the right-hand part (upper staff) is an expression of the pitch set I-1 and the vertical ordering of each three-note group follows the I version of the "register set" scheme just given; the left-

EXAMPLE 10–7.   Serial approach, through "register sets," to three-note simultaneities in M. Babbitt, *Three Compositions for Piano*, No. 1, measure 11.

hand part (lower staff), built from the pitch set RI-1, forms its simultaneities according to the RI version of that scheme.

In his *Composition for Twelve Instruments*, Babbitt went further to integrate the pitch and durational components of his music by deriving a "duration set" from the pitch set and composing in terms not only of a twelve-*tone* system but of a twelve-*duration* system as well. Example 10–8 shows (a) the prime pitch set, with each note defined by, first, its *order number* and, then, its *pitch number* (the latter measured in semitones up from the first note of the set); (b) the pitch set transposed up two semitones, thus altering the pitch number of each tone; and (c) the duration set, based on a sixteenth-note unit that corresponds to pitch set P-2 (its first pitch number, 2, being thus represented by an eighth note—equaling two sixteenths; its second, 3, by a dotted eighth; etc.).

EXAMPLE 10–8. Pitch and duration sets in M. Babbitt, *Composition for Twelve Instruments* (1948).

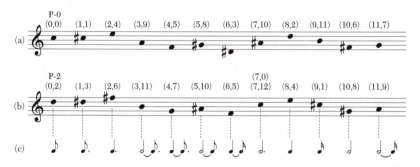

The musical expression in *Composition for Twelve Instruments* is one emphasizing single-impulse events; the pointillistic texture has been likened to a bank of multicolored lights, of varied wattage, flashing on and off at different rates. Later works by Babbitt have demonstrated that other textures, other expressive qualities, are perfectly possible with his systematic serialism. One knowledgeable admirer emphasizes this when he writes:

> Immersion in the music of Milton Babbitt leaves one with an impression of overwhelming variety. From the compact intensity of *Post-Partitions* [1966; NW CD 80466] to the broad lyricism of *Philomel* [1964; NW CD 80466] or *The Joy of More Sextets* [1986; NW CD 80364], from the intimacies of *The Widow's Lament in Springtime* [1950] to the vast canvases of *Relata* [(*No. 1*, 1965; NW CD 80396)] or the Piano Concerto, we are constantly invited to explore new realms of musical expression.[8]

---

[8] Andrew Mead, *An Introduction to the Music of Milton Babbitt* (Princeton: Princeton University Press, 1994), 5.

Babbitt's works for voice tend to have a frankly *espressivo* line, as in the song cycle *DU* (1951); *Two Sonnets*, for baritone, clarinet, viola, and cello (1955); and the *Composition for Tenor and Six Instruments* (1960). In these, duration is not serially organized, Babbitt believing that correct prosody should be the primary rhythmic determinant. Nevertheless, various linked chains of pitch relationships exist in them, as can be heard in the opening measures of *DU*, which also can exemplify Babbitt's expressive, sensitively rhythmed and contoured vocal line, reminiscent of the lyric art of Webern.

"Wiedersehen," the first song of *DU*, is based on a set that is all-combinatorial and is furthermore an "all-interval" set, in that it can be presented in such a way that every possible interval within an octave occurs once, and only once (Example 10–9). Such a set ensures a variety of interval structures in the music and allows a linear deployment free from built-in symmetries and other form-dictating repetitions.

EXAMPLE 10–9.   The all-interval set of M. Babbitt's *DU*.

The singer's first four phrases, each of three notes, expose the prime form of the set (Example 10–10). Each three-note phrase is accompanied by piano music with the nine other chromatic notes; vertical dotted lines in Example 10–10 show the four twelve-tone aggregates thus created. Within each aggregate, three-note interval structures are formed by voice and piano (circled in Example 10–10); they are the *same* structures within each aggregate; in the first aggregate, for example, the four interval structures ("molecules" might be an appropriate word for them) are all based on the intervals of a major third (or its inversion, a minor sixth), a minor second (or major seventh), and a perfect fifth (or perfect fourth). Finally, the nature of the accompaniment is such that we hear it as having three "voices": a high-register voice beginning B–F♯–A, a middle-register voice (E–G–D), and a low-register voice (A♭–C♯–B♭). Tracing each of these voices through the excerpt, we discover that each is itself a twelve-tone set, related directly to the prime set of the singer. Moreover, within each of the four chromatic aggregates, each of the accompanying voices is a different form of the singer's three-note phrase: the piano's high-register "voice" is an intervallic retrograde, the middle-register voice an inversion, and the low-register voice a retrograde inversion. These linear relationships have been bracketed in Example 10–10.

Through such extensions of the serial principle, Babbitt created music with a staggeringly complex network of interrelationships. His later works became increasingly witty (reflected in punning titles such as *Sheer Pluck* *[Composition for Guitar]*, *Four Play* for a foursome of players [both 1984], and *None But the Lonely Flute* [1991; NW CD 80456]) and seemingly playful, virtually improvisatory—yet in them the complexity of these relation-

EXAMPLE 10–10. M. Babbitt, *DU* (Hillsdale, NY: Boelke-Bomart, Inc., 1957), measures 1–5. Quoted by permission.

ships became ever greater. (The preceding discussion hardly scratches the surface.) But not only are these relationships complex; they *are* the music. The interlocked components are inseparable, and it is no longer meaningful to speak of one, or to hear one, separate from the others; the music, approaching "total organization," challenges listeners to total hearing.

Not only was Babbitt an articulate formulator and codifier of serial concepts; he was also an influential and much beloved teacher of younger composers, at Princeton University and the Juilliard School. Among those who, taught by both Sessions and Babbitt, constitute what has been called a "Princeton school" are Peter Westergaard (b. 1931), Henry Weinberg (b. 1931), Donald Martino (b. 1931), Benjamin Boretz (b. 1934), and J. K. Randall (b. 1929). Of these, Martino—who leavened his Princetonian serialism with Italianate lyricism through two years' study in Florence with Dallapiccola—has the broadest range compositionally; his *Seven Pious Pieces* (1972; *NW* CD 80210), *a cappella* settings of poems by Herrick, though atypical in some respects, exemplify his versatility and wit; more characteristic are *Parisonatina al'dodecaphonia*, for solo cello and written for Aldo Parisot (1964; *CRI* CDs 564 and 762), and the work that won him the Pulitzer Prize for 1974, *Notturno* for six players. Boretz distinguished himself as a theorist and editor: he was the prime mover and for twenty years (1962–82) coeditor of the journal *Perspectives of New Music*, considered by many as ultrasympathetic to the Princetonians' musical ideas.

ELECTROACOUSTIC MUSIC

Babbitt's interest in "total control" over musical materials led him perhaps inevitably to the medium of electroacoustic music, and in the late 1950s he became one of the directors of the first major American electronic-music studio, cosponsored by Princeton and Columbia universities and an outgrowth of the studio established at Columbia in 1953.

Electroacoustic music—music made or altered electrically (as opposed to acoustic music, made by mechanically vibrating or resonating bodies)—had a prehistory from the late nineteenth century and experiments arising out of early telegraphy. Effective composition of such music, however, had to await the development of reliable and easily handled recording techniques; essentially, it was only with the perfection of magnetic-tape-recorder technology after World War II that electroacoustic music was of interest to many composers. The pioneers in *musique concrète* (composition based on prerecorded sounds, often sounds of nature or machinery, stored on tape, then electronically manipulated, reassembled, and retaped) were a few French composers, notably Pierre Henry, working in the Paris studios of Radio France (the French national radio) in the late 1940s. The pioneers in *elektronische Musik* (composition based on electronically generated sound materials stored on tape, then—as with *musique concrète*—manipulated, reassembled, and retaped) were a few Germans, notably Herbert Eimert and Karlheinz Stockhausen, working in the Cologne studios of Westdeutsche Rundfunk (the West German national radio) in the early 1950s. John Cage was the first American actually to prepare a piece on magnetic tape (*Imaginary Landscape No. 5*; 1951–52), but two other composers began about the same time to work more systematically in tape-music composition: Otto Luening (1900–1996) and Vladimir Ussachevsky (1911–90), both on the faculty of Columbia University at the time.

Working singly and together, Luening and Ussachevsky had produced enough compositions by the fall of 1952 to present the first American tape-music concert, at the Museum of Modern Art in New York City. Luening's first tape pieces were *musique concrète* based on solo flute sounds: *Fantasy in Space*, *Low Speed*, and *Invention* (all 1952; all on *CRI* CD 611). Ussachevsky's early work culminated in *A Piece for Tape Recorder* (1956; *CRI* CD 611), which combined electronically generated sounds with prerecorded sounds on file in a library of sound-on-tape maintained at the Columbia studio; some of the sounds he had used for his earlier pieces *Sonic Contours* and *Underwater Waltz* (both 1952; *Sonic Contours* on *CRI* CD 611). The two composers collaborated in 1954 in two "concertos" for tape-recorded sounds and orchestra, *Rhapsodic Variations* and *A Poem in Cycles and Bells*, and in other works through the 1960s.

The basic equipment for these composers of early electroacoustic music consisted of two or more tape recorders; an electronic generator of sound signals, whether sine-wave (a fundamental pitch with no overtones), square-wave (fundamental with odd-numbered upper partial tones), or sawtooth-wave (fundamental with all upper partials); a generator of noise, whether the hissing, steamlike sound of "white noise" (an infinite number of signals over the entire range of the audible sound frequencies) or the cloudlike band of sound of "colored noise" (an infinite number of signals within a limited range of frequencies); various sound-filtering and reverberating devices; and scissors, razor blade, splicing block, adhesive tape, and a supply of magnetic tape. With such equipment the composer was in an extraordinary and unprecedented position—for a composer (though one that painters, sculptors, and writers had always enjoyed)—permitting the artist to create directly and concretely in the desired medium, not having to submit to interpretation, through a different medium, by a performer.

Understandably, Edgard Varèse, who more than thirty years earlier had dreamed of "instruments obedient to [his] thought" and of music invigorated by science, turned enthusiastically to tape music, completing two major works in the new medium before his death. One was *Déserts* (completed 1954), for a group of winds, piano, and percussion instruments alternating with "organized sound" material on tape, in a big A B A C A B A form—"A" standing for the sections played by instruments; "B" for tape music based on raw sounds collected by Varèse in a foundry, a sawmill, and several factories; and "C" for tape music based on percussion-instrument sounds.

The electroacoustic interpolations broaden the expressive range of Varèse's "sound-mass" techniques of the 1920s, and the music has a power of almost terrifying dimension.

In 1957–58, working together with the architect Le Corbusier for the Brussels World's Fair pavilion of the Philips Corporation (a Dutch radio and electronics firm), Varèse composed *Poème électronique*. Here finally all his ideas of music as spatial, of sound as "living matter," could be realized. The work was planned for tape-recorded performance through 425 loudspeakers arranged in 15 "tracks" and embedded in the looping curves of the ceiling and walls of Le Corbusier's building; the sound actually swept in great circles around and overhead, at different speeds and along various tracks simultaneously. Varèse composed the piece in a great variety of sounds, including the human voice, which lends an awesome presence to the work. In *Poème électronique*, Varèse approached the realization of his vision for a work never finished (*Espace*)—an apocalyptic sound montage in space: "voices in the sky, filling all space, crisscrossing, overlapping, penetrating each other, splitting up, superimposing, repulsing each other, colliding, crashing together."[9]

At the early Columbia University studio, as elsewhere in the 1950s, electroacoustic-music composition was a tedious task, involving recording and re-recording sounds on magnetic tape, then manually splicing together bits of tape to really "compose" a work. A great step in reducing such laborious techniques was taken with the development by the Radio Corporation of America of an electronic sound synthesizer (originally designed for use in speech synthesis), an advanced model of which, the Mark II, was installed in the Columbia studio in 1959 as the keystone of a Columbia-Princeton Electronic Music Center under the direction of Luening, Ussachevsky, and Babbitt. The RCA Synthesizer allowed Babbitt (and others of his compositional persuasion) to pursue the ideal of a totally organized music, for it made possible the most precise control of not only the pitch components but also those of rhythm, dynamics, and timbre, and including such details as the "attacks" and "decays" of sounds. The result, in works by Babbitt such as *Composition for Synthesizer* (1961) and *Ensembles for Synthesizer* (1964), was a music of great lucidity and unique sonic and architectonic qualities (in striking contrast to the music of both Luening and Ussachevsky, which seldom lost sight of its nonelectronic musical sources).

Other works by Babbitt combined synthesized sound with live performance: *Vision and Prayer* (1961; CRI CD 521), *Philomel* (1964; NW CD 80466), and *Correspondences* (1967). "Philomel," a wondrously musical poem by John Hollander on the transformation into a nightingale of the ravished and speechless Philomela, is set by Babbitt for live voice, taped and electronically altered voice, and synthesized sound. Composed for the remarkable soprano Bethany Beardslee (whose performance is preserved on NW LP

[9] Quoted in Chou Wen-chung, "Varèse: A Sketch of the Man and His Music," *MQ* 52 (1966): 151–70.

307), the music of *Philomel* is as precisely ordered and as full of structural subtleties as any of Babbitt's; at another level it is a profoundly moving, accessibly "expressive" work. One enthusiastic critic remarked that Philomela's "final triumphant phrase [Example 10–11], her ultimate recognition of her vocal powers, celebrates Mr. Babbitt's new-found voice as well."[10] The later *Phonemena* (1975; *NW* CD 80466), for soprano and tape or soprano and piano, is a playful encore piece dedicated "to all the girl singers I've known"; the text consists entirely of phonemes—twenty-four consonant sounds and twelve vowel sounds (numbers not haphazardly chosen but obviously related to serial structural concerns).

EXAMPLE 10–11. M. Babbitt, *Philomel*, last 11 measures (live-voice part only). Copyright © 1964 (Renewed) by Associated Music Publishers, Inc. (BMI). International Copyright Secured. All Rights Reserved. Reprinted by Permission.

A grant from the Rockefeller Foundation enabled the Columbia-Princeton Center to invite many composers to use its facilities; in 1969, a brochure accompanying the record album *Columbia-Princeton Electronic Music Center Tenth Anniversary* listed 225 compositions made at the center by more than 60 composers from 11 countries. A few composers closely identified with the center (besides its directors) rose to special prominence. Walter (later Wendy) Carlos (b. 1939) produced the first "hit" of electronic music, the synthetically recomposed Baroque works on the best-selling recording *Switched-On Bach* (1968). Mario Davidovsky (b. 1934), originally from Argentina, began with some purely electronic studies (1961 and 1962) but then concentrated on an integration of electronic sounds with music for live performers, in a series of eight dialogue-like pieces, each entitled *Synchronism* (No. 5, with percussion, on *CRI* CD 611; No. 6, with piano, on *NW* CD 80412 and *CRI* CD 707; No. 9, with violin, on *CRI* CD 706). Jacob Druckman (1928–96) also emphasized live/electronic confrontations in some

[10] Richard F. French, in "Current Chronicle," *MQ* 50 (1964): 382–88.

brilliantly conceived, powerful, almost theatrical works such as *Animus I* (trombone and tape; 1966), *Animus II* (female singer, percussionists, and tape; 1968; *CRI* CD 781), and *Animus III* (clarinet and tape; 1969). Charles Wuorinen (b. 1938), a virtuoso pianist and conductor (especially as codirector of the Group for Contemporary Music in New York from 1962 into the 1980s) and a prolific composer of nonelectronic music, was able easily to turn his rigorously serial style to the electronic medium (*Orchestral and Electronic Exchanges*, 1965); his *Time's Encomium* (1968–69) won the 1970 Pulitzer Prize in music—the first one awarded to a wholly electronic work, existing only in recorded form.

Even if, as mentioned, the RCA Synthesizer marked a great step forward in reducing the laborious, time-consuming job of electronic composition in a "classic" studio, it was a supercostly, bulky, and literally unique machine. However, during the mid-1960s, technologists, aided by the invention of tiny transistors and solid-state circuitry, developed smaller, less expensive, and easier-to-operate synthesizers. These were based on a principle of voltage control and consisted of a group of modules—sound generators, sound modifiers (filters, amplifiers, mixers, reverberators, and the like), control voltage generators, and control voltage processors. The first such modular synthesizers were those of Robert Moog (b. 1934), working in upstate New York, and Donald Buchla (b. 1937), of the San Francisco area; other makes were soon on the market. It is hard to say whether these small synthesizers came into existence out of composers' needs or whether their invention spurred composers into making electronic music—probably a bit of both. But by the early 1970s, electronic-music studios built around modular equipment were to be found all across the country; electroacoustic-music composition had entered a new phase of widespread practice.

Some composers associated with this development should be mentioned. Morton Subotnick (b. 1933) was one of the founders of the pioneering San Francisco Tape Music Center and directed it from 1961 to 1965. He and other composers in the area—notably Pauline Oliveros (b. 1932) and Larry Austin (b. 1930)—actually collaborated with Buchla in the development of his synthesizer equipment. Subotnick's *Silver Apples of the Moon* (1967) symbolized the new status of electronic music and was in fact a "first": in a happy and (with hindsight) seemingly inevitable marriage of technology, commerce, and art, it was specifically commissioned by the enterprising firm of Nonesuch Records and was planned to fill the two sides of a long-playing disc recording. A second Nonesuch commission, *The Wild Bull* (1968), and *Touch* (1969; for Columbia Records) shared with *Silver Apples* Subotnick's fondness for lengthy sequential patterns and multiple ostinatos (arising partly, at least, out of characteristics of the Buchla equipment). The prolific Kenneth Gaburo (1926–93) turned to the live/electronic medium in a series of compositions aptly entitled *Antiphony* (the earliest dating from

1958); among them *Antiphony III* (1962), composed at the Yale and University of Illinois studios, is a brilliant concerto-like work for sixteen voices and tape. Roger Reynolds (b. 1934), one of a lively group of composers in the San Diego area, moved beyond live/electronic antiphony into "multi-media" in *Ping* (1968), which calls for slide projections, film, and combined instrumental, *concrète*, and electronic sound in a highly personal realization of a story by Samuel Beckett. Reynolds's *Traces* (1969) is for piano, flute, cello, and six channels of taped sound (both *concrète* and electronic), so planned that a rich tapestry of combination tones, difference tones, and other by-products or "residues" (traces) of musical events is woven. His later *From Behind the Unreasoning Mask* (1975; NW LP 237) suggests how the virtually infinite sonic and timbral range of the new synthesizers stretched composers' ideas of the possibilities for live music: Reynolds's piece is scored only for trombonist and percussionist (the latter aided by an assistant) plus four-channel prerecorded tape, but the variety of the instrumentalists' sounds is immense, and the high incidence of silence among the sounds invites the ear to revel in them.

The late 1950s saw the beginning of the use of digital computers to aid both the recording of music and its composition. Record manufacturers were slow to make commercial use of computers; only in the mid-1970s did some companies begin to put computers to work in the process of making master tapes. The first serious experiments in computer-aided composition had been carried out, however, two decades earlier, by the composer-and-mathematician team of Lejaren Hiller (1924–94) and Leonard Isaacson, working with an Illiac high-speed computer at the University of Illinois. Their first product was a four-movement *Illiac Suite* (1956) for string quartet, each movement entitled "Experiment" and intended to show the compositional possibilities of one or another aspect of computer programming. Anything but radical in sound and structure, the *Illiac Suite* was more a technological breakthrough than an artistic masterpiece.

More fruitful than Hiller's approach were those of some other composers who developed methods for actually synthesizing sounds by means of computers. Early work was done at the Bell Telephone Company laboratories in New Jersey, where sound-synthesizing computer programs were developed by Max Mathews (b. 1926) in 1957. By the mid-1960s these programs were the basis for computer-music composition in such academic studios as those at Stanford University, where John Chowning (b. 1934) was a pioneer, and Princeton University, where J. K. Randall produced a number of works, including *Quartets in Pairs* (1964), *Mudgett: Monologues by a Mass Murderer* (1965; for voice and computer), and *Lyric Variations* (1968; for violin and computer). The Princeton studio was also where Charles Dodge (b. 1942) composed *Earth's Magnetic Field* (1970), probably the first work of computer music to be commissioned (by Nonesuch Records).

MUSIC OF CHANCE AND INDETERMINACY;
JOHN CAGE AND COLLEAGUES

At precisely the same time that composers of electroacoustic music (such as Babbitt and Ussachevsky) and computer music (such as Hiller and Dodge) were increasing the composer's personal control over musical materials and their realization in sound, an apparently opposite impulse was leading other composers in a different direction. In their music, the will and the determination of the composer were reduced: either they found ways of producing their music by chance or random methods (thus minimizing their role in the choice of the notes to be played or sung) or they produced not the actual note-symbols in ordered relationships but just musical raw material, to be ordered—"composed," in effect—by the performer; for some works, not even the raw material was provided, only suggestions about the physical activity to initiate it or about the environment in which it was to take place.

Several adjectives have been used to define this music: *aleatory, indeterminate, chance, improvisational,* and *random* are some of them. The different connotations of each of these may be subsumed under the more general term *experimental,* as precisely defined by John Cage: "An experimental action is one the outcome of which is unforeseen."[11] (The "action" here is that of musical composition; the "outcome" is the musical performance.) Cage's preferred term for this music has not, however, been generally accepted; perforce, others are also used here.

Undisputed leader of such "experimental" music from the early 1950s was Cage himself. In the summary of his compositional methods partially quoted previously (p. 251), Cage lists the postwar "paths [of his] musical thought":

> ... composition using charts and moves thereon (1951); composition using templates made or found (1952–); composition using observation of imperfections in the paper upon which it is written (1952–); composition without a fixed relation of parts to score (1954–); composition indeterminate of its performance (1958–).

Underlying all these means for reducing his dominance over the musical experience, including his compositions themselves, and letting the music "happen" was Cage's discovery in 1951 that there is no silence.[12] Previously, he had organized his music on the assumptions that the opposite of sound was silence; that duration was the only characteristic of sound measurable in

---

[11] "Composition as Process," three influential lectures given in September 1958 (at one of the annual postwar *Ferienkurse für neue Musik* in Darmstadt, West Germany); reprinted in Cage, *Silence* (Middletown, CT: Wesleyan University Press, 1961), 18–55.

[12] Cage's influence on the mixed-media, improvisational form of theater called *Happenings* was very great, following his organization at Black Mountain College in 1952 of an event involving painting, dance, piano playing, poetry, films, slides, phonorecordings, radios, and a lecture by Cage himself. See Michael Kirby, *Happenings* (New York: Dutton, 1965).

terms of silence; that therefore any valid musical structure (a work of sounds and silences) must be based not on frequency, as traditionally it had been, but on duration. Then one day Cage entered a soundproof and anechoic chamber, as silent as technologically possible. He heard two sounds, one high, one low; the engineer in charge explained that the high sound was his nervous system in operation, the low sound his blood circulating. In the chapter "Experimental Music" of his 1961 book *Silence* (a totally ironic title), Cage voiced his reactions to this discovery:

> There is no such thing as an empty space or an empty time. There is always something to see, something to hear. In fact, try as we may to make a silence, we cannot.... Until I die there will be sounds. And they will continue following my death. One need not fear about the future of music.[13]

The most dramatic, certainly the most famous, application by Cage of these ideas is the work known as *4'33"*, a piece in three movements for any instrument or combination of instruments; its score consists of the headings "I," "II," and "III," each followed by the word "TACET" (for musicians an instruction to "remain silent"). In its premiere performance on August 29, 1952, the pianist David Tudor appeared and seated himself at a piano, stopwatch nearby; he indicated the beginning of each part of the piece by closing, the end by opening, the keyboard cover; and he played... nothing. (The performance took four minutes and thirty-three seconds, hence the title by which the work is known; it is in fact untitled, or rather, as Cage puts it in the score, "The title of this work is the total length in minutes and seconds of its performance.") But if the performer (or performers) of *4'33"* makes (or make) no intentional sounds, there are other sounds to be heard, and the audience, in the traditional listening situation of a recital, is invited to listen to them. As Tudor puts it, "It is one of the most intense listening experiences one can have. You really listen. You're hearing everything there is. Audience noises play a part in it. It is cathartic—four minutes and thirty-three seconds of meditation, in effect."[14]

Cage could hardly repeat himself as a composer of "silent" music. From the theoretical and philosophical position so vividly dramatized by *4'33"*, and aided by certain ideas of Zen Buddhism and other oriental and speculative sources, he sought to find other ways to remove himself—his memory, taste, and will—from the act of "composition" in a traditional sense. The "charts and moves thereon [and the] templates made or found" that he mentions were themselves prepared by chance operations, typically by tossing coins and translating the results into visual diagrams according to an intricate system based on the Chinese *I Ching* (Book of Changes); the diagrams were then translated into conventional notation. Such was the composing

---

[13] *Silence*, 8.
[14] Quoted in Harold Schonberg, "The Far-out Pianist," *Harper's* 130 (June 1960): 49.

method for *Music of Changes* (1951) for piano (Parts III and IV on *NW* LP 214). Coin tossing together with notational "decisions" made on the basis of the inevitable minute imperfections on the surface of music paper provided the basis for the score of *Music for Piano 21–52* (1955), two groups of sixteen pieces that may be played alone or together in an indeterminate time span; the duration and dynamics of individual notes are free.

Another score-producing method was to suggest the notes by dropping an *I Ching*–derived stencilled diagram onto graph paper and then plotting the result in "graph notation," from which the performer might make any specific sonic version he or she wished. *Music for Carillon* [*No. 1*] (1952) is an example: Cage published it in graph notation and also in two different conventionally notated versions. For the *Concert for Piano and Orchestra* (1957–58) there is no master score; indeed, the work may be realized as a piano solo (the pianist being "free to play [from a 'book' of eighty-four kinds of composition] any elements of his choice, wholly or in part, and in any sequence") or as a chamber work, a piece for symphony orchestra, one for piano with orchestra, and so on. This is a work, in other words, not only "without a fixed relation of parts to score" but also "indeterminate of its performance." Together with the *Concert* may be performed an *Aria*, in which Cage leaves many aspects of performance undetermined. The *Aria* may also be sung with the tape-music piece *Fontana Mix* (1958), itself experimental in that the "sound sources, their mechanical alteration, changes of amplitude, frequency, overtone structure, the use of loops [for continuous repetition of taped material], special types of splicing, etc. may be determined" from graph-notated drawings and point-speckled transparent sheets. The voice-tape montage "is intended seriously to be fun, to provoke the audience to audible response, to break down the standard notion of performance in one dimension and an audience confined silently in another dimension." [15]

With such a conception, Cage had reached that point of indeterminacy where composer, performer, and listener meet and mingle in producing the musical experience. The means for obtaining such an experience were refined in such later works as *Theatre Piece* (1960), and Cage attained his ideal of non-self-expression as a composer: "I have no desire to improve on creation." [16] The paradox of that sentence is that in it lies perhaps the most creative aspect of Cage's "many paths": a profound humanism aimed at freeing human beings by removing the artificial barriers of their own making and permitting them to experience life with reawakened sensitivity. Cage's essential goal was, as he once said to me, "to introduce us to the very life we are living."

Three composers closely associated in New York with Cage and his ideas about music and life in the 1950s were Christian Wolff (b. 1934), Morton Feldman (1926–87), and Earle Brown (b. 1926). Both Wolff and Feld-

[15] Peter Yates, "Music," *Arts and Architecture* 77/7 (July 1960): 4, 32.
[16] Quoted in *Time* 75/12 (March 21, 1960): 46.

man took up Cage's ideas about setting sounds free, free from intended interrelationships. Wolff spoke of "a concern for a kind of objectivity, almost anonymity—sound come into its own. The 'music' is a resultant existing simply in the sounds we hear, given no impulse by expression of self or personality."[17] In a number of chamber pieces, some indeterminate not only as to duration of tones but also as to instrumentation, Wolff developed a notation whereby the players, responding to one another spontaneously—as basketball or hockey players do (if that analogy does not seem too far-fetched)—could seem to pass notes to one another, loosing them as an arrow is loosed rather than propelled. (He spoke of a "parliamentary participation" of performers, who responded to one another's "cues.") Typically, Wolff's music in performance includes more "silence" than sound, the notes hovering separately in the air almost as autonomous intelligences.

Feldman, too, developed in the early 1950s new notations for allowing the sounds to be "free," often suggesting through graphic means generalized areas (of register, for instance: high, medium, or low) within which the performer has a free choice of specifics: in 1951 a series of works, each entitled *Projection*, for various small groups; another similar series of works, each called *Intersection*; and *Marginal Intersection*, for orchestra. By the 1960s he had achieved "a more complex style in which each instrument is living out its own individual life in its own individual sound world," often by virtue of Feldman's having chosen "intervals that seemed to erase or cancel out each sound as soon as we hear the next"[18] (as in the series of five chamber pieces entitled *Durations*, 1960–61). In *The Swallows of Salangan* (1961), for wordless chorus and instruments, all the performers are given a music of successive notes; no rests are specified; there are precise pitch indications but no rhythmic ones. The conductor initiates the performance with a slow downbeat, then gives no others. Within the general tempo thus cued, the performers move through their parts, determining for themselves the actual durations of the slow, successive tones. The result, different in detail with every performance, is something like a cloud mass, the outlines of which are constantly, almost imperceptibly, shifting from moment to moment but a mass that retains its identity as it moves through space. Although various details of Feldman's music of this period were "experimental" (their exact results unforeseen), he obviously had a clear generalized image of each work. His musical personality was a distinctive one as well, tending to favor slow rhythms, very soft dynamics, and what Cage called "tender" sonorities. In some later pieces—one of the first was *Structures* for orchestra (completed 1962)—Feldman returned to notating rhythms and pitches precisely, but in such a way as to create the same kind of ethereal but intense atmosphere, the

[17] Quoted by Cage in "History of Experimental Music in the United States," *Silence*, 68.

[18] Feldman, jacket notes for *Durations I–IV* and other pieces on Time LP 58007/S-8007; rel. 1963.

weightless but clustered density, the nonperiodic but fluid rhythmic flow, of his chance music.

Earle Brown was influenced in his musical ideas by artists, especially the sculptor Alexander Calder and the painter Jackson Pollock. In the mobiles of Calder he saw the possibilities of a work never being the same twice yet always being the same work. In Pollock's drip-or-pour "action" paintings he saw possibilities for a musical work's being spontaneously realized on the basis of graphic cues given by the composer. In a remarkable group of compositions published under the title *Folio* (1952–53), Brown presented his first "open-form" music on the mobile principle: *1953* for piano, a study for the larger *Twenty-five Pages*. The score may be read either side up; the pages may be played in any sequence; the two-stave systems may be read in either treble or bass clef; the duration of each system is to be determined by the performer. Thus in many ways this music is "mobile." The notation, original with Brown, is "time notation": the horizontal length of a note suggests its duration relative to other notes and to the time span determined for each system. *Folio* also includes Brown's first Pollock-like pieces, *MM 87* and *MM 135* for piano ("composed very rapidly and spontaneously and … in that sense performances rather than compositions"), and the celebrated work *December 1952*, the score of which is reproduced as Example 10–12. "Score" is not quite the word: *December 1952* is a single page of plain paper (Example 10–12 "frames" it in gray) on which are drawn lines and rectangles, both horizontal and vertical, of various lengths and thicknesses. The lines and rectangles may be read as implying direction, loudness, duration, and pitch. This page constitutes both/either score and/or parts for (any) performer(s), who are to "track" their way around the page (which may be held in any position), realizing spontaneously (or under the control of a conductor reacting to the sheet as to a score) the sonic implications of the markings and the "tracks" chosen. Vaguely reminiscent of an artist's drawing—by Mondrian, for example—*December 1952* has been exhibited as a work of graphic art and is historically significant as the first wholly graphic music (at least since the staffless neumes of the early Middle Ages).

Utilizing various idioms of experimental and nonexperimental music and various methods of notation, Brown developed further his mobile, open-form ideas in such works as *Available Forms I* for chamber ensemble (1961) and *Available Forms II* for "large orchestra four hands" (i.e., two conductors). In each of these works, Brown composed a number of brief musical events, sharply differentiated in character. These may be sounded in any order, repeated, combined, cut off in the middle, taken at different tempos, all at the discretion of the conductor—who thereby realizes one version of the work from the "available forms" that are imagined by her or him. Such works offer maximum possibilities of transformation and mobility (as with Calder), and they are formed spontaneously in performance (as with Pollock).

EXAMPLE 10–12. E. Brown, *December 1952*. Copyright © 1961 (Renewed) by Associated Music Publishers, Inc. (BMI). International Copyright Secured. All Rights Reserved. Reprinted by Permission.

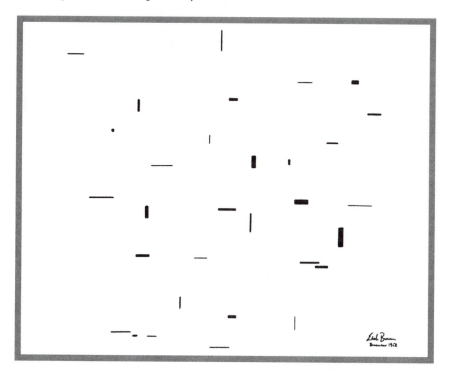

MUSIC AS PROCESS AND ACTION

Clearly, the "experimental" music of chance and indeterminacy by Cage and his New York colleagues of the 1950s and early 1960s completely changed the traditional relationships between composers and performers. One critic put it this way:

> Experimental music engages the performer at many stages before, above and beyond those at which he is active in traditional western music. It involves his intelligence, his initiative, his opinions, and prejudices, his experience, his taste and his sensibility in a way that no other form of music does.... For while it may be possible to view some experimental scores only as concepts, they are, self-evidently, (specific or general) directives for (specific or general) action.[19]

[19] Michael Nyman, *Experimental Music: Cage and Beyond* (New York: Schirmer Books, 1974), 13.

Not only were composer-performer relationships changed; so were those between listeners and performers: in the most extreme instance, Cage's *4'33"*,
the listener *is* the performer—is, in fact, both performer and composer. And
the "musical work" itself was a different thing: no longer a *work*—an object—it was a *process*, different from performance to performance.

A number of composers in the late 1950s and 1960s based further
developments on these altered relationships and their implicit redefini-
tion of "music" itself. They viewed it as necessarily leading to a sort of
Gesamtkunstwerk-like Happening; they were radically antiestablishment,
and reminiscent—in their humor and mockery of the Establishment—of
Dadaists earlier in the century; and they joined other artists in sound-and-
environment events so diverse as to make generalization about them, or categorization of them, almost impossible. New York City was a major center, with
an American wing of an international group called FLUXUS particularly active,
but similar groups existed in Ann Arbor, Michigan (the ONCE group), Seattle
(DIMENSIONS OF NEW MUSIC), and elsewhere in the country. The subtitle of
An Anthology (1963) edited by the composer La Monte Young (b. 1935) suggests the diversity of this movement toward music as process and action:

> Change operations / Concept art / Meaningless work / Natural disasters /
> Indeterminacy / Anti-art / Plans of action / Improvisation / Stories / Dia-
> grams / Poetry / Essays / Dance constructions / Compositions / Mathemat-
> ics / Music

Among the contributors (who included Cage, Brown, and Wolff) were Joseph
Byrd, Toshi Ichiyanagi, Richard Maxfield, Nam June Paik, and James War-
ing. Young himself included a number of his compositions of 1960; his *Composition 1960 #10* is reproduced as follows, in its entirety:

> Draw a straight line and follow it.
>
> October 1960

In New York in 1961, I heard Young's *Composition 1960 #7* 🎼 "to be
held for a long time"—performed by a string trio. The duration of that performance was forty-five minutes; it evoked a large number of ancillary sounds
(mostly audience noises) but also revealed to those who continued to listen

a whole inner world of fluctuating overtones in the open fifth as sustained by the players.

Among the ONCE group composers, Robert Ashley (b. 1930) and Gordon Mumma (b. 1935) were the leaders. A typical 1960s piece by Ashley was *Public Opinion Descends upon the Demonstrators* (1961), for a single operator of complex electronic playback equipment (with a large variety of prerecorded sounds on tape) ... and an audience. The audience is seated unconventionally so that its members are facing one another and the operator can observe their reactions. The operator determines the sounds of the piece according to audience activity and produces different sound complexes in response to any of the following actions "performed" by a member of the audience: (1) leaving the auditorium, (2) walking around in the auditorium, (3) speaking aloud or laughing, (4) whispering (audibly or noticeably), (5) making any kind of exaggerated gesture, (6) making any kind of secretive gesture, (7) glancing "meaningfully" at another member of the audience, (8) seeking a remote visual diversion (looking out the window or at the ceiling), (9) looking toward a loudspeaker, (10) making an involuntary physical gesture (yawning, scratching, adjusting clothing, etc.), (11) showing an enforced physical rigidity (waiting it out). Things get lively as soon as the audience members begin to understand that in some mysterious way they are creating the piece: exhibitionists, angry resenters, and shrinking violets all contribute to a lively interaction between "audience" and "performer" in which traditional roles are thoroughly confused and no one is certain who the "composer" really is.

Like Ashley, Mumma was concerned with activating the musical experience: *Meanwhile, A Twopiece* (1961) for two performers (of a piano, percussion instruments, and "another instrument on which one of the performers is proficient") and prerecorded tape is written in a notation that indicates only the physical gestures to be made by the performers, with cues for them to move from instrument to instrument at certain points. In speaking of the ideology of such a piece, Mumma suggested other reasons than Cage's ideological ones for the rise of such "music as process and action." The physicality, free choice of sounds, and interaction between performers in *Meanwhile*, he said, were partly a reaction to the impact of the new recorded-sound technology: "With the widespread use of 'canned' music (radio, phonograph, and tape playback in serious music, commercial popular music, jazz, and electronic music) the visual or theatrical aspect of the performance of music has lost much of its significance."[20] In *Meanwhile* and similar works, such as *Gestures II* for two pianos (1962) or *Cybersonic Cantilevers* for audience and cybersonics (1973), Mumma vehemently reasserted such significance, as did Ashley and other composers of process and action music.

[20] Private communication, February 23, 1962.

JAZZ: THE EMERGENCE OF BEBOP

The onset of World War II tended to inhibit the free development of various kinds of American music, but perhaps especially jazz, as the nation tightened its collective belt to some degree and nightlife diminished accordingly. Another kind of inhibition was a very real and practical one: in August 1942 James C. Petrillo, head of the powerful musicians' union, the American Federation of Musicians (AFM), called a strike banning AFM members from making any recordings until the record manufacturers agreed to pay a fee to the union for every recording they made. The strike not only created a vacuum between jazz musicians and listeners; more important, it eliminated a major source of communication among jazz players themselves—the phonorecording that had in effect served as text and teacher to the jazz community. Decca Records signed an agreement with the AFM late in 1943, but not until the fall of 1944 did RCA Victor and Columbia, the other two giants in the record-manufacturing industry at that time, capitulate.

When jazz recordings began to reappear, and especially when the end of World War II in 1945 brought a lifting of restrictions on the use of materials needed for record manufacture, a new species of jazz seemed to burst on a public unaware of the developments that had in fact been going on— almost underground, it seemed. Some of these developments could be viewed as reactions to certain aspects of prewar jazz in the swing era, especially the very bigness of the big bands and the pressures on such bands to cater to public and commercial taste. The development of a concert culture for jazz meant a broadening of its base of patronage; but just as in the development of a concert culture in art-music a century or more earlier, one result was a growing lag between the musical thought of the advanced performer and the public. After-hours "jam sessions," in which jazz musicians played for one another rather than for the public, became important proving grounds for new jazz expression. The most lastingly important of these—engaged in almost exclusively by black-American jazz musicians—reflected another sort of reaction: resentment and anger on the part of blacks against commercial exploitation (whites consistently being paid more than blacks and, typically, under more stable contractual terms) and social discrimination (being relegated to "colored" hotels and boarding houses, their families and friends often not able to gain entrance to the very nightclubs and dance halls in which they were applauded).

At the same time, blacks saw jazz being even more highly esteemed as a self-sufficient music, and one that they viewed (not entirely wrongly) as a music of their invention and propulsion. Out of such feelings as these arose, among some black-American musicians' experimentation in after-hours sessions, the initially exclusive and self-consciously progressive style of *bebop* (or simply *bop*), which developed in New York early in the 1940s and emerged to public consciousness by about 1945.

Among the leaders in the crystallization of bop were the alto saxophonist Charlie Parker (1920–55)—with Armstrong and Ellington one of the most supremely inventive musicians in the history of jazz—the trumpeter Dizzy Gillespie (1917–93), and the drummer Kenny Clarke (1914–85).

Gillespie contributed much to an expansion of the harmonic language of early bop. In such a work as his famous recording of the popular ballad *I Can't Get Started with You* (*SCCJ* CD 3), he can be heard almost forcing the other members of the combo into uncharted terrain with chord substitutions and distant excursions from the song's basic harmonies; and the wicked but humorous harmonic surprises of *Shaw 'Nuff* (1945; SCCJ CD 3; NW LP 271), in which he and Parker display a dazzling virtuosity in unison duets, are probably of his invention.

Parker, on the other hand, burst on the jazz scene with an unprecedented improvisatory flair and melodic virtuosity, in a style that was asymmetrically phrased, full of chromatic surprises, and built up by unpredictable combinations of the briefest ejaculatory motifs and very long, very fast, looping lines. Despite the aggressive novelty of his language, Parker's art was rooted in jazz tradition: a large number of his recordings, no matter what their titles are, are twelve-bar blues; most others are based on jazz "standards" (tunes, and more importantly their basic harmonic progressions, known to all jazz musicians) or the harmonies of a few popular songs, especially the Gershwins' *I Got Rhythm* (for example, the *Shaw 'Nuff* just mentioned, which is credited jointly to Parker and Gillespie) or *How High the Moon*, on which is based Parker's celebrated *Ornithology* of 1946.

Bebop drummers such as Clarke and Max Roach (b. 1924) gave up the incessant four-beat bass-drum thudding of the swing style, reserving that instrument for occasional "bombs" dropped irregularly into a new ride-cymbal-dominated, shimmering background beat.

One of the most common conceits of bop musicians was to base a piece on the harmonies of a well-known song but substitute for its original melody a new one in bop style and then retitle the work. Thus, the really knowledgeable would recognize Gillespie and Parker's *Anthropology* as a reworking of Gershwin's *I Got Rhythm*, or Gillespie's *Groovin' High* as the old popular song *Whispering* (1920) without the original melody. Example 10–13 shows the beginning of *Whispering* and of its bop derivative, *Groovin' High*, transcribed from the 1945 recording of Gillespie and Parker. The curt two-note figure that opens *Groovin' High* is a characteristic bop motif; some say that the term *bebop* originated as a verbalization of such a figure.

A revival of the Dixieland style of early jazz also occurred in the 1940s. This began on the West Coast, where the Yerba Buena band of Lu Watters (1911–89) made some recordings in faithful imitation of the early discs of Louis Armstrong. Actually, the New Orleans jazz revival was only one of many signs of a growing American nostalgia for the 1920s: before long, young Americans were once again dancing the Charleston and getting their parents'

EXAMPLE 10–13. A bop-style melody and its source. (*a*) John Schonberger, Richard Coburn, and Vincent Rose, *Whispering*. Copyright 1920 Miller Music Corporation, New York, NY. Copyright renewal 1948 Miller Music Corporation and Fred Fisher Music Co., Inc., for the United States and Canada. Rights throughout the rest of the world controlled by Miller Music Corporation. Used by permission. (*b*) Dizzy Gillespie, *Groovin' High*. After a transcription of Rondolette recording A-11 by Frank Tirro.

Note: In Gillespie's performance, ♩♩ = approximately ♩ ♪ , more precisely ♪. ♪

raccoon coats out of mothballs, enthusiastically acting out their rosy imaginings of life in the prosperous, "secure" 1920s.

THE REVOLUTION IN POPULAR MUSIC: FROM POP TO ROCK

If jazz underwent rapid changes in the three decades after World War II, an even more violent upheaval occurred in American popular music. With the exception of a continuing undercurrent of sweet, romantic, conservative, virtually "traditional" song—heard from such older performers as Lawrence Welk (1903–92), Bing Crosby, Perry Como (b. 1912), and Frank Sinatra (1915–98)—American popular music was transformed entirely, from "pop" to "rock."

As had happened before in American popular music, one main source of the transformation was the music of black Americans, this time their "rhythm-and-blues" on recordings.[21] Actually, the term covered several kinds of music American blacks were making and enjoying in the postwar years: big- and small-band jazz, essentially in the swing style; urban blues; and the songs of small vocal groups, most of them all-male quartets.

The strong-rhythmed dance music of big bands, rooted in the Kansas City swing style (such as those led by Andy Kirk, Jay McShann, Erskine Hawkins, and above all Count Basie), was important as a source of rhythm-and-blues. But the union-musicians' recording ban of 1942–44 and the increasing economic constraints on maintaining big bands had led to a greater importance for the small "jump" bands, with one or two rhythm players backing up one or two melody leaders. One of the most successful of these was the Timpany Five, led by the singer and sax player Louis Jordan; their *Choo Choo Ch'Boogie* (1946; NW LP 261) was Jordan's first big hit. Another group that helped the "race" music of blacks cross over into national popularity was the King Cole Trio, led by the creamy-voiced Nat "King" Cole (1917–65), whose early jazz work was eclipsed in popularity by such novelty songs as *Straighten Up and Fly Right* (1943; NW LP 261) and such smooth ballads as *It's Only a Paper Moon* (1943) and *The Christmas Song* (1946).

Another type of music identified with rhythm-and-blues was urban blues, both that of band-backed showmen in big-city dance halls and auditoriums (Chicago being a major center) and that of soloists on small-group recordings. Their roots were, of course, the deep-South rural blues and the recordings of such songsters as Charley Patton from Mississippi and Blind Lemon Jefferson from Texas, and later Leroy Carr, Bukka White, and Robert Johnson. Traditional black bluesmen such as T-Bone Walker (1910–75), who traveled widely in the South and West in the 1930s and 1940s, gradually shifted from acoustic to electric guitar. In Walker's case, the specific source is known—the solid-body electric instrument developed and played by Les Paul (b. 1915). Walker's classic *Call It Stormy Monday* (1947; NW LP 261) shows his assimilation of the more powerful and versatile amplified instrument, which was to become standard for rhythm-and-blues groups. Muddy Waters (1915–83) was another rural bluesman who traveled north—to Chicago in 1943. Not particularly identified with rhythm-and-blues, he nevertheless had an enormous influence on its style of performance with pieces such

---

[21] "Rhythm-and-blues" was a name coined in the late 1940s by the record industry; the popular-entertainment magazine *Billboard* proposed it as a substitute for "race music," which with the growing social consciousness of the postwar period had come to be viewed as offensive.

as *Hoochie Coochie Man* (1952; NW LP 261). One knowledgeable rock critic penned a vivid characterization of *Hoochie Coochie Man;* it can serve to
describe the mature rhythm-and-blues style in general: "... whining treble
electric-guitar fills around the melody, a slurring, muttering, shouting delivery of the lyric; rolling drum rhythms underpinned by a near-contrapuntal
bass line and a call-and-response riff pattern, [and] a beat that socks away
unmercifully."[22]

Most of these blues singers were men, but a few women also came to
prominence as rhythm-and-blues singers, among them Willie Mae "Big
Mama" Thornton (1926–84)—who had to wait, however, for national recognition until Elvis Presley recorded in 1956 his version of *Hound Dog* (by
Jerry Leiber and Mike Stoller, both b. 1933) and made it into a huge hit: her
version (1952; NW LP 261) was obviously Presley's model. (She was later to
be the model for another white star: Janis Joplin.)

Yet another wing of rhythm-and-blues was occupied by small vocal
groups—"sidewalk singers," they have been called—whose formation was
encouraged both by the instrumental recording ban of the 1940s and by the
growing popularity of black gospel music, which had a considerable tradition of male "quartets" (which actually varied in number of performers). An
early prototype was The Mills Brothers, who began singing in the 1920s,
made successful recordings in the 1930s, and then had a spectacular national hit in 1943 with *Paper Doll*. Similar to them stylistically were The Ink
Spots, who had risen to national fame in 1939 with *If I Didn't Care*. Less
close to white popular-music styles were other groups, many formed originally as gospel-music quartets. One was The Golden Gate Quartet, which
easily gained a secular audience with the irresistible (and danceable) drive
and precision of such songs as *The Sun Didn't Shine on Calvary* (1941;
NW LP 261). Several others were "bird" groups, among them The Ravens
and The Orioles.

If black rhythm-and-blues, in its various guises, was one major source
of the new American popular music, the other was the "hillbilly" music of
southern upland whites—or as it would be called when it became known
more widely, "country-and-western" music (or "country-western," or just
"country"). Originally a folk music rooted in the Anglo-American songs and
dances of the nineteenth century, country music was first viewed as a commercially viable music in the early days of radio and the rise of the recording industry, in the 1920s. The songs of Hollywood's cowboy heroes—Gene
Autry, Roy Rogers, Tex Ritter—were related in style to the southeastern
up-country music and "put the 'western' into country-and-western music."[23]
World War II turned it from a music of wide but mainly rural appeal into a

---

[22] Don Heckman, liner notes for the New World Records repressing just cited.

[23] As country-music historian Bill Malone remarks, in his lengthy and illuminating *SCCCM*
liner notes ("Born Country: A Personal Reminiscence").

national phenomenon. The first great star of this "new" popular music was Hank Williams (1923–53), known especially for a mournful, forlorn singing style that somehow touched people's hearts. An especially poignant example is the slow waltz *I'm So Lonesome I Could Cry* (1949; *SCCCM* side 10); 1949 was also the year Williams had his first hit, *Lovesick Blues* (*SCCCM* side 10), a gently rolling song projected by Williams with an appealing self-mockery underscored by swooping yodels.

At about the same time, a subgenre of country music—"bluegrass"— was being defined by Bill Monroe and his Blue Grass Boys; it was in fact named after the group. Bluegrass was a livelier music than most country, and more predominant in it was a rollicking, hell-bent-for-leather instrumental undergirding; syncopated banjos and mandolins added a sparky twang to the softer plucked-string sound of acoustic guitar and bass; instrumentalists often vied with one another in jazzlike exchanges. *Why Did You Wander* of 1946, from the first recording session of Monroe's group (*NW* LP 225), typifies the style; the spectacular three-finger banjo-picking of Earl Scruggs (b. 1924)—who with the mandolinist-singer Lester Flatt broke away from the Blue Grass Boys in 1948 to form the Foggy Mountain Boys—is heard to even better advantage in *Earl's Breakdown* (1951; *SCCCM* side 13) or *Randy Lynn Rag* (*NW* LP 235).

These two kinds of music—rhythm-and-blues and country-and-western—had some stylistic characteristics in common that made their marriage a potentially happy one. They both emphasized a highly personal, grassroots earthiness of vocal style; they both were based rhythmically on a powerful and danceable instrumental background; and they both tended to favor the guitar, whether the electrically amplified guitar of the urban blues singers, the natural "acoustic" guitar (long prominent as a rural, folkish instrument) of rural blues and bluegrass, or the steel guitar, sometimes amplified, of country-and-western music.

The transformation of American popular music through the marriage of black rhythm-and-blues and white country-and-western was owed primarily to a new phenomenon in American society: a self-conscious, selfaware, and economically strong "youth culture" of rebellious teenagers—a generation of Americans born just before World War II or during the baby boom immediately after it, raised in the postwar economic boom, and reaching adolescence in the 1950s. It was during that decade that rhythm-andblues records began to attract white teenagers, especially as a music for dancing. A few alert disc jockeys began to program the records for a general audience, not just for the black community; one of them, Alan Freed, broadcasting in Ohio during the early 1950s, was instrumental in popularizing the name "rock 'n' roll" for this music. Soon record manufacturers were marketing rhythm-and-blues/rock-and-roll recordings generally, not just to blacks. And soon they were employing white musicians to "cover" black hits— to perform them in their own versions, usually smoother-edged, somewhat

diluted, and generally more successful commercially than the black origi-
nals—and were searching for white musicians whose styles were based on,
or close to, black music. White rock-and-roll hits in turn awakened interest
in the black music and musicians they imitated. Before long, much American popular music was moving in the direction of rock-and-roll.

The first indication at the national level of the change in popular-
music taste was the appearance in 1953 of a rock-and-roll song on the weekly "chart" of best-selling popular-music recordings published in *Billboard*
magazine: it was *Crazy Man Crazy*, by Bill Haley and his Comets (a white
group). Haley (1925–81) was even more successful the following year with
Shake, Rattle and Roll (a cover for black Joe Turner's recording of it earlier
in 1954 [*NW LP* 249]). Neither of these songs, however, approached the
success of Haley's *Rock Around the Clock* in 1955. Used as theme music for
the movie *Blackboard Jungle*, which dealt with juvenile delinquency, it came
to be identified with youthful rebellion.

Haley's was primarily a northern style based on the heavy rolling beat
of rhythm-and-blues (and its powerful "backbeats" on notes 2 and 4 of a $\frac{4}{4}$
measure), with, however, a slight twang of guitars from country-and-western.
The opposite balance typified the songs of his successor in popularity (and
in fact the most spectacularly successful rock-and-roll star of the 1950s and
early 1960s), Elvis Presley (1935–77), born in Mississippi. Presley sang (and
played guitar to) a music blending a dash of rhythm-and-blues with large
amounts of country-and-western—some called the style "rockabilly," others
"country rock." He recorded first for Sun Records, a Memphis firm, and
built a reputation as the nation's most promising country musician; in mid-
1955 he reached No. 1 on *Billboard*'s country-music chart for the first time
with *Mystery Train* (*NW LP* 207), an infectious blues. In early 1956, newly
under contract to RCA Victor, he recorded the song *Heartbreak Hotel*; the
company arranged for television appearances and put together a long-playing
record album by him, partly from material recorded earlier.[24] Within a few
weeks, both the single of *Heartbreak Hotel* and the LP album were leading
Billboard's pop-music chart. A few months later, a disc with Presley's cover
of Big Mama Thornton's *Hound Dog* on one side rose to the No. 1 position
not only on the pop chart but also on the rhythm-and-blues and
country-music charts. Presley had reached the top; for eight years, into 1963,
he was to remain there.

If Presley and other early white rock-and-roll stars—notably Pat
Boone (b. 1934), Jerry Lee Lewis (b. 1935), and Buddy Holly (1938–59)—

---

[24] The album's songs clearly reveal Presley's models: *Blue Suede Shoes* (based on an original by the white country-and-western singer Carl Perkins), *I Got a Woman* (originally recorded in 1955
as a rhythm-and-blues number by the black Ray Charles), *Tutti Frutti* (a rock-and-roll hit by another black, "Little Richard" Penniman), and *Money Honey* (originally recorded in 1954 by the black
gospel-influenced group The Drifters). (In addition, there were rockabilly-tinged slow ballads and even
a version of Rodgers and Hart's *Blue Moon*, from the 1934 movie musical *Hollywood Party*.)

were the national favorites, some black musicians were more inventive. One whose originality, power, and wit can be measured by his enormous impact on later musicians was Chuck Berry (b. 1926). His first record, *Maybellene* (1955; *NW* LP 249), was about sex and speed; others spoke directly to, and for, the youth culture, such as *School Day* (1957), *Sweet Little Sixteen* (1958), and *Almost Grown* (1959) ("... Don't bother me, leave me alone, / Anyway I'm almost grown"). In *Roll Over Beethoven* (1956), Berry opted for popular as opposed to high culture ("... Roll over, Beethoven, and tell Tchaikowsky the news") in an unconscious echo of earlier American vernacular-culture champions (see p. 120). He sounded other notes of protest in his songs, and with his powerful shouting-blues voice, the brassy sounds of his amplified guitar, and his drummer's bombshell backbeats he helped to confirm rock-and-roll as a music of the rebellious youth culture.

Bo Diddley (b. 1928), Fats Domino (b. 1928), Sam Cooke (1931–64), and Little Richard (b. 1935) were other blacks who, although heard mainly within the black community during the 1950s, were to provide material for nationally—even internationally—popular covers later. (Many in the black community complained bitterly—and justly—about this cultural, and economic, robbery.) More versatile than his black precursors, able to adapt to a variety of styles (popular ballads, gospel songs, and jazz as well as rock-and-roll) and thus able to win a national audience more easily, was Ray Charles (b. 1930). He was a versatile, blind, black singer and pianist who along with Presley dominated the pop-music field in the early 1960s with a style of song and singing often so heavily tinged with the idioms of black gospel music that it invited a new categorization—"soul" music. A performance such as his 1959 version (*NW* LP 249) of Hank Snow's *I'm Movin' On* owes as much to church practices—the furious tempo, the ecstatic vocalization, the back-up singing group—as to the country-music origins of the song or to rhythm-and-blues in general. This aspect of Charles's art was immensely influential among younger black pop singers of the later 1960s such as Aretha Franklin, Stevie Wonder, Steve Winwood, and James Brown.

By the late 1950s a new trend in popular music—clearly related to rock-and-roll—was visible: an increased interest in folk music, especially that of the American past, and in folkish songs newly written. Pete Seeger (b. 1919) and The Weavers, strongly influenced by the leftist, Depression-era folk singing of Woody Guthrie (1912–67), turned *Goodnight, Irene*—which had been recorded in 1943 by the country-blues singer Huddie Ledbetter, known as Leadbelly (1885–1949)—into a hit as early as 1950. But it was not until several years later that folk music, or folk-derived music, began to rival rock-and-roll in national popularity. The Kingston Trio's *Tom Dooley* (1958), based on a late-nineteenth-century ballad, was a landmark. By the middle 1960s, the folk-music revival had progressed so far that perhaps the most universally well known song in the country was an earlier labor-movement song with a tune of uncertain origins, its words adjusted by Pete Seeger and others to

EXAMPLE 10–14. *We Shall Overcome*. Musical and lyrical adaptation by Zilphia Horton, Frank Hamilton, Guy Carawan, and Pete Seeger. Inspired by African American Gospel Singing, members of the Food & Tobacco Workers Union, Charleston, SC, and the southern Civil Rights Movement. TRO - © Copyright 1960 (Renewed) and 1963 (Renewed) Ludlow Music, Inc., New York, International Copyright Secured. Made in U.S.A. All Rights Reserved Including Public Performance For Profit. Used by Permission. Royalties derived from this composition are being contributed to the We Shall Overcome Fund and The Freedom Movement under the Trusteeship of the writers.

the major sociopolitical drives of the time for civil rights and world peace: *We Shall Overcome* (Example 10–14).

Among the leading figures in the folk revival were Harry Belafonte (b. 1927), who popularized the calypso style of the West Indies in 1957; Joan Baez (b. 1941), who came to prominence in 1960 with her first LP album (including *Donna, Donna* and *House of the Rising Sun*); the trio of Peter, Paul, and Mary, whose first hit album (1962) included *Cruel War* and a version of Pete Seeger's *Where Have All the Flowers Gone?*; and a young man known as Bob Dylan.

Dylan (b. 1941 as Robert Zimmerman) began his career as a New York coffeehouse balladeer in 1961. His model was Woody Guthrie; he sang in a high, harsh, somewhat tuneless voice that sounded very "old-timey," very "country," and he played an acoustic guitar, sometimes punctuating his songs with wails on a harmonica hung on a frame around his neck. He had a unique poetic sensibility, and a number of his songs expressed unforgettably some major themes of the 1960s—at least those of the disillusioned, alienated youth, sick of the country's domination by a military-industrial complex, its undeclared wars, and its racial strife. Some of these were *Blowin' in the Wind* (1963), against racial prejudice; *A Hard Rain's a-Gonna Fall* (1963), against the nuclear bombing threat; *It Ain't Me Babe* (1964), about superficial boy-girl relationships; *Mr. Tambourine Man* (1965), about alienation; and *Subterranean Homesick Blues* (1965), about the absurdity of it all.

Among many others influenced by Dylan was the team of Paul Simon and Art Garfunkel (both born in 1941). They treated topics as timely as Dylan's, if in a less poetically unique and musically uncompromising and individualistic way, in such songs as *The Sounds of Silence* (1964), *Scarborough Fair/Canticle* (1966), and *Mrs. Robinson* (from the film *The Graduate* of 1968).[25] In fact, one of the most striking things about the new popular songs of the later 1960s was the quality and significance of their lyrics: they spoke of serious matters both timely and timeless, often in a more poetically artful way than had the popular songs of a generation earlier.

Ironically, the team of musicians that most clearly personified the intersections of black and white, urban and country, folk and pop, and pop and art in American "popular" music of the later 1960s—a team that even surpassed Presley in popular success—was not American at all but British: The Beatles (John Lennon, Paul McCartney, George Harrison, and Ringo Starr). Early in 1964 their recording of *I Want to Hold Your Hand* reached No. 1 on the *Billboard*, *Cashbox*, and *Variety* magazines' charts; during one week in March, the top five recordings were all by them; and for the whole period from February to July, songs by them led all others. This fantastic popularity, without historical precedent, was maintained by The Beatles for years, virtually until the group dissolved in 1970; it was due to several factors, among them the inventiveness of Lennon and McCartney as songwriters; canny management and promotion of the group; and its studied eclecticism, always seeming to be one step ahead of the expanding stylistic range of rock-and-roll.

BIBLIOGRAPHICAL NOTES

The music discussed in this chapter (and the following three) is also treated in Eric Salzman's companion volume, *Twentieth-Century Music: An Introduction*, 3rd ed. (Upper Saddle River, NJ: Prentice Hall, 1988). More narrowly focused on composition in concert music is Kyle Gann's *American Music in the Twentieth Century* (New York: Schirmer Books, 1997). Leonard B. Meyer's *Music, the Arts, and Ideas* (Chicago: University of Chicago Press, 1967) is an important critical-aesthetic contribution.

Riegger's life and music are briefly but knowledgeably discussed in Stephen Spackman's *Wallingford Riegger: Two Essays in Musical Biography* (ISAMm 17 [1982]).

Elliott Carter's many writings are gathered in *Elliott Carter: Collected Essays and Lectures*, ed. Jonathan W. Bernard (Rochester, NY: University of Rochester Press, 1996). They may best be complemented, concerning Carter's music, by the "authorized" study of his former pupil David Schiff (see note 7).

[25] Hollywood was slow to adopt the new pop music: Columbia made *Rock Around the Clock* with Bill Haley and the Comets in 1956, but thereafter, other than the many films with Elvis Presley as the male lead (beginning with *Love Me Tender* of 1956), few Hollywood products used rock-and-roll on their sound tracks until the late 1960s. The first film with an all-rock score was Richard Lester's *A Hard Day's Night* (1964), a British production starring The Beatles (and their music).

The first significant essays on the work of Milton Babbitt appeared in a sixtieth-birthday celebration in *PNM* 14/2–15/1 (Spring–Summer/Fall–Winter 1976); a seventieth-birthday follow-up appeared in *PNM* 24/2 (Spring–Summer 1986): 10–128, with a refreshing essay by Joseph N. Straus (with accompanying cassette). Babbitt's theories are in effect summarized in a very clearly written practical manual by Charles Wuorinen, *Simple Composition* (New York: Longman, 1979); his eloquence as a lecturer/teacher captured in *Milton Babbitt: Words About Music*, ed. Stephen Dembski and Joseph N. Straus (Madison: University of Wisconsin Press, 1987); his compositional development outlined in Andrew Mead's *Introduction* (see note 8). His most famous *general* essay, which appeared in *High Fidelity Magazine* 8/2 (February 1958) under an editor's invented, and regrettable, title ("Who Cares If You Listen?"), was reprinted in the expanded edition of Elliott Schwartz and Barney Childs's anthology *Contemporary Composers on Contemporary Music* (New York: Da Capo Press, 1998) and, under Babbitt's original title, "The Composer as Specialist," in *Classic Essays on Twentieth-Century Music*, ed. Richard Kostelanetz and Joseph Darby (New York: Schirmer Books, 1996), 161–67.

On the origins of electroacoustic music, Otto Luening speaks from a position of authority in chap. 24 ("Electronic Music 1906 to Present") of his autobiography, *The Odyssey of an American Composer* (New York: Scribner's, 1980). Still valuable is Barry Schrader's *Introduction to Electro-Acoustic Music* (Upper Saddle River, NJ: Prentice Hall, 1982), especially its interviews with composers Luciano Berio, Pauline Oliveros, Morton Subotnick, Jean-Claude Risset, and Gordon Mumma, each centered on one of their works. "Developments in Technology: Electronic Music," chap. 22 of Robert P. Morgan's *Twentieth-Century Music* (W. W. Norton, 1991), and chap. 10 ("Electronic Music") of Kyle Gann's *American Music in the Twentieth Century* are both trustworthy (and complementary) accounts.

John Cage's essays and lectures are unparalleled sources for his ideas on the music of chance and indeterminacy; they are listed (along with much other material) in *A John Cage Reader*, ed. Peter Gena, Jonathan Bent, and Don Gillespie (New York: C. F. Peters, 1982). Cage embodied his later thought in Norton Lectures at Harvard University, published as *I–VI* (Cambridge: Harvard University Press, 1990). The German journalist Walter Zimmermann compiled the massive *Morton Feldman Essays* (Cologne, Germany: Beginner Press, 1985), with three articles and an epilogue about Feldman plus twenty-three writings by Feldman himself; see Carol J. Oja's perceptive review (contrasting Feldman's writings with those of composer Ned Rorem in his *Setting the Tone* [1984]) in *AM* 5/2 (Summer 1987): 205–8.

La Monte Young's *An Anthology [etc., etc., etc.]* (see p. 290) is not easy to find but worth the search, for examples of the music of process and action. Only slightly less elusive are the issues of the periodical *Source: Music of the Avant Garde* (1969–77), which tend to be multimedia productions themselves, as well as essays and articles; a helpful guide to its contents is Michael D. Williams's *Source[:] Annotated List of Contents and Cumulative Indices*, in the Music Library Association's Index and Bibliography Series (1978; distributed by Scarecrow Press [1/800/462-6420]). Richard S. James discusses ONCE in "ONCE: Microcosm of the Musical and Multimedia Avant-Garde," *AM* 5/4 (Winter 1987): 359–90.

The transition in jazz from swing to bebop is considered in Scott DeVeaux's masterly *The Birth of Bebop* (cited on p. 253 n. 15); bebop itself is central to Thomas

Owens's *Bebop: The Music and Its Players* (New York: Oxford University Press, 1995). Gary Giddins writes briefly but with authority in *Celebrating Bird: The Triumph of Charlie Parker* (New York: Beech Tree Books, 1987); Carl Woideck's *Charlie Parker: His Music and Life* (Ann Arbor: University of Michigan Press, 1996) is exceptionally strong on the music. Also valuable is Martin Williams's sensitive criticism in his collection *Jazz Masters in Transition 1957–69* (New York: Macmillan, 1970).

For rhythm-and-blues, turn first to Charles Keil, *Urban Blues* (Chicago: University of Chicago Press, 1966), and Arnold Shaw, *Honkers and Shouters: The Golden Years of Rhythm & Blues* (New York: Macmillan, 1978). Still the best book on country music is Bill C. Malone's *Country Music U.S.A.*, rev. ed. (Austin: University of Texas Press, 1985); a more recent, complementary approach is Richard A. Peterson's *Creating Country Music: Fabricating Authenticity* (Chicago: University of Chicago Press, 1997). Besides *The Rolling Stone Illustrated History of Rock & Roll*, ed. Jim Miller, rev. ed. (New York: Random House/Rolling Stone Press, 1980), still valuable are Greil Marcus's *Mystery Train: Images of America in Rock 'n' Roll Music*, rev. ed. (New York: Dutton, 1982), and Ed Ward, Geoffrey Stokes, and Ken Tucker's *Rock of Ages: The Rolling Stone History of Rock & Roll* (New York: Rolling Stone Press/Summit Books, 1986). Clinton Heylin's *Bob Dylan: Behind the Shades* (New York: Summit Books, 1991) is more than a biography; see the review of it (and other Dylaniana) by Craig Russell in *[MLA] Notes* 50/3 (March 1994): 929–33.

ELEVEN

INTERSECTIONS, INTERACTIONS, PROJECTIONS: FROM THE 1960s TO THE MID-1970s

Each of the suggestive nouns in the title of this chapter might be found as a heading for a musical work of the 1960s or early 1970s. The first decade or so after World War II had seen extraordinary activity in American music, along widely divergent lines; beginning in the 1960s, however, it seemed there might be some new syntheses developing—or if that term suggests too strongly mergers wholly completed, at least some "intersections" and "interactions" among different kinds of music, and perhaps these "projected" some syntheses lying ahead. In all the areas of American music—jazz, popular music and musical theater, concert music—one of the most striking trends of the 1960s and early 1970s was the intermingling of musical techniques, languages, and even worlds that had seemed separate before.

Those nouns of this chapter's title say something, too, about the period: abstract, cool, detached, antiexpressionist and antiromantic in implication, they bespeak a kind of "laid-back" acceptance of the ups and downs and absurdities of modern life. As one composer-critic of the period put it, "For the younger composers, and many of the older ones, the barriers are down, the categories destroyed. ... Any kind of statement is possible."[1]

---

[1] Eric Salzman, *Twentieth-Century Music*, 2nd ed. (Upper Saddle River, NJ: Prentice Hall, 1974), 200; he elaborated on this perception in the 3rd edition (1988), 245–46.

POST-BEBOP JAZZ AND THE "THIRD STREAM"

In jazz, three principal types of the period—cool jazz, hard bop, and free jazz—arose from interactions of attitude and intersections of style.

The beginnings of cool jazz are often identified with a famous series of recordings made in 1949–50 by a nonet led by the trumpeter Miles Davis (1926–91). Based on sophisticated arrangements, many of them by Gil Evans (1912–88), this was chamber jazz of great musical elegance, but also of great restraint expressively, compared with the contemporaneous bebop style. The ruminative, often relaxed, understated soliloquies of Davis and the thin, pale tone of alto saxophonist Lee Konitz (b. 1927) were characteristic. Davis's collaboration with Evans was exceptionally fruitful: following the nonet recordings (reissued as the Capitol album *Birth of the Cool*) came the albums *Miles Ahead* (1957), *Porgy and Bess* (1958), and *Sketches of Spain* (1959–60). In *Miles Ahead*, Davis plays both trumpet and flugelhorn; the album also includes early examples of "modal jazz," with improvisation based not on a "tune" or its "changes" but on a nontraditional music scale (or "mode"). *Porgy and Bess*, inspired reworkings of songs from Gershwin's opera, includes a remarkable transformation, at Evans's and Davis's hands, of *Summertime* (*SCCJ* CD 4).

Pianist in the performances, on *Birth of the Cool*, of *Venus de Milo* by Gerry Mulligan (1927–96) and his own *Rouge* was John Lewis (b. 1920). In 1952, Lewis founded the Modern Jazz Quartet; its light sound (piano, vibraphone, bass, and drums) and a style including contrapuntal niceties like canon and fugue (*Versailles*, 1956; *Concorde*, 1963) and such unusual source materials as Elizabethan harpischord music (*The Queen's Fancy*), music by Johann Sebastian Bach (*Vendôme*), and old English carols (*God Rest Ye Merry, Gentlemen*) made it the epitome of cool jazz.

Related to the Modern Jazz Quartet in breadth of style sources was the music of a quartet headed by the pianist Dave Brubeck (b. 1920), who had studied with Darius Milhaud; it featured the improvisatory brilliance of the alto saxophonist Paul Desmond (1924–77). Typical of their work was a version of *Perdido*, recorded in 1953 during a concert at Oberlin College; this includes witty and apparently spontaneous quotations from a 1928 Broadway show tune (*Crazy Rhythm*, from *Here's Howe*), a silly popular song of 1935 (*The Music Goes Round and Round* [NW LP 248]), and Stravinsky's *Petrushka*, plus a fugal exposition in the manner of Baroque-era music. Brubeck also broke out of the traditional $\frac{4}{4}$ meter of jazz with such pieces as *Take Five* (in $\frac{5}{4}$) and *Blue Rondo à la Turk* (in $\frac{9}{8}$, the eighths divided 2 + 2 + 2 + 3).

Even more eclectic, sophisticated, and intellectualized was the work of the pianist-composer Lennie Tristano (1919–78), noted as a teacher of vanguard jazz style in the 1950s. His *Subconscious Lee* (1949; *SCCJ* CD 4), based on Cole Porter's *What Is This Thing Called Love?*, exemplifies the melody-dominated style of his recording groups, this one displaying amazing unison playing by Konitz and Tristano (in the opening and closing choruses) plus complex solos by them and guitarist Billy Bauer. In the same year, Tristano's quartet "stretched almost to the breaking point" the harmonic underpinning of Jerome Kern's *Yesterdays* (NW LP 216; the quotation is from Gunther Schuller's liner notes).

Perhaps in reaction to such a cultivated chamber jazz, there emerged in the mid-1950s a hard, harsh, leather-lunged style sometimes called "hard bop" or "funky" jazz. The latter term, an old colloquialism for "smelly," with sexual implications like the original ones of "jazz" itself, suggested the back-to-the-roots quality of the style. As conceived by Horace Silver (b. 1928), pianist and leader of the Jazz Messengers with drummer Art Blakey (1919–90), by Blakey himself, and by the alto saxophonist Cannonball Adderley (1928–75), hard bop combined the chromaticism, the asymmetrical phrases, and the sharp punctuation of the bebop style with the old earthiness of New Orleans jazz, plus an accessible intensity related to black rhythm-and-blues. The result was a tough, angular, honking music as complex harmonically as bop and cool jazz but also as expressively fervent and powerfully communicative as the early jazz of the 1920s. Well-known and widely successful examples of hard bop include Silver's *Stop Time* (1954; NW LP 271) and *Nica's Dream* (1956; NW LP 242). The Horace Silver Quintet's *Moon Rays* (1958; SCCJ CD 4) begins deceptively as a quiet, balladlike piece, but each of its solos—by tenor-sax player Clifford Jordan, trumpeter Art Farmer, and Silver himself—unrolls with expressionistic intensity and soulfulness.

Two musicians related to hard bop but so independent and inventive that they resist classification were Charles Mingus and Thelonious Monk.

Charles Mingus (1922–79) was an extraordinary double-bass player and a visionary composer. In the mid-1950s he organized a Jazz Workshop with which to develop his ideas—a four- to eleven-piece band usually including the drummer Dannie Richmond (1931–88) and often the vanguard alto-sax player Eric Dolphy (as in the angry political satire *Original Faubus Fables* of 1959, referring to Orville Faubus, the segregationist governor of Arkansas; a 1960 recording [NW LP 242] includes an angry, sneering text). Mingus's visionary concepts sometimes led him to a music difficult to claim as jazz in any traditional sense—for example, *Eclipse* (1953; NW LP 216), with its unconventional contrapuntal use of unconventional instruments (flute, cello) in an unconventional form, with unconventional lyrics appearing (unconventionally) to begin and end the piece. On the other hand, he could inspire a group to a roaring, ripsnorting riot of tradition-based riffs and solos, such as *Hora Decubitus* (1963), which also exemplifies his fondness, as a composer, for dense textures, low-pitched ensembles, and acrid dissonance.

Thelonious Monk (1917–82) had been one of the architects of the bebop style in New York in the mid-1940s but almost immediately veered off on a purely personal path, highly influential if also almost inimitable—as can be heard in such early works as the blues transformation *Misterioso* and the original version of *Evidence* (both 1948; both on SCCJ CD 4). Monk's mature piano style was so iconoclastic in its spare, spastic, broken-rhythmed, angular melody, often seeming at odds with the harmony (itself full of strange-ness and surprise), and the whole feigning a kind of uncertain awkwardness, that many listeners and critics were deceived into thinking that he couldn't really play the piano. Ultimately, however, Monk's absolute mastery was ac-knowledged universally. One jazz critic, thinking of such unique re-creations as Monk's coruscating, awesomely original solo on the blues-based *Bag's Groove* (recorded by Miles Davis's All Stars in 1954; *SCCJ* CD 4) or his 1957 recording of the ballad *I Should Care* (*SCCJ* CD 4), has written,

> His compositions and his playing were of a piece. His improvisations were molten Monk compositions, and his compositions were frozen Monk impro-visations. ... His medium- and up-tempo tunes are stop-and-go rhythmic struc-tures [which] move irregularly through sudden intervals and retards and broken rhythms. His balladlike tunes are altogether different. They are intense and graceful art songs, which move slowly and three-dimensionally. ... He filled us with his noble, funny, generous music.[2]

With the appearance in the late 1950s of the saxophonists John Coltrane (1926–67) and Ornette Coleman (b. 1930) and the pianist Cecil Taylor (b. 1929), some jazz approached the ultrachromatic, atonal style of certain concert music. This *free jazz*—"the new thing," "atonal jazz," "the new wave" were other attempts to name it—gave up the traditional basis of jazz in a preexistent "tune" (or the progression of harmonies underlying a tune) and a steady, even beat, turning instead to an almost wholly spontaneous, rhap-sodic, and passionately expressive style—"speechlike cries, squawks, moans, and cackles ... slurring, burring, braying, crying" was one early critical re-sponse—in which the players almost seemed to rely on extrasensory per-ception to follow one another's ideas.[3] Coleman's dirgelike *Lonely Woman* (1959; *SCCJ* CD 5) reveals an almost Ivesian dissociation between the soloists (Coleman on alto sax, Don Cherry on trumpet) and the backup bass and drums; his *Free Jazz* of 1960 is an extraordinary thirty-six-minute achievement in collective free improvisation by a double quartet (a ten-minute excerpt is on *SCCJ* CD 5). The aims of such music were related to ideals of personal freedom and self-expression: the players sought to "speak" instrumentally with one another, and to their listeners. In *Alabama* (1963; *SCCJ* CD 5), Coltrane ruminates meditatively on a speech by the black leader Martin Luther King, Jr.; in the fourth part ("Psalm") of one of his most celebrated works, the suite *A Love Supreme* (1964), he "recites" with his tenor sax a

---

[2] "Notes and Comment," *The New Yorker* (March 1, 1982): 37–38 (an obituary article, un-signed but most probably by Whitney Balliett).

[3] The quotation is from Nat Hentoff, "The New Jazz—Black, Angry, and Hard to Under-stand," *New York Times Magazine* (December 25, 1960): 10, 36–39. Only much later did analyses make clear the strong structural foundations of some so-called free jazz; see especially Lewis Porter's discussions in his definitive study *John Coltrane: His Life and Music* (Ann Arbor: University of Michi-gan Press, 1998), generously reviewed by Zbigniew Granat in [*MLA*] *Notes* 55/2 (December 1998), 363–66.

prayer (printed with the liner notes of the CD reissue [Impulse! CD GRD-155; rel. 1995]).

Some free-jazz musicians, notably the saxophonists Albert Ayler (1936–70) and Archie Shepp (b. 1937), identified the searing expressionism of free jazz with the struggles of American blacks and with the militant black nationalism of the 1960s. Ayler commented, "It's not about notes anymore. It's about feelings!" The poet and playwright LeRoi Jones (who later took the Black Muslim name Amiri Baraka) said, "You hear ... poets of the Black Nation."[4] One of Shepp's early pieces had the title *Rufus*; this was an abbreviation for *Rufus Swung His Face at Last to the Wind, Then His Neck Snappe*d, and the idea behind the piece was a lynching.

As a vanguard music, free jazz eluded the popularity or even the acceptance of other jazz. This was especially true of the music of free jazz's most determined, uncompromising, conceptually "far-out" exponent, the pianist Cecil Taylor. His unprecedently energetic, intense, violent, percussive, asymmetrical, and unpredictable performances brought him critical acclaim but few jobs. Even repeated hearings of such works as the thirty-minute *Holiday en masque* (*NW* CD 80201) or the almost hour-long *3 Phasis* (*NW* CD 80303) leave most listeners, not excluding jazz aficionados, bemused.

Several composers of the period moved freely from jazz to concert music or the reverse. Gunther Schuller (b. 1925) saw in the intersection of these two mainstreams of American music possibilities for a "third stream," a term he coined in the late 1950s. There had been plenty of interaction between contemporaneous vernacular- and cultivated-tradition music during the twentieth century, from Ives and his ragtime pieces through Carpenter and Copland to Blitzstein—and in the opposite direction, from Joplin and his ragtime opera and ballet scores through Gershwin to Duke Ellington. Schuller's perception, however, was that postwar jazz had achieved a sophisticated language and freedom of form that made it possible to imagine, if not a true fusion, at least a happy marriage between jazz and nonjazz. His own *Transformation* (1957; *NW* LP 216), for an eleven-piece jazzlike ensemble, "begins as a straight twelve-tone piece ... and is gradually transformed into a jazz piece ... only to succumb to the reverse process."[5] Schuller's *Conversations* and *Concertino* (both 1959) set a jazz quartet (with the makeup of the Modern Jazz Quartet) against, respectively, string quartet and full orchestra. In these works the two styles are kept discrete; they intersect but are not fused. In other works by Schuller, such as *Seven Studies on Themes of Paul Klee* (1959), the First Symphony (1965), and the opera *The Visitation* (1966), Schuller moved closer to a real synthesis.

A number of other composers also utilized jazz elements. Their incentive seemed to spring not from any "Americanist" ideal, nor from pursuit of the third-stream ideal envisioned by Schuller (an ideal that was never

---

[4] Both quotations are from the liner notes of *The New Wave in Jazz* (Impulse LP A-90; recorded 28 March 1965).

[5] Schuller, liner notes for *Mirage: Avant-Garde and Third-Stream Jazz* (NW LP 216).

really to be realized). Some of them, practicing jazz musicians themselves, simply found the repertory of jazz idioms and inflections to be natural, viable foundations for more formal composition. Among these were Hall Overton (1920–72) and Francis Thorne (b. 1922); the latter's witty chamber work punningly entitled *Seven Set Pieces* (1967; *CRI* CD 586) combines jazz-derived ideas easily and convincingly with serial techniques, even in two helter-skelter movements based on the idea of "jam sessions" (and so titled). Thorne's later works—mostly abstract instrumental pieces but also his cunning one-act opera *Mario the Magician* (1991–93)—tended not to make such allusions. Salvatore Martirano (1927–95) first came to notice as a conventionally schooled twelve-tone composer (*Mass*, for double chorus, 1952–55; *NW* CD 80210) but began to exploit his background as a jazz keyboardist in the late 1950s—as in his *Ballad*, for a miked and amplified singer working over popular songs of the 1930–50 period; or *O, O, O, O, That Shakespe-herian Rag* (1958; *NW* CD 80535), the title from T. S. Eliot, the text from Shakespeare, and the music, for chorus and instrumental ensemble, a "so elegant, so intelligent" commentary on the verses.

Another emergent composer well versed in ragtime and jazz as a pianist, and a connoisseur of American popular music in general, was William Bolcom (b. 1938). This orientation influenced much of his career. He and the mezzo-soprano Joan Morris achieved both critical and popular success with recitals and recordings of American pop songs of the Tin Pan Alley era, in serious, stylish, "period" presentations. Collaboration among the two of them and the poet Arnold Weinstein led to several stunning sets of deceptively light *Cabaret Songs* (1985–97) by Bolcom, who summarized them as "little dramas, vignettes, stories, jokes, laments, regrets, celebrations." Bolcom also helped to spark a ragtime revival in the early 1970s, as a performer of old rags and newly composed ones such as his *Seabiscuits* (1967) and the poignant *Graceful Ghost* (1970). Together with William Albright (1944–98), he wrote *Brass Knuckles* (1969), a rollicking rag studded with cluster-chord crashes. (Albright himself contributed rags to the repertories of both pianists and organists, notably his *Grand Sonata in Rag* [1968] and *Dream Rags* for piano [1970]—one of them the grand panoramic [and pianoramic!] *Nightmare Fantasy Rag: A Night on Rag Mountain*—and several witty *Organbooks*.)

Bolcom's works in larger forms reveal a cheerful, purposeful eclecticism, beginning with his first major composition, *Dynamite Tonite* (1963)—a "cabaret opera for actors" to text and lyrics by Weinstein. These seemed to culminate in his massive setting of forty-six poems by William Blake, *Songs of Innocence and of Experience* (1956–84) for soloists, choruses, and orchestra—itself culminating in a blues-tinged Jamaican-reggae-derived finale, over a swinging ostinato, on Blake's *A Divine Image* ("Cruelty has a Human Heart/And Jealousy a Human Face"). But Bolcom went on to even more impressive works, notably the opera *McTeague* (1992), to a libretto by Weinstein, and an operatic collaboration with Arthur Miller and Weinstein based on the playwright's *A View From the Bridge* (1999).

THE ROCK ERA RAMPANT

By the late 1960s, variants of rock-and-roll were multiplying so fast, each seeming another step removed from the ultimate source (rhythm-and-blues/country-and-western), that the new music came to be called simply "rock," plus one of any number of qualifying adjectives. There was folk rock (The Byrds, The Band, Country Joe & The Fish, The Mamas and the Papas, and especially the work, from the mid-1960s on, of Bob Dylan and Neil Young). There were blues rock (Ike and Tina Turner, The Righteous Brothers), soft rock (James Taylor, Bread, The Carpenters), and hard rock (The Doors, The Jimi Hendrix Experience). There was acid rock (or psychedelic rock) from San Francisco groups such as Jefferson Airplane and The Grateful Dead. (The adjectives referred to LSD and other hallucinatory drugs; to songs that spoke positively of such drugs—*White Rabbit*, by the singer Grace Slick—or hinted at their use; and to the delirious experience of rock concerts, which combined ear-splitting, mind-numbing amplification, hypnotically repetitive rhythms and static or constantly revolving harmonies, and bizarre, kaleidoscopic "light shows.") There were southern-white rock (The Allman Brothers, Lynyrd Skynyrd) and northern-black rock ("Motown"—the rock-related black popular style named after Berry Gordy's publishing and recording company in Detroit and typified by Diana Ross and the Supremes, Martha and the Vandellas, Marvin Gaye, and Stevie Wonder). There were Bach rock (*A Whiter Shade of Pale*, by the British group Procol Harum) and Renaissance rock (*Pavan for My Lady*, by the short-lived American one, Ars Nova). In reaction to the "British invasion" in the later 1960s of groups such as The Beatles, The Rolling Stones, and The Who, there was self-consciously angry, violence-tinged punk rock (The Ramones, Black Flag, X). There was a rock of artistic pretensions dubbed art rock (The Velvet Underground, later the "new wave" group Talking Heads). There was even rock that was not—or as one critic described it, "unpopular pop": the complex, Varèse- and Stravinsky- and Cage-influenced music of Frank Zappa (1940–93) and his group, The Mothers of Invention;[6] their early concerts were precursors of the cynical grotesqueries of rock called variously rock-'n'-rouge, deca-rock (for "decadent"), or glitter rock: the homoerotic, sadomasochistic, chaotic unisex spectacles of performers such as like David Bowie and Alice Cooper (both males).

Rock was diffused primarily by recordings and airplay (on the radio). It also became a major kind of concert music, for a huge and almost exclusively youthful audience all across the country. Especially after The Beatles filled the giant Shea Stadium in New York in the fall of 1966, rock concerts and festivals became a commonplace, in both outdoor arenas and immense

---

[6] The characterization is that of Lawrence Gushee, in an unpublished paper of 1972. David Walley implies the same thing in the title of his book on Zappa, *No Commercial Potential* (New York: Outerbridge and Lazar, 1972).

interior halls ("rock palaces") such as Fillmore Auditorium in San Francisco and Fillmore East in New York. The peak of rock-concert productions occurred in a field near Woodstock, New York, in the summer of 1969, when about 450,000 young people gathered for a three-day "festival of love" and music; perhaps the nadir was reached later that year at Altamont Speedway, east of San Francisco, when many members of an audience of 300,000 experienced bad drug "trips," violence, and rioting (with a few deaths).

By the mid-1970s, it seemed that this glut of rock in all its variant versions might be presaging the decline of the genre and the dawn of a new cycle of American popular music. One critic forecast a renaissance of melodious lyricism, seeing worthy successors to the songs of Gershwin, Kern, and Rodgers in those of Joni Mitchell (in the albums *The Circle Game, Clouds, The Ladies of the Canyon*), Carly Simon (*Anticipation, No Secrets, You're So Vain*), Carole King (*Now That Everything's Been Said, Writer, Tapestry*), and Randy Newman (*Randy Newman, 12 Songs, Sail Away*).[7] And perhaps this lyric renaissance would come out of the musical, which had finally begun to reflect the transformation of American popular music.

THE MUSICAL

The rock revolution had effected a diffusion of the geographical centers of popular music (in performances, recordings, and publishing): Nashville, New Orleans, Memphis, Detroit, and San Francisco had become as important as New York as breeding grounds and distribution centers. The American musical comedy, however, with its center of gravity at Broadway and Times Square, remained dominated by New York's tendency to a narrow if sophisticated insularity and for a long time tended to maintain the aesthetic and the style of pre–World War II musical theater. Only in 1967, in *Hair* (music composed by Galt MacDermot), did the popular lyric theater begin to catch up with the new pop music of rock. *Hair*, although not the revolutionary work it seemed at first to be (partly because of one seminude scene), was at least perceptibly tinged with rock, in such songs as *Aquarius* and *Good Morning, Starshine*, and with rock's themes of protest from the youth culture.

One brilliant new composer of musicals (as well as other kinds of works) had appeared in the immediate postwar years: Leonard Bernstein (1918–90). A Harvard graduate with prodigious natural talents as a pianist, conductor, teacher, and composer, Bernstein moved easily from one to another of America's worlds of music, "classical" and popular. His Second Symphony, "The Age of Anxiety" (1949), includes a lengthy jazz-tinged piano solo; his ballet score *Fancy Free* was amplified into a musical, *On The Town* (both 1944). With a style that might be described as "by Copland out of

---

[7] Don Heckman, "You Like to Recognize the Tune? You Will," *New York Times*, September 24, 1972.

Stravinsky" and with complete fluency in popular-music idioms, Bernstein created in *West Side Story* (1957) the freshest musical of the early postwar period. A recasting of the Romeo and Juliet story in terms of the ethnic melting pot of Manhattan's upper west side, *West Side Story* was an evocative portrait of postwar urban America; its finely balanced interaction between drama and ballet owed much to the choreographer Jerome Robbins (who had also conceived the dances of *Fancy Free*). And with *Mass* (composed for the opening in 1971 of the Kennedy Center for the Performing Arts in Washington, D.C.), Bernstein wrote a work that had some relationship, at least, with avant-garde impulses toward a new, "third music theater" (see p. 322). (Bernstein's career as a composer of concert music and opera was somewhat uncertain; as a conductor championing such then-underplayed composers as Mahler and Ives courageous; and as a teacher—the first to capitalize charismatically on television—nothing less than spectacular.)

The only other postwar musical to rival (and even outdo) the success of *West Side Story* was *My Fair Lady* (1956), composed by Frederick Loewe (1901–88) to the book and lyrics of Alan Jay Lerner (1918–86) after George Bernard Shaw's *Pygmalion*. Perhaps the American audience that responded by the millions to this near-operetta was identifying with the guttersnipe-turned-lady of the heroine; musically speaking, it had little to identify with, for like all the other musicals of the late 1950s and most of the 1960s, *My Fair Lady* shared in no way in the popular-music revolution.

By the early 1970s, another figure seemed especially promising as a composer of musicals: Stephen Sondheim (b. 1930). Sondheim had written the lyrics for Bernstein's *West Side Story* and Jule Styne's *Gypsy* (1959). Later he went on independently to write both the lyrics and the music for a series of musicals of high inventiveness and artistry: *A Funny Thing Happened on the Way to the Forum* (1962), *Company* (1970), *Follies* (1971). With *A Little Night Music* (1973), a fresh and elaborate work, he entered a newly sophisticated phase: almost every song in its unique score was in one or another type of triple meter (especially waltzes); its rich harmonic language was evocative of Richard Strauss's *Der Rosenkavalier*; and it reveled in contrapuntal duets and trios, a quartet, and even a double quintet. All this suggested once again (as with *Oklahoma!* almost thirty years earlier) that the American musical might be aspiring to a new high-mindedness. Sondheim went on to an even more ambitious, virtually operatic musical-theater work in *Sweeney Todd* (1979), and to an experimental, developmental score for *Sunday in the Park with George* (1984)—which won the Pulitzer Prize for drama, and, along with *Into the Woods* (1987), was "generally considered to have taken the musical into more profound dramatic territory than many would have dreamed possible."[8]

---

[8] Stephen Banfield, *Sondheim's Broadway Musicals* (Ann Arbor: University of Michigan Press, 1993), 55.

THE NEW VIRTUOSITY

Virtuosity had long had a role in American music—but virtuosity of a circumscribed and conventionalized sort. This was especially true in concert music, where the very term "virtuoso" connoted simply a performer who had a more spectacular technical command than others over traditional methods of vocal or instrumental production. But much of the new concert music put brand-new demands on performers. The post-Cage process-and-action music called for improvisatory skills and a new responsiveness to the situation at hand. Serial music, obeying the dictates of intervals, rows, sets, and subsets, often simply disregarded the assumed limits of performer capabilities (especially in melodic contour, dynamics, range, and articulation, each of which tended not only to be extremely varied but also to change with unprecedented rapidity). Electroacoustic music had stretched all the boundaries of traditional music—and in doing so had affected composers' ideas of what they might try to get out of live performers. And the intersections and interactions among various kinds of music, coupled with the increasing range of musical experience possible to get from recordings (not just early, middle, and late music of the Western tradition but also folk and traditional music from all over the world), had stimulated the imaginations of both composers and performers.

One result was that composers demanded more and different things of performers; another was that performers demonstrated to composers that more and different things were possible. And out of these developments came a new virtuosity, displayed dazzlingly by specialist singers and instrumentalists (and a few conductors)—and counted on by composers. Among the singers, preeminent were Bethany Beardslee (b. 1927), Cathy Berberian (1925–83), Jan DeGaetani (1933–89), Paul Sperry (b. 1934), Phyllis Bryn-Julson (b. 1945), Susan Davenny Wyner (b. 1945), and Joan La Barbara (b. 1947); among the instrumentalists, flutist Harvey Sollberger (b. 1938); clarinetist William O. Smith (b. 1926); trumpeter Gerard Schwarz (b. 1947); trombonist Stuart Dempster (b. 1936); cellist Fred Sherry (b. 1948); double bassist Bertram Turetzky (b. 1933); percussionist Max Neuhaus (b. 1939); and pianists David Tudor (1926–96), Paul Jacobs (1930–83), Robert Miller (1930–81), Frederic Rzewski (b. 1938), and Ursula Oppens (b. 1944).

Rzewski, a composer as well as a pianist, joined with fellow composers Richard Teitelbaum (b. 1939) and Alvin Curran (b. 1938) in organizing one of the many new-music chamber ensembles that developed to meet the challenge of the new virtuosity: Musica Elettronica Viva, founded in Rome in 1966 to specialize in live/electronic music. Among other such ensembles were the Contemporary Chamber Players (Chicago, established 1954), the Group for Contemporary Music (New York, established 1962), Speculum Musicae (New York, established 1971), Parnassus (New York, established 1974), the New Music Consort (New York, established 1975), and others in almost every substantial city and university—not to mention string quartets that specialized in the new-music repertory, such as the Juilliard, Composers, Concord, Emerson, and Kronos quartets (and later the all-female Colorado Quartet). Some conductors, too, won acclaim as specialists in new music, among them Gunther Schuller, Thomas Nee (b. 1920), Ralph Shapey (b. 1921), Arthur Weisberg (b. 1931), Dennis Russell Davies (b. 1944), and Michael Tilson Thomas (b. 1944).

A number of leading younger composers of the period were identified with one or another of the new-music ensembles, often as organizers or conductors, and usually performers as well. Charles Wuorinen, for example, co-founded with Sollberger the long-lived Group for Contemporary Music—it celebrated its twenty-fifth anniversary in 1986—and often served as its pianist and conductor. As a composer, he remained a dedicated serialist, inclined to "a very detailed structuring of events [in a composition] down to a very small scale, as well as on a very large scale" (thus adhering to Babbitt's serial approach); on the other hand, he believes that "since even the most detailed score still represents an assemblage of generalities... it should always be possible to reinterpret compositions"[9]—thus coming down on the side of the interpretive performer. The overwhelming majority of Wuorinen's works have been for live performers, especially for virtuoso soloists; it was ironic, then, that his Pulitzer Prize was awarded to an all-electronic composition (see p. 282). More characteristic are his *Piano Variations* (1964), chamber concertos with different solo instruments (cello, flute, oboe, and others), the one-act opera *The Politics of Harmony* (1966–67), and the *Bassoon Variations* (1972; *NW* CD 80517). The last-named is particularly accessible and attractive sonorously, the bassoon being "accompanied" by an unusual duo—harp and timpani. Wuorinen writes a music sometimes of ferocious intensity and furious activity, sometimes of complex lacy delicacy, that both responds to and demands more of the new virtuosity, approaching at times the outer limits of interpretive possibility and perception.

The response of composers to the new virtuosos' capabilities is well illustrated by such works as *Inflections I* (1969), for unaccompanied double bass, by Robert Hall Lewis (1926–96) and *General Speech* (1969; *NW* CD 80541), for unaccompanied trombone, by Robert Erickson (1917–97). Lewis said, "I was reluctant at first to attempt a composition for an instrument I had considered rather limited. ... When I received a tape from Bert [Turetzky], however, on which he demonstrated more technical possibilities and resources than I had known existed, my imagination was awakened.[10] And Lewis proceeded to write a ten-minute work of staggering virtuosity for an instrument usually considered one of the most recalcitrant (and seldom thought attractive or interesting enough sonorously to hold its own all alone).

---

[9] Both quotations are from Benjamin Boretz, "Conversation with Charles Wuorinen," *Contemporary Music Newsletter* 3 (November–December 1969): 4–8.
[10] This and the following quotation are from the liner notes to *NW* LP 254, which includes recordings of both works cited here.

Erickson's piece was commissioned by Stuart Dempster; it is a "setting" for trombone of General Douglas MacArthur's retirement speech in which the trombonist must "merge his playing of precisely notated (and often difficult) musical events with verbal articulation[—]into the instrument[—]of a phoneticized version of the speech." The result is not only a marvel of virtuosity but also a savage parody, turning MacArthur's "Duty! Honor! Country!" oratory into belching, growling gobbledygook. (Recall that in 1969 American sentiment against the country's involvement in the Vietnam War was at a peak.)

Equally demanding of performers' virtuosity but more accessible was the music of George Crumb (b. 1929), whose early works were so well received that he was unquestionably the most highly acclaimed "young" American composer of the early 1970s. (Already by 1968 he had won the Pulitzer Prize, for the orchestral piece *Echoes of Time and the River*, in which the musicians must move about the stage, as they play, in a carefully worked-out ambulatory choreography.) A large number of Crumb's earlier works are settings of the picturesque image-laden Spanish poems of Federico García Lorca, among them four books of *Madrigals* (1965–69; Books I–IV on *NW* CD 80357); *Songs, Drones and Refrains of Death* (1968); *Night of the Four Moons* (1969; *CRI* CD 760); and *Ancient Voices of Children* (1970). Later, Crumb turned to cosmic images, as in *Makrokosmos I* and *II* (1972, 1973), each a set of "Twelve Fantasy-Pieces after the Zodiac for Amplified Piano," and *Star-Child* ("A Parable for Soprano, Antiphonal Children's Voices, and Large Orchestra"; 1977). All these reveal an extraordinarily subtle and adventuresome tonal imagination, a unique "ear," especially for tiny and delicate shades of timbre.

To realize his sonic visions, Crumb called on an immense range of new performance techniques: humming into wind-instrument mouthpieces, vocalizing into undamped (and amplified) piano strings, whispering, shouting, "bending" of pitch microtonally (by, for example, turning the tuning pegs of a double bass), and so forth. And from the world of popular music he borrowed many instruments: banjo, mandolin, toy piano, jew's harp, musical saw, cowbells, electric guitar, and other amplified instruments. *Black Angels* ("1970, *in tempore belli*" ["in wartime"] is the composer's dating, referring to the war in Vietnam) is for electric or amplified-acoustic string quartet; *Vox Balaenae* (1972; *NW* CD 80357) is for flute, cello, and piano, all amplified. In the latter work, the players are to wear black masks; the depersonalization of the human components eerily increases the "personalization" (à la Elliott Carter) of the music.

Another, older composer who came to new prominence in the 1960s after building an earlier reputation as a neo-Classic prodigy was Lukas Foss (b. 1922). In 1957, inspired by the improvisatory vitality of jazz, Foss organized an Improvisation Chamber Ensemble in Los Angeles, hoping to develop principles of nonjazz improvisation. This ensemble had a marked effect on the music that he composed. *Time Cycle* (1959–60), for example—four songs on texts having to do with time, clocks, or bells—appeared in two different versions, one of them for soprano and orchestra with improvisatory interludes between the songs (the other without them).

The score of Foss's *Echoi* (1961–63), for piano, percussion, clarinet, and cello (the instruments in Foss's improvisation ensemble), includes not only conventionally "precise" notation but also "proportional" notation, which, barless and beatless, requires the performers to view the entire score and to follow one another's playing; it also includes passages of "no coordination" and free reordering of given pitches; passages with random, aperiodic assortments of dynamics, articulations, and pitches; and passages with headless notes—stems and beams only—suggesting the general contour of a line but not specifying either the pitches or, for the percussionist, the instruments to strike or the order in which to strike them. Toward the end of *Echoi*, two prerecorded but uncoordinated tape tracks, one of clarinet music, the other of cello music, are turned on, and the live clarinetist and cellist are to echo in a free manner the taped sounds of their own instruments. There are other aspects of choice and chance in *Echoi* (no two performances will ever be the same), but the composer's ideas dominate throughout. Example 11–1 suggests some of the aspects of notation I have mentioned: the notation is proportional; large notes stand for longer time, small notes for shorter; dotted lines show the moments of coordination among performers; "c. 1s." (in the piano part) represents a rest of "about one second"; headless notes in the vibraphone staff indicate general melodic contour but no specific pitches.

EXAMPLE 11–1. L. Foss, *Echoi*, first-movement excerpt. © Copyright 1964 by Carl Fischer, Inc., New York. Reproduced by permission.

COLLAGE, SPATIALIZATION, MULTIMEDIA, AND MUSIC THEATER

Intersection and interaction are by definition the common ground among several other kinds of works that became increasingly important in the postwar period: collage pieces (from the French word for "pasteup"), mixed-media productions, and a new kind of music theater closely related to mixed media. Although many influences conjoined to stimulate the rise of such works, most were indebted, to some degree, to precepts and examples offered by John Cage.

In composing—or, rather, giving directions for—such a work as his *Imaginary Landscape No. 4* (1951) for twelve radio receiving sets (twenty-four performers), Cage effectively set the stage for a collage piece. The musical *objets trouvés* ("found objects") to be pasted up—comparable to the bits of wood, newspaper, ribbon, and whatnot in a collage by Picasso or Braque (or, more relevant to Cage, his contemporary artist-friend Robert Rauschenberg)—are bits of broadcast sound picked up by the various radios from different stations. Like the musical "quotations" in works of Ives (who must be considered the American ancestor of collage technique) or the pre-recorded materials of a *concrète* piece, these sonorous "objects" make for a double level of perception: one experiences a new work but at the same time is invited—or forced, willy-nilly—to perceive or remember others.

One of the first major collage-technique works of the postwar era— a drastic and startling one—was the third movement of *Sinfonia* (1968) by Luciano Berio (born in Italy in 1925; a musically influential American resident from early in the 1960s until 1972). Against a playing of the scherzo of Gustav Mahler's Second Symphony, countless fragments of other music proliferate—some spoken or sung, some played—by Bach, Schoenberg, Debussy, Ravel, Strauss, Berlioz, Brahms, Berg, Hindemith, Beethoven, Wagner, Stravinsky, Boulez, Stockhausen, Ives, Berio himself, and others. Berio remarked that the movement could be considered "a documentary on an *objet trouvé* recorded in the mind of the listener."[11] The surrealist effect of *Sinfonia* is common also to Foss's *Baroque Variations* (1967), based on material "found" in Handel, Bach, and Scarlatti; Foss described its third variation, "Phorion" ("booty," "spoils," even "stolen goods"), as "torrents of baroque semiquavers, washed ashore by ocean waves, sucked in again, returning." Foss's *Geod* (1969) is also based on *objets trouvés*: different patriotic/national tunes are to be borrowed for use in it, depending on the location of the particular performance.

---

[11] From disc-jacket notes by the composer for *Sinfonia;* on Columbia LP MS-7268.

More subtle is the collage technique in Crumb's *Ancient Voices of Children*, where evocative fragments of other music—flamenco, *Bist du bei mir* from the Little Clavier Book for Anna Magdalena Bach, a bit of Mahler—emerge from the matrix of the composition like flickerings of memory, and in a number of works by Michael Colgrass and Jacob Druckman. Colgrass (b. 1932) broke from strict serialism in 1966 with *As Quiet As*, an orchestral work using a theme from a sonatina by Beethoven transformed in manners reminiscent, successively, of Haydn, Stravinsky, Webern, and Count Basie. The very titles of Colgrass's *Déja vu* (1977; *NW* CD 80318) and *Flashbacks* (1979) suggest collage; the former is a brilliant quarter-hour-long piece for four percussion soloists and orchestra that transforms a single borrowed phrase into various styles (including big-band jazz). Both the title and the contents of Druckman's *Delizie contente che l'alme beate* (1973), for woodwind quintet and tape, derive from an aria by the seventeenth-century opera composer Francesco Cavalli, who also provided similar source material for Druckman's *Lamia* (1975), for soprano and orchestra. Druckman's Pulitzer Prize–winning *Windows* (1972; *CRI* CD 781) is mosaic-like, with "fragments of 'old music'—galant dances, wisps of chorale, hints of waltz—cunningly placed";[12] another orchestral work by him, *Aureole* (1979; *NW* CD 80318), is described by the composer as centered on a "constant but shifting, shimmering melody from which all the music springs": the "Kaddish tune" from Bernstein's Third Symphony.

Related to musical collage is another postwar approach to structure explored by some American composers—musical "spatialization," so to speak. Traditionally, Western music has been thought an exclusively temporal art: time is the only continuum in which music has generally been considered to exist. However, some post–World War II composers have conceived of music as spatial as well as temporal. (Ives had such a vision, as had Varèse. And they weren't the first: think of Giovanni Gabrieli's polychoral panoramas. And some music by Ross Lee Finney, too, hinted at such a vision; see p. 265.) In such works, the spatial separation of performers or other sound sources creates an effect of multiple musics, similar to the multiple and varied materials of which works of plastic-art collages are made.

In some works, physical space itself became crucial, as in Carter's Second String Quartet (1959), where the players are to be more widely separated than usual, or Crumb's *Ancient Voices of Children*, with its placement of a boy soprano offstage. In several imaginative works by Roger Reynolds, including *The Emperor of Ice Cream* (1962; rev. 1974) and *Blind Men* (1966), not only is the spatial distribution of the performers specified

[12]Andrew Porter, in a *New Yorker* review of February 10, 1975, reprinted in his *Music of Three Seasons: 1974–1977* (New York: Farrar, Straus & Giroux, 1978), 92.

but also the score indicates their movement from one area of the concert stage to another.

In other works, however, the "spatialization" is a matter of composition, not performance procedures. The musical discourse is not shaped according to principles of harmonic continuity or of underlying omnipresent "beat" but is essentially one of discrete sounds, or blocks of sounds, shaping time rather than being shaped by it. The result is an effect of sound in space more than in time, for the whole perception of time's passing is altered and attenuated by the discreteness of the sonorous events. Some composers no longer even speak of "sonorities" (let alone "chords" or "harmonies") but of "densities," "sound structures," or "sound objects"; and their ideas of musical form often rest on the intersection and interaction of such sound structures or on the equally spatial images of textures thick or thin, fluctuating or constant, combined or opposed. High–low contrasts are planned or emphasized in spatial terms, as are timbral shifts.

Not surprisingly in this ambience, the older composer Henry Brant (b. 1913), who had long been interested in the separation and spatial disposition of instrumentalists and singers in halls, auditoriums, and even the out-of-doors, achieved new recognition. Spatialization was the very basis of such works as *Antiphony I* (1953; rev. 1968), for five orchestral groups; *The Grand Universal Circus* (1956), a theater piece calling for eight solo voices and thirty-two choristers; *Fire in Cities* (1961), for choruses and instrumental groups; and *Voyage Four* (1963), a "total antiphony," with musicians not only onstage but also against side and back walls and beneath the floor. *Verticals Ascending* ("After the Rodia Towers" [the "Watts Towers" in Los Angeles]; 1967) is for double wind ensemble; for the recording on *NW* CD 80211, the two bands, led by two conductors, were placed back-to-back on opposite sides of the stage, separated by a sound wall and fifty feet of space.

Ralph Shapey similarly divided performers into subgroups and disposed them in spatially separated positions. Thus his *Ontogeny* (1958) divides a full orchestra into seven suborchestras, repositioned onstage. Another orchestral work, *Rituals* (1958; *CRI* 690), is similarly conceived, and one critic spoke of its conveying "not what is called organic growth, but rather ... a sense that the whole piece exists at once and that a listener's (and the performers') progress through it in time is kin to viewing central, unchanging images from different aspects, under different lights, against different backgrounds."[13] A similar quality informs slighter works by Shapey that do not call for spatial separation of the players, such as the duo for flute and piano, *Configurations* (1964; *NW* LP 254). In speaking of his *Incantations*

---

[13] Andrew Porter, "Musical Events: Affirmation," *The New Yorker* (July 9, 1979): 76–78.

(1961) for soprano and ten instruments, Shapey articulated his spatial concept of music as being made of "sound-objects":

music as an object in Time and Space

aggregate sounds structured into concrete sculptured forms

images existing as a totality from their inception, each a self-involved unit of individual proportions

related, inter-related, and unrelated images organized into an organic whole

permutations occurring only within each self-contained unit. ... .[14]

Both the collage technique and the compositional idea of "sounds structured into concrete sculptured forms" are naturally inviting ones for live/electronic music, especially because it lends itself so well to a kind of abstract musical drama: juxtaposition of totally different sound sources can easily suggest dramatic opposition and conflict. Man-against-machine is embodied in the last movement of Foss's *Echoi*, when the live performers struggle against prerecorded tapes of music on their own instruments. Man-against-machine is also the theme of Druckman's *Animus I* (see pp. 281–82); the composer described the dramatic result:

After the first splitting off of the tape and the ensuing dialogue the [trombone] player sits while the electronic sounds move too quickly for him to compete. The man begins again with angrier, more animal-like material; the tape again enters ... this time driving him off the stage. The tape exhausts itself, the man reenters, the two finish in a tenuous balance.[15]

Similar to collage in purposeful juxtaposition of discrete, disparate materials, but extending them beyond sound to other media, are *multimedia* productions. The term came into existence as a generalization for amalgamations of several art forms other than the traditional ones in, say, opera or ballet. Some multimedia (the terms "mixed media" and "intermedia" are used by some) had origins in the Happenings of the 1950s and early 1960s and in the action-and-process music of the ONCE, FLUXUS, and other such groups. Some also reflected, or at least paralleled, the multiple bombardment of the senses of a rock concert. Some were probably an attempt, if unconscious, to make up for the loss of the visual and human elements in electroacoustic music. And of course some flowed from a dictum of Cage's:

[14] Quoted in "Music Programs and Notes," University of Illinois 1965 Festival of Contemporary Arts, 23.
[15] Liner notes for *Electronic Music III* (Turnabout LP TVS-34177; rel. 1967).

"Relevant action is theatrical (music [imaginary separation of hearing from the other senses] does not exist)."[16]

Cage himself was coproducer with Lejaren Hiller of one of the most spectacular multimedia events, *HPSCHD* ("harpsichord" in a computer-convenient abbreviation), which was premiered at the University of Illinois in May 1969. The production, with all events systematically randomized, lasted about five hours; it involved seven harpsichordists; computer-generated sounds on fifty-two tapes; projections from fifty-two slide projectors; a battery of colored spotlights; and an audience of several thousand who sat, stood, danced, or wandered through the environment. The sound materials of the work, and their organization, were an extraordinary mix. Three harpsichordists played material based on Mozart's *Musical Dice Game* (K. 294d/K. Anh. C 30.01); two others began with material by Mozart and moved on through music by Beethoven, Chopin, Schumann, Gottschalk, Busoni, Cage, and Hiller; another played any Mozart music of his or her choice (or any of the composers' pieces the other soloists happen to be playing); and the seventh played a twelve-tempered chromatic single-line melody in ever changing dynamics and note lengths. Meanwhile, the fifty-two tapes, constituting a "tape orchestra" surrounding the harpsichords, were based on different equal-tempered divisions of the octave, from five to fifty-six tones (but excluding the conventional one of twelve).

The West Coast seemed to encourage such multimedia work. (Cage, of course, came from there originally, as did Partch, whose invented instruments, as mentioned earlier, have an awesome physical presence, calling attention to themselves visually as well as sonically.) Two figures mentioned previously (p. 282) as San Francisco tape-music composers—Morton Subotnick and Pauline Oliveros—went on to compose intriguing multimedia works. In the mid-1960s Subotnick wrote a series of diverse pieces entitled *Play!* Each combined live-music performance with tape-music performance, often with other media as well—films, slides, other props, and sometimes actors—and usually with the musicians performing unusual physical activities (lowering their heads, raising their arms, turning to one another as if in surprise or doubt). In *An Electric Christmas* (1967), Subotnick organized one of the most unusual multimedia presentations of the late 1960s. Evocative of a rock concert in its setting and format, *An Electric Christmas* was an evening-long event that mingled medieval music played by the New York Pro Musica (an early-music ensemble), rock by the group Circus Maximus, Subotnick's own electronic music (played by him on the keyboard of a synthesizer), film projections, and a light show; it culminated in a joyous, semi-improvisatory version by the whole crowd of *Douce dame jolie* ("Sweet, Pretty Lady"), a love song—to be interpreted, on this occasion, as addressing the

---

[16] John Cage, "Experimental Music: Doctrine," in his *Silence* (Middletown, CT: Wesleyan University Press, 1961), 13–17.

Mother of the Christ Child—by the fourteenth-century French composer Guillaume de Machaut.

In that same decade of the 1960s, in which multimedia peaked as a compositional ideal, Oliveros organized similar productions. One was *Valentine for SAG* (1968), the acronym referring to the Sonic Arts Group, which developed out of ONCE. This work centered on a game of hearts played on-stage, with the four players' heartbeats amplified, while at the same time a narrator discusses the history of card games, two carpenters build a picket fence downstage, a croquet player hits a few balls, and projections of giant playing-cards are displayed.

Robert Ashley (see pp. 291, 354) turned almost entirely to mixed media (and continued to be a leading-edge vanguardist into the 1990s). He worked with dramatic live/electronic combinations—as in *The Wolfman* (1964), in which Ashley himself, heavily miked, shouts "with maximum amplification against a deafening electronic roar"—and also with advanced video projections, instrumental and vocal music, lecturelike narration, and various graphic enhancements—as in his operas *Atalanta* (1982) and *Perfect Lives (Private Parts)* (1977–83).[17]

Obviously, there is an element of theatricality in virtually all the works we have been considering here. The composer-critic Eric Salzman (b. 1933) claimed that they tended toward a "third music theater—neither opera nor musical—that [is] in the process of finding itself[:] a primarily non-verbal art integrating sound, movement, image, music, language, idea, thinking, feeling."[18] Salzman himself pursued this vision by organizing in 1970 a music-theater group called Quog to perform such works as his own *The Nude Paper Sermon* (1968–69), "tropes" for actor, Renaissance consort, chorus, and electronic music. He later collaborated with Michael Sahl (b. 1934) in small-scale, pop-related, music-theater pieces, of which *Civilization and Its Discontents* (1980) was especially well received. In these works, just as media were mixed, so were musical styles, in a dramatic (and theatrical) response to the empirical modern situation, in which everyone has access through modern technology to a virtually limitless range of musics. As Salzman put it,

> Multi-track, multi-layer experience becomes the norm: Ravi Shankar, John Cage, the Beatles, Gregorian chant, electronic music, Renaissance madrigals and motets, Bob Dylan, German Lieder, soul, J. S. Bach, jazz, Ives, Balinese gamelan, Boulez, African drumming, Mahler, gagaku, Frank Zappa, Tchaikowsky, Varèse ... all become part of the common shared experience.[19]

[17] The quotation is from the sympathetic chapter on Ashley in John Rockwell's *All American Music* (New York: Knopf, 1983), 96–108.

[18] *New York Times*, December 12, 1972.

[19] From the composer's liner notes for *The Nude Paper Sermon* (Nonesuch LP H-71231; rel. 1969). The same point, put in a surprisingly similar way, was made by the composer Ben Johnston in a thoughtful essay, "On Context," *Source* 2/2 (July 1968): 44–45: "Machaut, the Beatles, Wagner, Ravi Shankar, Pete Seeger, Bach, and Xenakis meet ... only as far from me as my record player."

THE NEW EXPRESSIONISM

One of the most powerful, if paradoxical, effects of the new ideas of time and space in music of the mid-1960s to the mid-1970s—of "concrete sculptured forms," of the new virtuosity, and also of the music involving chance and performer choice in a context of composer-controlled image of sound—was a new expressionism. In this music, it was not the composer's feelings that seemed to be loosed (as in the post-Romantic expressionism of a Strauss or a Schoenberg) but in part those of the performers—and, even more potently and extraordinarily, those of the *sounds themselves*. Not only did the performers seem more alive, flexible, and responsive to one another, but also in a peculiarly palpable way the music itself took on an unprecedented sentience, personalization, and vitality. Hear Lukas Foss, speaking of the second movement of *Echoi*:

> ...vibraphone shadowing clarinet (close canon at the unison) sticks to him like glue. clarinet should make futile attempts to escape its own shadow, like an insect trying to extricate itself from a spider web. cello joins in the pursuit. ... pitchless percussion also shadowing, imitating. everyone wanting to get in on the act.[20]

Or hear Chou Wen-chung (b. 1923)—a composer whose Chinese origins allow him to relate what seemed new in American music to some very old oriental ideas—speaking of his orchestral works *All in the Spring Wind* (1953) and *And the Fallen Petals* (1954):

> a tonal brushwork in space—with ever-changing motion, tension, texture, and sonority.... The ancient Chinese musician believed that each single tone or aggregate of tones is a musical entity in itself and a living spark of expression as long as it lasts. Therefore, it was also believed that the meaning in music lies intrinsically in the tones themselves, that maximum expressiveness can be derived from a succession of tones without resorting to extraneous procedures.[21]

Or think of the abstract musical drama in Druckman's *Animus I* (see p. 320), when the tape drives the trombonist offstage but then "exhausts itself," or of the musical self-commentary inherent in quotation and collage techniques.

Many American composers in the period were building a whole new musical aesthetic on an assumption of the potential liveliness—in a literal sense—of sounds themselves. This was especially true of those working in electronic or concrète music, who no longer had to think, and who chose not to think, in terms of twelve-tone equal temperament, Classic-Romantic or "neo-" tonalities, metrical rhythm, traditional instruments, standardized instrumentation, or even "performance" itself. Suggestive in this connection is

---

[20] "Work-Notes for Echoi," *PNM* 3/1 (Fall–Winter 1964): 54–61.

[21] "Towards a Re-Merger in Music," *Contemporary Composers on Contemporary Music*, ed. Elliott Schwartz and Barney Childs with Jim Fox, expanded edition (New York: Da Capo Press, 1998), 308–15.

a set of hints to beginning electroacoustic-composition students for shaping their works, a guide written by Laurie Spiegel (b. 1945), at the time a young composer herself who was teaching even younger composers. She suggested working toward any of four "forms": static, evolutionary, climactic, and dialog. "Dialog form" she defined as "two or more distinctly separate sounds or textures brought into interaction." This interaction could be realized in different ways; some that she suggested were the following (and note the personalization):

    a. they [the sounds] begin as separate but eventually merge into one, or find some relationship to each other;

    b. one of several equals [one of the sounds] eventually dominates over others;

    c. one texture breaks up into several components which exhibit increasing individuality;

    d. a sound originally by itself begins to be accompanied (or possibly attacked) by another. ... [22]

MINIMALISM

The 1960s saw the beginning of an important new movement in American music—*minimalism,* a term borrowed from art critics, who had applied it to contemporaneous works by such artists as the painter Frank Stella, the sculptor Donald Judd, and the versatile Robert Morris. Most of the composers called minimalists rejected the term, but they were in the same position as Schoenberg, who rejected the term *atonal* for his music—they were stuck with it.

    In the background of minimalism were various musical trends of the 1950s. In both the serialist and the aleatoric camps, certain *reductive* tendencies were important—for example, the post-Webern composers' fondness for isolating single tones and giving them a microcosmic identity all their own (also true of Wolff's and Young's music, as noted), or, among the New York school composers, Feldman's unchanging, uninterrupted, murmuring low-level volume and slow-motion rhythms. Also important was Cage's having wiped the slate clean, so to speak, with 4'33" and its invitation to listeners simply to listen—to anything in the environment that caught their attention. The insistent, powerful pulse and the cyclical, variation-like structure of most jazz were also important, as was the insistent beat of almost all versions of rock. Technology, too, counted for a lot—the technology that had reduced much of the world to a nonstop jet flight and had led to a percep-

---

[22] "Some Possible Shapes for Sound Composition" (unpublished). I am grateful to Laurie Spiegel for permission to quote from this.

tion of it as a "global village." Technology had also, of course, led to such new recording media as magnetic tape and the long-playing disc (and, soon to come, the compact disc produced from digital recording)—making possible an unprecedented range of exotic music, distant or ancient, much of it based on very different principles of structure and continuity from those of the Western art-music tradition; it also made it possible for composers to work directly with the materials of composition and to manipulate, alter, repeat, and adjust them at will.

Interest in so-called third-world cultures—on the rise during the 1960s, among musicians as among others in the Western world—also fed into the minimalist aesthetic. Cage had emphasized the impact of Zen Buddhism on his thought and had used the Chinese *I Ching* to guide his composition. The great Indian sitarist Ravi Shankar had toured widely in the United States in the 1950s and moved here in the 1960s. The development, by Cage, Cowell, Harrison, and younger composers, of all-percussion music had stimulated interest in Indonesian gamelan groups and North African drumming. Yoga was newly popular; so was meditation, and also mind-altering drugs, used partly as aids in inducing meditative states.

Additionally contributing to the rise of minimalism was an increasing disillusionment by the 1960s with the compositional method espoused predominantly within the musical "establishment" (especially the academic establishment)—the twelve-tone technique, which though challenging intellectually to composers remained resolutely incomprehensible to most listeners.

The early minimalist leaders, all in their thirties, were La Monte Young, Terry Riley, Steve Reich, and Philip Glass.

Young (see pp. 290–91) began in the mid-1950s to introduce into his serial compositions unusually long-held notes and lengthy silences. His Trio for Strings (1958), a nonserial work, is famous (or notorious) as an extreme example. Lasting more than fifty minutes, it is based on a "dream chord" (Young's term) that he had heard singing in telephone wires. The work's first event consists of the viola's introducing a middle-C♯ without vibrato, *ppp*, and holding it, then the violin's adding an E♭-above-middle-C without vibrato, *p*, and holding it, and then the cello's adding a D-below-middle-C *sul tasto* without vibrato, *pp*, and holding it. This happens *very, very* gradually, over the course of about 45 $\frac{1}{2}$ measures in $\frac{8}{8}$ meter at ♪ = MM 80—or almost five minutes. (There follows a long half-minute of total silence.) By 1960, influenced by Cage's radical ideology, Young was making such conceptual works as *Composition 1960 #7* and *Composition 1960 #10* (see p. 290), which were typically realized as "static" drone-based pieces. But, to anyone who listened carefully, they were not in fact static: like "real" music, they pulsed and "moved" with a strange inner life of minutely shifting timbres arising from the slight variations of overtone structure in the tone(s) sounded—as, for example, when a violinist's bow moves across the string with very slight changes of pressure not willed by the performer but simply the result of human "imperfection."

Young made other dronelike pieces that revealed a different bent— a growing preoccupation with just intonation and nontempered tuning systems (confirmed by lengthy study later, in the 1970s, with the Indian master Pandit Pran Nath). One example is the piece entitled *The Second Dream of the High-Tension Line Stepdown Transformer*, from *The Four Dreams of China* (1962). Its pitch material is simply four tones, in the frequency ratios 36:35:32:24. Example 11–2 (a) gives two possible realizations of the tones (in *approximate* pitch: just intonation is to be used; the interval 36:35, smaller than a semitone, is implied by the arrows in the example). Example 11–2 (b) illustrates the just-intoned second (36:32 = 9:8), fourth (32:24 = 4:3), and fifth (36:24 = 3:2) that are produced between three of the four pairs of sounding tones. In the performance of the composition, strict rules dictate which tones may be sounded together; otherwise, each tone may enter or exit at will. A "harmonic" music results, harmonic in the sense of the intervals formed—not only between the basic tones but also between their upper partials—and of the combination tones produced when these simple fundamental tones are dwelt on. Example 11–2 makes the piece look static—this is *music?*—but, to the degree that the performers develop an acute sensitivity for the resultant "harmonies," and the listener does also, the music is not at all static; a strange, hypnotic, dreamlike succession of delicate sound-images unfolds in shimmering, floating procession.

EXAMPLE 11–2.   Basis of L. M. Young's *Second Dream of the High-Tension Line Stepdown Transformer* (1962). (*a*) Pitches to be sounded (approximate; just intonation is to be used). (*b*) Interval ratios produced between three of the four pairs of tones.

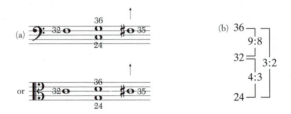

Terry Riley (b. 1935) was an associate of Young's on the West Coast and later in New York; he, too, became a student of Pran Nath. In the early 1960s he supported himself partly as a jazz pianist, and his background in jazz fed into one of the seminal minimalist works, his *In C* (1964). This is a work for any number of musicians, playing any melodic instruments, each musician running in order through a series of fifty-three melodic motifs and phrases—repeating each, however, as many times as she or he wishes before moving on to the next one.[23] The total length of *In C* and its moment-to-moment details (as well as its instrumentation) are variable, which suggests a Cage-derived aleatory randomness. But this factor is offset by the repetitive element and by a strictly controlled tempo, governed by a continuous, metronomic pulse drummed in octave C's (heard nakedly at the very beginning of the work, and then on throughout it); these latter aspects are jazz-related.

Steve Reich (b. 1936) also became interested in music based on the repetition of brief modular patterns (when he, like Riley, was working at the San Francisco Tape Music Center in the mid-1960s). Reich was especially intrigued by the possibilities of "phase-shift" patterns—created when identical, repeated phrases, at first played simultaneously, gradually get out of phase ("out of sync") as one part moves ever so slowly ahead of the other. (These he had noticed by chance in the minute differences in speed of two tape recorders playing a single piece.) Capitalizing on his discovery, he composed the *concrète* works *It's Gonna Rain* (1965) and *Come Out* (1966), each based on a single, short spoken phrase by a black American ("It's gonna rain!" a preacher; "Come out to show them" a Harlem youth), and both built up from endless repetitions of their basic phrases, with multitrack tape techniques used to create pileups of the gradual phase shifts. The resultant pulsation of out-of-phase tape tracks produces a kind of rhythmic combination-tone effect: as the parts, initially in phase, gradually go out of phase, and as the number of tracks increases to four, then eight, a thick tapestry of multiple pulsations, at different pitches, is perceived, as hypnotic and euphoric rhythmically as Young's music is harmonically.

Reich developed techniques for live performance of such phase-shift-based music in *Piano Phase*, for two keyboardists (1967); *Four Organs*, for electric organs and maracas (1970); and *Phase Patterns* (also 1970), for four or more identical keyboards. Example 11–3, the opening of *Piano Phase*, can suggest the principle involved: player 1 repeats a one-measure figure throughout the piece (except at the very end, a coda), maintaining an absolutely steady tempo; player 2 repeats the same figure but, after repetitions of measure 1, gradually accelerates until he or she is one sixteenth note ahead of player 1 (but back in phase, at measure 3). The same gradual phase shift occurs after the in-phase repetitions of measure 3, and so on throughout the piece.

Philip Glass (b. 1937) had a conventional but thorough musical training in this country and in France (with Nadia Boulanger). In Paris in 1965 he had an especially significant encounter with Indian music, through Ravi Shankar and the tabla player Allah Rakha; this profoundly affected his musical thought and set him on the so-called minimalist path. Like Riley and

---

[23] All fifty-three were printed on the jacket of the first recording of *In C* (Columbia LP MS-7178; rel. 1968) and reprinted in Salzman, *Twentieth-Century Music*, 3rd ed., as Appendix Example 19–2.

EXAMPLE 11–3. Steve Reich, *Piano Phase* (1967), beginning (basic module and first three phase shifts). © Copyright 1980 by Universal Edition (London), Ltd., London. © Copyright renewed. All Rights Reserved. Used by permission of European American Music Distributors Corporation, sole U.S. and Canadian agent for Universal Edition (London), Ltd., London.

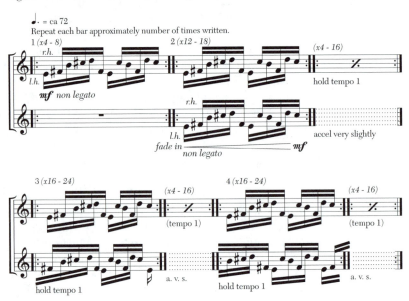

Reich, Glass began building pieces by repetition of melodic cells—varying the repetitions, however, by occasional additions or subtractions of minuscule units within them, as in *Strung Out* (1967), for amplified violin, and *Two Pages* (1968), for two amplified keyboard instruments. An excerpt (Example 11–4) from *Music in Fifths* (1969) suggests the principle: each numbered figure is to be repeated as many times as the players wish (or their leader determines); at an agreed-upon cue they move to the next figure, which is a tiny variant of the first; after similar repetitions of that figure, on to the next, which is yet another minutely varied version of the basic figure; and so on through the piece. The radicalism of Glass's works lay not only in their emphasis on repetition but also in their rejection of polyphony (in favor of monophony or two-note parallelism), their rejection of harmony, and their diatonic melodic vocabulary; they sound superficially like five-finger exercises.

The early minimalist music of these composers had a number of things in common: (1) radical reduction of the compositional material for each work; (2) extensive repetition of such material (accepting, in Young's case, a drone as repetition carried to the *n*th degree) and, moreover, repetition with virtually unchanging timbre, pitch, pace, and level of volume; (3) static, euphonious, nonmodulatory harmony (if any at all); (4) lack of "drama"—that

EXAMPLE 11–4.   P. Glass, *Music in Fifths* (1969), modules 13–19. Copyright © 1969 (Renewed) by Dunvagen Music Publishers, Inc. International Copyright Secured. All Rights Reserved. Reprinted by Permission.

is, lack of contrast, opposition, argument, climax, patterns of tension and release. As a result of all these factors, the music has an *apparent* accessibility, lack of complexity, denial of intellectuality, and lack of expressiveness or emotionality. Moreover, one might claim that the concept of the overall musical work is replaced by the notion of process. Reich, especially, was interested in this idea: in his essay "Music as a Gradual Process" (1968), he said, "I do not mean the process of composition, but rather pieces of music that are [themselves], literally, processes"; Glass said somewhat similarly that in his work of this period he "took rhythmic structure and made that more or less the subject of the work."[24]

The works of the 1960s by these composers were greeted with incredulity, hostility, and disdain. The academic serialists accused the minimalists of artistic nihilism; the aleatoric avant-garde accused them of aesthetic fascism. The critics largely ignored the music—and could afford to, at least during the 1960s and early 1970s, since it was performed most often in nonestablishment performance spaces (artists' lofts, art galleries, museums) and unknown even to most musicians, let alone the general public. Its early supporters were mainly visual artists who shared the minimalist aesthetic and who collaborated enthusiastically with their musical counterparts. Not until the

[24] Reich's essay appeared first in his *Writings About Music* (Halifax: Press of the Nova Scotia College of Art and Design; New York: New York University Press, 1974), 9–11; reprinted in *Contemporary Composers on Contemporary Music* (the edition cited in note 21), 421–24. Glass is quoted in Robert Palmer, "Philip Glass Comes to Carnegie Hall—At Last," *New York Times* (May 28, 1978): "Arts and Leisure," 13, 15.

mid-1970s, in fact, did the existence of musical minimalism rise to public consciousness; two landmarks were the opera *Einstein on the Beach* (1976) of Glass and stage director Robert Wilson, which sold out two performances at the Metropolitan Opera House (rented for the occasion), and Reich's *Music for 18 Musicians* (also 1976), the 1978 recording of which sold more than 20,000 copies within a year. (Both works are discussed in the next chapter; see pp. 335–36.) By then, the so-called minimalist pioneers (with the exception, in some ways, of La Monte Young) had moved on stylistically to a music that no longer seemed "minimal" at all.

BIBLIOGRAPHICAL NOTES

The redoubtable jazz critic Martin Williams was one of the first to see artistic value in the postbop "new thing"; see his *Jazz Masters in Transition, 1957–69* (New York: Macmillan, 1970). Gary Giddins's equally valuable criticism during this era (mostly from *The Village Voice*) is collected in *Riding on a Blue Note* (New York: Oxford University Press, 1981); and see also parts 5 and 6 of his big collection *Visions of Jazz* (same publisher; 1998). Still authoritative on free jazz is Ekkehard Jost's *Free Jazz* (Graz, Austria: Universal Edition, 1974; repr. New York: Da Capo Press, 1981). Lewis Porter's book *John Coltrane* (cited in note 3) is superlative. Ronald Radano's chap. 16 in *The Cambridge History of American Music*, ed. David Nicholls (Cambridge: Cambridge University Press, 1998), 448–70, is also excellent.

Third-stream music is discussed, along with many other topics, in Gunther Schuller's collection of essays *Musings: The Musical Worlds of Gunther Schuller* (New York: Oxford University Press, 1985).

By far the best brief account of "the rock and roll era" is the chapter thus titled, by Robert Walser, in *The Cambridge History of American Music*, 345–87. Still valuable are Greil Marcus's *Mystery Train: Images of America in Rock n' Roll Music* and *The Rolling Stone Illustrated History of Rock & Roll* (both cited earlier; see p. 303). Richard Kostelanetz put together a generous anthology, *The Frank Zappa Companion* (New York: Schirmer Books, 1997).

Although critical literature of substance on the American musical is quite thin, a major exception is Stephen Banfield's brilliant approach to Stephen Sondheim's music (cited in note 8). The books by Gerald Bordman cited earlier (see p. 230) are reliable, as is Andrew Lamb's adroit article "Musical" in *AmeriGrove*. Two unusually perceptive explorations into the complicated Leonard Bernstein are David Schiff's "Re-Hearing Bernstein," *Atlantic Monthly* (June 1993): 55–76, and David Denby's "The Trouble with Lenny," *The New Yorker* (August 17, 1998): 42–53.

Two representatives of the new virtuosity, Charles Wuorinen and Frederic Rzewski, write authoritatively (and interestingly) on "Performance" in the *Dictionary of Contemporary Music*, ed. John Vinton (New York: Dutton, 1974).

Wuorinen's work to the late 1990s is sensitively and sympathetically discussed by fellow composer Hayes Biggs in *[C. F.] Peters Notes* 3/2 (Spring 1998): 1, 6–7. George Crumb is well served in *George Crumb: Profile of a Composer*, ed. Don Gillespie (New York: C. F. Peters, 1986).

Stephen Husarik discusses not only *HPSCHD* but other multimedia pieces as well (especially Cage's *Musicircus* of 1967) in "John Cage and Lejaren Hiller: HPSCHD, 1969," *AM* 1/2 (Summer 1983): 1–21. New music-theater developments, an area of special interest for Eric Salzman, is reflected in his *Twentieth-Century Music*, 3rd ed. (Upper Saddle River, NJ: Prentice Hall, 1988), especially chap. 21.

Especially strong and authoritative on vanguard music of various kinds from 1960s on are the last few chapters of Kyle Gann's *American Music in the Twentieth Century* (cited earlier; see p. 301); David Nicholls's chapter "Avant-garde and experimental music" in *The Cambridge History of American Music*, 517–34, is also valuable. Self-explanatory is Maria Anna Harley's title "An American in Space: Henry Brant's 'Spatial Music,'" *AM* 15/1 (Spring 1997): 70–92; Brant himself contributed the important essay "Space as an Essential Aspect of Musical Composition" to the 1998 edition of *Contemporary Composers on Contemporary Music* (cited in note 21), 221–42.

Excellent on the "classic" minimalists (Young, Riley, Reich, and Glass) is K. Robert Schwarz's *Minimalists* (London: Phaidon Press, 1996). Edward Strickland's *Minimalism: Origins* (Bloomington: Indiana University Press, 1993) is a book-length attempt to relate early minimal music and art; briefer but perhaps equally valuable are H. Wiley Hitchcock, "Minimalism in Art and Music: Origins and Aesthetics" (1986), in *Classic Essays on Twentieth-Century Music* (cited earlier; see p. 302), 308–20, and Jonathan Bernard, "The Minimalist Aesthetic in the Plastic Arts and in Music," *PNM* 31/1 (Winter 1993): 86–133.

William Duckworth and Richard Fleming are editors of the very helpful anthology *Sound and Light: La Monte Young/Marian Zazeela* (Lewisburg, PA: Bucknell University Press, 1996)—Ms. Zazeela, a lightwork and calligraphic artist, being Young's wife. Richard Kostelanetz has edited a similarly wide-ranging anthology, *Writings on [Philip] Glass: Essays, Interviews, Criticism* (New York: Schirmer Books, 1997); notably valuable (and lengthy) is an interview with Glass conducted by Ev Grimes in 1989. A very thorough study of Reich's work into the 1970s is K. Robert Schwarz's "Steve Reich: Music as a Gradual Process," *PNM* 19/1–2 (Fall–Winter 1980/Spring–Summer 1981): 373–92 and 20/1–2 (Fall–Winter 1981/Spring–Summer 1982): 225–86.

TWELVE

ENTERING THE PLURALISTIC
POSTMODERN ERA: FROM THE MID-1970s
TO THE MID-1980s

As discussed earlier, the period immediately following World War II was one of seemingly simple dualities in American music; from the mid-1940s to the mid-1960s, new music appeared to center on pairs of opposite camps: twelve-tone music and serialism vs. the music of chance and indeterminacy; bop vs. swing; rock-and-roll vs. pop. The period that followed, from about the mid-1960s to the mid-1970s, was one of intersections and interactions that seemed to project new syntheses. But from the mid-1970s to the mid-1980s, things moved in different directions—many of them. Multiplicity and cross-currents, diversity of aesthetic aims and practical means, confusion and profusion seemed to reign. One type of music was termed "new age," but the era was hardly one that prized newness as such; instead, it embraced both the new and the old, the close and the distant, the high-artistic and the popularesque, often in startling juxtapositions. Lines once clearly drawn in American music between conservative and radical, between avant-garde and traditional, between modernist and mainstream, were sketchy at best. It was a period of pluralistic *postmodernism.*

One young composer, in describing his new opera, wrote,

> This music is Postmodern in the sense [in which] the term is applied to architecture. ... Postmodernism debunks inevitability or unity of voice—all

moments in history, [including] the present as well, exist with equal weight, share equal value, can rub shoulders with each other. ... The timeliness of the music does not lie in its Modern elements but in the juxtaposition—and, hopefully, balance and reconciliation—[of] a range of elements drawn from the continuity of our present-into-past.[1]

Noah Creshevsky (b. 1945), whose works include a considerable number in the *musique concrète* tradition, spoke rather similarly of his entertaining potpourri of a piece, *Drummer* (1986):

> *Drummer*'s familiar Times Square sounds ... have been compositionally manipulated to form the happy deception of intentionality. [The work] is a kind of sleight of hand, insisting on making order where there is none. Which of us has not hoped that ... the evident chaos around us is a pattern whose order eludes us?

Creshevsky's *Strategic Defense Initiative* (1986)—its title borrowed from the official name for President Reagan's proposed "Star Wars" space-based defense program—is also built up by extreme and unpredictable juxtapositions of sonic source materials. At first seeming funny, reminiscent of the musical satires during World War II of Spike Jones (1911–65) and his band (the City Slickers), it eventually projects, in the course of ten minutes, an eerie, uncomfortable atmosphere of a world in torment (an atmosphere contrived by the composer, of course, in exquisitely precise details and timings).

The composer-conductor Lukas Foss found something of the same sort of unmodulated, hard-edged adjacencies in William Bolcom's *Songs of Innocence and Experience*:

> When we [modernist composers] use something borrowed we feel we have a duty to transform it, which we call "making it our own." But [Bolcom] puts each style in its own ambiance. Melting pot does not quite describe it, because the ingredients are not melted.[2]

Note that there is no suggestion here of a *synthesis* of styles but rather a pluralistic juxtaposition and coexistence. (Perhaps not surprisingly, the American composer whose work had first seemed to celebrate such juxtapositions—Charles Ives—reached a new popularity in the mid-1970s, symbolized by the international festival-conference organized in 1974 around his music (see p. 171). Composer George Rochberg sized up the situation generally; in

---

[1] Conrad Cummings, "Notes on the Music of 'Eros and Psyche'" (unpublished typescript, ca. 1983), kindly provided me by the author.

[2] Quoted in Will Crutchfield, "Bolcom Sets Blake to Several Kinds of Music," *New York Times*, January 9, 1987.

an essay on his Third String Quartet (1971) and his shift to a neotonal style, he wrote,

> We can no longer live with monolithic ideas about art and how it is pro-
> duced.... On the contrary, the twentieth century has pointed... toward a dif-
> ficult-to-define pluralism, a world of new mixtures and combinations...replete
> with juxtapositions of opposites (or seeming opposites) and contraries.[3]

POSTMINIMALISM

The radical minimalism of the late 1960s and early 1970s, as produced by Young, Riley, Reich, Glass, and others, had far-reaching influence on various kinds of music of the later 1970s and 1980s. The early minimalists them-selves, however (with the exception of La Monte Young, who maintained a singularly pure and constant ideal), changed with the times: perhaps they too were caught up, to some degree, in the pluralistic currents that were washing over so much of American culture. Thus, although their music re-mained unmistakably rooted in the minimalist aesthetic, it developed a greater complexity, a wider range of expression, and a swifter rate of change—which made it seem hardly minimalist anymore. If "maximalist" is too strong a term for it, "postminimalist" may serve.[4]

Terry Riley seemed to disappear for a time, having gone to both Eu-rope and India; increasingly, he emphasized improvisatory performances, and he recorded only on obscure European labels. However, with the CBS LP album *Shri Camel* (released in 1980; the music composed in 1975–76), he reasserted his presence in American musical life. All four compositions on the album are performed by Riley himself, on an electric organ partially re-tuned in just intonation to permit the subtlest of India-influenced shadings of pitch; thus they have a new complexity of intonation. A different kind of complexity arises from multiple-track recording techniques, with as many as sixteen digital-delay channels allowing a rich tapestry-like improvisatory in-teraction as well as an exceptionally broad range of polyphonic voices and dynamic levels. In a number of later works, especially a series for string quar-tet commissioned by the Kronos Quartet, Riley returned to tempered tun-ing and wrote for acoustic instruments performing in real time (as in *Cadenza on the Night Plain* of 1984).

---

[3] "On the Third String Quartet," in George Rochberg, *The Aesthetics of Survival*, ed. William Bolcom (Ann Arbor: University of Michigan Press, 1984), 239–42; repr. in Elliott Schwartz and Bar-ney Childs's anthology *Contemporary Composers on Contemporary Music*, expanded edition (New York: Da Capo Press, 1998), 403–7.

[4] For a slightly different view of postminimalism as a more precisely definable *movement*, see Kyle Gann's section discussing it in the following chapter.

Steve Reich's phase-shift and process-driven music had already begun to expand and become more variegated and complex in the early 1970s; characteristic was *Drumming* (1971)—a sort of giant étude based on the single rhythmic phase

(on different-pitched drums, suggested by the stemming) but with changing timbres and instrumentation (including wordless voices) supporting its ninety-minute length and delineating a big four-section structure. *Music for Mallet Instruments, Voices, and Organ* (1973) introduced even sharper contrasts—of timbres, of sustained notes against pulsatile repeated ones, of accelerating patterns superimposed on decelerating ones—and for the first time in his career, Reich used harmonic shifts both gradual and abrupt as a structural element. With the hour-long *Music for 18 Musicians* (1976), these tendencies peaked in a multilayered, colorful work of immense attractiveness (as was confirmed in the extraordinary success, for a piece of new "classical" music, of its 1978 recording; see p. 330).

Yet another phase in Reich's career began with *Tehillim* (1981), in which for the first time since his student days he set words to music. *Tehillim* is a four-movement work for voices and chamber group (adapted also for full orchestra) on Hebrew psalm texts. ("Tehillim" is Hebrew for "Psalms.") Reich's postmodern expansions on his earlier music are here extended not only to medium (texted voices and polychromatic instrumental ensemble) but also to melody—no longer short-breathed, modular, and repetitive but arching, varied in phrase shapes, and fully responsive to both the structure and the meaning of the psalm verses; the work ends with a jubilant blaze of hallelujahs. The percussive background, however, maintains a typical Reichian pulse.

Even more ambitious and tending even more to "mainstream" modes of expression (including chromatic, cyclic harmony) were Reich's *The Desert Music* (1983), a five-movement setting, for a twenty-seven-member chorus and an instrumental ensemble of eighty-nine players, of parts of poems by William Carlos Williams, and *Three Movements for Orchestra* (1986), scored for conventional symphony orchestra (but with prominent mallet-instrument and piano parts).

The music of Philip Glass after the mid-1970s followed a rather similar curve in the direction of greater variety, complexity, and accommodation to traditional modes of thought and expression, but in forms and media different from those favored by Reich—specifically operas, works for dance, and film scores. Glass's meeting in 1974 with the experimental-theater writer and director Robert Wilson, who shared his interest in expanded timescales and other means for altering the perception of time's passing, had led to their unique theater work *Einstein on the Beach* two years later. Glass and Wilson termed it an opera, but perhaps it is better described as an unprecedented combination of mime, dance, and abstract music, with incidental spoken texts. The four-act piece (five hours long, and without intermissions) is basically plotless, though images and objects related to Albert Einstein and his epochal discoveries are the basis for the sets, props, lighting, and stage action. Five substantial interludes for instruments and wordless chorus serve as intermezzi—prelude, entr'acte pieces, and postlude—which are connective and articulative tissue (Glass called them "knee plays") and also provide the main musical substance of the work. There are no solo singers, and the twelve-member chorus, prominent throughout, enunciates only numbers or solfège syllables, describing its music by counting the beats and pulses or naming the pitches. The "orchestra" consists of the small Philip Glass Ensemble, made up of amplified woodwinds and keyboards plus wordless solo voice.[5]

The artistic success in Europe and the United States of *Einstein on the Beach* turned Glass definitively in the direction of theatrical and cinematic works. It became the first in a trilogy of operas, each centered on a historical figure of outstanding importance in world history, each representing a different arena of human action. *Einstein on the Beach* represents science, especially the terrifying scientific advances of the nuclear age ("on the beach" evoking Nevil Shute's apocalyptic novel of that title); *Satyagraha* (1980), subtitled "M. K. Gandhi in South Africa 1893–1914," revolves around racial and ethnic politics; *Akhnaten* (1984), named for the Egyptian pharaoh who was the first leader to espouse monotheism, explores themes of religion. If *Einstein* is primarily a work of mime and dance, *Satyagraha* is one of solo and choral song undergirded by a relatively modest orchestra of woodwinds, strings, and organ; *Akhnaten*, one of singing by soloists, two small vocal ensembles, and a large chorus, with a full orchestral component. Thus the progression is one of increasing conventionality of forces—also of dramaturgy, for *Einstein* is essentially timelessly surreal; *Satyagraha* moves back and forth among past, present, and future; and *Akhnaten* proceeds in a straight-line conventional chronology.

The minimalist composers' first supporters and enthusiasts had been "downtown" artists.[6] By the late 1970s, however, the minimalist composers had developed remarkably large audiences among others as well—especially young people more comfortable with rock than with "serious" music. Glass,

---

[5] Glass discusses *Einstein* in detail, and includes its libretto and "The Action—as Remembered by Robert T. Jones," in his *Music by Philip Glass*, ed. Jones (New York: Harper & Row, 1987), 24–84.

[6] The term initially indicated only an area of Manhattan south of Greenwich Village in New York City. After World War II, however, when there developed a concentration of artists living and working there in low-rent lofts in ex-industrial buildings, it came to connote "experimental" or "vanguard," in contradistinction to the more conventional art of the "uptown" galleries, museums, and concert venues north of 42nd Street.

especially, had a fruitful relationship with rock musicians, notably David Byrne and the group Talking Heads (see p. 348). Among the most unusual of his slighter works of the 1980s was the recorded song cycle *Songs from Liquid Days* (1986), for which he commissioned lyrics from Byrne and other popular or crossover artists (such as Paul Simon and Laurie Anderson). These he set with an expanded version of the Philip Glass Ensemble as accompaniment, and he recorded them with a variety of specially chosen singers, some from the popular-music world (Linda Ronstadt; the female trio The Roches). Although the recording was immensely successful, with sales that put it on *Billboard* magazine's "charts" of best-sellers, critics remained puzzled and wrote quizzically about the hybrid character of the cycle.[7] Similar reactions greeted a new collaboration by the makers of *Einstein on the Beach,* an operatic extravaganza titled *the CIVIL warS; a tree is best measured when it is down* (portions presented in 1983); nor were critics kind to *Koyaanisqatsi: Live* (tour version of 1987), a multimedia event pairing Godfrey Reggio's 1983 film and Glass's music for it. (Both works achieved, however, sold-out houses.)

As the influence of early minimalism fanned out, the number of composers described indiscriminately as "minimalists"—by one critic or another, at one time or another, in connection with one work or another—was very large indeed. The term has served as a catchall for many kinds of reductive compositions: for works by Alvin Lucier (b. 1931) that explore the acoustic characteristics of physical spaces, such as *I Am Sitting in a Room* (1970) or *Music on a Long Thin Wire* (1977–79); for works by Jon Gibson (b. 1940) that combine modular structures with improvisation, such as *Cycles* (1973) for pipe organ; for self-defining works by Tom Johnson (b. 1939) such as *An Hour for Piano* (1971), *The Four-Note Opera* (1972), or *Nine Bells* (1979), and his purely visual compositions produced by a music typewriter (*Symmetries* of 1981; several reproduced in the I.S.A.M. *Newsletter* 18/1 [November 1988]); for the early open-structure works of Harold Budd (b. 1936), such as *The Candy-Apple Revision* (1970), which may be played by any instrument(s) and consists solely of a D♭ major triad; for the visually oriented "eyescores" of William Hellerman (b. 1939), such as *To the Last Drop* (1974; reproduced as Figure 23 in the *AmeriGrove* article "Notation"); for some of the "political" works of Frederic Rzewski, such as two inspired by the 1971 prisoners' revolt at Attica (New York) State Prison, *Coming Together* and *Attica* (both 1972); for the "sonic meditations" of Pauline Oliveros, such as *Deep Listening* (1988), for her accordion, Stuart Dempster's trombone, and Panaiotis's voice; for the Amerindian- and Mexican-music-influenced works of Peter Garland (b. 1952), such as the set, for two violins and gourd rattles, of six *Matachin Dances* (1980–81) or the six-movement solo

---

[7] One conscientious reviewer, in concluding his uncertain critical comments, wrote resignedly, "Oh, what the hell, go ahead and buy it. You'll hate yourself in the morning, but so what?" (A[ndrew] S[tiller], in *Opus* 3/2 [February 1987]: 17).

piano work *Walk in Beauty* (1989); for almost all the compositions of Phill Niblock (b. 1933); et al.; etc., etc.

The younger composer who by the mid-1980s seemed most strongly to represent postminimalist sensibilities, and seemed to have found, more successfully than others, ways to bridge the gap between minimalist and more traditional styles and aesthetics, was John Adams (b. 1947). He combined a driving, pulsatile, minimalist rhythmic sense with a rich harmonic palette and carefully planned, through-composed structures expressed typically through conventional instrumental forces with more than a hint of influence from the Classic-Romantic concert-music tradition. The sympathetic critic Michael Walsh, writing of such works as *Phrygian Gates* (1977) for piano; *Shaker Loops* (1978) for string septet; *Harmonium* (1980) for chorus and orchestra; and *Grand Pianola Music* (1981–82) for two pianos, two singers, and chamber ensemble, described the result:

> Adams' music represents less of a conscious break with the past than either Reich's or Glass's; instead [he] draws inspiration from composers like Beethoven, Mahler, Sibelius and Stravinsky. His works have a lushness and emotional depth largely absent in the ascetic though fundamentally cheerful sounds of Reich or the giddy, explosive rhythms of Glass.... Adams has forged a big, strong, personal style, expressed in complex forms that employ a more extensive use of dissonance than other minimalists.[8]

Another critic was not quite so sympathetic: referring primarily to such works as *Harmonielehre* and *Light Over Water* (both 1984–85), Edward Rothstein wrote that "John Adams' sole accomplishment is to join the Minimalist audience with the mainstream, offering condescendingly accessible works that speak to both.... [He] marks, in a peculiar way, the end of Minimalism."[9]

New-Age Music

Related to minimalism and hovering on the edge of the pop-music world was new-age music, a phenomenon that rose to prominence in the late 1970s and early 1980s and relied almost exclusively on recordings that drew on the latest in high-tech sonic clarity and nuances. Its name derived from an organic-food and naturopathy magazine called *New Age*, and it had close connections with the increased American interest in such Asiatic traditions as yoga and meditation. New-age music was improvisatory, modal or microtonal, open-ended, tensionless, climaxless, trancelike—essentially amorphous music that was strangely calming: "music from the hearts of space," as the title of one radio series put it. Much of it was based on piano or acoustic guitar or gentle synthesized sounds; all of it was quiet and faceless. Some have

---

[8] Walsh: "Music[:] The Heart Is Back in the Game," *Time*, September 20, 1982, 56–58.
[9] *The New Republic*, December 2, 1985, 26–28.

claimed that the 1964 LP album *Music for Zen Meditation* (1964), with improvisations by the clarinetist Tony Scott (b. 1921) aided by two Japanese classical musicians, heralded new-age music; not for another decade, however, did the genre reach significant dimensions. Then dozens of minor new-age composers and composer-performers appeared on such specialist record labels as Windham Hill and Private Music. Perhaps best known were the pianist George Winston (b. 1949), whose 1982 album *December* was an immense success; the keyboardist Steven Halpern, who produced a series of albums collectively titled *The Anti-Frantic Alternative* ("music for relaxation, meditation, and pure listening pleasure"); the Swiss harpist Andreas Vollenweider (*Down to the Moon*, 1986); and the Japanese electronic-music composer known as Kitaro (real name Masanori Takahashi), who by 1986 had issued no fewer than seventeen albums of new-age music.

THE NEW ACCESSIBILITY

George Rochberg was quoted earlier (p. 266) as having cried out in 1963, "Now that the question arises on all sides: after abstractionism, what next? the answer rings out clearly: the 'new romanticism.'" He was looking back at a recent past dominated by the formalism of neo-Classic composers, the intellectualism of serial composers, and the impersonality of chance-music composers. But he was also speaking, with extraordinary prescience, of the future: exactly twenty years later a major festival of new music was centered on the theme "Since 1968, a New Romanticism?" This was Horizons '83, the first of a series of annual festivals organized by the New York Philharmonic's composer-in-residence at the time, Jacob Druckman; in the program book of the festival, Druckman wrote,

> During the mid-1960s the tide [shifted, in] a gradual change of focus, of spirituality and of goals. ... One can discern a steady re-emergence of those Dionysian qualities [of] sensuality, mystery, nostalgia, ecstasy, transcendency.

Druckman's use of the term "New Romanticism" was widely applied to much American music of the period from the mid-1970s on. For many, however, his purposely general definition was too narrowly redefined: "New Romanticism," with a capital "R," immediately suggests the nineteenth century—the age of Beethoven, Schumann, Liszt, Wagner, Mahler. But the qualities cited by Druckman informed other music than that of the nineteenth-century Romantics, and thus the term "New Romanticism" was not a comfortable one. Another may be more suitable.

Coexistent with minimalism, postminimalism, and new-age music were, of course, other types of American music, some conceived along more "traditional" lines, some pursuing a post-Cageian path of experimentalism, some moving into technological no-man's-lands. No one could lump all these under such a term as "New Romanticism." But a great many of these otherwise variegated and widely differentiated musics shared one aspect: *accessibility*. The antimodernist tendencies of postmodernism were expressed in various ways, but almost all of them shared a new warmth, emotionality, revival of traditional tonal harmony, and—especially—accessibility. It was as if, in an age of technological revolution, of social and racial unrest, of dire poverty amid unprecedented plenty, of the threat to all of nuclear annihilation, artists were reaching out to audiences rather than communing only with themselves and hoping that posterity would get their message. Thus a major trend of the period might be termed "the new accessibility."

Neo-Romanticism and Neo-Mannerism

Some of the music of "the new accessibility" did indeed merit the term neo-Romantic, in that it overtly related to, and sometimes even quoted or was based on, music of the Romantic era. Druckman chose 1968 as the dawn of a possible neo-Romanticism perhaps in recollection of a key work of that year, *Sinfonia* by Luciano Berio, the premiere of which, by the New York Philharmonic, had had an immense and immediate impact. Not only was the collage technique of the third movement startling (see p. 317); even more of a surprise—and this was true of all the movements—was the accessibility of Berio's musical language. Similarly, Rochberg's return to tonality (mentioned earlier) was accomplished with many explicit references to such composers as Beethoven and Mahler, not only in the Third String Quartet but in later works by him as well, such as the "Concord" quartets (nos. 4–6, 1977–78); their musical language of tonal design, harmony, and rhythm justifies the term "neo-Romantic." Moreover, in some works not only by Rochberg but by a number of others as well, more important than mere quotation of themes or reinterpretation of earlier harmonic/rhythmic language was the adoption of an immense *range* of expression and gesture evocative of the nineteenth century. This was the main characteristic of the music of Druckman himself, especially a series of orchestral works—following his *Windows*—including *Incenters* (1973) and two works relating to the dramatic myth of Medea, *Lamia* (1974) and *Prism* (1980).

Many works by still others shared this broad gestural expansiveness, such as the birdsong-inspired orchestral *Auroras* (1982) of Robert Erickson; the ballet score *Ulysses' Bow* (1983) of John Harbison (b. 1938); the Clarinet Concerto (1977) and the *Three Hallucinations* (1981) of John Corigliano (b. 1938); the orchestral *Sequoia* (1981) and the Piano Concerto "Homage to Beethoven" (1985) by Joan Tower (b. 1938); the *Adagio for Oboe and String Orchestra* (1977) by Tison Street (b. 1943); the overture *Parachute Dancing* (1984) and Symphony No. 1 ("Water Music"; 1985) of Libby Larsen (b.

1950); the symphonic poem *Aftertones of Infinity* (1979) by Joseph Schwant-
ner (b. 1943); a number of compositions by Ellen Taaffe Zwilich (b. 1939),
including her Symphony No. 1 ("Three Movements for Orchestra"; 1983);
and the symphony *RiverRun* (1984) by Stephen Albert (1941–92). (The last
three works cited won Pulitzer Prizes, Zwilich's—which has a "Mahlerian
glow and intensity [and a] mystery-laden slow movement"[10]—being the first
ever awarded to a woman.) Some of Frederic Rzewski's works, too, moved
far from a minimalist-narrow range of expression—notably the fifty-five-
minute-long set of variations for piano on an antitotalitarian Chilean popular song, *The People United Will Never Be Defeated!* (1975), of which the
critic John Rockwell wrote, "The overall idiom suggests romantic piano writing, with an idiomatic felicity in that writing that has warmed the hearts of
piano buffs and provides some rattling virtuoso passages."[11]

The pervasiveness of the aesthetic of the new accessibility was suggested in the music of one young composer trained by three modernists
(Wuorinen, Carter, and Babbitt): Tobias Picker (b. 1954), who combined
thoroughgoing serialist structural techniques (mostly unheard) with an exuberant, eclectic audible surface in such works as his Violin Concerto of 1981;
Symphony of 1982; and his Piano Concerto No. 2, "*Keys to the City*" (1983;
CRI CD 554), a celebratory piece for the centennial of the Brooklyn Bridge.

Some older composers, too, whose music had been criticized in the
modernist era as being out of step with musical evolution and old-fashioned
in its conservative tonal language, rhythmic simplicity, and traditional forms
and expressive gestures—in short, anachronistic—achieved a new regard and
respect in the context of the new accessibility. William Mayer (b. 1925) spoke
for them, viewing with ironic surprise his new "respectability" as he recalled
that "to be a tonal composer in the '60s ... was a deeply dispiriting experience. One was shunned as the last teen-age virgin."[12] Now, however, Mayer
and, even more, Samuel Barber, who had been seen as throwbacks, impossible neo-Romantics, suddenly emerged as prophets; their works, always successful with audiences, now got favorable notices from critics as well.

Others, too, who had similarly been quietly working away as competent "conservative" composers—and doing so quite successfully in terms of
publication, performance, and recording, though not in critical acclaim—
were belatedly acknowledged. This was true, for example, of Ned Rorem
(b. 1923), who, though hailed regularly as a composer of many grateful songs
and as a first-rate (and saucily forthright) diarist—*The Paris Diary* (1966), *The
New York Diary* (1967), *The Final Diary* (1974)—had been considered a
fair-to-middling conservative composer until the 1970s. Then he began to
be recognized as an elegant and versatile composer, even something of a

---

[10] As put in a review by Andrew Pincus in the *New York Times*, October 12, 1986.

[11] *All American Music* (cited in the first paragraph of this chapter's Bibliographical Notes),
86, in a chapter centered on Rzewski.

[12] "A Tonal Composer in Atonal Times," *MadAminA!* (1998), 9.

proto-postmodernist in such works as the symphonic poem *Lions* (1963), with its hallucinatory evocations (by a supplementary onstage jazz combo) of the pop-song style of Billie Holiday and the swing era.

Robert Starer (b. 1924) similarly emerged from the shadows of critical neglect into a sunny glade of recognition, after many years of turning out shapely, broadly expressive works with the versatility and assuredness possible only to an artist thoroughly in command of his craft. Like Rorem, Starer was applauded most as a composer of vocal music—particularly for a series of works to texts by the novelist Gail Godwin, including *Journals of a Song-maker* (1975); the opera *Apollonia* (1978); and the poignant, powerful monodrama *Anna Margarita's Will* (1979; *CRI* CD 612).

Another composer identified with song and opera but thought to be a conservative Minnesotan and little else, Dominick Argento (b. 1927), began to reap critical and national plaudits with the full-length one-act opera *Postcard from Morocco* (1971; *CRI* CD 614) and the 1975 song cycle *From the Diary of Virginia Woolf* (which won the Pulitzer Prize). Carlisle Floyd (b. 1926), composer of *Susannah* (1954), *Of Mice and Men* (1969), and seven other regionally successful operas, came to be viewed no longer with critical condescension but with genuine admiration, as well as local-audience affection: by 1998, his opera *Susannah* had enjoyed more than 750 performances in 230 productions, even including one by New York's snobbish Metropolitan Opera Company.

One composer whose name was inevitably mentioned in connection with the New Romanticism, new tonality, new accessibility, or whatever term the writer preferred, was David Del Tredici (b. 1937), especially in relation to a long series of big works inspired by Lewis Carroll's Alice's *Adventures in Wonderland* and *Through the Looking Glass*. Composed over eighteen years (1968–86), much of this Alicead is scored for amplified soprano (who both sings and declaims), "folk group" (saxophones, mandolin, banjo, and accordion) or rock group, and extremely large orchestra.[13] Del Tredici's handling of these forces is virtuosic, reminiscent of Strauss or Mahler. Those composers, and Wagner, are also the sources of the harmonic style, which is straightforwardly tonal, as well as of the basic melodic materials and, to some degree, their pervasive, transformational usage.

On the other hand, in such works as *An Alice Symphony* (1969; *CRI* CD 688) or *Final Alice* (which won the Pulitzer Prize for 1976), as in Wonderland itself, all is skewed, distorted, exaggerated, unbalanced, full of weird juxtapositions and dizzying tangential swoops. Fragments of melody repeat themselves obsessively, crazily; long, ardent, arching vocal phrases are often

---

[13] "Alicead" is Andrew Porter's witty term; see his collection of criticism, *Music of Three Seasons: 1974–1977* (New York: Farrar, Strauss & Giroux, 1978), 558–63. The tangle of Del Tredici's "Alice" pieces is unraveled in a helpful listing (with dates and places of first performances and approximate timings) in Porter's *Musical Events: A Chronicle 1983–86* (New York: Summit Books, 1989), 496–501.

placed so high in tessitura, against such a welter of instruments, that the soprano can only bawl them out. The vocal range demanded of her is immense, and now and then she has to traverse its entirety in a sudden, surprising belcantoesque burst of virtuosity; crescendos rise, over great stretches of time, to feverish, hysterical climaxes, maintained long after their emotional peak can be sustained.

The first few measures of the "Simple Alice" song of *In Memory of a Summer Day* (1980) shows how Del Tredici suddenly skews a promissory antecedent-consequent phrase structure in foursquare metrical shape by dropping or adding a beat (Example 12–1 [a]). In the same work, a luscious altered-seventh chord on E, scored for strings and harp—a chord termed by the composer the "Chord of Rapture"—turns into one of "Regret" with the addition of a "stingingly dissonant F natural in stopped horns" (Example 12–1 [b]) in a "two-measure distillation of the sentiment of the entire piece.[14] A private, semisecret self-reference concludes *Final Alice*, when over a sus-

EXAMPLE 12–1. David Del Tredici, *In Memory of a Summer Day* (1980) (*Child Alice*, Part I). (*a*) Song, "Simple Alice." (*b*) Chord of Rapture and Regret. © Copyright 1980 by Boosey & Hawkes, Inc. Reprinted by permission.

[14] From liner notes (by Del Tredici himself) for the recording of *In Memory of a Summer Day* (Nonesuch LP 9-79043-4 G; rel. 1983).

tained A, which grows ever softer until it concludes with the orchestral oboe's
"tuning A" that began the work, the singer counts slowly to twelve in Italian
and adds a whispered "tredici" (i.e., thirteen).

This handling of historical style elements in a readily recognizable
but purposefully distorted, imbalanced, and private way—turning common practice into an involuted, highly personal language—is more "neo-
Mannerist" than neo-Romantic (using the term "Mannerist" as art
historians do, in reference to, say, mid-sixteenth-century Italian art as opposed to the Renaissance classicism of the early sixteenth century—Pon-
tormo and Bronzino as opposed to Leonardo da Vinci and Raphael). Thus
it would seem more appropriate to term works such as the Alice pieces of
Del Tredici "New Mannerism" rather than "New Romanticism"; the distinction is worth making. Similarly, most of the pieces in a set of 25 *Waltzes
by Contemporary Composers*, compiled in 1976–78 by Robert Moran
(b. 1937)—by such diverse composers as Babbitt, Cage, Glass, Harrison,
Sessions, Tower, and Moran himself—are better described as neo-Man-
nerist than as neo-Romantic, despite their obvious roots in waltz styles
from Schubert to Ravel.

CONSERVATISM AND NOSTALGIA
IN THE POPULAR-MUSIC WORLDS

Not surprisingly, the currents of accessibility that led to stylistic retrospection in the concert-music world were also visible or audible in popular music
and jazz. Older performers (Frank Sinatra, Willie Nelson, Barbra Streisand)
continued to maintain a toehold on the "charts." There even arose, by the
1980s, a counterrevolutionary pop nostalgia resurrecting older styles, such as
rockabilly, big-band jazz, and prerock pop songs, as in the LP albums *What's
New* (1983) and *Lush Life* (1984) by Linda Ronstadt (b. 1946) and the sensuous renderings of "standards"—*Star Dust, When You Wish Upon a Star*,
and the like—on the album *Hot House Flowers* (1984) by the jazz trumpeter
Wynton Marsalis (b. 1961). Reissues of earlier recordings proliferated: in
1976, among almost seven hundred "new" jazz recordings, nearly half were
reissues; and within a few years rock-record manufacturers also were reissuing
"golden oldies" (e.g., a twelve-album Capitol Record set of 1985 tracing rock-
and-roll from the early 1950s through the early 1970s) and biographies of
dead stars (e.g., the Hopkins-Sugerman 1980 biography of Jim Morrison [of
The Doors] and Albert Goldman's *Elvis* of 1981).

Broadway, in the late 1970s and early 1980s, seemed host to almost
more revivals than new musicals (despite Sondheim's continued innovative
efforts)—such as Rodgers and Hammerstein's *Oklahoma!* (revived 1979)
and Rodgers and Hart's *On Your Toes* (revived 1983)—and to revues built

around songs of older composers, such as *Ain't Misbehavin'* (1976; music mainly by Fats Waller), *Eubie* (1978; by Eubie Blake), and *Sophisticated Ladies* (1981; by Duke Ellington).

Country music, never inaccessible, reflected the new mood in its own ways. On the one hand, the identity of much country music became blurred, its edge and bite softened, by submission to the influence of rock, particularly the electronic technology of rock; crossover successes—country-music hits also rising to the top of the rock charts—were not infrequent. On the other hand, there was at the same time a nostalgic return to simple soulful songs eschewing the backup strings and vocal choruses that had come to characterize the "Nashville sound" of the nationally popular country-and-western repertory. One older leader of the revisionist rebels was Willie Nelson (b. 1933), who achieved immense crossover success in the mid-1970s with giant rocklike festivals and such albums as *Red Headed Stranger* (1975), which included the most popular country-music song of the year, *Blue Eyes Crying in the Rain* (*SCCCM* CS side 16). Younger figures who resisted the country-pop style in favor of a more traditional hard-core rural and honky-tonk approach included Moe Bandy (b. 1944), with such songs as *It Was Always So Easy (to Find an Unhappy Woman)* (1974; *SCCCM* CS side 16), and Ricky Skaggs (b. 1954), in such songs of the early 1980s as *Crying My Heart Out Over You* and *Heartbroke*.

JAZZ AND ROCK

Even if there were currents of nostalgia, revivalism, and retrospection in various areas of jazz, rock, and pop, these fields were not at a total standstill: the period from the mid-1970s to the mid-1980s saw important other developments.

The free jazz of the 1960s seemed almost to go underground in the next decade, overwhelmed by the rock revolution, and it never became the major voice of jazz. It did, however, lead to such exciting music as that of the Association for the Advancement of Creative Musicians (AACM), a loosely organized, Chicago-based cooperative, founded in 1965 by the pianist Muhal Richard Abrams (b. 1930). And out of the AACM came the important and long-lived Art Ensemble of Chicago (AEC), which produced some twenty LP albums in as many years, that of early 1985 being called *The Third Decade*. Though centered on a traditional core of saxophones, trumpet, double bass, and drums, the AEC played also on literally hundreds of other instruments, from many cultures, and burst the traditional boundaries of jazz in appearing in costumes and makeup; offering dance, mime, and theater skits; and drawing on a huge repertory of black music, old and new. Also from the Middle West, and branching out from free jazz into eclectic individual styles, were the woodwind player and composer Anthony Braxton (b. 1945) of Chicago and the saxophonists Oliver Lake (b. 1942), Hamiet Bluiett, and Julius Hemphill (of the Black Artists Group of St. Louis), who joined with the Californian David Murray to form the World Saxophone Quartet in 1976.

In something like a spirit of "If you can't lick 'em, join 'em," large numbers of jazz musicians borrowed ideas and instruments from rock, and the most striking general development in jazz of the 1970s and early 1980s was the music known as "jazz rock," "electric jazz," or "fusion." Throbbing rock rhythms, heavy amplification, and the use of electric piano and keyboard synthesizers typified this brand of jazz, which had been forecast as early as the late 1960s by Miles Davis (in the albums *In a Silent Way* and *Bitches Brew*). Jazz rock of the 1970s was led primarily by musicians associated at one time or another with Davis, especially Herbie Hancock (b. 1940) in such albums as *Headhunters* (1973); the group Return to Forever led by Chick Corea (b. 1941); and Weather Report, a group formed in 1970 around the keyboardist Joe Zawinul (b. 1932) and the saxophonist Wayne Shorter (b. 1933).

Influences flowed in the opposite direction, too, in the 1970s, for several strands of rock borrowed from jazz and the blues, especially "hard rock," but also to some degree "heavy metal" and "art rock." Hard rock, as typified by the group Lynyrd Skynyrd (centered on the singer Ronnie Van Zant), was essentially electrified blues with a pile-driving southern-rock beat. Even more noisily aggressive was "heavy metal," characterized by one critic as "blues chords plus high-pitched male tenor vocals singing lyrics that ideally combined mysticism, sexism, and hostility," the performers "decking themselves out in leather and studs, growling and grimacing for all they were worth, turning concerts into exercises in high-decibel rants."[15] Heavy metal's prototype had been the British group Led Zeppelin, sedulously imitated by such American bands as Aerosmith (with *Dream* and *Walk This Way*, both 1976), Blue Oyster Cult (*Agents of Fortune*, 1976), and Grand Funk Railroad (*All the Girls in the World Beware*, 1975; *Born to Die*, 1976). Key works by somewhat later heavy-metal musicians included Van Halen's *Runnin' with the Devil* (1978), Ozzy Osbourne and Randy Rhoads's *Suicide Solution* (1981), and the virtual song cycle *Seventh Son of a Seventh Son* (1988) by the band Iron Maiden.

Art rock, as the name implies, had aesthetic pretensions higher than other types; its pedigree went back not only to the first "concept album" of interrelated songs by the Beatles, the LP album *Sgt. Pepper's Lonely Hearts Club Band* (1967), and the self-conscious artiness of another British group,

---

[15] Ken Tucker, in Ed Ward, Geoffrey Stokes, and Ken Tucker, *Rock of Ages: The Rolling Stone History of Rock & Roll* (New York: Rolling Stone Press, 1986), 485. That contemporaneous (and journalistically simplistic) description is balanced by the impressive musico/social study of Robert Walser, *Running with the Devil: Power, Gender, and Madness in Heavy Metal Music* (Hanover, NH: Wesleyan University Press, 1993).

Emerson, Lake & Palmer, but also to such American bands as Frank Zappa's Mothers of Invention and The Velvet Underground. The Zappa bands were independently establishing an art-rock tradition at about the same time, which perhaps peaked with a commission to Zappa from the French composer-conductor Pierre Boulez: *The Perfect Stranger*, a seven-movement set of "preposterously non-modern" pieces (recorded in 1984 by Boulez, conducting the Ensemble InterContemporain of Paris and the Barking Pumpkin Digital Gratification Consort—Zappa's band under a mockingly "arty" new name).

Several subgenres of rock sputtered into existence in the 1970s, were exploited furiously on rock-oriented radio stations and recordings, and then fell victim to their own overcommercialization. The main one of these was "disco," which took its name from discothèques—the nightclubs, popular since the 1960s, where patrons danced to recorded music. It was a relentlessly rhythm-dominated, designed-for-dancing music; in its background were the black-American soul music of the Detroit-based Motown recording company (the songs, for instance, of the Temptations, Diana Ross and the Supremes, Smokey Robinson and the Miracles, Stevie Wonder, and the Jackson Five) and the pop-soul issues of Philadelphia International Records, like Motown a black-owned firm. There were musicians who rode to stardom on the disco wave—notably Donna Summer (b. 1948) with the erotic *Love to Love You Baby* (1975) and The Bee Gees' album from the sound track of the movie *Saturday Night Fever* (1977). The real star of disco, however, was the disc jockey: using two turntables to segue seamlessly from one record to another, the deejay built "sets" that rose inexorably in tension and excitement until they peaked climactically. This development led, in New York in the late 1970s and early 1980s, to the even more creative deejays' "scratching"—backspinning records by hand and using other collagist techniques to create a harsh, percussive background for the incredibly athletic, solo "break dancing" or for the improvisatory streetwise rhyming dialogue called "rapping." A landmark in the early recorded history of rap was the LP album *Run-D.M.C.* (1984) by the pair of hip-hoppers who called themselves just that.

By about 1979 the fad for disco had peaked and passed, giving way to a grittier species of black-inspired rock: funk. That term, as we have seen (p. 306), had been applied to some jazz of the 1950s; it was also used to describe the harsh, howling athleticism of the 1960s soul music of James Brown (b. 1933). Now it served to describe a rock style considerably more intricate rhythmically than disco, and in fact inspired in part by African polyrhythms (as well as call-and-response techniques). A number of funk groups emerged in the wake of Sly and the Family Stone, a group headed by Sly Stone (b. 1944)—among them Kool and the Gang, the Ohio Players, and Earth, Wind and Fire. But the prototypical funk artist was George Clinton (b. 1940), who headed a constantly changing cast of rock musicians under the group names The Parliaments and Funkadelic, producing wild extravaganzas, three and four hours long, marked by songs with such titles as *Maggot Brain, America Eats Its Young*, and *Free Your Ass and Your Mind Will Follow*—musical equivalents of the contemporaneous belittlings of American white-dominated society by the black actor and comedian Richard Pryor. Highly successful albums by "P-Funk" included *Tear the Roof Off the Sucker* and *Mothership Connection* (both 1976) and *Funkentelechy vs. the Placebo Syndrome* (1977).

By the mid-1970s, rock was the principal dialect of American popular music (having even affected the folkish speech of country music) and was no longer identified with rebellious youth or a counterculture; it was, in fact, the mainstream of the establishment's popular music. Perhaps inevitably, this contributed to the nonconformist punk-rock reaction from within the ranks (see p. 310). In the hands of such groups as the New York Dolls and the Ramones, and in the lyrics and voice of Patti Smith, this was a deliberately outrageous, primitive, raw, raunchy, revisionist rock. It in turn gave way to a less ragged but still lean and hard-edged rock termed "new wave," typified by the group Talking Heads, led by the versatile David Byrne (b. 1952). Self-consciously artistic (the original group had been formed as students at the Rhode Island School of Design) but drawing deep from the well of black soul and even African music (though they themselves were all white), Talking Heads issued a series of albums produced by the sophisticated recording-studio technologist Brian Eno (like Byrne, British-born)—*Talking Heads '77*, *More Songs about Buildings and Food* (1978), *Fear of Music* (1979), and *Remain in Light* (1980)—which, surprisingly in view of their uncompromising, noncommercial eccentricity, turned into successes.

Elaborate studio productions also helped a rock artist who emerged as a figure as olympian and summarizing for the 1970s and early 1980s as Elvis Presley had been for the 1950s (and the Beatles for the 1960s): the singer-songwriter Bruce Springsteen (b. 1949). His LP album *Born to Run* (1975) catapulted him to national prominence, which he not only maintained but even exceeded a decade later, when *Born in the U.S.A.* (1984) sold more than 7 million copies in a year. The opposite side of the Springsteen coin in the 1980s was Michael Jackson (b. 1958), who broke out of a collaborative role in Motown's Jackson Five with the superhit albums *Off the Wall* (1979) and *Thriller* (1982). As one critic put it,

> Ultimately, the ascendance of Springsteen and Michael Jackson summons up the spirit of Elvis Presley. ... In Springsteen, we could hear and see Presley's heroic humility, his regular-guy sense of humor, his implied spokesmanship for the American lower middle class. In Jackson, we could observe Presley's smoldering sexuality, his artful, sometimes disturbing eccentricity, his gospel-music roots, and his enduring love for the florid pop ballad. Together, they offered ... rock music imbued with a sense of history, but invigorated by fresh innovation.[16]

---

[16] Ward, Stokes, and Tucker, *Rock of Ages*, 612–13 (in a chapter written by Tucker).

TIMBRAL, TONAL, TEMPERAMENTAL, AND TECHNOLOGICAL OUTREACH

The title of this section is intended to suggest areas in which American composers extended the musical boundaries of sound during the decade of the mid-1970s to mid-1980s: the quality or color of sounds (*timbre*) and the repertory of sounds, especially in terms of different tuning systems (*tonal* divisions, including microtones, and systems of *temperament*—alterations of acoustically perfect intervals to form musically viable scales). Many of those related to—and in most instances were made possible by—new *technology* (especially the electronic technology behind synthesizers and computers). Above all, a more ecumenical attitude toward musical possibilities—literally a matter of *outreach*—proved inspiriting and fruitful.

The new virtuosity (see p. 313 ff.) was important in broadening concepts of what was possible sonically, whether in music produced by the human voice or by instruments (acoustic or with electronic transformations). A second generation of the "new virtuosos" was characterized by a more personal, often theatrical approach to performance and by the composer-performers of "performance art." Thus, although Joan La Barbara gained an early reputation as a virtuoso singer who both inspired and interpreted music by others, she went on to compose music for herself as soloist, most often live/electronic music with tape. More boldly theatrical was the work of Diamanda Galas (b. 1955), who exploited stunning and startling costuming, lighting, makeup, and onstage behavior, together with her operatic voice (extended electronically to superhuman limits, either by live signal processing or by prerecorded tape), to produce a gabbling, babbling, roaring turmoil of female vocalization. The titles of works by her such as *Wild Women with Steak Knives* (1981) and *The Litanies of Satan* (1982)—and, much later, *Malediction and Prayer* and *Nekropolis* (both 1998)—suggest accurately her aura of "a demonic soul in torment" (as one critic wrote); she has said that she attempts to illuminate the outer limits of human emotions, "extremes of incandescent beauty and unmitigated ghastliness ... extremes encroaching upon [each] other within microseconds."[17]

The epitome of the performance artist of the period was Laurie Anderson (b. 1947), a winsome, deceptively fragile- and innocent-looking woman of great versatility: poet, sculptor, photographer, singer, storyteller, violinist, composer, lyricist, and electronic high-tech wizard. Her way with rocklike "songs" (with texts that are apt to deal, however glancingly, with cosmic matters), which she performed with the panache and the split-second timing of a great stand-up comedian, brought her abruptly to international attention in 1981; in that year her recording of *O Superman* (backed by *Walk the Dog*)

---

[17] Quoted in K. Robert Schwarz, "Young American Composers: New York's 'Downtown' Music," *Music and Musicians*, July 1985, 10–11. See also Galas's own comments, "Intravenal Song," *PNM* 20/1 (Fall–Winter 1981): 59–62.

became a pop hit in England and won her a national tour in the United States. These two songs and almost eighty others—plus a dizzying variety of little narratives, skits, comic turns, Chaplinesque shuffling and robotic dance steps, giant backdrops with slide projections, and other visual props—she stitched together into an extravagant four-part, two-evening-long "solo opera" called simply (if grandly) *United States* (1983). A few years later she had moved on, to make the feature-length film *Home of the Brave* (released 1986), a strangely compelling, episodic concertlike work in which, as she put it,

> …there are no plots. The strategy of this film is to use technology to criticize itself. Machines are the fall guys. Animals are the straight men. The people are everyone else.[18]

Closely related to performance art were "text-sound compositions"— works that hovered on the borderline between literature and music, their "sound" being primarily manipulated texts; the term "lexical music" was sometimes applied to them. Among the important makers of text-sound compositions were Jackson Mac Low (b. 1922), Beth Anderson (b. 1950), and Charles Amirkhanian (b. 1945). Mac Low combined verbal, musical, and visual elements—taking what he called a "multilevel approach to language, sound, and action"—in such works as *Musicwords (for Phill Niblock)* (1978) and *Unstructured Meditative Improvisation for Vocalist and Instrumentalist on the Word "Nucleus"* (1982). Anderson's text-sound compositions (the words of which she wrote herself) include *Torero Piece* (1973), *I Can't Stand It* (1976), and *Yes Sir Ree* (1978). Many of Amirkhanian's pieces teetered on the edge of the humorous or the ironic—for example, *Church Car* (1980–81), in which two speaking vocalists tangle in increasingly complex counterpoint as they pile up repetitions of such minimal phrases as "Church car," "box car," and "auto-bump car" (all spoken very fast), or *Maroa* (1981), with its playful offsetting of liquid words (such as the title) with a jazzy hard-edged drum-synthesizer background.

Text-sound composition arises from a fascination with, and an exploration of, the compositional possibilities of individual sounds—from the sentence and phrase level down to the most minimal syllables, vowels, consonants, and phonemes. A similar fascination and exploration had led in the late 1960s to instrumental *multiphonics*—the production of two or more notes simultaneously on a single wind instrument—which quickly became one of the resources of the new virtuosity. In the 1970s, the singer-composer David Hykes (b. 1953) found means for achieving *vocal* multiphonics. Inspired by the *hoomi* ("throat") singing of western Mongolians and the resonant chanting of Tibetan Buddhists, Hykes trained himself and a half-dozen other singers (whom he named the Harmonic Choir) in similar "harmonic

---

[18] Laurie Anderson, "'Hi, We Need $1 Million for a Film,'" *New York Times*, April 20, 1986.

singing" and in fact raised it to new levels of subtlety, variety, and precise control. His *Hearing Solar Winds* (1977–83), *Current Circulation* (1983–84), and other works are partially improvisatory and made up of wordless, shimmering streams of groaning fundamentals, eerie flutelike upper partials, and long "chordal" glissandos swooping slowly up, down, and around. This was not exactly performance art, but for obvious reasons it was best experienced live in large resonant spaces such as the giant Cathedral of St. John the Divine in New York, where the Harmonic Choir was in residence.

Hykes's group produced its unearthly vocal multiphonics by virtue of an acoustically pure *just intonation*. In this it shared with a small but growing community of American performers and composers an interest in tuning systems other than twelve-note equal temperament, which had dominated Western music for several hundred years. Some musicians were inspired by exotic music (especially Asiatic) based on other tunings; some were freed by electroacoustic means of sound production from any necessity to think in terms of "12-equal" temperament.

After Partch, a pioneer in just intonation and alternative tuning systems was Lou Harrison. His interest in Asiatic music arose naturally from residence on the West Coast, tutelage by Cowell, and early involvement with Cage. In the early 1960s he studied traditional music in Japan, Korea, and Taiwan; later, collaborating with William Colvig (who became his life partner), he built many instruments and even entire gamelan—instrumental ensembles based on those of Indonesia. (Harrison has declared unequivocally, "A good gamelan is the most beautiful musical ensemble on the planet."[19]) For gamelan and varied combinations of unusual instruments, Harrison has produced a very large body of work, much of it stylistically inspired by Asiatic or ancient music. Harrison has also been extremely influential as a teacher and practitioner of this sort of musical outreach.

Some compositions by Harrison for hybrid ensembles of both Eastern and Western instruments lie on the borderline between the two worlds, such as the charming pair *A Joyous Procession and a Solemn Procession* (1962), for wordless high and low voices, trombones, tambourines, handbells, great gong, and bass drum. Each of these processional pieces is based on a different heptatonic mode in just intonation; according to the published score (a facsimile of Harrison's exquisite calligraphy), they may be used for "different celebrations by various religious and civic groups, but may not be used by the military." Harrison has also written more conventional music, to which he brings an extraordinarily refined ear and masterly orchestration, as in the *Concerto on G* (1961; *CRI* CD 715) and the brief tone poem *At the Tomb of Charles Ives* (1964), both for orchestra, and the Concerto for Organ with Percussion Orchestra of 1973. The Concerto for Piano and Orchestra (1985),

---

[19] Quoted in Leta Miller and Fredric Lieberman, *Lou Harrison: Composing a World* (New York: Oxford University Press, 1998), 157.

though conventional enough in structure and expression, is based on a 12–*unequal* tempered scale known as "Kirnberger II" after the disciple of J. S. Bach who invented it; in his program notes for the concerto, Harrison writes,

> This astonishing tuning contains almost the whole history of "Western Music" from Babylonian times to the middle of the last century, because its flat series produces perfectly tuned fourths and fifths (the whole Middle Ages) and the white keys are, with the exception of a very slightly raised pitch A, in perfect Renaissance and Baroque just intonation.

Another older composer much affected by Asiatic musics (if not, however, with alternative tuning systems) was Alan Hovhaness (b. 1911). Since the 1940s, when he first became interested in Armenian music (he is of Armenian and Scots descent), and especially since about 1960, when Far Eastern elements began to infuse his music, Hovhaness has produced a staggering number of works, primarily instrumental. (Cage is supposed to have said that Hovhaness is "a music tree who, as an orange or lemon tree produces fruit, produces music.") By the summer of 1986 his production of symphonies alone had reached No. 61 (the "Mount St. Helens" symphony), and his total oeuvre by then numbered well over four hundred compositions, all determinedly tonal and accessible, if also tinged with a personal mysticism.

Equal temperaments other than 12-equal have interested some composers. The Hiller-Cage extravaganza *HPSCHD* had included, as mentioned (p. 321), tapes based on about fifty different alternative equal temperaments except "12-equal." Microtonal divisions of the octave interested some composers: Tui St. George Tucker (b. 1924) worked with quarter tones (= 24-equal) in *Little Pieces for Quarter Tone Piano* (1972), *Quartertone Recorder Duets* (1973), and *Indian Summer* (1983). Easley Blackwood (b. 1933) took advantage of the tuning potential of a synthesizer in his set of twelve *Microtonal Etudes* (1982) for keyboard synthesizer, each étude based on a different division of the octave, from 13-equal to 24-equal. John Eaton (b. 1935) used quarter tones as well as just intonation and 12-equal temperament in his opera *Danton and Robespierre* (1978). Ben Johnston (b. 1926), interested in microtones (and in developing a music notation to express them), also wrote extensively in just intonation, but usually for traditional Western instruments (some of which—the piano, for instance—must be retuned). His *Sonata for Microtonal Piano* (1965; NW CD 80203) demands a retuning in chains of just-tuned nontempered triads that leave only seven of the eighty-eight piano keys with octave equivalents—in other words, there are eighty-one different sounds available (not just twelve, as on the usual keyboard).

The upsurge of interest in non-Western music and in alternative tuning systems has meant an expansion of instrumental possibilities—not only the importation of third-world folk and traditional instruments but also the adaptation of conventional instruments (new fingerings, for example, for wind instruments; extra valves for brass; extra keys for keyboards) and the invention of others (those of Harry Partch, for instance [see p. 250]), or the thirty-one-tone just-tuned zoomoozophone of Partch's former student Dean Drummond). A very special case is that of Conlon Nancarrow (1912–97), who from the late 1940s composed almost exclusively for player piano (in conventional 12-equal temperament). Frustrated by the difficulty of finding performers able to execute his rhythmic ideas, Nancarrow taught himself to punch piano rolls, note by note, and wrote—for one or both of a pair of modified uprights in his Mexico City studio—a unique series of more than forty one-movement "studies." The principal structural basis of these is canon, each voice of the canon usually proceeding at its own rate of speed. The character of Nancarrow's studies is well described in composer Philip Carlsen's *AmeriGrove* entry on the composer:

> [They] fully exploit the player piano's potential for rhythmic complexity and textural variety; they are showpieces of virtuosity far beyond the capabilities of human performers [yet] many of the studies have an elegance and spontaneity that belie their mechanical origins.

Without question, the most overwhelmingly significant element in virtually every kind of the new American music of the later twentieth century was *technology*. Technology has affected the musical experience of virtually everyone—composers, performers, and listeners alike. Radio, recordings, television, and especially electronic and computer technology have altered the very perception of what music is or can be—in the direction of limitlessness, of unbounded choice, of cosmic possibilities. John Cage foresaw this development with astonishing clarity as early as 1937, when he began a lecture—printed much later in his book *Silence* of 1961—called "The Future of Music: Credo" with these words:

> I believe that the use of noise to make music will continue and increase until we reach a music produced through the aid of electrical instruments which will make available for musical purposes any and all sounds that can be heard. Photoelectric, film, and mechanical mediums for the synthetic production of music will be explored. ... The present methods of writing music, principally those which employ harmony and its reference to particular steps in the field of sound, will be inadequate for the composer, who will be faced with the entire field of sound.

Prescient as that statement seemed in 1937 in the world of "serious" music, technology had been crucial in the history of popular music for many decades. Popular music thrived on early commercial radio and the budding recording industry of the 1920s (and vice versa), including hillbilly music and "race records" for the black community. The crooners of the 1930s such as Rudy Vallee and Bing Crosby, and even more the great jazz vocalists (Mildred Bailey, Billie Holiday, Ella Fitzgerald, and especially Sarah Vaughan), revolutionized popular-song vocalism by special microphone techniques that gave them an extraordinary range of vocal timbres, in live performance as well as on radio and recordings. Electrically amplified guitars were available in the early 1930s, and when major artists such as the jazz guitarist Charlie Christian (1916–42), the blues singer and guitarist Muddy Waters, and the country guitarist Les Paul (b. 1915) began to use them (see p. 295), the door was opened for a popular-music revolution centered squarely on technology. Jazz of all eras, rhythm-and-blues, rock-and-roll, later rock, disco, country, and other popular-music subgenres are unthinkable without electronic reproduction, amplification, and other technological components. Concert music and opera were occasionally hosted on television, but the only new television-music genre to have emerged is the music-video short, great numbers of which have been produced by rock and pop artists for telecasting over twenty-four-hour-a-day music-video cable channels (such as MTV [Music Television] and VH-1 [Video Hits One]) and even over regular network channels.

Some concert-music composers, also, were leaders in exploiting—and in some cases actually developing—technology in the service of musical art. To a few of these we turn, to conclude this chapter.

To video art, which beckoned as one of the least-explored new media, some composers turned. One pioneer was Nam June Paik (b. 1932), who beginning in the mid-1960s had experimented with videotape, often in notorious collaboration with the occasionally topless cellist Charlotte Moorman (1933–91), to produce such works as *Opéra sextronique* (1967), *TV Cello* (1971), and *Global Groove* (1973). Another major figure was Robert Ashley, whom we met earlier as a founder of Once (see pp. 291, 322). From the beginning, much of Ashley's work was theatrical, and in the 1970s, he started to concentrate on mixed-media performance-art and video-art projects. Ashley also generously documented the personalities and work of a group of fellow composers in the set of video portraits *Music with Roots in the Aether* (1976). He considered this to be as much a "piece" as anything else he had done; it focuses successively on David Behrman, Philip Glass, Alvin Lucier, Gordon Mumma, Pauline Oliveros, Terry Riley, and (breaking the alphabetical ordering) Ashley himself.

The technological tool whose potential for composers and performers of all kinds—and for that matter, ultimately listeners—is probably greater than any other is the digital computer. By the mid-1980s, the authors of a major guide to the world of so-called computer music could begin their preface this way:

Computer music activity ... has grown from its somewhat specialized origins as an interdisciplinary subfield of electronic music, digital signal processing, and experimental music to occupy an increasingly central position in the technologies of professional recording and home audio, as well as electronic music synthesis and composition. The expanded use of digital electronics in music ... may be only the beginning of an era in which computer technology predominates in all aspects of the reproduction and synthesis of music.[20]

My phrase "so-called computer music" is intended to downplay the implications that this music was actually *composed* by a computer. That is possible, but so far the results have been of limited interest—to practitioners and listeners alike. Much more significant, at least to the present, have been various uses of the computer as an aid to composition of electroacoustic music, as a particularly effective source of synthetic sounds, and of course as a necessary resource for "digital recording" (which made possible, beginning in 1983, the commercial production of compact discs—"CDs"—and their flawless reproductive sound quality).

A major problem for composers attempting to use early digital-computer programs had been to hear quickly the results of their work, or to alter, amend, and edit it. This was solved by about 1970 with the development of digital synthesizers; these combined the sound-generating and -processing capabilities of such analog synthesizers as the Moog and Buchla instruments (see p. 282) with the progammability of digital computers. Somewhat later, high-speed computer technology made possible astonishing uses of computers in real-time musical performance.

I commented earlier on the pioneer work in developing computer programs for the synthesis of musical sound (see p. 283). Among the composers to have concentrated from the late 1960s through the mid-1980s on computer music with critically acclaimed results are Barry Vercoe, Roger Reynolds, and Charles Dodge.

Barry Vercoe (b. 1937) wrote excitedly about the 1970s' new possibilities for a composer to capitalize on computer technology; he related his experience in composing *Synapse for Viola and Computer* (1976) at the M.I.T. Experimental Music Studio (which he established in 1971): the two computers there, he said,

> are capable of synthesizing a large orchestra-like sound. The composer controls this performance by communicating with the computer in traditional musical terms. Thus, when he "plays" a section of his score at the keyboard, the computer will "listen" and then display those notes in music notation on a screen. The composer can ... make modifications as he or she goes. Upon request, the computer will synthesize and play back any segment of that score, and can print copies of the score and parts for individual players.[21]

---

[20] Charles Dodge and Thomas A. Jerse, *Computer Music: Synthesis, Composition, and Performance* (New York: Schirmer Books, 1985), ix; the preface (hence also the passage quoted) reprinted in the book's 2nd edition (1997), xiii.

[21] Jacket notes for a recording including *Synapse* (*CRI* LP SD-393; rel. 1979).

Reynolds, whose searching musical mind we have met earlier (see p. 283), first added computer technology to his arsenal of compositional resources in a series of quadraphonic tape-music works collectively titled *Voicespace—Still* (1975), *A Merciful Coincidence* (1976), *Eclipse* (1979), and *The Palace* (1980). Of them, he wrote:

> Electronics—at first analog, later digital systems—offered rather precise control over auditory space (a particular sound's size, location, distance, the character of the host space in which it was heard. ... The four works ... share a concern with the potential of auditory imaging. ... They attempt to create a personal theater through the mind's ear.[22]

The "personal theater" that resulted is one of uncommon richness, resonance, and compelling expression. These are settings of texts by, respectively, Coleridge, Beckett, other writers (from whose works a collage of fragments is drawn), and Borges; but "settings" is a meager term for the extraordinary reshapings, the virtuosic manipulations, the consummate technological mastery (in the service of expressive aims) with which Reynolds builds the compositions. They are experienced as virtually "auditory operas"—some of the vocal materials being performed live (but amplified), some prerecorded and reverberated, some still natural but "enhanced," and some thoroughly transformed electronically through the processing capability of a computer-music system. Reynolds went on, in such works as *Archipelago* (1982), *Transfigured Wind II* (1984), and *Vertigo* (1986) to even more sophisticated usage of computers in the compositional process.

Charles Dodge, who founded the Center for Computer Music at Brooklyn College, was one of the pioneers in computer synthesis of musical sound. For a number of years, beginning in the early 1970s, he concentrated on compositional applications of speech synthesis by computer, producing an impressively varied series of pieces—beginning with *Speech Songs* (1972), *The Story of Our Lives* (1974), *In Celebration* (1975), and *Cascando* (1978). Each of these originated with Dodge's "reading" a text into a computer (by means of an analog-to-digital converter); the computer was then used to analyze in infinitesimal detail the vocal sounds, in order to define very precisely each of their many attributes ("parameters") in time segments as brief as milliseconds. Dodge could then alter any parameter he wished, independently, then put together (literally "compose") a synthetic voice or texture of voices, and to combine or repeat or manipulate them in any imaginable way. Finally, after editing (in the computer, no longer needing "hard copy"), he transferred onto audiotape, by means of a digital-to-analog converter, the finished composition with its resynthesized vocal sounds.

The four little *Speech Songs* are amusing études, and *In Celebration* transforms a single speaker's reading into multiple voices, composed into a

---

[22] Jacket notes for *Voicespace* (Vital Records LP VR-1801/2; rel. 1982).

work full of dark surprises. *The Story of Our Lives* and *Cascando* (originally a radio play by Samuel Beckett) are dramatic dialogues; in both, a nonhuman "character" in the drama (a book in *The Story of Our Lives*, "Music" in *Cascando*) is made by Dodge to "speak"—in eerie, unforgettably unique sonorities, which nevertheless relate to the resynthesized human vocal sonorities, thanks to the analytic/synthetic precision of Dodge's computer-music techniques. Similar relationships are literally built into the exquisite live/electronic piece *The Waves* (1984), for soprano and tape, based on the first paragraph of Virginia Woolf's novel of that title. Composed for Joan La Barbara, *The Waves* has a synthesized accompaniment derived from computer-aided acoustical analysis of her voice, reading the Woolf text and using extended vocal techniques. Thus, in the work as performed by La Barbara (on New Albion NA-043–CD), the live voice and the tape accompaniment are ineluctably related to each other.

Few composers working in computer-aided composition were as skillful as those just discussed in "humanizing" their work, in being able to overcome the tendency of electronically generated sounds to seem abstract, lacking in sentience and vitality, machine-made—in short, dehumanized. And just as with earlier electroacoustic-music composers, many composers of "computer music" soon combined synthetic sound with live performers, perhaps in an attempt to guarantee such humanization. Technological development soon made possible computers that operated so swiftly that there was virtually no time lag between instructing the computer and hearing the results; the computer's output could thus be used directly in concert performance. Such computers were termed "real-time digital synthesizers." Understandably, some composers have leaped at the opportunity to exploit such instruments, putting them onstage and, with the composer "playing" them, having them interact instantaneously with live musicians. Two pioneers in such real-time performance electronics were Morton Subotnick and Daniel Lentz.

Subotnick was, as noted earlier (p. 282), one of the first composers to work extensively with analog synthesizers. Later, in a series of works beginning in the late 1970s, he explored the possibilities of real-time electronics: *Two Life Histories* (1977), for male voice, clarinet, and electronic sounds produced in real time; a female counterpart, for soprano, chamber ensemble, and real-time electronics, is *The Last Dream of the Beast* (1978). *The Double Life of Amphibians* (1982–84) deepened the electronic involvement: it is scored for pairs ("doubles") of amplified acoustic instruments (cellos, clarinets, trombones, percussion, pianos) and real-time digital synthesizer, which is in fact controlled by the cellos and is wholly dependent on what *they* do for its own manner of "performance." As the piece unfolds, the relationship between "instrumental" and "synthetic" sounds becomes more and more symbiotic, until by the end (as the composer explains in the score) "the two become a single homogeneous texture."

A number of works by Daniel Lentz (b. 1942) sound superficially close to minimalist music, and some even to new-age music: they contain very little harmonic and rhythmic variety; much repetition of perpetual-motion motifs (often arpeggios) in foursquare phrase structures; very slow changes of texture; very little sense of "development" or motion toward climax; and hardly any sense of contrast, tension, rivalry, or struggle. Yet usually by the end of a work by Lentz, one realizes that something considerable has happened, that a piece has evolved, materialized, become a piece.

This was, in fact, an aesthetic ideal of Lentz's—to shape his music in what he calls "spiral forms," with the musical material kept in a spiraling, additive state of becoming rather than in a static state of being. This was especially true of Lentz's vocal works, which often reveal their full texts very slowly, sometimes only at the very end of the piece, after having been introduced partially, in tiny fragments (often only single phonemes), which are instantly repeated together with different, dovetailing fragments, and those re-repeated with still other fragments added—until finally, like a jigsaw puzzle, the entire text is spread out before the ear. Along the way, interesting, unpredictable verbal and sonic juxtapositions, configurations, and even meanings not present in the full text emerge.

An early example was *O-Ke-Wa* (*North American Eclipse*) (1974), a thirteen-minute piece for twelve solo singers (with handbells), rasps, and drums. (The Amerindian title is the Seneca word for the tribe's dance for the dead, and the brief text, by Kit Tremaine, is a nostalgic lament for the "dark murmuring Indians," occupants now of "wispy hidden graves.") Each singer has her or his own melodic line and selection of text fragments. The singers introduce the fragments additively in repetitive cycles—text fragment/singer 1, then text fragments/singers 1 + 2 together, then text fragments/singers 1 + 2 + 3 together, and so on, until all twelve voices are sounding and the text is complete. (The ritualistic repetitive cycles are especially apt, given the nature of the text; and ideally the piece is to be performed in darkness, with the singers moving around the audience in a slow shuffle.) Example 12–2 shows the fourth cycle: singer 4 enters; singers 1–3 repeat their phrases as before; singers 5 and 6 hum (▲) and singers 7–12 whistle (△) in heterophonically supportive accompaniment; handbells, rasps, and drums are to be understood.

There is a limit to which such procedures are possible, or effective, in live-only performance. But electronic technology is perfectly suited to them, and already in the early 1970s Lentz began exploring its possibilities, especially analog echo systems (familiar to rock keyboard-synthesizer players). In his *Missa Umbrarum* ("Mass of Shadows") of 1973, for example, an eight-voice chorus (SSAATTBB) unfolds the five sections of the Latin Mass text fragmentarily and in repetitive echo cycles, dovetailing new fragments with the repetitions ("sonic shadows") of ones already introduced, by means of a multiple tape-loop process. A similar record-and-repeat-with-tape-delay technique is used for the single reciting voice in the brief *Song(s) of the Sirens* (1975), accompanied by clarinet, cello, and piano. This is based on the voluptuous sirens' song in the *Odyssey* ("Listen to our voices, / Listen to the music

EXAMPLE 12–2. Daniel Lentz, *O-Ke-Wa* (1974), cycle No. 4. Reproduced by permission.

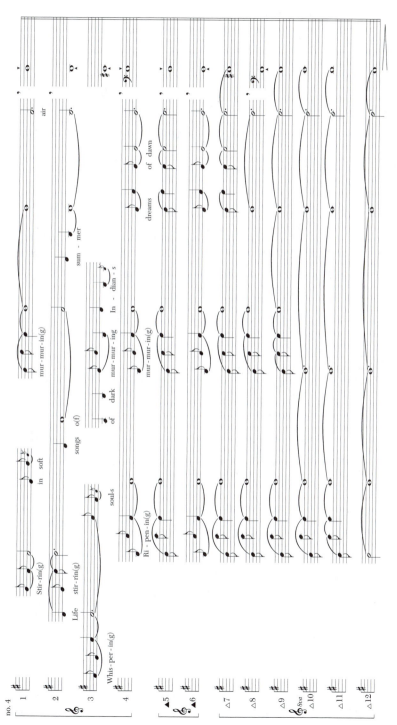

which sounds from our lips, sweet as honey / ..."); the ambiguous plural in Lentz's title implies the ten cycles of replays-with-additions required for the "song" text to materialize in its entirety.

More sophisticated computer/synthesizer technology underlay later work by Lentz, such as *On the Leopard Altar* (1983–84), *Wild Turkeys* (1985–86), and *The Crack in the Bell* (1986). For these, he employed his own ensemble of one or more vocalists and several electric keyboardists at synthesizers; he himself sat at a small (but very powerful) real-time digital processor and mixing console, hooked up to the other performers. Using half-inch tape, he could record on more than sixty tracks and mix down, in real time, with uncanny speed and accuracy. In effect, he had at his disposal, under his own two hands, an electroacoustic- and computer-music studio and a recording studio as well, and he acted as composer, music editor, producer, and recording engineer—all virtually at the same time, on the spot.

On the Leopard Altar expands on the plan of *Song(s) of the Sirens*: from a matrix text, six brief "songs" are lifted, then performed in spiral-form additive fashion, until with the sixth "song" the entire matrix text is unveiled. *Wild Turkeys* (for several keyboardists) is an étudelike work built from a reservoir of myriads of modular figures (based exclusively on fifths, hence the punning title), all related to a basic rapid pulse, which are looped repetitively and successively. The keyboardists have precise scores to read, but many aspects of the sonic realizations of what they are to play—aspects of timbre, register, harmonic-partial structure, octave doublings, relative intensity of "simultaneities," and others—are governed by Lentz at the console. Despite the heavy reliance on technology and "recording," the resulting piece has all the vitality and spontaneity of wholly live music (no two performances are ever quite the same) and is potent, powerful, and propulsive—sheets of kicky-rhythmed, pulsatile, postminimal patterns that flicker and surge and are electrifying in their effect.

The Crack in the Bell by Lentz is based on E. E. Cummings's sonnet "next to of course god america i / love you land of the pilgrims' oh." It was the composer's response to a commission from the remarkable West Coast new-music patron Betty Freeman (b. 1921). Lentz's text-analytic penchant, together with a strain of black humor and wry cynicism, resulted in a provocative and lively work, slyly satirical but also deeply felt—matching Cummings's verses themselves and their ambiguous "heroic happy dead / who rushed like lions to the roaring slaughter."

It seems appropriate, in concluding this chapter's final section on American music from the mid-1970s to the mid-1980s, to call attention to such pieces as those by Daniel Lentz. They share with the other music discussed in the chapter the vivaciously pluralistic postmodernism of the era—the postminimalism, the text-sound composition, the new accessibility; they represent a new phase of the "new virtuosity" and relate, in their real-time spontaneity, to jazz's improvisatory approach to music making. And, in their spirited interaction between human performers and products of technology, they reaffirm that, as always in the past (come to think of it)—whether harp-sichord music, the music of string or symphonic orchestras, of valved brass-es, of pipe organs or kazoos, of grand or player pianos—man and machine can make vital music together.

BIBLIOGRAPHICAL NOTES

John Rockwell's panoramic but sharply focused *All American Music: Composition in the Late Twentieth Century* (New York: Knopf, 1983) is especially valuable in connection with the material in this chapter, as are William Duckworth's com-ments and interviews in his *Talking Music: Conversations with … Five Genera-tions of American Experimental Composers* (New York: Schirmer Books, 1995). Also valuable are the relevant portions of Kyle Gann's *American Music in the Twen-tieth Century* (New York: Schirmer Books, 1997); John Schaefer's *New Sounds: A Listener's Guide to the New Music* (New York: Harper & Row, 1987), which has more on new-age music than any other source; and sections on American music in Elliott Schwartz's *Music Since 1945: Issues, Materials and Literature* (New York: Schirmer Books, 1993).

K. Robert Schwarz presents sensitively the shift from "classic" minimalism to early postminimalism in "Process vs. Intuition in the Recent Works of Steve Reich and John Adams," *AM* 8/3 (Fall 1990): 245–73; on Adams's earlier music and ideas, see Schwarz's "Young American Composers: John Adams," *Music and Musicians*, March 1985, 10–11, and "John Adams: Music of Contradictions," *New York Times*, January 11, 1987, section 2, 25. Geoff Smith and Nicola Walker Smith (eds.) offer a prepublication excerpt from *New Voices: American Composers Talk About Their Music* (Portland, OR: Amadeus Press, 1995) in "John Adams Speaks His Mind," *American Record Guide*, September/October 1995, 20–24, 47; see also "John Adams: *An Interview* with Aaron Jay Kernis" in *Conjunctions* (New York: Random House, 1992), 174–90.

Stephen Holden was perhaps the first to note the phenomenon of "Pop Nostalgia: A Counterrevolution," *The New Republic*, April 1985, 121–22; Bill C. Malone touches on it in his masterly *Country Music U.S.A.*, rev. ed. (Austin: University of Texas Press, 1985), which is complemented by his *Southern Music/American Music* (Lexington: University Press of Kentucky, 1979).

Ronald Radano (see p. 330) revised his brilliant dissertation as *New Musical Fig-urations: Anthony Braxton's Cultural Critique* (Chicago: University of Chicago Press, 1993). Robert Walser (see p. 330) published a remarkable book-length study of heavy metal (cited in note 15). Impressive in its comprehensiveness is the Ward-Stokes-Tucker collaborative history of rock (also cited in note 15), though it lacks bibliography and has an unhelpful index. Steven Hager's *Hip Hop: The Illustrat-ed History of Break Dancing, Rap Music, and Graffiti* (New York: St. Martin's Press, 1984) is lively and illustrated generously. Soul is the subject of Gerri Hirshey's well-written, enthusiastic *Nowhere to Run: The Story of Soul Music* (New York: Times Books, 1984).

John Rockwell discusses Laurie Anderson in chap. 10 of his *All American Music*; William Duckworth offers informed commentary on her as well as a generous in-terview in his *Talking Music* (cited near the beginning of these notes), 368–85.

The growing interest in microtones and alternative tuning systems is reflected in the journal *Pitch: for the International Microtonalist*, which began in autumn 1986. Douglas Leedy's *AmeriGrove* article "Tuning Systems" is authoritative. The ideas of one influential microtonalist are to be found in Lou Harrison's delightful *Music Primer* (New York: C. F. Peters, 1971); this is complemented generously in various chapters of the Harrison biography cited in note 19.

On Conlon Nancarrow, the most thorough account is Kyle Gann's *The Music of Conlon Nancarrow* (Cambridge: Cambridge University Press, 1995); Philip Carlsen's study, *The Player Piano Music of Conlon Nancarrow* (*ISAMm* 26 [1987]), though slighter, complements Gann's in several ways. Also valuable are Roger Reynolds's "Conlon Nancarrow: Interviews in Mexico City and San Francisco," *American Music* 2/2 (Summer 1984): 1–24, and Peter Garland's "Conlon Nancarrow: Chronicle of a Friendship," in his *Americas: Essays in American Music and Culture* (Santa Fe, NM: Soundings Press, 1982).

Robert Ashley's fourteen-hour video piece *Music with Roots in the Aether* is discussed and described by Norbert Osterreich in *PNM* 16/1 (Fall–Winter 1977): 214–28.

The pioneering book cited in note 20 includes many bibliographical citations and discusses some of the music by Vercoe, Reynolds, Subotnick, and Dodge touched on here. Harold W. Whipple's "Beasts and Butterflies: Morton Subotnick's Ghost Scores," *MQ* 69 (1983): 425–41, is not easy to read but worth it. Roger Reynolds writes a fascinating account of his own philosophy and procedures in *A Searcher's Path: A Composer's Ways* (*ISAMm* 25 [1987]).

Joseph Kerman discusses Lentz's *Song(s) of the Sirens* perceptively in his *Listen*, 3rd ed. (New York: Worth Publishers, 1980), 479–82.

THIRTEEN

NEW CURRENTS COALESCE: SINCE THE MID-1980s

by Kyle Gann

If the 1960s were a time of deep cultural revolution in America, the early 1980s brought a pervasive technological revolution whose ultimate effects may prove to be even more radical. The primary event affecting musical activity at this time—and most other activity as well—was, of course, the development and mass distribution of the personal computer. Moreover, digital technology brought a host of musical devices in its wake: sequencing and notation software, drum machines, the sampler, the near-universal application of MIDI (Musical Instrument Digital Interface) standards—not to mention the replacement of the vinyl record by the compact disc, and the promised replacement of the compact disc by the instant download.

Many composers born before 1950 were little affected by the changes, but those born after 1970 inherited a musical outlook that earlier generations would hardly have recognized; those born in between struggled to adjust. In addition, American composers who matured after 1975 could hardly escape (though they sometimes rebelled against) the pressure to work vernacular elements of America's ubiquitous rock culture into their music.

The technological changes brought a new way of life. By 1985 or so, it was possible for a composer with only a few thousand dollars of disposable income to build a private home studio that greatly surpassed the great electronic studios of the 1960s in which many composers worked together. It has become not only viable but also attractive for radical individualists such as Charles Amirkhanian, Laurie Spiegel, Carl Stone, and Henry Gwiazda to pursue composing careers completely independent of performers and musical institutions. Even for composers who did not work primarily in electronics, the attendant philosophical changes were decisive.

Consider the following tendencies common in the 1990s, all of them bringing certain aesthetic similarities to otherwise diverse bodies of musical practice:

1. With so much compositional work being done by means of sequencing software, notation lessened in importance as a compositional intermediary. As a skill, reading music has never been as highly prized in America as in Europe, and the new music software allowed even amateurs to create music of considerable sophistication without ever putting a note on paper. To a certain extent, this was a healthy change. In mid-century, composers had too often fetishized the score, considering the look of the notes or their relationships more important than the actual sound or audibility of a work's structures. The new priority of recording over notation corrected that balance, but it also threatened to lead to superficiality, as detailed analysis waned and sound production took precedence over content.

2. For composers who used electronics, the sampler changed a fundamental thought pattern: the smallest musical unit was no longer the note but the sample, which might be a complex noise structure, an excerpt of environmental sound, or even a quotation from a previous piece of music. A sampler can record any sound, play it back at any speed or pitch level, and allow the musician to manipulate it, play it backwards, blend it with other sounds, and so on. Where tape splicing had encouraged the musical atomism of serialism, the sampler encouraged collage and gradual metamorphosis, as well as a more holistic approach to sound material.

3. The dominance of European influences on American music faded exponentially; the young American composer of the 1990s was just as likely to base his or her music on Balinese, Indian, or Japanese musical conventions as on European. In part this was due to the explosion of ethnomusicological courses in American universities of the 1970s; it was also due to increased immigration of Asian and African musicians, as well as to a widespread (if little remarked) perception that European music had stagnated since the high-water mark of serialism in the 1970s. By the 1990s, rare was the young American composer who hadn't borrowed something from a non-Western culture, and many were highly trained in techniques of some Asian or African tradition. Intensifying this tendency was the fact that music education had been dropped from many American public schools, further lessening early exposure to European tradition.

4. Providing an opposing centripetal force to the diversity of musics found in the 1990s, the experience of growing up with rock music was nearly universal among composers born after 1960. Few entirely escaped the pressure to use the materials of rock or at least emulate rock's pounding macho energy

(though some contrary influences, such as that of Morton Feldman's quiet music and the Asian use of music for meditation, provided counterbalancing tendencies).

5. The impression of a unified contemporary-music scene has been dissipated by the daunting multiplicity of subcultures that have arisen with the increase in population. Artists universally admired within one subculture—theater composers, film composers, concert-music composers, computer composers, deejays, alternative rockers, jazzers, free improvisers, and so on—may be entirely unknown in all the others. The Internet both exacerbated and fed this tendency by allowing the members of one subculture to locate and communicate with one another within a transcontinental virtual neighborhood.

Although musical trends began to reformulate in this period, the arts in general were forced into low profile during the 1980s and 1990s. In the conservative atmosphere of the time, federal funding for liberal social programs was reviewed and cut back. The National Endowment for the Arts was particularly targeted, and it barely survived by redirecting its funding strategies from individual artists toward large institutions.

Composers and musicians suffered along with other artists. Between 1990 and 1995, funding for the arts dwindled rapidly; over that period the annual number of new-music concerts in New York City alone dropped by more than 50 percent. Instead of giving concerts close to home, composers found it more efficient to put the money from their daytime jobs into making compact discs, and then publicizing them by touring Europe, which seemed always glad to receive them. Energy sapped from concert life was redirected into the Internet. American orchestras lost funding and audience support, and began closing down at the rate of several a year. Those that remained became even more skittish about programming music not written by widely recognized brand names. The marginalized, divided life that Charles Ives felt forced to live became, for many composers, the only survivable strategy.

Nevertheless, American creativity is distinguished for its ability to thrive in hard times. According to one survey made about 1990, there were 40,000 Americans who identified themselves as composers, whether of film music, concert music, jazz, or whatever. The era was characterized by rampant diversity and was generally treated in critical writings as too diverse to characterize. However, a number of identifiable trends resulted from the impacts of technological change, rock hegemony, and ethnomusicological interbreeding. One notable change was that twelve-tone music came to seem discredited and suffered a precipitous decline in the 1980s parallel with the fall of Communism and the Berlin wall. The preeminent status of the European tradition could no longer be assumed; the positive corollary to this was that the American tradition from Ives through Cowell, Partch, Cage, and others was finally becoming recognized as one of the world's great traditions.

ART ROCK; ROBERT ASHLEY

As late as 1975, most classically oriented composers felt that rock, jazz, and classical music were separate worlds, not to be mixed. Increasingly, though, young musicians trained in more than one tradition came to resent this separatist state of affairs, and the boundaries began to fall away. First of all, minimalism—with its motoric rhythms and simple harmonies—eased the way for a conciliation with rock. Composers trained to value complex pitch relationships had distrusted rock's harmonic simplicity, but the even more extreme simplicity of some minimalist works offered a new, more rhythmic and conceptual approach to harmony. Once rock artists such as Brian Eno or the group Yes began working minimalist melodies and textures into their music, the door was open to a fertile interchange.

A great many perceptions switched suddenly in 1981 when Laurie Anderson (see p. 349) hit the British pop charts with her performance-art song *O Superman*, which spun off a sampled and relentlessly repeated one-syllable "ha." Technologically innovative enough to seduce mass audiences, Anderson worked minimalism, performance art, rock, and political commentary into a mixture all her own. Likewise, Robert Ashley (see pp. 291, 322)—known for such aggressive avant-garde assaults as *The Wolfman* (1964)—began writing television operas based on open rhythmic structures that allowed for rock accompaniments. *Perfect Lives* (1978–83), *Atalanta* (1983), and the mammoth tetralogy *Now Eleanor's Idea* (1984–93) relied to varying extents (*Perfect Lives* most of all) on improvised rock accompaniments provided by the pianist "Blue" Gene Tyranny and others. As aficionados despaired of making a distinction between rock and the new "classical" music, Ashley ventured one: "If it's under five minutes it's rock, over five minutes it's classical."[1]

Rhys Chatham (b. 1952), who had once tuned pianos for La Monte Young, wrote a work called *Guitar Trio* in 1977, which consisted of rhythmic pulsations on the overtones of a single pitch on three electric guitars. This was a simplistic attempt, but minimalism and rock had now fused for the first time. He followed this with a more complex work, *Drastic Classicism* (1981), tuning his guitars to the same intervals as La Monte Young's *Second Dream of the High-Tension Line Stepdown Transformer* (see p. 326). These works brought into existence a new type of rock—art rock, highly structured and arising from a classical sensibility.

During this time, Chatham fell in with Glenn Branca (b. 1949), an erstwhile surrealist playwright and punk rocker, who also started working with great masses of noise from mistuned guitars. In such early works as *Dissonance* and *The Spectacular Commodity* (both 1979), Branca mistuned his guitars randomly, but he soon became so fascinated by the masses of clash-

---

[1] Conversation with the author, 1981.

ing harmonics his group achieved that he undertook an extended investigation of acoustic principles. His works grew large enough that he began calling them "symphonies"; of the eleven symphonies he wrote between 1981 and 1998, eight were scored for electric guitars plus drummer. Numbers 3, 4, and 5 are written in the pure tunings of just intonation. Starting with No. 6 ("Devil Choirs at the Gates of Heaven"), he abandoned pure tunings as too impractical, although he continued to approximate the overtone series by using microtones.

Branca's music attracted a huge underground following among rock fans seeking the ultimate mystical electric-guitar experience. It was not uncommon to see listeners at his concerts fall into a sort of trance, spasmodically jabbing their fists in the air at climactic downbeats. For all his masses of volume, however, Branca remained more interested in a kind of Dane Rudhyar–influenced mysticism than in grandiose rock spectacles. Proof came in his Symphony No. 9 (1993) for conventional orchestra with two wordless vocalists. In this work, Branca created an ever moving polyphonic form whose transformations came from the inside out, almost too slowly for the listener to notice (Example 13–1). His paired Symphonies Nos. 8 and 10 (1992, 1994) for electric guitars, though, returned to an idiom Bergian in its atonality, massive in its rock momentum, and Nancarrovian in its internal canonic devices, the last barely audible amid the 120–decibel turmoil. With Branca's Symphony No. 11 (1998), premiered in Europe, he realized a long-held dream of combining electric guitars with orchestra.

Not to be outdone by Branca's symphonies, Chatham countered with a series of works scored for a hundred electric guitars, the first being *An Angel Moves Too Fast to See* (1989). In any group of a hundred guitarists culled from one city, a certain percentage are guaranteed not to read music, and Chatham's compositional methods used ingenious minimalist-inspired devices to overcome the problem—such as having each section play simple chords in repetitive cycles of different lengths. Whereas Branca pursued a single idea with monomaniacal intensity, Chatham's music ranged from minimalist brass pieces (*Waterloo No. 2*, 1986) to trumpet works with computer interaction (*Manifeste*, 1987), to microtonal expansions of serial technique, to experiments in quotation collage (his Symphony No. 4 applied cut-and-paste techniques to Brahms's Fourth Symphony). Meanwhile, in an increasing spiral of one-upmanship, Branca announced plans for a work for two thousand electric guitars; even though, as Chatham noted, "A hundred electric guitars can't really be louder than three."[2]

Parallel to Branca, the astonishing singer Diamanda Galas (see p. 349) gained her own following among rock fans. With consummate control over a powerful vocal range of three and a half octaves, she could have easily had a conventional operatic career, and in fact she did start out in Europe

---

[2] Conversation with the author, June, 1997.

EXAMPLE 13–1.   G. Branca, Symphony No. 9, measures 1–4. Quoted by permission.

performing avant-garde works by Iannis Xenakis, Vinko Globokar, and others. But Galas quickly turned to her own disturbing brand of music theater, creating dark vocal works (such as *Wild Women with Steak Knives*) that delineate the dialectic of oppressor and victim. When the AIDS crisis came along, bringing with it the death of her brother, the performance artist Philip Galas, she found the issue on which she based her work from the 1980s on.

Galas's largest work has been *The Masque of the Red Death* (official dates: "from 1984 to the end of the plague"), a theatrical trilogy consisting of *The Divine Punishment, Saint of the Pit,* and *You Must Be Certain of the Devil.* Masked in frightening makeup, she plays the piano (phenomenally well), sings into microphones through processors that distort her voice, croaks passages from the Old Testament that condemn homosexuality, weaves angry poetry around the text of the Catholic Mass, and performs parodies of country-music and rock idioms:

> In Kentucky Harry buys a round of beer
> To celebrate the death of Billy Smith the queer
> Whose mother still must hide her face in fear.
> Let's not chat about despair.[3]

Despite or because of her evil-woman persona, Galas put together a devoted cult audience made up, apparently, of liberal Democrat heavy-metal fans—a larger group than one might have imagined. Later works such as *Insecta* (1993) and *Schrei X* (1996) have turned away from explicit protest to the wordless use of chilling vocal effects, more abstract but still redolent of death, sickness, and satanism.

Meanwhile, Robert Ashley's career took a crescendo into the 1990s, his significance slow to emerge partly because of the difficulty of getting his operas produced, partly because of the alternately attractive and off-putting opacity of his texts. A complete—though unstaged and un-video-produced—premiere of his tetralogy *Now Eleanor's Idea* waited until 1994, by which time he already had a series of newer operas awaiting production. The four operas—*Improvement: Don Leaves Linda, Foreign Experiences, eL/Aficionado,* and the title opera *Now Eleanor's Idea*—describe Ashley's universe from four different points of view. Moving away from the rock-beat improvisations of *Perfect Lives*, he developed obsessive verbal and pitch structures of split-second timing held together by the singers listening through headphones to click tracks. What were audiences to make of high-speed, sometimes obscene monologues like the following (from *Foreign Experiences*)?

> All the world's people revel in oral sex
> We had to stop asking the question except the British
> We don't do it OK you don't do it and we know why
> Nobody takes a bath Jane Austen didn't take a bath

---

[3] Liner notes for *You Must Be Certain of the Devil* (Restless/Mute 7 71403-2; 1988).

She wrote her ass off but she didn't take a bath
Mr. Darcy never took a bath Disraeli never took a bath
The whole place smelled to high heaven whole
Cults jumped on boats to the New World they knew
Something was amiss Charles Dickens never took a bath
Until he met Mark Twain who kidded him so bad about stinking
That he took a bath he hadn't seen his own legs in 15 years.[4]

Ashley took inspiration for these operas from literary sources as diverse as the financial section of the *New York Times*, the Hispanic-oriented *Low Rider* magazine, and Frances Yates's writings about Renaissance Neoplatonism. In particular, he took the Renaissance notion of the Theater of Memory as a model for his operas, deriving them from carefully structured tone rows deployed over the largest scale possible. "Of course," he once said of his generation, "I'm a serialist! What else could I do?"[5] Despite that self-identification, Ashley created a compelling, highly original model for vernacular American opera that younger composers are only beginning to assimilate.

FREE IMPROVISATION

Jazz and American classical music had always shared an active, if uneasy, mutual influence, even if the distinction between scored and improvised musics remained in place. In the late 1950s, however, "classical" musicians such as Terry Riley and Pauline Oliveros began experimenting with free improvisation. Then, in 1965, Muhal Richard Abrams founded the Association for the Advancement of Creative Musicians (AACM) in Chicago (see p. 345). Musicians from the AACM, devoted to what they termed not jazz but Great Black Music, began working with structured improvisation free from jazz's traditional harmonic patterns and formal structures. Besides Abrams, these included Anthony Braxton, Leroy Jenkins (b. 1932), and Roscoe Mitchell (b. 1940), among many others. By 1980, white and black free-improvisation styles were largely indistinguishable—as was proved when the Knitting Factory in New York began presenting both—and in the next decade they unleashed a frenetically active "free improv" movement on America's major cities.

Ironically, however, the 1980s found AACM musicians left out in the cold by the very musicians whose support they had once counted on. In tune with the conservatism of the time, jazz turned toward the preservation of a "classic" tradition, with an emphasis on black-American contributions to the art that downplayed the contributions of great white jazzers such as Bill Evans (1929–80). After the extraordinarily popular but traditionally main-

---

[4] Unpublished manuscript.
[5] Quoted in Kyle Gann, "Shouting at the Dead: Robert Ashley's Neoplatonist TV Operas," *Village Voice*, October 8, 1991, 89.

stream jazz trumpeter Wynton Marsalis cofounded Jazz at Lincoln Center in 1987, musicians from the AACM tradition, too, found themselves marginalized by the jazz world, and sometimes more welcome in circles devoted to new classical music (and by performers such as Ursula Oppens and the Kronos Quartet).

Thus, although black AACM figures such as Braxton, Abrams, Jenkins, and Mitchell remained heroes to young improvisers, they themselves began writing fully notated scores and even operas, such as Braxton's mammothly complex *Shala Fears for the Poor* (1996) and Jenkins's *Mother of Three Sons* (1991). Braxton, whose music had taken a Stockhausenesque fragmentation as its early starting point, continued to run through a dazzling array of styles. He did much of his best work of the 1980s touring Europe with a fine quartet: himself on sax, Marilyn Crispell on piano, Mark Dresser on bass, and Gerry Hemingway on drums. Many of his works with this group and afterward are "collage form structures" (his own term) in which different works can be played simultaneously.

Despite the maximalist aura of most of Braxton's music, he had cultivated an interest in minimalism, starting in 1971 with his *104° Kelvin* series for solo saxophone, the first of which is dedicated to Philip Glass. In the 1980s this interest in repetitively pulsing textures grew into what he called "pulse track musics," long works grounded in a relentlessly reiterative beat. By the mid-1990s, the trend climaxed in a series of ghost trance musics. For example, *Composition No. 185* (1996) is a dense, trance-inducing sextet of staccato notes, often running up and down scales. Hired to teach at Wesleyan University in 1990 and given the prestigious MacArthur "genius" Fellowship in 1994, Braxton was well certified as black improvisation's guiding Protean figure.

More publicly visible, however, and more explicable in his musical processes, was Anthony Davis (b. 1951), who became the most prominent proponent of a black-American compositional idiom. His best music may be his improvisations with the ensemble Episteme. He has received more attention, though, for his operas, especially *X: The Life and Times of Malcolm X* (1985). An effective series of vignettes laced with famous quotes from the radical black leader ("The chickens have come home to roost," he sings after Kennedy is shot) and climaxing in the hero's own assassination, the work leaves breathing room for some effective improvised cadenzas by soloists in the orchestra. (Similarly, Leroy Jenkins's *Mother of Three Sons* is enlivened by Jenkins's own violin improvisations from the orchestra pit.) Davis followed *X* with other, less sensational operas: *Under the Double Moon* (1989), *Tania* (1992), and *Amistad* (1997).

The best-known white improviser of the 1980s, and also the least typical, was John Zorn (b. 1953). Inspired by television cartoons, heavy-metal rock, and the European serialist avant-garde, Zorn invented methods to improvise fast-paced collages. Recognizing the major pitfalls of free improvisation—formal amorphousness, the inability to make sudden changes in ensemble texture, and self-indulgence—he invented strategies for overcoming them, such as cue cards and hand signals given by ensemble members acting as temporary conductors. *Cobra* (1984), a mammoth collage of abstract and referential sound bites, was the most successful of Zorn's early works, and remained for years a staple of downtown Manhattan performance. Subsequent recordings such as *The Big Gundown* (1986), a wacky arrangement of movie tunes by Ennio Morricone, brought Zorn a larger audience and also led to a breakdown of high-art/low-art boundaries within the music world.

Zorn led a hectic free-improv scene in the 1980s in New York that spilled over into centers such as Chicago and Los Angeles. His most active colleagues in New York included Elliott Sharp (b. 1951), a self-styled "science nerd" whose highly structured yet raucously noisy works often derived from principles of biology and chemistry; Anthony Coleman (b. 1955), a Thelonious Monk–influenced jazz pianist who brought a jazz-improv approach to abstract, classical materials; and Shelley Hirsch (b. 1952), a fluid vocalist who drew stream-of-consciousness collages from her growing-up experiences in the New York suburbs. These leading figures attracted an intense group of improvisers, including the drummer Robert Previte, pianists Marilyn Crispell and Myra Melford, pianist-vocalist Robin Holcomb, and guitarist Wayne Horvitz—some of whom gravitated back toward more traditional jazz in the 1990s as the free-improv movement began to lose steam.

In fact, rock, jazz, and classical music, after a free-wheeling decade of genre-mixing, disentangled themselves to some extent in the 1990s, partly for the very practical reason that although the musicians may have liked to combine their diverse talents, the hard-core audiences for rock, jazz, and classical music simply were not enamored of one another's genres. New phases in this slow fusion process, however, were bound to follow.

POSTMINIMALISM; MORTON FELDMAN

Following its enormous splash in the 1970s, minimalism seemed to have run into a dead end; despite the continued and even increasing popularity of Steve Reich and Philip Glass, minimalism played little part in musical politics during the 1980s and 1990s. However, minimalism had not really died but, rather, had gone underground, to give birth to a new musical language. Postminimalist composers—heavily influenced by and building on minimalism but not adhering to the style's original strict principles—have not been widely recognized as constituting a movement because they did not form a close-knit group as had the original minimalists. Nevertheless, a highly unified style of music emerged in the 1980s, indebted to minimalism yet different from it, which gave the vague 1970s term "postminimalism" a more specific meaning based in a close-knit group of style characteristics.

Postminimalism can be identified as having begun about 1980 in works by William Duckworth (b. 1943), Janice Giteck, and Daniel Lentz. Perhaps the first major, identifiably postminimalist work was Duckworth's *The Time Curve Preludes* (1977–78), a piano cycle of twenty-four pieces. Although they retained the static tonality (or, rather, modality) and numerical rhythmic processes of classic minimalism, they eschewed minimalism's self-evident structural processes. *The Time Curve Preludes* relied on mysterious inner processes (such as additive or subtractive sequences, often based on the Fibonacci series, and self-retrograding rhythms) that drew each work to a naturally closing perceptual spiral. Where minimalist works were notable for their great length and repetitiveness, postminimalist works were more conventional in length and less repetitious. The style aimed not at audible process but at internal consistency in a language marked by diatonic scales, mostly consonant harmonies, and almost always a steady beat based on an unchanging unit (eighth note—or sixteenth note or quarter note).

It is typical of postminimalism that although *The Time Curve Preludes* absorbed traits of not only minimalism but also bluegrass music, early rock-and-roll keyboard style, Erik Satie, Olivier Messiaen, Indian ragas, Bach, and medieval music, it fused them all into a seamlessly consistent musical language. In a profound way, postminimalism was the antipodal opposite of serialism. Whereas serialist syntax was abrupt, discontinuous, angular, arrhythmic, opaque, and generated from a single source-principle, postminimalist syntax was precisely the opposite: smooth, linear, melodic, gently rhythmic, comprehensible, and drawn from diverse sources. Yet the two diametrically opposed styles had in common the search for a consistent musical language, a cohesive syntax. The postminimalist-generation composers, mostly born in the 1940s, had grown up studying serialism and had internalized many of its values. Although minimalism inspired them to seek a more audience-friendly music than serialism, they still conceptualized music in terms familiar to them from twelve-tone thought—as a language with rules meant to guarantee internal coherence.

Duckworth followed *The Time Curve Preludes* with other large cycles, such as *Southern Harmony* (1980–81; a choral work based on shape-note hymns) and *Imaginary Dances* (1985/88, for piano), climaxing in the late 1990s with *Cathedral*, the first major interactive work written for Internet performance. *Cathedral* is made up of works for diverse synthesized ensembles, and most of the movements are characterized by Duckworth's poignant major-minor ambiguity. (See Example 13–2, from *Mysterious Numbers*; 1996.) In addition, there are pages in the Web site that allow listeners to send in their own MIDI materials, which are then worked into the musical fabric that flows back from the Web. *Cathedral* demonstrated in dramatic terms Duckworth's ability to synthesize a wide variety of materials in a smooth, piquant continuum.

The mature postminimal style of Janice Giteck (b. 1946) began with *Breathing Songs from a Turning Sky* (1980). If anything, her range of influences was even wider and more international than Duckworth's: Eastern European, American Indian, Jewish, and especially Javanese performance traditions appear in her magnum opus of the 1980s, *Om Shanti* (1986), a

EXAMPLE 13–2. W. Duckworth, *Mysterious Numbers*, mm. 19–27. Copyright © 1997 by Monroe Street Music, 666 Fifth Avenue (No. 232), New York, NY 10103. International Copyright Secured. All Rights Reserved. Used by permission.

meditatively prayerful work dedicated to victims of AIDS. Another post-minimalist, Elodie Lauten (b. 1950 in Paris but resident in New York City after 1972), wrote improvisatory keyboard pieces and mystical theatrical works based on a personal cosmology drawn from the Indian Vedas; it correlated scales, keys, and rhythmic patterns with hexagrams from the *I Ching*, signs of the zodiac, seasons, even animals. She first achieved recognition with a video opera of muted, mystically repetitive textures, *The Death of Don Juan* (1987)—a retelling of the Don Juan myth from a feminist standpoint. She devoted the late 1990s to an even larger work, *Deus ex Machina*, for singers and Baroque-instrument ensemble.

Perhaps the most publicly acknowledged postminimalists have been Ingram Marshall (b. 1942) and Paul Dresher (b. 1951). Influenced by Indonesian repetitive patterns and Scandinavian atmospheres such as that of Sibelius's symphonies, Marshall achieved fame for his early works *Gradual Requiem* (1979–81) and *Fog Tropes* (1979/82), which used tape delay to create filmic, slowly transformational textures of lovely melancholy. In Dresher's early works, such as *Channels Passing* (1981–2), he seemed a card-carrying minimalist, but more recent works such as *Double Ikat* (1988–90, for violin, piano, and percussion) are more mercurial, if still rhythmically propulsive.

Postminimalism is such a widespread movement that it is impossible to do much more here than list some of the other major composers involved: Paul Epstein (b. 1938), David Borden (b. 1938), Phil Winsor (b. 1938), Jonathan Kramer (b. 1942), Stephen Scott (b. 1944), Peter Gena (b. 1947), Guy Klucevsek (b. 1947), Bernadette Speach (b. 1948), Thomas Albert (b. 1948), Mary Jane Leach (b. 1949), Wes York (b. 1949), Joseph Koykkar (b. 1951), Peter Garland (see p. 337), Sasha Matson (b. 1954), and Mary Ellen Childs (b. 1957). In fact, one thing working against the recognition of postminimalism as a movement is the far-flung and isolated situation of the major figures, who range from Seattle to Florida and from Maine to Mexico.

Garland is best known for his groundbreaking work as the editor of the journal *Soundings* (in which he first published scores of Harry Partch, Conlon Nancarrow, James Tenney, Lou Harrison, and other seminal figures). His music is quietly rhythmic in a modal idiom marked by frequent but irregular repetition of motives and pitches; examples include his String Quartet No. 1, "In Praise of Poor Scholars" (1986), *Jornada del Muerto* for piano (1987), and *Roque Dalton Songs* for ensemble (1988). Gena, a Chicago postminimalist, broke into the style with *McKinley* (1983), a dashing trio based on political songs. Later he used computers to derive music from the structure of DNA chains, as in his *Beta Globin* (1994). Scott, like Nancarrow, has written much of his music for a single peculiar medium: bowed piano, played by an ensemble bowing the strings with nylon threads. His gently shimmering *Rainbows* (1981) became one of the most popular works of the 1980s. Kramer's early works reduced the pitch spectrum to only five, six, or seven pitches, including his *Moments In and Out of Time* for orchestra (1981–83) and *Atlanta Licks* for ensemble (1984). In *Notta Sonata* (1992–93), however, in search of a postmodern idiom that would break with the traditional idea of authorial consistency, he veered off into his own strangely effective brand of a collage of styles. Klucevsek, an expert accordionist, wrote some charming music with odd titles ("*Viavy Rose" Variations*, 1989; *Flying Vegetables of the Apocalypse*, 1988) and was responsible for the widespread presence of the accordion in postminimal music. And Leach found her niche writing beautiful works for *a cappella* vocal ensemble, including her *Mountain Echoes* (1987) and *Bruckstück* (1989).

Postminimalism received a powerful impetus from one composer whose significance did not fully emerge until after his death in 1987: Morton Feldman (see p. 286ff.). Long known as a sidekick of John Cage who wrote all his works "as soft as possible," Feldman moved to the State University of New York at Buffalo in the 1970s and began writing works of ever more astonishing length. By and large, these works remained unknown until the 1990s. At the time of his death, Feldman was known only through about a half-dozen recordings and few live performances. By one of those regrettable ironies of reception history, more than three dozen compact discs of his music appeared in the following decade. Their impact on younger composers was enormous.

As evidence of Feldman's interest in ever longer musical essays, take the three works he wrote for flutist, percussionist, and keyboardist. The first, *Why Patterns?* (1978; *CRI* CD 620), is a half-hour long; the second, *Crippled Symmetry* (1983), is an hour and a half; and the third, *For Philip Guston* (1984), is five hours. Tired of what he saw as a modernist cliché, the twenty-minute piece, Feldman sought to move from the level of form to that of scale. In *For Philip Guston*, a seminal motive—C G A♭ E♭, with the first interval descending and the others ascending—reappears every twenty-five minutes or so, creating an unusual feeling that you are exploring a large, labyrinthine house and occasionally stumble back into the room you started in. In one section, the music is funneled down to a small segment of the chromatic scale for twenty minutes of deadening sensory deprivation, then suddenly opens up across the entire piano range in glorious C major, eliciting an audience reaction of unexpected relief. Such unprecedented time-expanding and -contracting effects opened up a wealth of new territory for younger composers to explore—not always with happy results, since not every composer has the Feldmanesque sensitivity to write a rewarding two-hour work for, say, cello and piano. Feldman's monochromaticism, too, coming as it did after an exhausting era of serialism's every-possible-effect-in-every-piece, gave postminimal composers permission to develop entire works from a specific set of chords, or a specific dynamic or rhythmic device. Especially stunning in their impact were two of Feldman's largest works, his opera *Neither* (1977), based on a few lines given to him by Samuel Beckett, and his swan song, *For Samuel Beckett* (1987), a forty-five-minute orchestral work in which dense thickets of echoing harp and piano notes fade away in disconsolate sadness.

TOTALISM; CONLON NANCARROW

A number of currents converged in the late 1980s to form the dominant, or at least the most characteristic, new style of the 1990s; this acquired, in certain circles, the controversial name of totalism. The composers involved, mostly born in the 1950s, grew up with rock but had been of an age to discover minimalism in college, and also to take advantage of the explosion of ethnomusicology in the 1970s. Accordingly, they inherited static forms, gradual process, and unison ensemble performance from minimalism, but had little interest in minimalism's (or postminimalism's) pretty tonalities or rhythmic simplicity. They wanted the energy of rock and the rhythmic liveliness of Indian, Balinese, or African music. And they got it.

Thus the overriding characteristic of totalist music is a bracing rhythmic complexity, often derived from superimposition of tempos or rhythmic cycles and expressed in harmonic contexts sufficiently stripped down to keep the rhythmic friction in central focus. The music is just as likely to be harshly dissonant or noisy as it is to be purely consonant, or anything in between; the totalist generation had tired of the consonance-versus-dissonance fights of its teachers' generation, and refused to put much emphasis on the distinction. Totalist complexity is rhythmic, and the complexity is always beat-related, within well-defined tempos. The word "totalist" carries connotations of having your cake and eating it too; in this case, having in your music the raw energy to appeal to rock fans, but also background structures intricate enough to intrigue cognoscenti. The term arose when it became evident, about 1992, that composers including Mikel Rouse, Michael Gordon, John Luther Adams, Ben Neill, David First, Evan Ziporyn, Diana Meckley, Larry Polansky, and Arthur Jarvinen were all using similar beat-shifting and multitempo rhythmic structures in their music.[6]

Starting out in a rock or jazz band seemed de rigueur for young composers in the 1980s and 1990s. Rouse headed a band called Tirez Tirez. Gordon played keyboard for Peter and the Girlfriends. First formed a trio called the Note Killers, describing it as "Steve Reich meets Jimi Hendrix." Ben Neill went in the other direction, crossing over into ambient music and gaining a rock following.

Mikel Rouse (b. 1957 in rural Missouri) moved to New York City in 1979 and studied both African music (through A. M. Jones's famous book of 1959, *Studies in African Music*) and Joseph Schillinger's composition technique before forming an instrumental rock band called Broken Consort capable of playing his Schillinger-inspired tempo labyrinths. One of his first works for the group, *Quick Thrust* (1984), sets an untransposed twelve-tone row against itself at different tempos and with lumbering rock dynamism. Michael Gordon (b. 1956) followed the example of Reich and Glass and

---

[6] For the first use of the term in print, see Kyle Gann, "After-Ugly Music," *Village Voice*, June 1, 1993; for an early definition, see Kyle Gann, "Totally Ismic," *Village Voice*, July 20, 1993, 69.

formed his own group, The Michael Gordon Philharmonic. He christened the ensemble with *Thou Shalt!/Thou Shalt Not!* (1983; *CRI* CD 636), minimalist in its relentless repetition of gestures but not in its disintegrating conflict between quarter notes, dotted quarter notes, and triplets. Evan Ziporyn (b. 1959) developed a divided career by playing in both jazz bands and Indonesian gamelans, eventually becoming director of Gamelan Galak Tika at the Massachusetts Institute of Technology. John Luther Adams (b. 1953), who uses his middle name to distinguish himself from the John Adams who wrote *Shaker Loops*, discovered Feldman and Varèse from liner notes by the eccentric rocker Frank Zappa. The Los Angeles composer Art Jarvinen (b. 1956) is the only member of the group not based on the East Coast (more of him shortly). Ben Neill (b. 1957 in North Carolina) studied with La Monte Young before veering in the direction of ambient music. As music director at the Kitchen in New York City, he brought the burgeoning ambient scene of the 1980s in contact with the avant-garde, and his ambient computer environments have become as popular with rock fans as with new-music fans.

Despite the diversity of these artists in temperament, materials, and concerns, they all share a tendency to use phase shifting as a basic structural paradigm: the phase shifting of different tempos, beats, phrases, or repeating patterns. This represents an American legacy with multiple roots: the idea was first suggested in Henry Cowell's *New Musical Resources* (1930) and taken up from the late 1940s by Conlon Nancarrow; it also stems from the phase shifting of Steve Reich's early pieces such as *Come Out* and *Piano Phase* (see p. 327). In totalism, minimalism and the rhythmic experimentation of Cowell and Nancarrow have flowed into a rich common stream. One of the clearest examples of phase shifting as a shaping force is Jarvinen's *Murphy Nights* (Example 13–3), in which the bass and the electric keyboard play two phrases against each other, one in $\frac{33}{16}$ meter and the other in $\frac{8}{4}$ or $\frac{32}{16}$.

The most publicly successful manifestations of the totalist generation have been the festivals of Bang on a Can and the operas of Mikel Rouse. Bang on a Can—founded in 1987 by Michael Gordon, Julia Wolfe (his wife), and David Lang—has been a major showcase for works by composers born in the 1950s whose music had been too long ignored by the more conventional musical institutions.

Rouse turned from the geometric number abstractions of his Broken Consort music to a vocal overdubbing technique he called "counterpoetry" (by analogy with "counterpoint"), in which several voices speak or sing the same text in highly structured rhythmic counterpoint. With this technique he wrote *Failing Kansas*, his first opera—using "opera" in the loose, downtown Manhattan sense, in this case performed solo by Rouse with taped background and video projections. *Failing Kansas* obliquely tells the story of the same murders on which Truman Capote based his gripping novel *In Cold Blood*. Example 13–4 (from which a complex percussion track is omitted) shows a clear example of both counterpoetic technique and phase shifting, as a phrase four beats long is heard against two phrases each six beats long.

EXAMPLE 13–3. A. Jarvinen, *Murphy Nights* (a coda to "Johnny Sprays"), opening measures. Copyright 1989, Leisure Planet Music. Quoted by permission.

The words come from the diary of Perry Smith, one of the novel's murderers. Rouse followed *Failing Kansas* with a more ambitious opera, *Dennis Cleveland* (NW CD 80506), in the form of a talk show: Rouse walks around the room with a microphone singing and speaking as other vocalists rise from the audience to enact their roles. Since at first the real audience members don't know the actors from the audience, the piece is a dazzling feat of operatically breaking down the fourth wall. The work's 1996 premiere at the Kitchen in New York City was the first performance ever to draw scalpers to that venerable experimental venue. And yet the music is complex enough to

EXAMPLE 13–4.   M. Rouse, *Failing Kansas*, measures 56–59. © 1995 Mikel
Rouse. Published by Club Soda Music.

My mo-ther was al - ways drunk.

In Fris - co I was con - tin - u - ous -

I had start-ed to run a - - -

contain bitonal passages, intricate isorhythms, and even tempo canons. Perhaps no other totalist squeezed so much complexity into a smooth rock idiom.

Michael Gordon came close, however. His *Four Kings Fight Five* (1988; *CRI* CD 636), dedicated to Glenn Branca, opens with a loud, Branca-ish melody, and adds on different tempos by means of nested two-against-three relationships until at its thickest point there are eleven tempos going at once. Peaks in Gordon's career have included his *Van Gogh Video Opera* (1991), based on the artist's letters, and *Trance* (1995), an hour-long continuous cross-rhythm fest that culminates in ecstatic prerecorded samples of chanting by Buddhist monks and Arabic *muezzins. Trance* represents for the totalist movement what Reich's *Drumming* did for minimalism—a major work that proves the validity of the style in its purest form.

A highly regarded composer across the country, John Luther Adams is associated with his home state of Alaska, and his music has been pervaded by both northern atmospheres and environmental issues. Heavily influenced by Feldman and Cowell, he typically creates textures of often repetitive phrases of different lengths running out of sync with one another (Example 13–5). In works such as *Dream of White on White* (1992), the mammoth *Clouds of Forgetting, Clouds of Unknowing* (1990–95; *NW* CD 80500), and his environmental opera *Earth and the Great Weather* (1993; *NW* CD 80459), such textures create an aura of meditative calm.

Arthur Jarvinen, mentioned earlier, has perhaps the most inventive timbral imagination among the younger composers. The rhythmic complexities of his *The Paces of Yu* (1990) are articulated by flicked window shutters, eight snapping mousetraps, the grinding of pencil sharpeners, and a spinning fishing reel; the hissing of spray cans punctuates his *Egyptian Two-Step* (1986). Larry Polansky, one of the designers of the computer language HSML, often writes algorithmic computer works in which tones from various overtone series pass each other in different tempos, such as *B'reysheet* (*Cantillation Study No. 1*) (1985). His array of compositional techniques, however, is vast, and one of his most powerful works is *Lonesome Road* (*The Crawford Variations*) (1988–89), a massive, ninety-minute set of variations

EXAMPLE 13–5.   J. L. Adams, *Clouds of Forgetting, Clouds of Unknowing*, measures 79–81. Copyright © Taiga Press 1996. Quoted by permission.

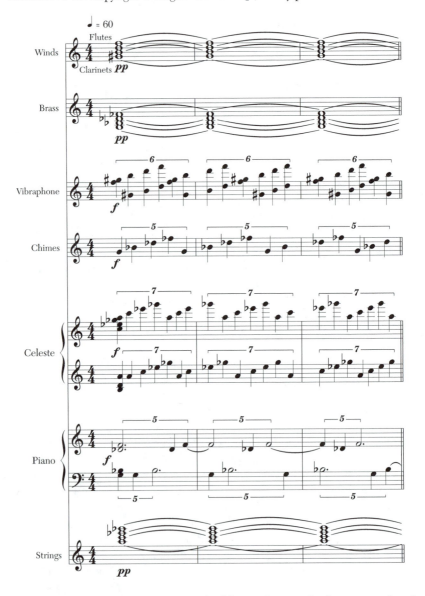

for piano based on a folk song transcribed by Ruth Crawford. Mercurial and extraordinarily difficult, the piece is a worthy successor to that other great American set of variations, Frederic Rzewski's *The People United* (see p. 341).

Two unusual composers have become known for their work with glissandos. Lois Vierk (b. 1951) is a rare example of an ethnomusicologist who became a composer, having studied the *ryūteki* in Japan with Sukeyasu Sheba, a famous gagaku player. Starting with *Go Guitars* (1981), for guitar and four overdubbed guitars ("go" being Japanese for "five"), she wrote a stunning series of works for multiples of a single instrument. Typically of Vierk's works, which often involve some kind of gradual, though often nonlinear, transformation, *Go Guitars* moves gradually from pingy tremolos to a texture of wild up-and-down glissandos. Her *Timberline* of 1991 for mixed septet is much more complex and subtle, though still tinged with glissandos evocative of Asian music.

Whereas Vierk does not depend on the same phase-shifting rhythms as the totalists, David First (b. 1953) has effectively exploited phase shifting in both pitches and rhythms. The central device of his music is ultraslow glissandos, often between synthesizers, whose gradual detuning causes shimmering arrays of modulating beat patterns capable of raising the hair on the back of one's neck. One of the most gorgeous of such works is *Jade Screen Test Dreams of Renting Wings* (1993)—one example of First's obscure but lovely titles. He also wrote an opera fusing glissando techniques with rock arias, *The Manhattan Book of the Dead* (1995).

Just as Feldman became a guiding spirit for the postminimalists, Conlon Nancarrow (see p. 353) gave an impetus to totalism. Although he had been writing his rhythmically virtuosic "studies" for player piano since the late 1940s, Nancarrow remained almost unknown until the late 1970s, and the sudden availability of his music in the early 1980s (thanks to scores published by Peter Garland in *Soundings* and recordings by Charles Amirkhanian for the 1750 Arch and, later, Wergo labels) opened a new phase in his influence. As Nancarrow's works became more available for study in the 1980s, his elegant sense of tempo structure and his clashes of tempos in ratios such as $5:6:7:8$ proved inspirational for the works of the totalists.

Equally important, Nancarrow entered a new phase in his music after 1970. Each of his first thirty-seven studies was based on a technical idea such as ostinato, isorhythm (the same rhythm over and over with different pitch rows), tempo canon, or acceleration. Starting with Study No. 40 and continuing through his amazingly fertile seventh decade, he began combining these discrete devices into a dauntingly complex yet elegant synthesis. In a wildly crashing work such as Study No. 48, for instance, with its unprecedented tempo clash of 60:61, acceleration and tempo canon support each other in a relentless crescendo of activity, so that the devices become difficult to discuss separately. Accelerating tempo canons of isorhythms underly passages in Studies Nos. 45, 47, and 49. The result is a new language in which large-scale form and melodic details are as intimately wedded as in the late works of Beethoven, and musical process becomes as audible as any minimalist could wish for. In addition, as Nancarrow became better known, performers began to commission him, and he wrote his first works for live performers since the 1940s. His *Tango?* (1983) for Yvar Mikhashoff, *Two Canons for Ursula* (1988) for Ursula Oppens, and String Quartet No. 3 (1987) for the Arditti Quartet brought a new level of rhythmic complexity to the repertoire through players willing to tackle and master the difficulties.

ELECTRONIC MUSIC; TRIMPIN

In the 1960s and 1970s, it was fairly clear what the term "electronic composer" denoted. Electronic composers worked collectively in studios full of expensive equipment and produced their work, more often than not, on magnetic tape. The personal-computer explosion of the early 1980s changed all that. Thereafter "electronic composer" could mean anything from someone who used a synthesizer in his or her otherwise acoustic-instrument works to someone whose music was produced on computer, to someone whose acoustic music was *composed* by means of computer, to someone who performed with simple electronic circuitry, to someone whose music relied on electronic processing. In fact, the term had become virtually meaningless: most composers born after 1950 were electronic in some sense or another. Still, there were plenty of composers incapable of producing a note during a power outage, and who spun their careers out of specific innovations in electronic equipment or software; these we can call "electronic composers" with minimal ambiguity, and it is to these that we turn now.

The speed at which the electronic-music network grew was vastly accelerated by the development (some would say imposition) of uniform industry standards. In 1983—a little-acknowledged watershed date in the history of music—technicians from Roland, Oberheim, and Sequential Circuits went public with the universal system they had developed: MIDI, or Musical Instrument Digital Interface. Thanks to MIDI, any IBM-compatible or Macintosh computer was able to control any synthesizer or sampler. Critics charge that MIDI is too single-note oriented and too keyboard oriented, that it imposes a conceptual grid on musical possibilities. Some composers, such as Tom Hamilton (b. 1946), rebelled by eschewing MIDI and continuing to work with older analogue synthesizers such as the Serge Modular and Oberheim Matrix 12. Hundreds of others have bowed to the prevailing circuitry, though many have turned to sophisticated specialist software that circumvents MIDI's note-by-note logic. Economics also entered the picture: the first sampler (the Fairlight CMI) appeared in 1980 for $25,000; by 1984, samplers were available for less than $1,300, and music was never to be the same again.

As it became more affordable, rock musicians began taking to new technology as fast as did classical composers, and in some cases faster. Trent Reznor (b. 1965) became the first to create a rock band at home on his computer; his CDs for his virtual band Nine Inch Nails, controversial for profanity and dark imagery, are made by means of software through collage techniques (though he puts together a live band to tour). Popular performers and bands such as Beck, Tricky, Faithless, the Chemical Brothers, and Radiohead have all used sampling techniques to intercut their music with noises, voices, and quotations. Makers of *techno music* and *ambient music*, two forms that swelled to mass popularity in the 1980s (if still underground), were highly dependent on computer technology for their dance grooves and for the samples and electronic phrases layered above them. Ambient music became the background for all-day events in which several ambient artists performed at once, often to the accompaniment of computerized (if usually fairly random) visual projections. Techno, as its name implies, was a mechanical music emphasizing heavy rhythmic grooves and synthesized sounds. One ambient composer, Terre Thaemlitz (b. 1968), even used technology to deconstruct (and criticize, in terms of sexual politics) the German techno group Kraftwerk.

At the same time, many acted as if the new technology freed up obsolete technologies for new purposes. Hip-hop swept the 1980s as dozens of black-American deejays—many of them denied conventional music training because of budget cuts in underfunded schools—began performing with vinyl records on old turntables. In the hands of the best, such as DJ Spooky and DJ Olive, the vinyl collage became—like rap music, the heavily verbal form of rock that developed in tandem with hip-hop—a form of social criticism. For instance, *Viral Sonata* by DJ Spooky (nom de gramophone of Paul D. Miller) is rich and sensuous, slickly cinematic in its slow moves from one texture to another, and with an occasional groove buried subliminally underneath. Within its new medium, it explores issues of timbre and continuity similar to those of 1960s *musique concrète*.

In the end, though, it little mattered whether the collages were made by twirling vinyl records simultaneously or combining samples from those records on a computer. Just as, in the nineteenth century, the invention of photography made painters redefine painting, the heavy and varied use of late-twentieth-century technology by vernacular artists challenged classical composers to think deeply about the premises of their work and to relocate outside the areas that the hip-hoppers and the DJs had claimed as their own.

The sampler has defined the direction of many careers, particularly those of Paul Lansky (b. 1944), Charles Amirkhanian (b. 1945), Noah Creshevsky (b. 1945), Neil Rolnick (b. 1947), Henry Gwiazda (b. 1952), and Carl Stone (b. 1953), each of whom puts the instrument to very different uses. Amirkhanian (see p. 350), best known as an aggressive champion of American music as music director of public radio station KPFA in San Francisco from 1969 to 1992, is perhaps the greatest sound purist. In tape homages such as *Walking Tune* (1986–87; homage to Percy Grainger) and *Pas de voix* (1987; homage to Samuel Beckett), he uses the Synclavier II to play unaltered samples up to three minutes long, creating snapshot collages of superimposed environmental sounds. In *Walking Tune*, footsteps in the gravel of Grainger's driveway form a background for a plaintive violin melody, cackling fowl, and a sung phrase of music by C. P. E. Bach. Beckett refused to let anyone, Amirkhanian included, record his voice, so for *Pas de voix* (French for "no voice") Amirkhanian recorded the sounds outside Beckett's apartment and mingled them with sounds suggestive of the playwright's works (the flushing of a toilet, for instance).

Henry Gwiazda has taken a similarly purist attitude toward found sounds, many of which he takes from sound-effects libraries and leaves unaltered. His sensitivity as a poet of natural sounds is beautifully evident in oddly capitalized works such as *whErEyoulivE* (1989) and *MANEAT-INGCHIPSLISTENINGTOAVIOLIN* (1990). More recently, however, he has become the leading artist involved in virtual audio. Using software developed to enable airplane pilots to deal with a multiplicity of radio-transmitted voices, he has made works that locate sounds at specific points in space—the drawback being that only one person can listen at a time, since the illusions work only at a specific distance from and angle to the loudspeakers. Thus, in *buzzingreynold'sdreamland* (1994), basketballs bounce toward you, troops march past you, a lazily cawing seagull circles from right to left and back. More disconcertingly, in *thefLuteinthewor Ldthef Luteis-theworLd* (1995), which must be listened to on headphones, someone seems to sneak up behind you and cut your hair.

More often, composers have prefered to alter the sampled sounds themselves. Carl Stone, for instance, began his career in the mid-1980s with software that could apply minimalist processes to prerecorded samples. With such software he could sit at a laptop computer and, tapping away, perform such works as *Shing Kee* (1986), in which a looped voice-and-piano sample is gradually lengthened until it becomes recognizable as a phrase from Schubert's *Winterreise*; the charming joke of the piece is that the singer (in the original recording sampled by Stone) was the Japanese pop star Akiko Yano, so that the timbre and inflections sound anything but Western-classical. *Hop Ken* plays in a less linear way with samples from Mussorgsky's *Pictures at an Exhibition*, gradually corralling its notes into rock-inspired rhythms of Stone's own making. (Stone titles all his works after restaurants, especially those that serve Asian cuisine.) Paul Lansky has likewise channeled samples in the service of an attractive minimalism, especially in his happily babbling electronic voice-pieces *Idle Chatter* (1985), *just more idle chatter* (1987), and *Notjustmoreidlechatter* (1988).

Perhaps the cutting edge of electronic music in the 1990s was that of interactive computers. After 1985 it became increasingly common to see a composer perform on a synthesizer whose MIDI data went into a computer, which would then spin its own variations on the input provided according to whatever software was engaged. Alternatively, a computer could also chart the pitch, rhythm, and dynamics of an acoustic trombone or violin, transforming pitch contour into dynamic contour, reacting to specific triggering frequencies, or anything else the composer-programmer imagined. Such conceptual acrobatics have absorbed the talents of David Behrman (b. 1937), Joel Chadabe (b. 1938), Richard Teitelbaum (b. 1939), Laurie Spiegel (b. 1945), David Rosenboom (b. 1947), George Lewis (b. 1952), Tod Machover (b. 1953), Nicolas Collins (b. 1954), and Ron Kuivila (b. 1955).

The first interactive works can be credited to Chadabe: *Drift* (1970) and *Ideas of Movement at Bolton Landing* (1971). In general, the music of each of the later composers can be characterized by the type of logic his or her computer systems employ. Teitelbaum's systems, for example, tend to crescendo in information until they overload and self-destruct; his major work is a series called *Golem* (the major one, an opera, from 1989), based on the Jewish myth about a Frankenstein monster who goes out of control. Rosenboom's systems, on the other hand, generate music organically according to seeds set forth in the beginning.

Rosenboom started out working with Terry Riley and La Monte Young, as is evident in one of his early minimalist works for Buchla synthesizer, *How Much Better If Plymouth Rock Had Landed on the Pilgrims* (1968). In *Systems of Judgment* (1987), he produced one of the most remarkable live-performed electronic works ever made. For one thing, Rosenboom not only controlled a table of electronic circuitry to create the piece but also played piano and violin, both virtuosically. In seven movements, the work moves through a three-dimensional conceptual space determined by three models of evolution. One model is that of a drone whose microscopic fluctuations, greatly magnified, eventually give rise to other tones; another is that of random white noise, within which aberrations inevitably suggest specific directions; and the third is a model of how we distinguish between "primitive" and "advanced" symbolic systems.[7] Within these models rides a "Theme of Wonderment" (Example 13–6), reminiscent of the "Theme of the Dawn of Eternal Time" from Young's *The Well-Tuned Piano.*

EXAMPLE 13–6.   D. Rosenboom, "Theme of Wonderment," from *Systems of Judgment.* Quoted by permission.

[7] Liner notes for (and by) David Rosenboom, *Systems of Judgment* (Centaur CRC 2077; 1989).

Of course, interactivity is the computer mode most closely related to improvisation, and intersections with free improvisation have become common. George Lewis is an AACM musician who has worked computers into free-improv situations, and Teitelbaum and Rosenboom have both worked closely with Anthony Braxton and other improvisers. San Francisco's collective The Hub—consisting of Mark Trayle, Tim Perkis, Phil Stone, Chris Brown, John Bischoff, and Scot Gresham-Lancaster—have taken computer interactivity as the basis for a new collectivism, sometimes performing improvisatorily together (even though located in different cities). Laurie Spiegel, a composer of gradual-transformation pieces involving amazingly rich sound palettes, is better known for her interactive software Music Mouse, a sophisticated program that creates music of different styles in extremely detailed complexity at the touch of a computer mouse.

A little-heralded genre that took firm root in the 1980s is the sound installation, a semipermanent sound-producing environment that encourages the listener to wander around and explore. After Alvin Lucier himself (see p. 337), two of his protégés, Nic Collins and Ron Kuivila, have been pioneers in this field. Collins performs with a computerized trombone that sends sounds to speakers around the performing space. So close does his work come to ventriloquism that it is appropriate that one major work of his is an opera (*Truth in Clouds*, 1999)—based on a seance and using the first Ouija-board-to-MIDI converter. Kuivila has often used video motion sensors to allow onlookers to unknowingly trigger noises, and has sent 12,000 volts through his *Spark Harmonicas* and *Spark Harps* to make noises with pure electricity. Tod Machover created a public stir with his 1996 *Brain Opera* in New York, which allowed audience members to create rhythms and speak phrases later incorporated in the audio surface. One of the most original installation artists is Maryanne Amacher (b. 1946), whose works are site-specific, taking over an entire house or building to create booming, slowly evolving noise environments. Her temporary, one-of-a-kind works are better supported in Europe than in America, though rare anywhere.

Perhaps the most forward-looking electronic musician of all has never produced a single electronic sound. Trimpin (b. 1951 in Germany but resident in America since 1980; he uses only his last name) is a unique engineer-composer and inventor of strange computer-controlled devices. His signal achievement is that he has invented machines to play, through MIDI, virtually any acoustic instrument, from violins and tubas to timpani and xylophones. His installations, which also double as instruments for performance, have included the following:

A microtonal xylophone six stories high running through the center of a spiral staircase in an Amsterdam theater, with computer-driven melodies rippling up and down

Bass drums, beaten by mechanical mallets, traveling across the room suspended from tracks on the ceiling (the mallets, vibrating on the drum heads, introduce a sustained tone impossible for human hands to achieve)

Water fountains dripping into glass receptacles, digitally timed to drip in complex rhythmic fugues

A gamelan with iron bells suspended in air, a system of photosensor and electronic magnets keeping the bells in an oscillating stasis in which, since they touch nothing, they ring with a phenomenally long decay

A quartet of extralong bass clarinets with extra keys spiraled around the instrument to make possible a scale of tiny microtones, the keys being played by computer (since humans have only ten fingers, and all the human performers do is blow)

A fire organ, with glass pipes made to vibrate by Bunsen-burner flames that make hot air rise through them, triggered by the pitch of a voice singing into a microphone

Trimpin avoids loudspeakers—not on principle but because the hundred-year-old design of current loudspeakers is inadequate to convey the richness of the full sonic spectrum he envisages. Mind-blowing as Trimpin's instruments are in conception, his music uses them for effects other composers only dream about: Nancarrovian tempo canons, spatial melodies flying around the room, quick echoes from one location to another, even audience inter-activity—and all with the dramatic presence of acoustic sounds. His instruments are so expensive to create and transport that chances to hear them remained infrequent in the 1990s; but in some future day of acoustically performed, note-perfect, multitempo, spatial music, we may look back to Trimpin as the first musician of the New Era. Meanwhile, in 1998 Trimpin received one of music's best-deserved "genius" fellowships from the MacArthur Foundation.

THE YOUNGER NEW ROMANTICS

Not all American composers of the century's last two decades are driven by new technologies; many have continued writing orchestral and chamber works in standard European genres. In fact, with the rapid decline of twelve-tone music in the early 1980s, a new breed of younger composers appeared who were not only willing to deal with symphony orchestras, string quartets, and the like but also able to infuse these old media with new energy from rock and world musics. Younger composers such as Peter Lieberson (b. 1946), George Tsontakis (b. 1951), Scott Wheeler (b. 1952), Stephen Hartke (b. 1952), Daniel Asia (b. 1953), Robert Carl (b. 1954), Michael Daugherty (b. 1954), David Lang (b. 1957), and Julia Wolfe (b. 1958) have brought a New Romanticism to traditional acoustic media. These are the composers who write for the extensive in-place resources of the classical-music establishment, and whom that world rewards with orchestra and academic-institution residencies, prizes and awards, foundation grants and fellowships, frequent commissions, and so on.

George Tsontakis studied with George Rochberg (see pp. 266, 333–34, and 339) and, like his teacher, broke away from the modernist aesthetic he had been taught. In his subsequent music, beginning with the Third String Quartet, "Coraggio," of 1985 (*NW CD 80414*), he has cultivated a Beethovenian logic within a personal and compelling rhetoric. The opening allegro of this quartet features motives that go out of phase in a quasi-totalist way, though the repetitions are not strict, and the resolution from E♭ to D has consequences that follow a classical pitch logic; the music gradually expands beyond the streamlined opening pitch set. Tsontakis followed this in 1988 with a mellow, mystical String Quartet No. 4, "Beneath Thy Tenderness of Heart (*NW CD 80414*)," stemming from a Russian hymn quoted in the opening measures. In its rhythmically sprung, diatonic but sometimes dissonant language, the work echoes the thoughtful serenity of the late Beethoven quartets without sounding at any point unoriginal (Example 13–7).

Tsontakis has called his music a "search for the timeless gesture," a gesture that might evoke earlier music but is here used in a new context. His *Four Symphonic Quartets* for orchestra (1996), based nonvocally on the *Four Quartets* of the poet T. S. Eliot, seem impressionist and romantic at once in

EXAMPLE 13–7.   G. Tsontakis, String Quartet No. 4, measures 32–36. Quoted by permission.

their orchestration and dissonance-tinged tonality. The way Tsontakis's music piles motive upon motive into irresistibly slow climaxes makes him the most convincing New Romantic of his generation.

The search for authentic vernacular styles on which to ground classical forms is a constant among the younger generation of New Romantics. David Lang, one of the Bang on a Can curators, wrote into his *Are You Experienced?* (1987; *CRI* CD 625), named after a Jimi Hendrix song, a tuba solo with amplified distortion analogous to that of Hendrix's guitar. Stephen Hartke's Violin Concerto, "Auld Swaara" (1992; *NW* CD 80533-2), molds its Stravinskian neo-Classicism around joyous folk-fiddling idioms, ending with variations on the Shetland Islands fiddle tune named in the subtitle. Julia Wolfe, another of the Bang on a Can curators, sometimes harbors rock influences in her otherwise postminimalist music; in a few works such as *Lick* for mixed ensemble (1994), echoes of Led Zeppelin become obvious in pounding gestures. Elsewhere, however, Wolfe is one of the premiere orchestral colorists of her generation, as evidenced in symphonic works such as *The Vermeer Room* (1989; *CRI* CD 628) and *Window of Vulnerability* (1991).

Other younger New Romantics have sought to bring classical music out of the academy and into popularly public concerns. Michael Daugherty has been foremost in this attempt, especially with his *Metropolis Symphony* (1988–93) based on characters from the Superman comic books, his string quartet *Sing Sing: J. Edgar Hoover* (1992), and his widely publicized opera *Jackie O* (1997). In quite another direction, Peter Lieberson—who besides composing teaches Tibetan Vajrayana Buddhism in Nova Scotia—has brought Asian religious themes into a Eurocentric idiom in his *Drala Symphony* (1986) and chamber opera *King Gesar* (1991).

PERFORMANCE ART

Economics shapes musical genres. Just as certain composers will always take advantage of the classical-music performance establishment because it is there, others will always perform their own music as soloists because support for music along radically experimental lines is *not* there. After the 1980s, more and more composers insisted on writing for ensembles again, but the tradition of the solo composer-performer—reborn in the 1960s with such figures as Pauline Oliveros and Robert Ashley—did not die out. Instead, it merged with both performance art and electronic music, and many composers continued using technology as an extension of their performance capabilities.

It is remarkable how many of such composers were women and, even more, how many of these women use their voices as their primary means of expression. Besides Diamanda Galas and Laurie Anderson, one could list Eve Beglarian, Elise Kermani, Laetitia Sonami, Joan La Barbara, Brenda Hutchinson, Shelley Hirsch, Pamela Z, Bonnie Barnett, Christine Baczewska, Lynn Book, and many others.

Beglarian (b. 1958) came from an "uptown" background at Princeton and Columbia but rebelled and burst onto the "downtown" scene in the early 1990s. Her works use high technology toward vernacular ends: for instance, she has digitally altered the pitch and the tempo of disco songs to make her own seamless collages, and she relies on more current pop idioms than practically any of her contemporaries. Her *No Man's Land* (1995), in which she intones a scathingly honest description of an ugly New York street corner over a gritty background of noises and pop ostinatos, is characteristic. When the opportunity has arisen, she has also written large ensemble works, such as her *FlamingO* of 1995: a groundbreaking work in which the live orchestra is engulfed by sampled noises.

The San Francisco performance artist Pamela Z (b. 1956) is similar if less abrasive, singing her gentle satires such as *Cultured Pearls* ("they go to the opera / they support the ballet") over rhythmic accompaniments wrung from her electronic equipment. Laetitia Sonami (b. 1957) is more mystical and less personal, intoning non-sequitur stories by Melody Sumner Carnahan while triggering noises in a complex field of computer-controlled sensors. Tape pieces by Brenda Hutchinson (b. 1954) are sadder and more humanist. She has recorded monologues by mental patients as sound material; she interviewed her mother about the latter's gambling addiction (in *Every Dream Has Its Number*, 1996); and in *How Do You Get to Carnegie Hall?* (1997–98), she drove around the country with a piano in a trailer, stopping by the road to elicit stories from bystanders about their early piano experiences. The results, superimposed on tape, are charmingly revealing.

Joshua Fried (b. 1959) and Phil Kline (b. 1956) have both made reputations with cheap tape equipment. Fried started out in New York clubs as a kind of totalist improviser by setting several tape loops going at once and mixing channels on the spot. He made a bigger splash, though, with his electrifying *Travelogue* (1991), in which a singer is asked to listen to noises and music over headphones and imitate them as closely and quickly as possible; the frantic attempt, as the audience hears the singer over a *different* tape, is riveting. Kline has set up series of boom boxes to record and overdub himself singing—or (in *Bachman's Warbler*, 1992; *CRI* CD 646) playing harmonica—to create crescendoing washes of sound. His moving sound sculptures of people carrying boom boxes through the streets (starting with *Carol*, 1991, which became a Christmas tradition in New York City) interlace geometric sound patterns into mellow, moving—in two senses of the word—symphonies.

It has become one of our defining paradigms to think of the late twentieth century as a time of dissolution, of falling apart and increasing chaos. So deeply ingrained is that notion that many have missed the fact that, at least musically, the chaos may be beginning to subside. Think of the nineteenth-century musical world being centered on the orchestra and the public concert, and of the twenty-first-century musical world being centered on the computer, the Internet, and the small ensemble amplified and extended by loudspeakers and technology. At some point, the earlier paradigm would have to dissolve and the new one begin to take form, in a period otherwise characterized by an impression of chaos and a feeling of not knowing what is coming next. For someone closely following new composers of the 1990s, the peak of that chaos appears to have been reached in the 1970s and 1980s. The shape of the future of American music never looks certain at any point, but its trajectory looks clearer today than anyone could have foreseen twenty years ago.

BIBLIO-DISCOGRAPHICAL NOTES

A good overview of electronic music into the 1990s is Joel Chadabe's *Electronic Sound: The Past and Promise of Electronic Music* (Upper Saddle River, NJ: Prentice Hall, 1997). Kyle Gann's *American Music in the Twentieth Century* (New York: Schirmer Books, 1997) is the first general history of its subject; it deals in depth with the last two decades of the century: more than three of its thirteen chapters are devoted to music since 1980.

Laurie Anderson's *Stories from the Nerve Bible: A Retrospective* (New York: Harper Perennial, 1994) is a generous compendium of her thought-provoking stories, with plenty of visuals that convey her multimedia imagination. Writings about Anthony Braxton can be as confusing as their subject, but among the best is Ronald M. Radano's *New Musical Figurations: Anthony Braxton's Cultural Critique* (Chicago: University of Chicago Press, 1993), which examines Braxton in his cultural context. As intuitive as Morton Feldman's works seem on the surface, they repay close analysis; the most extensive and thorough such treatment is contained in *The Music of Morton Feldman*, ed. Thomas DeLio (New York: Excelsior Music Publishing Company, 1996). (The more poetic mind will prefer Feldman's own essays, cited in the Bibliographical Notes for Chapter 10.) Steven Johnson's *"Rothko Chapel* and Rothko's Chapel," PNM 32/2 (Summer 1994): 6–53, is a close analysis of a single Feldman work.

The most fertile sources of first-hand information about recent composers are books based on interviews. William Duckworth's *Talking Music: Conversations with John Cage, Philip Glass, Laurie Anderson, and Five Generations of American Experimental Composers* (New York: Schirmer Books, 1995) is especially fine; his composer's mind draws the interviewees into unusually deep musical waters. More conventional but also full of rare information are Cole Gagne and Tracy Caras's *Soundpieces: Interviews with American Composers* (Metuchen, NJ: Scarecrow Press, 1982) and its sequel, *Soundpieces II* (Metuchen, NJ: Scarecrow Press, 1993); their posing the same questions to all the composers interviewed makes for a remarkably complete survey of late-twentieth-century musical issues and attitudes.

As the recording-industry establishment succumbed more and more to commercial pressures in the 1980s and 1990s, new and creative music was forced out, to be recorded on ever smaller and more independent labels. Just as composers of such music had begun to self-publish their scores, they began to self-record their music on compact discs as well. The music listed below exists mostly on small specialty labels; many of these, however, have marketed themselves effectively on the Internet, in lieu of widespread record-store distribution. The list is ordered according to the subchapter divisions, and by composer as discussed within each subchapter.

Art Rock; Robert Ashley

Robert Ashley, *Perfect Lives* (Lovely Music LCD 4917.3)
————, *Atalanta* (Lovely Music LCD 3301-2)
————, *eL/Aficionado* (Lovely Music LCD 1004)
————, *Improvement: Don Leaves Linda* (Elektra Nonesuch 79289-2)
Rhys Chatham, *Drastic Classicism* (Dossier DCD 9002)
Glenn Branca, Symphony No. 6 (Blast First ALP 10)
————, Symphonies Nos. 8 & 10 (Blast First ALP 12)
Diamanda Galas, *Divine Punishment; Saint of the Pit* (Restless/Mute 7 71423-2)
————, *You Must Be Certain of the Devil* (Restless/Mute 7 71403-2)

Free Improvisation

Anthony Braxton, *104° Kelvin* (New Albion NA 023)
————, *Composition No. 185* (Braxton House BH 001)
Anthony Davis, *X: The Life and Times of Malcolm X* (Gramavision R2-79470)

Postminimalism; Morton Feldman

William Duckworth, *The Time Curve Preludes* (Lovely Music LCD 2031)
————, *Southern Harmony* (Lovely Music LCD 2033)
————, *Imaginary Dances* (Lovely Music LCD 3051)
Janice Giteck, *Breathing Songs from a Turning Sky* (Mode 14)
————, *Om Shanti* (New Albion NA 054 CD)
Ingram Marshall, *Fog Tropes; Gradual Requiem* (New Albion NA 002)
Paul Dresher, *Double Ikat* (New Albion NA 053 CD)
Jonathan Kramer, *Atlanta Licks* (Leonardo LE 332)
Guy Klucevsek, *"Viavy Rose" Variations* (John Marks Records JMR 4)
————, *Flying Vegetables of the Apocalypse* (XI 104)
Mary Jane Leach, *Mountain Echoes; Bruckstück* (XI 107)
Morton Feldman, *Why Patterns?; Crippled Symmetry* (hat ART CD 2-6080)
————, *For Philip Guston* (hat ART CD 4-6104 1/4)
————, *Neither* (hat ART CD 102)
————, *For Samuel Beckett* (hat ART CD 6107; Newport Classic NPD 85506)

Totalism; Conlon Nancarrow

Mikel Rouse, *Failing Kansas* (New Tone nt 67640 2)
John Luther Adams, *Dream of White on White* (New Albion NA 061 CD)
Conlon Nancarrow, *Studies for Player Piano* (Wergo 60165-50; 60167-50)

Electronic Music; Trimpin

Charles Amirkhanian, *Walking Tune* (Starkland ST-206)
Henry Gwiazda, *whErEyoulivE; MANEATINGCHIPSLISTENINGTOAVIOLIN* (innova 505)
Carl Stone, *Shing Kee* (New Albion 049 CD)
Paul Lansky, *Idle Chatter; just more idle chatter; Notjustmoreidlechatter* (Bridge BCD 9050)

INDEX

BAKER & TAYLOR